ALSO BY BETTY FUSSELL

Mabel: Hollywood's First I-Don't-Care Girl

Masters of American Cookery

I Hear America Cooking

Eating In

Food in Good Season

Home Plates

The Story of Corn

The Story of Corn

Betty Fussell

*I believe in the forest, and in the meadow, and
in the night in which the corn grows.*

—HENRY THOREAU, "Walking" (1862)

ALFRED A. KNOPF

NEW YORK

1992

Library of Congress Cataloging-in-Publication Data

Fussell, Betty Harper.
The story of corn : the myths and history, the culture and
agriculture, the art and science of America's quintessential crop /
Betty Fussell. — 1st ed.
p.   cm.
Includes bibliographical references (p.   ) and index.
ISBN 0-394-57805-8
1. Corn.   2. Corn—America—History.   3. Corn—America—Folklore.
4. Corn—Utilization.   5. Indians—Folklore.   6. Folklore—America.
I. Title.
SB191.M2F87   1992
633.1′5′0973—dc20   91-58645
CIP

Manufactured in the United States of America

Published August 12, 1992
Second Printing, August 1992

Frontispiece: Maya mural painting of a corn stalk with human heads in the form of
the Tonsured Maize God, from east Temple Rojo, c. A.D. 700–900, at Cacaxla in the
province of Tlaxcala, Mexico. The elongated heads show grains of yellow corn
topped by tassels of corn silk. In J. B. Carlson's Center for Archaeoastronomy Technical
Publication No. 7 (1991). Photo copyright © 1992 by Bob Sacha.

FOR MY GRANDMOTHERS

Ellen Josephine Culver Kennedy
1857–1946

Carrie Hadassah Erskine Harper
1866–1955

ACKNOWLEDGMENTS

Many thanks to many people, not only to those named in the text, but to legions of others, among them: Eloise Alton, Robert Bird, Ruth Bronz, Judith Brown, Millie Byrne, Jack Carter, Keith Crotz, Phyllis Drozd, Mary Mills Dunea, Meryle Evans, Charlotte Green, Katherine Hamilton-Smith, Tiff Harris, Stan Herd, Carrie Hollister, Josefina Howard, Marcia Keegan, Barbara and Justin Kerr, Eli Klein, Kornelia Kurbjahn, Jan Longone, Katie MacNeil, Deborah Madison, Clark Mangelsdorf, John McElhaney, Steve Miller, Nicholas Millhouse, Edith Monroe, Alicia Rios, Alice Ross, Trevor Rowe, Cynthia Rubin, Drew Schwartz, Eugene Sekaquaptewa, Sarah Morgan Snead, Duff Stoltz, Terry Wilde and to archivists of collections, libraries, museums across the land.

Muchas gracias to friends in Peru: Marco Bustamante, Maria Elena Gonzalez Buttgenbach, Federico Perez Eguren, Luis Antonio Guerra, Betty Leyva, Hilda Linares, Ricardo Sevilla Panizo.

Thanks for untold mercies to George Andreou, Josephine Caruso, Don and Eleanor Crosier, Matthew Culligan, Roger Feinstein, Harry Ford, Sam Fussell, Tucky Fussell, Barbara Hatcher, Leah Holzel, Arlene Lee, Gloria Loomis, Patricia Rucidlo, Elisabeth Sifton, Fiona Stevenson, Kendra Taylor, Mia Vander Els.

Thanks to Gregory Thorp, who transmutes corn madness into photographic art.

And thanks, in memoriam, to Lloyd Wescott, who planted the seeds of this book in his stand of New Jersey corn.

Contents

ONE

*A
Babel
of
Corn*

*(overleaf) In a Classic Maya
image of fertility, corn sprouts
from the belly of a human sacrifice. Drawn from a carving on
Stela 11 at Piedras Negras,
Guatemala,* A.D. *731. In S. G.
Morley's* The Ancient Maya
(1946)
*In a contemporary American
advertising image, a corn ear
becomes a pencil to record bank-
book savings for farmers who
buy hybrid seed from Lynks
Seeds in Marshalltown, Iowa.*
Courtesy Lynks Seeds

Corn Mad

"At the end of the third quarter," the cabin steward announces over the loudspeaker, "the Cornhuskers are leading twenty-one to nineteen." The passengers burst into cheers. This United Airlines steward knows how to milk his audience. He got laughs at the beginning of the flight from O'Hare Airport in Chicago to Lincoln, Nebraska, when he asked us to don our Mae Wests "in the unlikely event that we should land in water." Now he congratulates our pilot on back-to-back perfect landings: "Let's show him our appreciation, folks." We burst into applause. We have just landed in the city named for America's favorite president, in the state that is the exact center of the United States.

My cousin Eleanor and her husband, Don, meet me at the airport dressed in Cornhusker red because on football Saturdays *tout* Lincoln paints the town red. "The State Capitol is one of the top ten Wonders of the World," says my cousin, "that's what they say." I've seen most of the classical seven but never the Capitol nor Nebraska nor my cousin, although I'm here for a reunion of cousins, the grandchildren of Parks Ira and Ellen Culver Kennedy, whose eight children were born in Nebraska. Most of the grandchildren are now grandparents themselves, most live in the Midwest, and all but one are strangers whom I've never met. I've been to Halicarnassus and the country of Peru, but never to the center of America, which boasts four Perus, one of them a small town in Nebraska where my mother taught country school. As a migrant bi-coastal American, old enough to be a grandmother, I have come at last to seek and to find, as my Grandmother Kennedy would have said, the center of my family, my country, my culture—founded and sustained on the cultivation of corn.

When I traveled around the United States in the early 1980s looking for the genus and the genius of American food, I discovered that American cooking was rooted in corn. But because I was looking then for the diversity of our hybrid cuisine, I focused on ports of entry around the perimeter—Boston, New Orleans, Santa Fe, Seattle. I spent less time in the center because it was the last land settled and the most Anglo-Saxon in its settling. Nebraska belonged entirely to buffalo and the hunters who pursued them until the last century, when pioneering folk like Grandfather Kennedy pushed west from Ohio and Iowa to turn the sod and dig wells and plant corn.

Nebraska wasn't even a state until 1867, when my grandfather was eleven years old. By the time he married another Scotch-Irish Presbyterian in 1880 and exchanged his "soddie" for the first of many frame houses he would build himself, the farming revolution had already begun to turn his small acreage in Wilcox into a notch in the world's Corn Belt. He would recognize the Wilcox I saw a century later, because it is still no more than a crossroads with a water-tower and a silo and a cluster of white frame houses, but the scale of the plane geometry of green that I saw from the air flying into Lincoln would have discombobulated him considerable.

My Grandfather Kennedy, who was born in 1856 in Benton County, Iowa, and died in Los Angeles, California, in 1947, experienced in his ninety-one years a revolution on land no less extraordinary than that in the air. "A lot of North Americans forget," Joel Garreau has reminded us in *The Nine Nations of America* (1981), "that the Breadbasket was the *last* frontier," and that the transformation of the Great American Desert into the World's Breadbasket took place only within the last hundred years.

A land and its people founded on corn.
Photo by Gregory Thorp

By the time my grandfather pushed west from Iowa into Nebraska, he had John Deere's "singing" Moline plow of wrought iron and steel to turn the sod and a single-row horse-drawn planter to deposit seed and dried manure in one drop. By the 1930s, when he left farming and well digging—he had dug the town well in Wilcox—for carpentry and retirement in California, he wasn't needed as a farmer anymore. His hands and his horses had been replaced by tractors and combines. A bushel that had taken him two to three hours to produce now took three minutes. The very seed he saved from open pollinated fields to plant again each year had undergone revolution. By the year he died, virtually all Midwestern corn grew not from farmer's seed saved year to year but from "factory-produced" hybrid seed. That seed nearly pentupled the amount of corn my grandfather could have harvested; he averaged perhaps 25 bushels an acre, but today he would average 120. Within the span of a single life, the pioneer farmer and his seed went under as quickly as the prairie sod, the plow and the horse.

While nearly all the Kennedy grandchildren were born on a farm or ranch (I on a California orange ranch), none of them farms today. Most have moved into cities, like the rest of America's farm population, which in the 1980s dropped another 11 percent. Today 97 percent of us live on what 3 percent of us farm. Small wonder that, in the age of service industries, corn is not always a major topic of conversation, even in Nebraska. When Cousin Eleanor introduced me to a friend as an Eastern writer, the friend asked with excitement, "What subject?" I told her, "Corn," and she groaned. "Why don't you write about something glamorous, something sexy?"

My days of innocence—before I understood the true sexiness of corn, before I learned the power of hidden corn—were nostalgic days, when Eleanor would tell me how her mother had canned hominy and her father had saved seed corn. He would take one kernel each from selected ears, wrap the kernels in a wet sheet to germinate and then throw out the ears of any kernels that had failed to sprout. They were days when I ate large helpings of caramel corn, scalloped corn and cornhusker bread, which Eleanor made from a can of cream-style corn, a can of whole corn kernels, two boxes of cornbread mix and simple nostalgic things like six eggs, a pint of cream and a cup of butter.

They were the days before I went corn mad. Even then, however, I could see that no matter what I touched, it turned to corn. Corn was everywhere.

"Sing a song of popcorn
When the snowstorms rage
Fifty little round men
Put into a cage.
Shake them till they laugh and leap
Crowding to the top;
Watch them burst their little coats
Pop!! Pop!! Pop!!"

—NANCY BYRD TURNER,
"A Popcorn Song" (1988)

Family snapshots in Nebraska showed cousins in their youth standing in cornfields higher than their heads. When I left Lincoln to drive through canyons of corn in Kansas, Iowa, Ohio, Illinois, I stumbled on corn folk I never knew existed. There was the cornhusking champion in Kewanee, Illinois—home of the Cornhuskers' Museum; the champion Corn Collector displaying his wares in Courtland, Kansas; the Omaha Indian and his wife at Macy, Nebraska, who hickory-smoked corn; the retired corn canner in Hoopeston, Illinois—home of the National Sweetcorn Festival; the pioneer hybrid-seed producer, Henry Wallace's brother James, in Des Moines, Iowa. Corn made the whole world kin.

Neither my Grandfather Kennedy nor my Grandfather Harper, a Kansas farm boy, ever went east of the Alleghenies or west of California. Their fathers on both sides were born and buried in the Midwest and fought Indians in between. Both generations shared territorial imperatives that ended with the oceans on each side, and they shared the politics of America First. My grandfathers would have been astonished to learn that today a farmer's income in the Corn Belt is tied, directly or indirectly, as Garreau has pointed out, "to the weather in Siberia." Today poke your finger anywhere in corn country and you strike corn one hundred, one thousand, ten thousand miles away.

Bantus in 1954 in East Cape Province, South Africa, flail cobs with poles to remove kernels, which they will grind into "mealies." Photo by A. M. Duggan-Cronin

The living plants at the Corn Belt center have roots that reach deep into the past and extend wide across the present. Following roots means exploring our earliest corn cultures in what is left of Indian territory in scattered patches in North Dakota, Oklahoma, New Mexico, Arizona. On the Second Mesa, I found Hopi grandmothers who grew blue corn and made piki bread as their ancestors had done centuries before a handful of Italians and Spanish beached their ships on a tropical isle, bit into the little yellow cakes offered them by the natives and wondered what this peculiar substance was. To find out what it was and where it came from, I had to explore the steamy rainforests of Mexico and the icy highlands of Peru. I had to talk in broken Spanish to Zinacotecans in Chiapas and Quechuans in Cuzco, places where the same breeds of corn had grown for two or even seven thousand years, and where corn bred and sustained sacred rites that still bind people to one another and to the land that nourishes spirits as well as bodies.

The corn culture of the Western world circled the globe a good four centuries ago, wherever the Spanish, Italians and Portuguese were foolhardy enough to go next. Today one can see—at a Polenta Festival in Gubbio, Italy, or in villages by the Great Wall of China outside Beijing—on both sides of the Eastern Hemisphere, rooftops, houses and walls that are compact with ears of drying corn. So quickly did the American corn revolution of this century spread that not only the Great American Desert was transformed, but also barren lands in Egypt and South Africa, India and China; today China, after the United States, is the world's largest producer of corn.

Geographic spread was only the beginning. Every item in Cousin Eleanor's cornhusker bread came from corn—not just the corn kernels but the eggs, cream and butter; even the baking powder, sugar and salt were touched indirectly by corn. My very flesh was compacted of corn and, at Eleanor's table, was beginning its own geographic spread. Everything that went into my mouth—including the fresh fruit and vegetables if they had been sprayed with insecticide—had been touched in one way or another by corn. To enter a supermarket was to step into cornland—all the items but the fresh fish having made contact with some product or by-product of processed corn, be it syrup, oil or starch in one of its multifoliate, mostly inedible forms.

Edible corn for humans, whether fresh, canned, frozen or in the form of cornmeal, makes up less than 1 percent of the American corn market, a tiny amount that nonetheless adds up to about three pounds of corn per person per day, a pound per meal in foodstuffs derived from converted corn. We are but one product of the Great Corn Conversion Chain that converts sun and water into animal, vegetable, mineral and synthetic. From the more than 200 million metric *tons* of corn that the United States produces each year, 85 percent is converted into cows, hogs and chickens in the proportion of 60 million cows, 100 million hogs and 4 billion chickens. As an index of corn's super conversion powers (double those of wheat), one bushel of corn in a mixed feed bag translates into 15 pounds of retail beef, 26 pounds of pork and 37 pounds of poultry. And this is still corn in a form we can recognize: fodder, silage, shelled grain or fibrous by-products.

Far more pervasive is the world of hidden corn, in which corn's living flesh is converted alchemically into industrial gold. Before my Grandfather Kennedy was born, the local gristmills of the East were already being replaced by Colgate's roller mills in Jersey City, which by 1844 extracted starch from corn in the process now called wet-milling. Twenty years later, starch was converted into syrup and sugar and, soon after that, into dextrose and the roasted starch called dextrin that turns corn into glue. After a century and a half of playing with the chemical constituents of corn, America has created an invisible and awesome corn network.

We expect to find corn oil in mayonnaise and even soap, but aren't apt to think of it in paint and insecticides. While corn syrup or sugar is not unthinkable in a jar of peanut butter, it is downright worrisome in baby foods, chewing gums, soft drinks, canned and frozen vegetables, beer and wine, crackers and breads, frozen fish and processed meats like hot dogs and corned beef hash. It is mind-boggling in cough drops, toothpaste, lipstick, shaving cream, shoe polish, detergents, tobacco, rayon, tanned leather, rubber tires, urethane foam, explosives and embalming fluid.

When we get to invisible cornstarch, it's cause for national alarm. Just how much so, Howard Walden told us in *Native Inheritance* (1966), when he pointed to corn's indispensability in World War II or indeed in any war. Starch or dextrin touches all dehydrated foods, powdered and granulated foods, aspirin tablets, antiseptics, the surgeon's gloves and sponges, shotgun shells, dynamite, cloth fabrics, adhesives, cigarettes, books and magazines, every paper product but newsprint, penicillin and sulfa, molded plastics, oil-well drills, battery dry cells, aluminum in every form from wire to airplanes, and metal molds of every type from gun carriages to tanks.

The list goes on. Think of the distilling industries, from whiskey to ethanol, and you must think corn. Think of all the metal and oil industries, and you must think corn. Think not only of what's in the supermarket but of the materials of which the store is built and the machinery that moves both you and the food in and out of the supermarket, and you must think corn. Think of the greenhouse effect at the end of the green revolution, and you must think how green *was* the corn. For the revolution in chemical farming that turned green plants into industrial plants hinged on corn.

One dip into Nebraska and my green corn days were over. If corn was everywhere and everything was corn, how could I find the perimeter or center of the maze? Where to begin? As the subject possessed me, my apartment dispossessed me by the mounting boxes of books, photographs, paintings, jewelry, rugs, recipes, ephemera and kitsch, bags of meal and grits, stacks of blue and white tortillas and dried ears of purple, black and green kernels. I found that corn, like Captain Ahab's monstrous whale, possesses its pursuers until it drives them mad. But I wasn't alone. America is full of corn madness.

The townsfolk of Mitchell, South Dakota, have built the world's only corn palace of kernel mosaics and minarets, like a prairie Xanadu. A field artist in Kansas has planted corn, sunflowers and sorghum to replicate, from the air, Van Gogh's *Sunflowers*. A noted geneticist in Massachusetts pats the leaves of his baby corn plants and asks them to talk to him nicely. A photographer in Vermont, when I telephone to ask about corn pictures, immediately puts down the phone and lets out a long "Whooooopeeeee!" A Nobel Prize winner in Long Island has said that the best thing about studying corn is that you become part of the subject. Corn breeds its own poets, lunatics and lovers. After five years of corn madness, I can't think of anything sexier than corn. Or more dangerous.

THE POPCORN CONNECTION

To KEEP a grain of sanity, I turned to food. What did corn mean to me? Popcorn. When I think of my Grandfather Harper, I think of popcorn. Or rather, I smell popcorn, with rivulets of real butter trickling down through the red-striped bag of hot roasted kernels, fresh from the electric popper that was a prominent feature of the lobby of the movie theater in California we attended every Saturday afternoon in the 1930s. When I think of my son in the 1960s, sprawled on the living-room sofa of our house in suburban New Jersey watching Saturday-afternoon football, I smell popcorn, heavily buttered and lightly salted in a large wooden bowl that I bought on my honeymoon in Cape Cod.

In the 1980s, with my son long gone and the honeymoon over, I still pop corn the old-fashioned way, in a cast-iron skillet, holding the lid slightly ajar while I shake the skillet back and forth over a high flame until the pop-pop-popping quiets and only an occasional late-bloomer explodes against the lid. I upend the skillet over the wooden bowl, dark now after four decades of oiled salads and buttered popcorn that gave luster to its intended function as a quahog chopping bowl. How curious that my grandfather in the West who died long before my son was born in the East should be linked to him, a continent and decades apart, by popcorn.

Popcorn is a truly indigenous fast finger-food that links all ages, places, races, classes and kinds in the continuing circus of American life. Popcorn is the great equalizer, which turns itself inside out to attest to our faith that color is only skin deep, and class superfluous. Popcorn connects toddlers and grannies, hard-hats and connoisseurs, moviegoers and sports fans, beer drinkers and tee-totalers, sharecroppers and industrialists, cops and robbers, even cowboys and Indians. Popcorn bags the past with the present and evokes even in old age the memories of childhood. We eat it not because it's good for us, which it is, but because it's joke food, and Americans love joke food. We eat popcorn for fun.

Each year every man, woman and child of us eats an average of fifty-six quarts, popped, from a total of 900 million pounds of kernels, unpopped. We

"The first thing I saw when I got into his house was a console TV entirely covered with popcorn. Above it, suspended from the ceiling, was a popcorn bra and a popcorn football."
—SPALDING GRAY, "Travels Through New England" (1986)

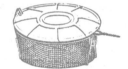

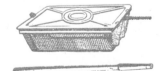

Corn poppers advertised in trade catalogue of Fletcher, Jenks & Company, 1889. From the Collections of Henry Ford Museum and Greenfield Village

The decorative possibilities of popcorn, exploited by the Aztec, are evident in this "tasselseed" mutant, grown and popped by Paul Mangelsdorf and R. G. Reeves in their 1939 researches into the origin of corn. Today, this popcorn "bouquet" decorates the Botanical Museum of Harvard University. Botanical Museum, Harvard University

love to pop corn because it explodes with the noise and violence of our language, our streets, our practical jokes. The late lamented puppet Ollie, despite his single dragon tooth, was addicted to it. Texas Junior Leaguers can't roast turkey without it. "You fill the cavity with kernels," Ruth Bronz explains, "seal it and bake it until the turkey blows its ass off." My cousin Don of Nebraska couldn't date college girls without it, in the days when they bought grocery sacks of popcorn and gallon jugs of root beer for a blanket party in the park. "Popcorn and root beer and it was impolite to belch," he remembers, "but you had to or it would have blown your head off."

Nebraska, I learned, is our number one popcorn state, although it feuds with Indiana for that title. Together they grow 65 percent of all processed kernels. Typically America has turned its favorite joke food into a $2-billion-a-year industry. That gives popcorn status as a cultural institution. Chicago is the home of the Popcorn Institute; Marion, Ohio, of the Popcorn Museum; Columbus, Ohio, features major Cracker Jackiana in its Center for Science and Industry; and men across the nation, vying for the title of Cracker Jack King, acquire "rare" Cracker Jack prizes with the same avidity Japanese show in acquiring Van Goghs.

In the last few years, popcorn sales have exploded, skyrocketing 25 percent in a single year. At a recent national foods show, I found new "fun flavors" like yogurt and jalapeño; innovative coatings like Jell-O and chocolate; fashion colors like black and blue (although the kernels always pop white); and "fun packaging" like disposable poppers, hot-air poppers, popcorn-on-the-cob. Merchandising is the name of the popcorn game and that, too, happened within the lifetime of my grandfathers.

If corn is the prime model of America's industrialization of crops at the production end, popcorn is the model at the distribution end, where packaging is all. By nature, popcorn has an edge, for each dull kernel comes equipped with its own snowy-white display. Popcorn's eye appeal is what Spanish soldiers and priests in the wake of Cortez noted when they saw Aztec virgins place "over their heads, like orange blossoms, garlands of parched maize, which they called *mumuchitl.*" This was "a kind of corn which bursts when parched and discloses its contents and makes itself look like a very white flower," wrote Father Bernardino de Sahagún in the 1560s, relating how Aztecs honored the god who protected fishermen and other water workers by scattering these white blossoms as if they were "hailstones given to the god of water." There was precedent for Thoreau's calling popped corn "a perfect winter flower hinting of anemones."

"Parched corn" is what Governor John Winthrop called it when he observed the natives of Connecticut stirring it in hot embers until it "turned almost the inside outward, which will be almost white and flowery." Parched corn is what Quadequina, Chief Massasoit's brother, is said to have brought in a deerskin bag to the first Thanksgiving feast. Parched corn is what Benjamin Franklin described a century later, when he approved the method of throwing grains into sand heated in an iron pot until "each Grain burst and threw out a white substance of twice its bigness." Four centuries later, an Englishman encountering parched or popped corn for the first time exclaimed, "How extraordinary—fluffed maize."

While all kinds of corn pop to some degree, not all will turn inside out to become light, white and fluffy. The two major types of popcorn grown commercially—"rice," with sharply pointed kernels, and "pearl," with smooth rounded crowns—contain such a high proportion of hard starch that their prime feature is popping expansion or, as the admen say, "poppability." As scientists say, expansion depends upon moisture within the grain that turns into steam when the kernel is heated, but which is held within the starch-protein matrix until it suddenly explodes. In popcorn types where the starch-to-protein ratio is somewhat low, steam leaks out without exploding. Poppability is best when the kernel's moisture is between 13.5 and 15.5 percent and when the kernel is heated in such a way that the water vapor can escape. For this reason, when you pop corn in a skillet, you should cover the skillet only partially with a lid or the kernels will reabsorb the moisture and become tough. Texture is the essence of popcorn flavor. "Ideally, it should be crisp but not tough," stated *Consumer Reports* (June 1989). "It should shear off cleanly and compress easily as you chew, but not pack the teeth too much. Once chewed, it should be easy to swallow, leaving few crumbled bits in the mouth."

Today popcorn is so easy to swallow that *Consumer Reports* has rated fifty-one brand-name varieties and has observed that sales have increased more than 50 percent in the last decade through the magic combination of a microwave in every kitchen and a TV in every bedroom. Americans eat 70 percent of their popcorn at home, and they microwave 60 percent of that for couch potatoes. Today's surge of popularity

Moche pottery corn poppers (A.D. 100 to 800) from the northern coast of Peru, where the Moche had developed extensive irrigation canals for farming. Field Museum of Natural History, Chicago

In his No. 1 Wagon of 1893, Charles Cretors put his steam-powered peanut roaster and corn popper machine on wheels and into the hands of street vendors, who found a ready audience for the theatrics of automated popping. C. Cretors & Co., Chicago

began, however, in World War II, when home-fronters sacrificed candy for our boys over there and chewed popcorn instead. In movie-theater lobbies in the 1940s we purchased corn popped in streamlined machines named "Majestic" and "Hollywood." Today we run to our microwaves during commercials.

If the earliest method of popping was simply to toss kernels into the embers of a fire, the method of popping in a sand-filled pot is as ancient as prehistoric Peru. A three-legged container with an open mouth on one side, an *olla canchera,* kept the heat in and let the steam out. While colonists substituted iron for clay, natives continued to pop corn in clay as late as this century. Buffalo Bird Woman of the Hidatsa tribe in North Dakota described parching hard yellow corn in the hot sand of "a clay pot of our own make," until "all the kernels cracked open with a sharp crackling noise; they burst open much as you say white man's popcorn does."

New England colonists improvised a popper by punching holes in a sheet-iron container shaped like a warming pan, a rare version of which was a pierced cylinder that revolved on an axle, like a squirrel cage, in front of the fire. In 1847, in his *Memoir on Maize, or Indian Corn*, D. J. Browne listed two "Modern Modes of Popping Corn," one of them by heating the kernels in a buttered or larded frying pan and the other by "a very ingenious contrivance" of recent invention:

It consists of a box made of wire gauze, with the apertures not exceeding one twentieth of an inch square, and is so constructed that the corn can be put within it, without being burnt, and can be held over a hot fire made either of wood or coal. The carburetted hydrogen gas, produced within the box by the decomposition of the oil in the corn, is prevented from explosion in a similar manner as *fire-damp,* in mines, is prevented from explosion by the safety-lamp.

While his chemical analysis and analogy may give us pause, Browne's is one of the first descriptions of the wire-basket corn popper that became a staple of American hearths until popcorn machines put popcorn vendors on every street corner.

Charles C. Cretors of Chicago was the first to develop a steam-driven machine in 1885 to pop corn in such volume that it could be sold from street wagons propelled first by hand, then by horse and finally by gasoline motor. Within the decade, Frederick William Ruckheim, also of Chicago, "improved" the popcorn he sold from his corner stand by sweetening it with molasses and calling it—from the same slang pool that gave us "swell" and "topnotch"—Cracker Jack. There was nothing new about sweetening parched corn with a native sweetener; Indians had been doing it for millennia. Nor was there anything new about using molasses candy to stick together toasted almonds or other kinds of nuts. With molasses candy, Ruckheim and his brother Louis stuck popcorn together with marshmallows and other sweets before they settled on popcorn and peanuts. Their inventiveness was not in cooking but in marketing, with the 1893 World's Columbian Exposition in Chicago for a launching pad.

At first the brothers sold their product in tins and barrels, until Henry Eckstein joined them in 1902 and developed a moisture-proof sealed box that contained the first "green stamp," a printed coupon redeemable for adult prizes like clothing and sporting goods. In 1912, the Ruckheims replaced coupons with children's prizes: miniature books, magnifying glasses, tiny pitchers, beads, metal trains—"a prize-in-every-package." In 1916 they capitalized on the fame of that year's naval Battle of Jutland by putting F.W.'s grandson Robert on the box in his sailor suit (with his pet dog Bingo) and calling him Jack the Sailor. In the 1930s they added presidential medals, movie-star cards, Mystery Club prizes. During World War II, Cracker Jack went to war, and the company was commended for "high achievement in the production of materials needed by our armed forces." In the 1960s the company was sold to Borden and moved into the modern age with the foil bag, the big party-pack tub, safety-tested toys, and automated plant machinery that pops eighteen to twenty tons of corn every day.

In the 1930s just plain popcorn had become popular enough to encourage a rival to the Cretors company in the person of William Hoover Brown of Marion, Ohio, known then as "Shovel City" from the success of the Marion Steam Shovel Company. Brown founded his Wyandot Popcorn company after he married Ava King, daughter of the shovel company head, whose family mansion was frequented by President Warren Harding, born and buried in Marion. At Harding's burial in 1923, the King mansion lodged for the occasion Henry Ford, Harvey Firestone and Thomas Edison. The conjunction was fortuitous in the history of the popcorn industry, for Brown adapted Ford's assembly-line method to mass-produce popcorn, which he then distributed by trucks, equipped with Firestone tires, to chain theaters, which showed the movies that Edison had helped to invent.

*Sailor Jack and Bingo in 1925
salute their prize package.*
Courtesy Borden, Inc.

In the 1960s the kernel itself was streamlined by a county extension agent in Indiana named Orville Redenbacher, who developed a hybrid popcorn seed he called "Gourmet Popping Corn." "It's a Snowflake variety," says Orville, with "higher popping volume" than other kinds—one ounce pops to a quart—and higher reliability—fewer of those unpoppable kernels the industry calls "old maids." Redenbacher put his smiling bumpkin face on a label and marketed his gourmet kernels from the back of a car until Hunt-Wesson bought up the company in 1974. Six-million-dollar television campaigns, plus clever microwave marketing, have made Orville's face and name ubiquitous.

The super-marketing of a Redenbacher leaves little room for popcorn farmers like Michael Della Rocco in Melrose, New York. A traditional crop farmer who had run into hard times, Della Rocco began experimenting in 1985 with popcorn types that might grow in New York's short season. "I wanted something I could grow and market so that I could take control of my own destiny," he says. "I wanted to have my name on it." The name was Dellwood Farm, but it's tough work going up against nationally known brands. "Look, I'm convinced my product is good, but you're looking at a farmer, and farmers aren't known for their marketing abilities."

Who knows anymore what a farmer is? It's as hard to imagine TV Time Gourmet Microwave Pop actually growing in dirt fields as it is to imagine popcorn, our clown of corns, at the center of the story of corn in America. Popcorn, I knew, linked my grandfather to my son, but I never dreamed that popcorn was the connection between Pop-a-Cobs for Couch Kernels and the cobs, no bigger than half a thumbnail, that were uncovered exactly one year before the summer on Cape Cod when I married a Harvard graduate student of English and bought a quahog chopping bowl to put our popcorn in.

It seems that on a hot August day in 1948, another pair of Harvard graduate students, one in anthropology and the other in botany, were digging in an abandoned rock shelter 165 feet above the San Augustin plain in Catron County, New Mexico. They were exploring Bat Cave, a site known to have been occupied by cave dwellers practicing primitive agriculture on the rim of an ancient lake three thousand years ago. In order to join his anthropologist

A former county agriculture agent in Indiana, Orville Redenbacher scrutinizes ears of the hybrid Snowflake variety he developed into his trademarked Gourmet Popping Corn. Orville Redenbacher and the Popcorn Institute, Chicago

friend Herbert Dick, the botanist Earle Smith had asked his professor in Cambridge for enough cash to pay for a round-trip bus ticket and a sleeping bag—$150. His professor was Paul Mangelsdorf, then director of Harvard's Botanical Museum, who later wrote, "Seldom in Harvard's history has so small an investment paid so large a return."

What they discovered in the Bat Cave's layers of trash, garbage and excrement, which had accumulated over two thousand years, were "766 specimens of shelled cobs, 125 loose kernels, 8 pieces of husks, 10 of leaf sheath, and 5 of tassels and tassel fragments." The deeper they dug, the smaller and more primitive the cobs, until they reached bottom and found tiny cobs of popcorn in which each kernel was enclosed in its own husk, the "pod popcorn" that Mangelsdorf identified as the genetic ancestor of a modern Mexican brown-skinned popcorn called Chapalote. Among these prehistoric kernels they found six that were partly or completely popped. Mangelsdorf and his colleague Walton Galinat took a few unpopped kernels and dropped them into a little hot oil to prove that two or three millennia later they could *still* pop. The Bat Cave find was, as Mangelsdorf said, "a landmark discovery." Not only was this the oldest known corn in America but, as later discoveries proved, popcorn was the oldest known corn in the world.

WHAT IS THE CORN?

FOR THOUSANDS OF YEARS before corn was popcorn, corn was grass. A century ago, Whitman asked, "What is the grass?" Fifty years ago, looking at the green heart of America where leaves of corn had replaced grass, Paul Mangelsdorf asked, "What is the corn?" The answer depends on who wants to know—in what mother tongue and in which mother culture. "*Mamaliga,*" says the Romanian. "Stir-about," says the Irishman. "*Makkal,*" says the East Indian. "*Welschkorn,*" says the Amish. "*Masa,* our daily bread," says the Mexican. "*Tâ'-a,* the Seed of Seeds," says the Zuni.

What kind of corn? my botanist father would have asked the questioner. To a botanist corn is maize or, better yet, *Zea mays,* one of three related grasses in the tribe Maydeae, a member of the family Gramineae. Since maize hybridizes so readily, it has more varieties than any other crop species. There are thousands of varieties of corn, so many that taxonomists, engaged in what is today called "systematics," group these varieties loosely into three hundred races for the Western Hemisphere alone. Earlier, when corn seemed simpler than it does today, textbooks divided it into six kinds: dent, flint, flour, sweet, pop and waxy. But today we talk about "racial complexes." Northern Flints, Great Plains Flints and Flours, Pima-Papago, Southwestern Semidents, Southwestern 12-row, Southern Dents, Derived Southern Dents, Southeastern Flints, Corn Belt Dents are the nine major racial complexes of corn in the United States, excluding popcorns and sweet corns.

Corn in what form? the Quechuan in Peru would ask. If you mean parched kernels, the answer would be *kancha hara*. If boiled kernels, *mote*. If young ears for roasting, *choklo*. If cut kernels cooked in corn husks, *shatu*. If corn soaked in lye to remove their hulls, *mote lyushki*. If ears boiled and dried, *chochoka*. If fermented corn, *hara togosh*. If corn fermented and dried for corn beer, *shura*.

Corn at what time of year? the Iroquois would ask. He would use a different Onondaga word for "corn" in each of its stages or aspects: She is dropping or planting the corn. She is doing first-corn-hoeing. She is doing second-corn-hoeing. The corn pollen is being shed. The corn is in the milk. She is plucking the green corn. She is plucking the ripe corn. She is husking corn. He is making a string of corn. The corn is hung over the pole.

Corn for what purpose? the Iowan would ask. If the whole plant is to be chopped up and used for animal fodder, the answer would be silage. If hybridized for planting, seed corn. If fermented for distilling, corn mash. If used for feed and other manufacturers, cash crop.

Corn in what culture? the mythographer would ask. Corn to the ancient Maya was embodied in One Hunahpu, one of the twin heroes who defeated the Lords of Death. Corn to the Inca was embodied in Manco-Paca, son of the Sun and founder of the dynasty of the Royal Lords of Cuzco. Corn to the Totonac of Central America was Tzinteotl, wife of the sun. Corn to the Aztec was the goddess Xilonen and the god Quetzalcoatl. Corn to the Chippewa was Mondawmin. Corn to the Pawnee was the Evening Star, the mother of all things, who gave corn to the people from her garden in the sky.

From the beginning of corn in Mesoamerica, its languages have been as varied as the races and languages of the peoples who grew it. The Taino that Columbus heard the Arawaks of the West Indies speak was but one of two thousand languages that had developed among the diverse peoples of the Western Hemisphere. In the centuries after Columbus, the Old World struggled to incorporate into languages rooted in Greco-Roman or Anglo-Saxon the flora and fauna of peoples who spoke in unknown tongues. The first act of the explorers was an act of linguistic imperialism—the naming of plants. If, as some historians have said, the New World was an invention of the Renaissance, shaped by the European imagination, so too the Old World's perception of the

New was shaped by European crops. Explorers and colonists alike spoke the language of wheat, oats, barley, rye and millet. Looking for similar grains here, they found none. They found instead a monster for which they had neither language nor understanding.

Characteristically, the first time the plant appeared in written form in the Old World, it appeared in imperial Latin: "*maizium, id frumenti genus appellant.*" So wrote Peter Martyr d'Anghiera of the grain we now call "maize." Peter was a cleric at the court of Barcelona in May 1493, when Columbus returned from his first voyage. Peter wrote excitedly to his patron, Cardinal Sforza, in Rome to tell him everything Columbus said of the strange islands of the Arawaks. "There were dogs that never barked," Columbus reported of the fauna, and of the flora, "All the trees were as different from ours as day from night, and so the fruits, the herbage, the rocks, and all things."

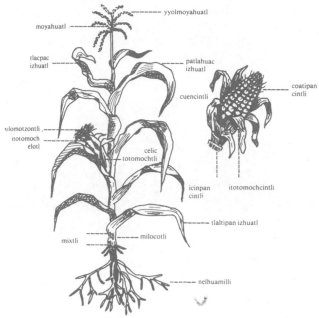

The naming of corn parts in the dialect of the Indians of Acatlán in Chilapan de Álvarez, Guerrero, one of dozens of corn dialects current in Mexico today. Museo Nacional de Culturas Populares, Mexico City

When the Arawaks had pointed to heaped ears of grain and the cakes they made from its meal, Columbus heard the word *mahiz.* Columbus amazed the court with details of its tapered ear longer than the span of a human hand and thick as an arm, its grains "affixed by nature in a wondrous manner and in form and size like garden peas, white when young." He delighted them with tales of black seeds which, when split open, revealed interiors whiter than snow. "*Fracta candore nivem exuperant,*" Peter wrote Cardinal Sforza about popcorn.

Peter's notes weren't published until 1511, in *De orbe novo decades,* and by that time Europeans were rendering the word *mahiz* in every way, in every language. While Columbus's journal of the first voyage circulated among many during this time, the original manuscript was eventually lost. Today, we must rely on abridgments by later chroniclers to learn that on November 6, 1492, Columbus sent two of his men, Rodrigo de Jerez and Luiz Torres, with a pair of native guides, into the interior of the island to search for the large Asian city and its emperor that Columbus expected to find. While they found no emperor, his men did find a city of a thousand people, who showered them with gifts, including "a sort of grain like millet, which they called *maize* [or *mahiz*], which it very well tasted when boiled, roasted, or made into porridge." Another version speaks of the grain "which the Indians called *maiz* but which

In a symbolic conjunction of New and Old Worlds in Florida in 1564, Chief Athore of the Timucua Indians displays to René de Laudonnière the fruits of field and forest before a column erected by Jean Ribault at his Huguenot colony. The scene was rendered by Jacques Le Moyne de Morgues in gouache on vellum. Collection of the late James Hazen Hyde, in the Print Collection, the New York Library

the Spanish called *panizo." Panizo* was the term Spaniards applied generically to the grains they knew, such as wheat, millet, barley, oats, sorghum.

In the next two decades, Spaniards and Portuguese spread variants of the name "maize" as rapidly as they spread variants of its seed through Europe, Africa, the Middle East and Far East. In 1516, when Portuguese sailors finally reached the Asian coast Columbus had sought, they deposited maize seeds in China. So quickly did these seeds take root wherever they were dropped, even in the most extreme climates, that patriots of Africa, Turkey, India and China alike claim corn as native. "So completely has India now appropriated the Makkal [maize]," wrote a nineteenth-century botanist, "that few of the village fathers would be found willing to admit that it had not always been with them as it is now, a staple article of diet." I know many Chinese today who insist, with some heat, that China was the onlie begetter of corn.

There are good reasons for confusion about the place of corn's origin. In the sixteenth and seventeenth centuries, as herbalists began to incorporate the world of newly discovered plants into their *Theatrum Botanicum,* as John Parkinson called his monumental book in 1640, plants were what you called them. An early Parisian botanist, Jean Ruel (or Ruellius), in his *De Natura Stirpium* (1536), called maize *Turcicum frumentum.* For centuries thereafter, Europe called maize Turkish wheat. Ruel may have thought the grain originated in Asia Minor, then under Turkish rule, or he may have wanted to distinguish "savage" maize from civilized wheat.

To this day, the French sometimes call maize *blé de Turquie,* despite the admonitions of one of their own botanists, Alphonse de Candolle, who as long ago as 1890 threw up his hands at the persistence of this misnomer. To call America's native grain *blé de Turquie,* he argued, was as silly as to call America's native bird *coq d'Inde* or "turkey." The English herbalist John Gerarde in his 1597 *Herball* was similarly exasperated, but he cited the authority of the ancients to show off his Latin and Greek, unaware that no ancient had ever heard of the plant:

Turkey wheat is called of some *Frumentum Turcicum,* and *Milium Indicum. Strabo, Eratostenes, Onesicritum, Plinie* and others, haue contended about the name heereof, which I minde not to rehearse, considering how vaine and friuolous it is: but leauing it vntill such time as some one *Oedipus* or other shall bewraie any other name therof that hath been described, or known of the old writers. . . . In English it is called Turky corne and Turky wheate: the inhabitants of America . . . do call it *Maizium* and *Maizum* and *Mais*.

But the English inhabitants of America never took to the word "maize." Rather, they adopted the term "Indian corn" to distinguish it from British corn, meaning all the grains known in Europe before Indians came into their ken. "Their Corn is of two sorts," John Harris reported in his *Voyages & Travels* (1748), "*English* Wheat . . . and Maize, or *Indian* Corn, which . . . grows in a great Ear or Head as big as the Handle of a large Horsewhip."

"Corn" in Old English meant a small worn-down particle, as, say, a grain of sand or salt; by extension, "corn" meant cereal grain in general and wheat in particular. When Biblical Ruth "stood in tears amid the alien corn," she was standing in a field of Mesopotamian wheat. Germans compounded the confusion by calling maize *Welschkorn,* after a botanist labeled it thus in 1539, saying it was "without doubt first brought to us by merchants from warm lands of fat soils." To the Turks during the period of the Ottoman Empire, on the other hand, maize, which they called *kukuruz,* signified barbarism. The Ottoman sultans erected a grain wall between their own people and those they ruled: the Turks ate wheat, while their Balkan and Hungarian subjects ate maize, which did nothing to elevate the status of "Turkey corn" in the rest of Europe. Portuguese muddled the names further by confusing maize with millet or sorghum. To this day the Portuguese term for corn is *milho,* a close derivative of *milhete,* "millet," and the South African name for maize, "mealies," comes from *milho.*

Contemporary anthropologists have made us aware that different societies live in different worlds, "not merely the same world with different labels attached." The Old World attached wheat labels to colonize an alien corn that was far more alien than it knew. Thirty years before the first English colonists landed in Plymouth, Gerarde's *Herball* set the tone of Europe's attitude toward New World corn for years to come:

Turky wheate doth nourish far lesse than either Wheate, Rie, Barly or Otes. . . . The barbarous Indians which know no better, are constrained to make a vertue of necessitie, and think it a good food; whereas we may easily iudge that it nourisheth but little, and is of hard and euill digestion, a more conuenient foode for swine than for man.

4 *Frumentum Indicum luteum.*
Yellow Turky Wheat.

6 *Frumentum Indicum cæruleum.*
Blew Turky Wheat.

5 *Frumentum Indicum rubrum.*
Red Turky Wheat.

From John Gerarde's Herball, or Generall Historie of Plantes *(1597).* Rare Books and Manuscripts Division, The New York Public Library, Astor, Lenox and Tilden Foundations

One hundred and forty years after the English landed, Josiah Atkins of Connecticut, following General Washington through Virginia in 1781, lamented that their want of provisions reduced them to eating coarse Indian meal. "This is what people live on chiefly in these parts & what they call Hoe cakes. However, we not being used to such bread nor such country . . . all these together make my trials unsupportable." So unsupportable, it seems, that Atkins died in Virginia that same year, at age thirty-two. The hoe-cake natives, on the other hand, thought British wheat vastly inferior to their own grain and were horrified when these aliens fed sacred Indian corn—stalk, leaf, husk and cob—to their cows, chickens and pigs.

From a wheat culturist's point of view, corn was peculiar indeed. First was the plant's ungainly height, which rivaled a man's and sometimes exceeded it, reaching twenty feet. Next was the clumsy arrangement of its seeds, clamped together into one or more thick clubs halfway down the stalk, instead of the numberless graceful tassels waving atop stalks of "orient and immortal wheat." Third were the bastard colors and shapes produced by a profligate copulation. Fourth was the cloistering leaf sheath that kept seeds chaste as nuns, *and* as infertile, until man violated the cob. Finally, corn was common, cheap and therefore vulgar.

From a corn culturist's point of view, these very peculiarities made corn a godsend and, to the Indian, literally divine. It grew tall with outstretched arms like its brother, man. For its brother's use, it sacrificed every part of its body. Its abundant seeds, massed and well anchored in a central stem, could be eaten as fruit, vegetable or cereal, and at every stage of their growing, green or mature, raw or roasted, whole or ground. It stored its own grain in a waterproof wrapper on the stalk and did not have to be harvested when ripe. In addition, it grew with great speed and abundance and with half the labor of the foreign grains.

From the point of view of nature, corn was unnatural. Botanists today call it a "hopeless monster," for it cannot reproduce itself without man's help. Not only does the husk wrap the seeds so tightly that they cannot disperse, but the seeds are so tightly massed that, if a shucked ear happens to be buried in earth, the young shoots die from overcrowding. On the other hand, since corn adapts more readily than other grains to extreme climates and varied soils, it grows in more places than any other of the world's grains. As an energy converter, it surpasses all—in yield, speed and edibility of the total plant.

This drawing made from a pottery vessel from the Chicama Valley, an early agricultural site (2500 to 1800 B.C.) on the north coast of Peru, renders a detailed botanical understanding of the corn plant: the internodes of the stalks, corn ears ending in silks, tassels with a central spike and branches. From Lehman and Doering, The Art of Old Peru, courtesy Paul Mangelsdorf

From the point of view of culture, corn is unique among the world's staples because the earliest corn we have found was man-made, a cultural artifact. Since it cannot reproduce unaided, its relation to man is without parallel. To its native cultivators, corn coexisted with man on equal terms, as if corn and men grew up together as children of earth and sky. "When you're working with a wheat plant, who cares?" asks a contemporary botanist, Garrison Wilkes. "But when you're dealing with a corn plant, it's different. It's of human height, and you can look it in the eye. It's one on one."

To English yeomen who settled Plymouth in hopes of bettering themselves, wheat stood for upward mobility from barley-and-oats peasantry. Wheat was a matter of class, and corn was beyond the pale. When Edward Johnson wrote home in 1654 to praise the *Wonder Working Providence of Sions Savior in New England,* he focused on the new egalitarianism of wheat: "Now good white and wheaten bread is no dainty, but even ordinary man hath his choice." When Preacher Edward Taylor looked for a metaphor to encompass the ineffable qualities of his Lord, he didn't speak of barley cakes or corn pone. God's Bread of Life was ground from "the Purest Wheate in Heaven, his deare-dear Son" to make "Heavens Sugar Cake." And when Mistress Anne Bradstreet poeticized "corn" in her elegy on the death of a grandchild, you can be sure she didn't mean the Indian corn outside her door but the grain of British poetry:

> And Corn and grass are in their season mown,
> And time brings down what is both strong and tall.

CORN, U.S.A.

How much the naming of corn mattered I discovered at the second reunion of the Kennedy clan, this time in Oklahoma City. I found that Oklahoma was the only place in the country where you could go to the National Cowboy Hall of Fame and the National Hall of Fame for Famous American Indians on the same day. Of course this is the only place in the country that even has a Cowboy or Indian Hall of Fame. It is also the only place in the country that has a town named Corn.

"The only way you git to Corn is if that's where you're going," Flo says. "Corn's not a place you just drive through." Flo Ratzluff Richardson is Corn born and bred, as were her parents, retired now from their farm in the "country," as she calls it, meaning the land around Corn. The town of Corn, including a Main Street two blocks long, is what I would call country. A few white bungalows line up like opposing baseball teams on either side of Main Street behind opposing churches, Mennonite Brethren on one side and Calvary Baptist on the other, flanked by the Corn Historical Society Museum and Post Office, the Dutch Touch Cafe, Albert Odefehr American Legion, Veal's Grocery, Corn Town Hall and a tall white grain elevator labeled "CORN" at the end of town. Beyond that is nothing but red earth and flat green fields. Red earth gave the state its name, from the Choctaw *humma* for red and *okla* for people. Green fields gave the town its name of Corn, but not for maize.

Corn is a Mennonite community of Dutch-German wheat farmers who spelled Corn with a "K" when they first settled here in 1893, because *Korn* is German for "grain" and the grain they raised was wheat. Earlier they had raised wheat in the Ukraine, where Catherine the Great had given their ancestors both land and religious freedom in the eighteenth century and where a century later Alexander II had taken both away. Migrating through Canada to Kansas and finally to Oklahoma, after the Indian Appropriation Act of 1889, they built a church of sod, then frame, then brick. Today their church of poured concrete is the center for Mennonite missionaries from around the world.

I got to Corn—population 483—by driving due west from Oklahoma City on I-40 for a couple of hours, then south on Route 54 until a watertower spelled "CORN" in green letters above a faded sign, "CORN BIBLE ACADEMY, A Christian High School." Mennonite Dirk Bouma, owner of the Dutch Touch Cafe, got to Corn from Holland. His wife, Shabnum, got here from India. The entire population of Corn drops in to Dutch Touch at least three or four times a day to eat *verenikas* and *schnetkas* with their coffee and to keep in touch with the day's events. No jail, no police, no saloon—everyone keeps an eye out for, and on, his neighbor. "You sacrifice privacy," says James Resneder, at thirty-four sole owner and operator of the *Washita County Enterprise*, where Flo works part-time. "But I like living in a small town," he says. "I like being able to pick up the phone, get a wrong number and talk anyway because you know who's on the line."

Flo likes the family gatherings, listening to stories of how folks used to come to town on Saturdays and park in the middle of the street to sell their eggs and get their haircuts. "I've always had a real soft spot for the old days when the whole family did everything together," she says. "It was a closeness."

Four miles south on Route 54 there's an even closer community, about half as big as Corn, named Colony. "We're two hundred and one, countin' the dogs," says the town mayor, John Kauger, whose German parents also came here from Russia but as Lutherans, not Mennonites. To the left of John's house are horses, to the right are cows, and dead ahead are three churches and a small adobe Indian museum founded by his daughter Yvonne. Colony took its name from John Seger's Indian Colony, built in 1872, when this was Cheyenne-Arapaho land in the midst of IndanTerritory.

Inside John introduces me to his wife, Alice, from Mississippi, and to a slender dark-haired girl who is dusting the chairs and the Indian paintings on the walls. She is Mary Haury, whose great-grandfather was an Arapaho chief at the time John Seger was a farmer working with the Bureau of Indian Affairs and trying to persuade Arapaho hunters to stay put and learn to farm. After the Dawes Act of 1887 reduced tribal homelands to allotments of 160 acres, and after the Land Run of 1889 brought in land-hungry ranchers, Seger built with the help of the Arapahos and in defiance of the Bureau a schoolhouse encircled by cottages—Seger's Indian Colony. The schoolhouse is a two-story, red-brick colonial affair of a certain grandeur, which it retains even now when its windows are boarded and its walls crumbling in the dusty oak grove where Cheyenne-Arapahos gather for their annual powwow in the fall. Even then, Seger's reign was brief, for he was caught in the crossfire between white Bureau chiefs and Cheyenne chiefs, and in 1905 was fired from the school. When he died in 1928 at the age of eighty-two, his friend Joe Creeping Bear delivered the eulogy:

> *Dear Mr. Seger is gone, his darling form no more on earth is seen.*
> *He is gone to live just o'er the sea on a shore that is ever green.*

Corn and Colony, the one named for wheat and the other for Indians, named the contradictions as America's midsection got settled and unsettled by a Babel of opposing tribes. "There's some animosity between Corn and Colony," says James Resneder of the *Washita County Enterprise*. "The land down there was poorer, so the farmers were poorer, until they found there was an underground river and they could irrigate." Colony is on the edge of a seven-mile-wide river that runs underground from Canada through central Oklahoma. Now while Corn grows wheat, Colony grows peanuts and prospers, but the Arapahos have gone. "Only two families left," says Mary Haury, "and so few gathered

"I took up a conversation with a gorgeous country girl wearing a low-cut cotton blouse that displayed the beautiful sun-tan on her breast tops. She was dull. She spoke of evenings in the country making popcorn on the porch. . . . And what else do you do for fun? I tried to bring up boyfriends and sex. . . . What do you do on Sunday afternoons? I asked. She sat on her porch. The boys went by on bicycles and stopped to chat. She read the funny papers, she reclined on the hammock. What do you do on a warm summer's night? She sat on the porch, she watched the cars in the road. She and her mother made popcorn."

—JACK KEROUAC, *On the Road* (1957)

for the powwow last year that they didn't even set up the tepee they used to call Big Church."

"When I was growing up, there were about thirty Indians to one white," says John, who graduated in 1932 from the first class of the high school that replaced Seger's schoolhouse. One of his classmates, Paul Bitchknee, served with the Army's 45th Division in World War II and when he landed in Sicily, John recalls, he raised his hand and said, "Columbus, I have come to return your visit."

Oklahoma is full of anomalies like the conjunction of Corn and Colony, and so is its history, like so much of history in this part of the world. When the fathers of my grandfathers crossed the Mississippi with a blueprint of the Promised Land in their heads, killing Indians when they had to in the name of the Peaceable Kingdom, they were driving roughshod over the graves of a civilization that was cradled eight thousand years before Moses was cradled in the bulrushes of the Nile. A hundred years before Christ was cradled in Bethlehem, the Hopewell Indians of Ohio had begun to build the giant circular earthworks of their ceremonial centers and to sculpt finely wrought effigies in copper and mica to bury in their domed mounds. A thousand years before the Kennedy clan reunited in Oklahoma, the Moundbuilders of the Mississippi had built from Maya blueprints the four-square tabernacle they named Cahokia, the largest temple complex in the world, larger by three acres than the Great Pyramid of Giza. When my grandfathers' fathers set out across the wilderness it was less virgin, as one historian says, than widowed.

From my cousins I learned that my Grandmother Kennedy was an eighth-generation Culver, descended from Edward and Ann, married in Dedham, Massachusetts, in 1638, to produce progeny named Zebulun, Ebenezer, Hezekiah, names sacred to the Biblical cultivators of wheat. Culvers may have been among the batch of English who landed on Cape Cod in 1620 and who fell on the stored grain they found there as if it were manna from Heaven, rather than the hard-won labor of civilized hands. Six years earlier, Captain Thomas Hunt had plundered the Nausets on Cape Cod not only of corn but of seven of their men, whom he sold as slaves in Spain. As heathen, these were assuredly agents of Satan and therefore fair game.

"The whole earth is the Lord's garden," Governor John Winthrop would tell Edward and Ann Culver at Massachusetts Bay, "and He hath given it to the sons of Adam to be tilled and improved by them." One of Satan's slaves who had escaped from Spain to England had learned enough English to help the colonists improve the Lord's garden in Plymouth, after he was sent back to Massachusetts, but Squanto too was an anomaly. The trick of fertilizing fields with alewives or other fish he had learned in England, where land was scarce. The native blueprint for corn was different.

"For Americans," Daniel Boorstin wrote, "discovery and growth were synonymous from the very beginning." From the very beginning, these words meant radically different things to the people of wheat and to the people of corn. From the very beginning, the wheat people's discovery of this new land was synonymous with the growth of a new language that fostered territorial exploration, discovery and change—the language of science. But what did "from the very beginning" mean? To the sons of Father Adam it meant one thing, to the sons of Mother Corn another. Those who had inhabited this land for at least twenty thousand years, who spoke the language of myth and metaphor and enacted it in ceremony and art, meant different things by "discovery," "growth" and "beginning."

From the very beginning of my search for the center of my own people, in Nebraska, in Oklahoma, I fell into the hotchpotch confusions registered in Arapaho Colony and Mennonite Corn. Not just conflicting worlds but self-contradictory ones, fractured and displaced. Improving the Lord's garden took its toll and I had ghosts to appease, including the ghost of a dead mother who did not find paradise in an orange grove in California and went corn mad for real. The Way West for some was the Trail of Tears for others, for settlers as well as natives, and I saw no way to reconcile the two. Still, there was my own discovery of the land's center. Still, there was the growth of corn. A beginning.

A mile west of the wheatfields of Corn I found a stand of Indian corn grown by a man who looked like my Grandfather Kennedy, farmer A. C. Hinz, whose gnarled hands and eyes blue as his overalls testified to eighty-three years of Oklahoma winds and weathers. Born in a dugout on this same land, Hinz grows at the far end of his wheatfields a little corn just for roastin' ears, he says. "If you want a good-tastin' roastin' ear, you use big yellow dent, the old-fashioned corn." Farmer Hinz has kept his dent seed pure for fifty years. "I don't detassel," he explains, "but corn, it's funny how it interbreeds so quickly, just that *poll*-en [poll as in pole] fallin' on the silks."

On the way to his cornpatch he points to a dam that beavers have built from good-sized boulders that fell in the creek, beavers weighing two hundred pounds, he says, big enough to move rock. He points to a cottonwood tree split in two by lightning. "That's a historical tree," he says. "Used to be Indian camps all along here and the cowboys and Indians were feudin', stealin' a few of each other's cattle, so the Indians tied a few boys to the tree, scalped 'em and burnt 'em, so the government sent in the Fort Wayne cavalry and killed them some Indians." That was in his father's day. The radio in his pickup truck is playing

The coupling of oil derricks and corn stalks, in a bas-relief on a public building in Chickasha, Oklahoma, is only one of the incongruities in the settling of Oklahoma. Photo by Gregory Thorp

a country song that warns, "Don't call him cowboy, Until you make him ride." That was in my day.

Not until I step into the red earth of his greening field do I begin to put the two together, his past and my present, my past and the country's present. The smell—dank and musty, yet fresh like the smell of corn silks when you first rip off the husks—is overpowering. "It's shooting for tassel," he says. And I see that this squadron of green ten feet tall, armed with outstretched blades, is helmeted by plumes of pale lavender, some malformed with bulbous flowers, others with hermaphroditic ears and tassels entangled in the same husks. Where a leaf joins a stalk I see a secondary shoot of leaves and, within, a delicate ear the length of my finger, lined with rows of tiny pointed kernels white as baby's teeth, each shooting a fine silken hair from its center, hairs that seem to grow as I watch, that seem to stretch for release from their tight sheath to burst like pale sea-green anemones into a cloud of pollen. Shooting for tassel.

Stripped of its green cloak, the silk lies as glossy and abundant as pubic hair. The sexiness of corn. Old World paintings of Danaë and Jove, coming in a shower of gold. New World photos of Culvers and Kennedys, coming to turn corn into cash. In farmer Hinz's cornfield in Corn, U.S.A, the corn silks smell of wet, fecund earth the color of dried blood. And I know that the growth of corn is not only up but down, down into the muck where roots stretch toward the darkness, toward the germinating seeds of life which are sown, as both Christians and Indians knew but knew differently, in blood.

(overleaf) A Mixtec drawing depicts a cornfield made fertile by ritual offerings of blood from above and a corpse below, curled like a seed in the earth. The germinating Goddess of Earth and of Maize is personified as "Maize Stalk Drinking Blood," in the Codex Vindobonensis (Codex Vienna), late fifteenth century. British Museum *Olaf Krans portrays* Women Planting Corn *in a settlement of Swedish religious dissenters at Bishop Hill, Illinois, c. 1875–1895. To achieve symmetrical rows, a pair of men move a string across the field while the women poke holes at evenly spaced intervals. Shown is Stanley Mazur's 1939 rendering of Krans's original painting.* Courtesy The National Gallery of Art, Washington, D.C.

The Language of Myth

THE SEED OF BLOOD

Blood is the color of the feast of martyred San Sebastian in the valley of Zinacantán near San Cristobal, in Chiapas, on January 21, "the very day of very day," as the Zinacantecs say. I stood on a hill by a shaman's cross festooned with pine and looked into a lake of red. On top of hair coiled at each ear like the hair of Gauguin's Tahitian beauties, women wore folded shawls in colors that burned the eyes—aqua, deep pink, red. Men wore flat wide-brimmed skimmers that burst into streamers of multicolored ribbons over pinstriped tunics of white and red. The tassels of their headcloths were exclamation points of fuchsia. The long black ponchos of the elders were banded with red at neck and shoulders and their turbans were tasseled with red. Two dozen elders, each with a stave of new wood, sat in a row at one side of the square, facing the church front covered in flowers—cloudbursts of white calla lilies, flames of gladioluses and chrysanthemums.

A mariachi band followed a procession of men and boys, carrying daisies and tapers, into the church. Inside, red and green banners spanned the nave beneath a ceiling painted blue, above a floor green with pine needles. Kneeling amid trays of white tapers, clustered families chanted before the tiny figure of San Sebastian on the altar, half swallowed by a wall of flowers and half suffocated by the scent of burning copal. Here and there a body sprawled face down, overcome by poche, the drink of fermented sugar cane ritually dispensed by shot glass from plastic demijohns. Outside, people flocked to stands of tamales and popcorn, Fanta and Pepsi, hovered around great round black fry pans, bubbling with strips of meat and ballooning frybread. A large bull, four legs tied together, waited with open eyes for the knife that would signal the beginning of the feast.

". . . all the historian can do is to reconstruct a myth based on his own selection of fact."
—LÉVI-STRAUSS

Suddenly, from a group of wooden crosses, a band of forest creatures, dangling scarlet penises, sprang into the center, dancing to the cries of beasts and birds. There was Jaguar in a spotted baggy jumpsuit next to the black-masked Spooks. With hand puppets of monkeys and squirrels, they taunted the crowds with obscene gestures. There were Spanish lords and ladies, men in drag, comically elegant in lace and velvet. There was Raven flapping his wings of painted boards and pointing his conical beak. His beak held an ear of corn, for Raven, or *K'uk'ulchan* in the language of Tzotzil, is none other than Quetzalcoatl, the Plumed Serpent of the Toltec, the god of wind and rain who first brought corn to man.

The dancers enacted their version of the story of San Sebastian, left for dead in the woods but saved by wild animals in order that he might captain the Spaniards and reign as patron saint of the Zinacantecs. Here Sebastian was Maya, and in his victory over death the Zinacantecs celebrated their triumph over the conquistadors, reaffirming in present ritual those collective memories that the Maya call dreams and Europeans call history and myth.

While the dancers danced, a group of men mounted horses and raced one by one through a leaf-covered chute. Like jousting knights, they charged with staves, which they aimed at the heart of the saint painted on a stick hanging between poles. It is said that only a pure Zinacantec can pierce his heart, for the Zinacantecs have absorbed the saint into their own pantheon of martyrs, holy martyrs like Quetzalcoatl, who absorbed earlier gods of corn.

Maize gods native to Central and South America were far more ancient than Christian saints or the crucified God whose image the Spaniards planted in maize fields red with the blood of conquest. For these Maya descendants, the association of maize with blood is as old as the oldest Maya memory, as old as the first planted seed. As their culture evolved, ancient Maya fertilized seeds of corn with the sacrificed blood of their enemies and the blood of their own kings. For the Maya a single kernel of corn is symbolic of what Christians symbolize by the holy cross—the tragic and monstrous truth that the seed of life is death.

Today, in the Maya ruins of Palenque in the Yucatán jungle, the Temple of the Foliated Cross reveals in its carvings what Christians call the Tree of Life. For the Maya, it is the World Tree in the shape of a cross, where the crosspiece or branches are formed by leaves and silk-topped ears of corn, each ear a human head. The corn sprouts from a trunk of blood rooted in the head of the Water-Lily Monster that floats on the primal waters of the Underworld. Here out of the monster's mouth a god is born—God K, the Young Lord, the Maize God.

The Foliated Cross at Palenque depicts the cosmos as a leafy corn plant, through which the life-blood of the universe flows, uniting the World Tree at the center with the kings on either side, the Underworld with the heavens, the living with the dead. Neg. No. 320486. Courtesy Department of Library Services, American Museum of Natural History

Today, Maya descendants in Chiapas, Yucatán and Guatemala live double lives between Christian and Maya crosses, Christian Axle-trees and Maya World Trees, Christian saints and maize gods, Catholic priests and shamans— lives colored by blood. "People, when they are dying, save their corn, which has beautiful grains," a modern Chorti told an interviewer in 1972. "They look for those with beautiful white grains, with black corn, with red corn. Because they say that that is the blood of Jesus Christ." In a kernel of red corn, a contemporary Maya sees not only the cosmic globe but a drop of blood that condenses all of human history into a single germ of life.

Above a tributary of Rio Motagua in western Honduras stands Copán, which Michael Coe calls "one of the loveliest of all Classic Maya ruins" and which the nineteenth-century archaeologist John Lloyd Stephens once bought for $50. The price included the perfectly preserved Ball Court, the Temple of the Hieroglyphic Stairway and four figures carved in green volcanic tuff that are among the finest pieces of Maya art—the busts of the Young Maize God.

One of these, carved around A.D. 775, in the Late Classic period, is a delicate boy whose upraised and downturned palms curiously suggest the hand gestures of Buddha Sàkyamuni. This Young Lord once adorned the temple-palace of Yax-Pac, last of the Maya kings. When the king entered the

Here the Young Corn God (shaped as a mold whistle in the Late Classic period) embodies the rhythm of regeneration as he dances between earth and sky, with the Witz or Mountain Monster beneath him and signs of the Moon Goddess in the leaf curls above his head. Private collection, photo by Justin Kerr

innermost sanctum of his acropolis, he walked through the mouth of a gigantic serpent, over its stone fangs and through its gullet, to reach the sacrificial altar within. Here from his penis and earlobes the king drew his own blood to fertilize the Young Maize Gods "growing" from clefts in the stone heads of the Cauac-Monsters that ornamented the cornices of the temple's exterior. A Maya would have seen in the face of the Young Lord an ear of corn: in his hair, corn silk; in his gesturing hands, waving leaves of corn; in his closed eyes, the silent teeming life within the plant. Even today this carved stone evokes the living plant. When the palace fell into ruin, wrote the authors of *The Blood of Kings* (1986), "the Maize Gods fell across the East Court like a ripened crop that was not harvested."

So subtle and complex is the ancient Maya language of corn, carved in stone, painted on walls and pottery and screen-folds made of beaten bark, that only in recent years have its mysteries begun to be decoded. We now see that the Maya Maize God, like the medieval Christian God, stands at the center of a cluster of images and symbols that evolved slowly but took primary shape in the third to ninth centuries after Christ, a period rich in Christian saints and Maya maize gods. Rich also in Maya script which recorded the history and destiny of a people as expressively as Christian Scripture. Maya hieroglyphs, once we can read them, may help us learn what "discovery," "growth" and "beginning" meant to a civilization built on the symbolic as well as the physical potency of maize.

Until 1952, epigraphers tended to misread Maya hieroglyphs by oversimplifying them. Ever since Bishop Diego de Landa in the mid-sixteenth century sketched an "alphabet" of twenty-nine signs, scholars had quarreled over their meanings by construing them as either exclusively a phonetic or exclusively an ideographic system. The breakthrough came when they were read as both—as phonetic letters or syllables *and* as ideograms or rebuses. Anagogic symbols were as typical of the New World as Aristotelian logic was of the Old, a logic compelled to divide what the mythic mind unites.

Divide and destroy, some might say, in view of Bishop Landa's torching in 1562 of the thousands of heathen texts—red and black drawings on bark paper bound in covers of jaguar skin—that recorded the Maya world. Only four such texts escaped the flames: three codices that we name for the European cities which house them—Madrid, Paris, Dresden—a fourth, the Grolier, which is the only one to remain in Mexico. Until recently, what we knew about the ancient Maya we knew principally from the encyclopedic work Landa proceeded to write about the life of the natives in post-Conquest Yucatán, *Relación de las cosas de Yucatán* (1566). Ironically, modern editions of Landa's work are illustrated with the blasphemous images of the Maya books that escaped his burnings.

Not only the books but the monuments of Classic sites are now read in a new way, as we see that Maya glyphs record history as well as myth, the history of dynasties contemporary with the early Christian martyrs in Rome and the close of the Han dynasty in China. When Linda Schele and Mary Ellen Miller explored the dynasties and rituals of Maya art in their *Blood of Kings,* they found that the Maize God depicted in the great carved Temple of the Foliated Cross was but a mask of the historical king who built the major temples of the Sun, Cross and Foliated Cross at Palenque in the seventh century.

Lord Chan-Bahlum, or Snake-Jaguar, who stands like a giant on the left of the Foliated Cross, became king in A.D. 684, after the death of his father, Lord Pacal, who stands on the right. Chan-Bahlum was believed to incarnate in mortal form a higher Lord, the Young Lord of Maize. At the same time, he stood as an embodiment of the Cross itself, the World Tree as a living corn plant, bearing human heads, rooted in the Kan-cross Water-Lily Monster, symbolic of the raised-field method of agriculture, with its ecology of canals, water lilies, birds, fish and corn plants, all flourishing together, though only with the aid of man. The Tree is crowned with Celestial Bird, or Vision Serpent Bird, symbolic of the vision quest by which the king communicated, on behalf of his people, with the Otherworld of gods and ancestors. Pacal offers to his son the Personified Bloodletter, by which Chan-Bahlum will draw blood painfully from his penis in order to evoke the beneficence of the gods and sustain the social order of man and the agricultural order of nature.

The Foliated Maize God, as he is called, is another form of the Tonsured Maize God, discerned by Karl Taube in the canoe images carved on bones found in the temple mausoleum of Tikal in Guatemala. The forehead of the god who sits in the center of the canoe has been shaved and the head flattened and elongated. The tonsuring separates a short brow fringe from his tufted top, as if his head were a husked corn ear and his hair, corn silk. On his head, he wears the Jester God, a personification of royal and sacred power that Maya kings wore as a crown of jade, shaped in three points like a jester's cap and signifying the Hero Twins of the *Popol Vuh*. His wrist at his forehead suggests

SACRAMENTS:
Guatemala City, 1775
"Nor do the Indians come to Mass. They do not respond to announcements of the bell. They have to be sought out on horseback in villages and fields and dragged in by force. Absence is punished with eight lashes, but the Mass offends the Mayan gods and that has more power than fear of the thong. Fifty times a year, the Mass interrupts work in the fields, the daily ceremony of communion with the earth. For the Indians, accompanying step by step the corn's cycle of death and resurrection is a way of praying; and the earth, that immense temple, is their day-to-day testimony to the miracle of life being reborn. For them all earth is a church, all woods a sanctuary.
—EDUARDO GALEANO, *Memory of Fire II: Masks & Faces* (1987)

Stingray Paddler   iguana   spider monkey   dead king   parrot   Kankin dog   Jaguar Paddler

The Tonsured Maize God in the middle of the canoe on his journey to the Underworld. From Linda Schele and Mary Ellen Miller, *Blood of Kings* (1986)

death, imaged by the sinking of his canoe into the waters of the Underworld. He is both Maize God and king, for the bone carvings celebrate the life of the historical Ruler A, buried with a royal treasury of pottery and jade in the mausoleum built after his death in A.D. 735.

Everywhere the phallus-shaped head of the Tonsured Lord is associated with fertility, corn and blood. Glyphs of the god show corn kernels, or "corn curls," as Maya iconographers say, affixed to his head or hands. Often the curls sprout corn leaves and cobs, like those of the Foliated God. We see both forms often in the imagery of Late Classic plates and vessels which depict the severed head of the Maize God floating in a pool of blood. The curving tassel at the back of his head suggests corn tassels, as his beaded necklace suggests drops of blood. On the rim of such plates are Kan-crosses, which bear both the phonetic value of the Kan sign and its ideographic value as the sign for Day, suggesting the color yellow, ripeness, maize.

The life cycle of maize was the great metaphor of Maya life, the root of its language, its rituals and its calendar. We now see that the many configurations of the Maize God evolved from the seed of life embodied in the Kan sign. Kan is only one of the twenty named days of the Maya calendar, but wherever the Kan sign appears in conjunction with a god, it refers to crops and the powers for good and evil that affect them. Kan is also the syllable *wah,* which denotes bread, tortilla, tamale. Bowls holding Kan signs may represent offerings of maize, and therefore blood offerings and other precious things—jade beads, drops of blood. The beaded streams that fall from the hands of the Tonsured Lord and king in Stela 1 at Yaxchilan suggest drops of blood falling as dynastic seed.

Sometimes from the Kan or kernel there sprouts a serpent's head with a single eye at the top. The Madrid Codex, which deals largely with farm ceremonies, includes a cartoon sequence of corn plants growing like serpents from godheads, from seeds in the earth, from Kan signs and from Ik, the sign of Breath or Life. As the serpentine leaves and stalks of the plant represent the fertility associated everywhere with the snake, so the kernel represents the originating breath we name the soul. In the Maya language, the word for "serpent" is a homonym of the word for "sky," and both are pronounced "Kan."

The earliest Maize Gods of the Olmec, named gods I and II by the iconographers, prefigure by a thousand years the later Maize Gods of the Maya, which culminate in the many guises of the Plumed Serpent. Like a many-leaved plant of corn, they spring from the same "Seed-corn Dot." The Olmec saw corn as a three-part plant, its vegetation sometimes sprouting from the round Dot, sometimes incorporated into the Bracket, a sign abstracted from the paired fangs and vegetation that bracket the mouth of God I. From the cleft head of God II maize sprouts from the cleft itself, from the forehead, from the eyes or mouth—sometimes as a phallic cone (Banded Maize), sometimes as a dot with three feathers (Feathered Seed), sometimes as a fleur-de-lis (Three-pronged Vegetation). Like a plant the symbols of the three-part seedling develop into the three-pointed headdress of the Maya Jester God, uniting the primal cleft gods of the Olmec at La Venta with the Foliated Maize Lords of the Maya at Copán.

Through such complex figurations of vegetation and violence, blood and maize, the Maya expressed the symbiotic exchange between corn and man, each imaging the other. The image of the tonsured and foliated head of the Maize God severed from its body is at the same time a phallic ear of corn stripped from its stalk. The ritual perforation of the penis with one of the sacred bloodletting instruments—the obsidian blade, stingray spine and flint knife—at the same time enacts the husking of the cob with sharpened wood or bone. At Palenque, the historical Lord Chan-Bahlum saw in the severed head of the Maize God a mirror image of his own tonsured head, in the pool of blood his own life stream, rising as sap through the World Tree that connects the Cauac Monster of the Underworld to the Celestial Bird of the Heavens.

What the Maya read as sacred, we read as art. Today, a fine version of the Beheaded God, incised in the lid of a cache vessel used to catch the blood in these perforating rituals, rests peaceably despite its horrific message in the Art Museum of Princeton University. Three bloodletting lancets sharpened from stone and bone, together with the signs of Kan-cross and bone-beads, mark the undulating wave patterns in the background as blood, on which the severed head appears to float.

Although I spent most of my adult life in the town of Princeton, I never saw this vessel and if I had, its figurations would have signified nothing to me. They would have meant little more, or so I imagine, to my Uncle Roy, my father's younger brother, when he attended the Presbyterian Theological Sem-

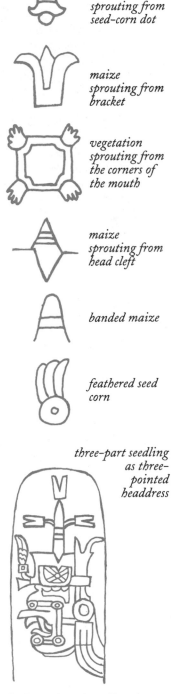

maize sprouting from seed-corn dot

maize sprouting from bracket

vegetation sprouting from the corners of the mouth

maize sprouting from head cleft

banded maize

feathered seed corn

three-part seedling as three-pointed headdress

Redrawn from Peter David Joralemon, "A Study of Olmec Iconography" (1971).

A drawing of the cache vessel lid (Early Classic Maya, A.D. 350 to 500) shows the decapitated head of the Maize God in profile beneath three bloodletting instruments—obsidian blade, stingray spine and flint knife—on top of a symbolic bloodletting bowl, marked with the sign for the sun. The Art Museum, Princeton University; lent anonymously; drawing by Lin Deletaille

inary at Princeton before setting off as a missionary for the jungles of Brazil. Had he seen the vessel, he might have thought of John the Baptist, but it's doubtful that he would have thought also of the corn he had husked as a boy in Kansas. And when he sang hymns for the jungle heathen, accompanied by his wife on her portable organ, it's doubtful that he would have seen any connection between his sacrificed God and theirs. He had brought them the Word of God by way of Calvin, a Word that severed the head of the Creator God from His creation and that damned at once the World, the Flesh and the Devil. He brought words and worlds unintelligible to savages who believed that it was now as it was in The Beginning, that men and gods were created one flesh, one blood, from the same vital substance of corn.

Maya Corn Language, from Tamales to Corn Gods

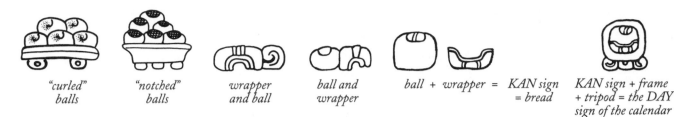

*"curled"
balls*   *"notched"
balls*   *wrapper
and ball*   *ball and
wrapper*   *ball + wrapper =
KAN sign
= bread*   *KAN sign + frame
+ tripod = the DAY
sign of the calendar*

Above left, drawings represent actual tamales, or balls of corn dough with fillings marked as "curled" or "notched." The dough and the wrapper of the tamale metamorphose into the Kan sign, which means bread or sacred offerings, and into the Kan glyph for Day. Below, corn kernels, ears and foliage are integrated in different ways with human heads and beaded streams to signify sacred corn gods and blood sacrifice.

     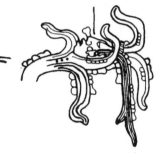

*corn ears as
human profile*   *corn curls and
foliage*   *corn curl and
foliage sprout
from head*   *corn ear
extends head*   *beaded
streams of
water*   *beaded streams
of blood*   *corn god as blood sacrifice*

At far left, a large ball of corn dough is unwrapped on a bed of banana leaves for a contemporary Yucatec communion feast. At near left, God K (from a West Court panel in Copán) holds a bowl of corn dough as an offering and sits on a bed of corn leaves, as if he were himself the communion tamale. Based on Karl Taube, "The Maize Tamale in Classic Maya Diet, Epigraphy, and Art" (1989)

CORN CANNIBALS

WHEN MY UNCLE ROY landed in São Paulo, the Tupinambas who had once occupied a two thousand-mile strip of Brazilian coast had given up the cannibal ways reported with a certain relish by Amerigo Vespucci in his *Mundus Novus* (1504–5), when he first encountered the savages of Brazil. "I saw salted human flesh suspended from beams between the houses, just as with us it is the custom to hang bacon and pork," he wrote, and added that the cannibals, for their part, wondered "why we do not eat our enemies and do not use as food their flesh which they say is most savory."

For two centuries, accounts of the cannibalism of the New World evoked the zeal of priestly converters even as they justified the greed of conquistadors. Even as late as this century, when the works of Father Bernardino de Sahagún were first published in English, a new wave of missionaries, Protestant and Catholic, was fired by his account of the cannibal stews of the ancient Aztec. After they had slain a captive, Sahagún reported, they cut him in pieces and offered the best piece of dark meat (a thigh) to Moctezuma. Then, at the house of the captor, "They made each one an offering of a bowl of stew of dried maize, called *tlacatlaolli*. . . . On each went a piece of the flesh of the captive."

How do Americans today respond when they learn that cannibalism was practiced by many of the tribes of our own continent? As late as 1756 there were reports of the Iroquois around Ontario eating captives taken in war, which jibed with Jesuit accounts from the sixteenth century. Jesuits who had witnessed the torture and ritual deaths practiced by the Iroquois and Huron on each other noted that the torturers seemed to act not in rage but in gentleness when they first burned different parts of the live victim, thrusting flaming brands down his throat and red-hot embers into his eyes, then cutting off several of his members, a foot here, a hand there, and finally the head "to carry it to the Captain Ondessone, for whom it had been reserved, in order to make a feast therewith." Commoners were content to make a feast of the trunk and whatever part they could carry home. When the feast was over, the Jesuits observed, "we encountered a Savage who was carrying upon a skewer one of [the victim's] half-roasted hands."

This drawing from the Florentine Codex underlines Sahagún's account of cannibal stews, eaten ceremonially with and without dried maize. Neg. No. 292757, Department of Library Services, American Museum of Natural History

None of the priests, adventurers, missionaries and criminals who busied themselves over four centuries with saving, civilizing and exterminating the brutes could have been expected to connect the cannibalism of "perfidious Savages," as Captain John Smith called them, with the cannibalism planted in the godhead of Christ. Whenever Christians celebrated the Eucharist, they consumed their Lord cannibalistically, but they had so long substituted wheat and grapes, in the form of bread and wine, for the primal connectedness of flesh and blood that the vegetative origins of cannibalism were as easily obscured as vows of chastity and poverty. How could Christians be other than horrified by savages who put a vegetable on equal footing with man and who believed that the primal being whose body had become and was now the world, flesh of their flesh, was incarnate equally in an ear of roasted corn and a half-roasted human hand?

"Then they surrounded those who danced, whereupon they went among the drums. Then they struck the arms of one who beat the drums; they severed both his hands, and afterwards struck his neck, so that his head flew off, falling far away. Then they pierced them all with iron lances, and they struck each with iron swords. Of some they slashed open the back, and then the entrails gushed out. Of some they split the head; they hacked their heads to pieces; their heads were completely cut up. . . . "

—From Bernardino de Sahagún, in the Florentine Codex, quoted by Nigel Davies, *The Aztecs* (1973)

The cannibal ways of the New World sprang from the strength and persistence of an ancient planting culture that had kept its roots intact. High civilizations, as we define them today, began when man with great daring risked burying wild seeds in the earth at one time of year in the hope that green plants would appear in the same place at a later time. By that one act of imagination, Paleolithic man radically altered his relation to earth and to time. In his dawning awareness that the fertility of the earth was related to the alternating light and darkness of the skies, he began to tame by his own selection the wildness of plants he found edible, just as he began to tame by his own selection the wildness of animals he found useful.

That, at any rate, is the scenario of modern science that divorces history from myth to call the one "fact" and the other "fiction." According to the time projections of history, for nearly two million years men hunted, fished and gathered before they planted seed. Then twenty thousand years ago or more, peoples hunting mammoths and giant bison crossed the narrow land-bridge of the Bering Straits and wandered south between two massive sheets of ice that once covered the waterways of Chicago. Archaeologists who have recently uncovered rock paintings in the caves of Pedra Furada in Brazil, and who believe that the charcoal found there came from cooking fires, claim a much earlier date. Indisputably Paleo-Indians were in the Western Hemisphere twelve thousand years ago, from Alaska to Patagonia, roasting over campfires

*"Corn is the only veg-
etable we eat that is
made entirely of seeds,
like a pomegranate. To
eat corn on the cob is to
eat life, like fish roe or
caviar, in which we
cannibalize the future in
the instant."*
—SAMUEL WILSON,
*The Inquiring
Gastronome* (1927)

the game they killed with the flaked stone points that have been found at Onion Portage in Alaska, Clovis in New Mexico, Ayacucho in Peru.

In the context of two million years of non-planting, the three agricultural matrices of the world may be said to have begun at roughly the same time, in 9000 to 5000 B.C. In each matrix, man's crucial act was to tame a wild grass into a domestic grain that could feed an increasingly settled and expanding community. The cultivation of wheat is thought to have begun in Mesopotamia in 9000 to 7000 B.C., the cultivation of rice in southwest Asia in 6000 to 4500 B.C. Three major discoveries by archaeo-botanists in the past forty years give evidence of the cultivation of corn in Mexico, between the highlands of Tehuacán and the tropics of Yucatán, in 6000 to 5000 B.C.

In a remarkable find in the 1960s, Richard MacNeish, encouraged by Paul Mangelsdorf, explored the caves of Tehuacán in the arid highlands of south-central Mexico, near Oaxaca and the ruins of Mitla, and uncovered 24,186 specimens of maize in a total of five caves. More than half of these were whole cobs, so that for the first time an evolutionary growth of seven thousand years could be arranged in sequence. The smallest of the soft cobs were even tinier than those found in New Mexico's Bat Cave and could be dated to 5000 B.C. At first, a jubilant Mangelsdorf announced that this was the wild corn he had known they would find somewhere, but his "discovery" was not unlike Columbus's "discovery" of India. Today, most archaeo-botanists believe that these prehistoric cobs are the earliest known relics of *cultivated* corn and that sometime around 2300 B.C. corn underwent the major evolutionary changes that made it the primary staple of Mesoamerica a thousand years later.

A recent discovery of fossil corn pollen in Oaxaca thought to be nine thousand years old (but pollen dating is extremely speculative) confirms Mexico as the seedbed of corn. So too does an earlier discovery of pollen samples taken by drill cores from depths of six to sixty-nine feet beneath the Palacio de Bellas Artes in the heart of Mexico City. The earliest remains of corn thus far found in South America are in Colombia and suggest a date around 3000 B.C., a thousand years earlier than the arrival of corn in the highlands of Peru. These "discoveries" of modern science confirm what native Americans have always known, that the New World was new only in the sense of Prospero's reply to Miranda, " 'Tis new to thee."

From their first seedbeds in Tehuacán and Yucatán, primitive forms of corn spread north, east and south: north to the Woodland native tribes of the Mississippi and Ohio valleys, east to the Arawaks and Caribs of the Antilles, south to the rainforest tribes of the Amazon and the highland tribes of the Andes. Wherever corn went, the local ecology—rainfall, soil fertility, weed growth—

determined how the crop was grown and what it was grown with. Slash-and-burn, the shifting-field farming called *milpa,* was the earliest and is still the chief method of corn cultivation in the tropics of Mexico and Central and South America. It was a method ideally suited to tropical lands because slashed and burned jungle growth could quickly regenerate itself and renew earth exhausted after two or three years of corn plantings. In recent decades, however, archaeo-botanists have discovered more and more evidence of intensive raised-field farming in ancient Mexico and South America. They have discovered how vast and intricate were the canals dug to create and to irrigate raised fields, which were fertilized organically by water plants and organisms, by water animals and water birds.

As agriculture developed, Mesoamerican Indians grew corn in partnership with plants domesticated earlier—squash, pumpkin, and chili—in a "seed agriculture." Peruvian Indians, on the other hand, grew corn in conjunction with earlier tubers like potatoes and oca in a "vegetable agriculture." The connecting link between the two agricultures, north and south, was corn.

Wherever corn went, civilization followed. When the Olmec erected two thousand years ago the earliest known ceremonial center in this hemisphere at La Venta in northern Tabasco, they connected the action of planting seeds in the earth with the movement of planets and stars in the sky. As corn grew, so did narratives and ceremonies that expressed man's new relation to the organic world when he entrusted his life to buried seeds as well as to migratory animals. Men felt a kinship to animals because they moved as men did across the earth's surface. The myths of the earliest hunting cultures dramatize the struggle between antagonists who are equal, hunter and hunted, alike independent and mobile creatures who rely on skill and speed to outmaneuver each other. Plants, in contrast, stay put. The myths of planting cultures reveal a new terror, an abandonment of human consciousness and immersion in the primeval ooze, the formlessness and flux beneath the earth's crust. Here all creatures breed, grow and decay in the same generative mud. Here man experiences more primally "the voracity of life, which feeds on life," as Joseph Campbell put it, and "the sublime frenzy of this life which is rooted (if one is to see and speak truth) in a cannibal nightmare."

Ritual cannibalism is as central to early planting cultures, Campbell found, as the image of a primal being whose body is the universe. Because for subsistence planters, survival depends directly upon the facts of organic life, their myths express and their ceremonies ritualize the dependency of that life upon death: in the plant world it is vegetable death that generates and sustains new life; in the world of man it is chosen death, self-sacrifice, that generates and sus-

Life from death imaged as the Tree of the Middle Place growing from the belly of a human sacrifice, representing the primal earth goddess. The quetzal bird on top devours the serpent, symbolic of transformation and rebirth. From the Dresden Codex, Maya Postclassic Period, c. A.D. 1300, redrawn by S. G. Morley, *The Ancient Maya* (1946)

tains social order. The tragedy for the conscious animal called man is that pain and death are not only inevitable but necessary. In the Western World, Nietzsche's birth of tragedy begins with the birth of corn.

In the Western World, a plant rather than an animal was the supreme symbol of the life-death connection. Because the New World domesticated few animals in comparison to the Old, its high civilizations retained their planting-culture origins, their primal sense of the mutual dependence of humankind and plant-kind, the interchange of blood with sap and flesh with grain. For the same reason, these civilizations adhered to cannibalistic rituals; animal flesh could not substitute for human flesh because animals did not cultivate plants, only people did.

At the same time, wild animals survived in the New World in unprecedented abundance across vast stretches of tundra, plain, prairie and desert, and their flesh sustained migratory human tribes. One of the oddities of the New World in contrast to the Old is that the ancient conflict between nomad and planter persists to this day. Joseph Campbell spoke of "the culture tides" that for centuries flowed in opposite directions after a few nomadic groups first turned to planting. Settlers widening their village centers to tame more land were in constant conflict with nomads invading those centers to take what others had so conveniently gathered. This cultural dichotomy was shaped and maintained by the topographical extremes of the American landscape. "The great problem of the cultural geography of America," Leo Frobenius said, "lies in the question of how, between the two prodigious negative fields of the northern hunting nomads and the southern forest and water nomads, the American high civilizations could have originated and developed at all."

Develop they did, as those of the Old World did, from the beginning of the Word. "This is the beginning of the Ancient Word" is the way the Sacred Book of the Quiché Maya begins, the Council Book, the *Popul Vuh*. This book, the codices and the post-Conquest *Book of Chilam Balam* are all collections of texts like the Bible or the Book of the Dead. They are both myth and history for a civilization that did not divorce the two but told the history of the gods and the mythos of mankind in a single narrative, as if the Old Testament began not with the genesis of man but with the genesis of the gods and "the emergence of all the sky-earth":

> *the fourfold siding, fourfold cornering,*
> *measuring, fourfold staking*
> *halving the cord, stretching the cord*

in the sky, on the earth,
the four sides, the four corners,

as if the gods were measuring out the entire universe as a cornfield.

The narrative begins with gods and ends with humans, in a collection of stories about the gods who prepared sky-earth before planting within its four sides and four corners the men and women of corn. The literatures of Mesoamerica attempt to chart time as well as place and so recount a series of creations, a fourfold staking of "world ages" from which man emerges at the end. In the *Popul Vuh,* we find that the gods were lonely and wanted someone with enough understanding to talk to but not enough to rival them. At the end the situation is reversed, and we find man worrying about how to keep in touch with the gods. Male and female alike share in the creation of humanity, which is at once a sowing of seeds and a dawning of light, connecting sky-earth by corn.

Corn also connects creation to sacrifice. The twins One Hunahpu and Seven Hunahpu are playing on the ball court when they are summoned by the Lords of Death who have already triumphed over their fathers. The boys are sent to the House of Gloom, given lighted pine sticks and rolled tobacco and told that they must bring them back whole at dawn. But alas, they burn the sticks for light and smoke the tobacco, and so at dawn they are killed. The Lords throw the head of One Hunahpu into a barren tree and instantly the tree is covered with yellow gourds as large as a man's head, the fruit of the calabash tree. A girl called Blood Woman, daughter of the Lord of the Underworld (named Blood Gatherer), sees the fruit and wonders if she should pick it. Then a voice in the branches tells her that the fruit is mere bone and asks her if that is what she wants. I want it, she says. As she reaches up, the bone spits in her palm and tells her that through his spit she will put flesh on the bone of his son. When her father sees that she is pregnant, he calls her a whore and commands the owl Keepers of the Mat to kill her and to bring back a bowl that contains her heart. The girl persuades the owls to fill the bowl with red sap from the croton tree, which looks just like blood, and she escapes to the Upperworld.

Here the girl, her stomach swollen, comes to the

"And so then they put into words the creation,
  The shaping
Of our first mother
  And father.
Only yellow corn
  And white corn were their bodies.
Only food were the legs
  And arms of man.
Those who were our first fathers
  Were the original men.
Only food at the outset
  Were their bodies."
    —*Popul Vuh,* Monro Edmundson
      translation (1971 edition)

house where the mother of the twins still lives. She calls the woman Mother and tells her that the sons of One Hunahpu are inside her. The woman, Xmucame, is outraged by this claim because she believes that her sons are dead. To test the girl, she tells her to fill a big net with corn from the field. In the field, the girl sees but a single corn plant and cries aloud, "Where will I get a netful of corn?" She begs for help from the guardians of the field—Generous Woman, Harvest Woman, Cacao Woman, Cornmeal Woman. She then stands before the tall green plant, takes the red silk of the ear in her hand and pulls it out, leaving the single ear untouched. When she lays out the silk in the net as if the strands were ears of corn, the net is filled. The animals of the field come running, take the net from the girl and parade down the path to the grandmother.

When she sees the full net, the old woman is astonished. "Where is this from?" she asks and storms down the path to the field, but when she gets there she finds only the single stock of corn as before and the place where the net was on the ground. "The sign is there," she says. "I see that you really are my daughter-in-law and that my grandsons will be soothsayers." And so Blood Woman gives birth to twins, whose fathers could not conquer the Lords of Death by strength but did so by guile. The spittle of One Hunahpu was at once corn seed and the flesh of his progeny, as his severed head was the head of the Young Maize God whose death brings the return of the Sun.

Now it becomes time for the grandsons, Hunahpu and Xbalanque, to play ball with the Lords of the Underworld, but they leave with their grandmother "a sign of their word," a sign that they will return: in the center of her house, each boy plants an ear of corn on the earthen floor; when the corn dries, they tell her, it is a sign of their death and when the corn sprouts, it is a sign of their life. In the Underworld, the boys outwit the Lords of Death and by guile recover the head of One Hunahpu and use it as a ball in the ball court. But since they have outwitted both the gods and monster animals sent to defeat them, the boys predict that the Lords of Death will build a great stone oven and burn them there. This death they choose and so they leap into the oven. They have told the seers Xulu and Pacam to grind their bones on a stone the way corn is ground and to sprinkle the bone meal in the river. When the seers do so, the ground bone sinks and after the fifth day the boys reappear—first as catfish, then as vagabonds who dance in various masks the dance of the heart sacrifice. With each sacrifice they bring themselves back to life, and the Lords of Death are so ravished by the dance that they too beg to be sacrificed. So the boys do as they ask, but do not bring them back to life.

When the boys burn in the oven, their grandmother cries out and burns

The Young Maize God of Copán (Maya Late Classic, c. A.D.*775), who is also One Hunahpu of the* Popul Vuh. Reproduced by courtesy of the Trustees of the British Museum

copal in their memory, for the corn plants they have planted in her house have dried up. When the corn plants sprout again, the grandmother rejoices and gives them names: Middle of the House, Middle of the Harvest, Living Corn, Earthen Floor, in order that they will never be forgotten. So today the Quiché Maya burn copal in the pair of shrines (the *uinel*) they place by their cornfields, and after praying that the seeds will sprout again, they pass the ears through the smoke and place them in the center of the house in harvest time. These ears are to be neither eaten nor used as seed corn, Dennis Tedlock has reported, for they are "the heart of the corn" that does not die but remains alive throughout the year, "between the drying out of the plants at harvest time and the sprouting of new ones after planting."

Today, the Quiché use the *Popul Vuh* as a divining book, like the Chinese *I Ching,* because it provides a way of seeing daily events within the unchanging cycles of sky-earth as they were measured at "The Dawn of Life" in "Our Place in the Shadows," when the dawning of seeds and the sowing of stars began. For the people of corn, dawning and sowing are metaphors of each other, for their stories also tell of the "one dawn for all tribes" in the birth of the gods who become sun and moon, Venus and Mars, charted in their cyclic course by the 20-day, 260-day and 52-year cycles of the Maya and Toltec calendars.

One of the twenty named days of the Maya calendar, like the day-sign Kan, is Net. When the old grandmother sees the imprint of the girl's net in the earth by the corn plant, she takes it as a sign that the evening star that rose on the day named Death will reappear as the morning star on the day named Net. The twin maize gods are also aspects of the evening star, the star-mask of Quetzal-coatl, whose heart at his fiery death was transformed into the bright planet that descends into the Underworld in cycles that parallel the cyclic life of corn—and of man. In the *Popul Vuh,* man who sprouts like a seed in the womb sees his birth as the dawn of life; man whose corpse decays in the earth sees his death as the dawn of spirit. Like the twin gods, like the Plumed Serpent, he is both seed and star.

The authors of the *Popul Vuh*—who called themselves "daykeepers" or "mother-fathers of the Word," in imitation of the first "mother-father of life"—recounted also the pilgrimage of the Quiché lords to the East—to the kingdom of the Plumed Serpent. They returned with the Council Book they call "The Light That Came from Across the Sea," which enabled them to found the pyramids and palaces of Rotten Cane. This was the historical citadel of Utatlán, near Chichicastenango on the Pacific side of Guatemala, which the Quiché-speaking Maya founded around A.D. 900, after the abandonment of Palenque and Copán and after the invasions of Nahuatl-speaking Toltec from

Tabasco spread the name and power of the Plumed Serpent. In the *Popul Vuh,* the first men of corn were created in the darkness in the East—at Tula Zuyua, Seven Caves, Seven Canyons—evoking both the historical capital of the Toltec in Tula and the far older capital of Teotihuacán in central Mexico. Here beneath the Pyramid of the Sun are seven underground chambers and here, the *Popul Vuh* says, began the split between the Nahuatl languages of Mexico and the many languages of the Maya, a Pyramid of Babel. In the *Popul Vuh,* as in the Book of Exodus, the story of man is one of exile and wandering, after the golden age at Tula, at the dawn of the many tribes of Mesoamerican civilization in their rising and falling.

Utatlán, which rose as other Maya citadels fell, flourished until 1524, when the Spanish soldiers of Pedro de Alvarado slaughtered most of the inhabitants. Thirty years later, "amid the preaching of God, in Christendom now," a few survivors translated Maya hieroglyphs into the Roman alphabet in order to preserve the *mythistory* of their lost kingdom. The Quiché manuscript survived until the beginning of the eighteenth century, when a Franciscan friar at Chichicastenango, Francisco Ximenez, copied down the text and translated it into Spanish. While the Quiché original was lost, Ximenez's manuscript was published in the mid-nineteenth century, first in Vienna and then in Paris, before it worked its way back across the Atlantic to the Newberry Library in Chicago (a city named, by the way, for the wild onions that grew there after the ice retreated and left fields for the planting of corn).

In this Mexican Huichol yarn painting of The Five Sacred Colors of Maize, *by Guadeloupe and Ramón Medina Silva, each corn stalk represents a sacred corn maiden watched over by the dove,* Our Mother Kukuruku. The Fine Arts Museums of San Francisco, Gift of Peter F. Young

The daykeepers of the *Popul Vuh* adopted the foreigners' alphabet as a mask, like the Zinacantec mask of San Sebastian, for the invaders' Word did not displace their own, any more than my Uncle Roy's Blood of the Lamb displaced the natives' Seed of Blood. As symbolic lambs absorbed actual human sacrifice in the Old World, so in the New World symbolic corn absorbed cannibal rites, but without a corresponding loss of vision. Corn remained both sentient and sacred. Even today a Maya farmer in Chichicastenango will warn that white and yellow corn left alone on the porch will copulate. If a farmer feels the earth quake as if a giant had turned over, he will comfort the corn in the field and tell it not to be afraid. To the north and south of the seedbed at Teotihuacán, the Word dawned wherever the seed of corn was sown.

THE CIRCLES OF CHACO CANYON

FAR TO THE NORTH and west of ancient Teotihuacán, the present ruins of Chaco Canyon in New Mexico are best seen from above, for only then can you grasp the scale of Pueblo Bonito. The weirdness you get right away, by driving north from Gallup toward Navaho country through miles of flat scrub desert before turning east on a straight and narrow track to nowhere. Chaco Canyon is mercilessly dry, hot, barren and seemingly empty even of ruins, for at a distance the layered stones are the color of sand and cliff, and not until you trace on foot the contours of ruined walls do you begin to sense the achievement of the Anasazi civilization that flowered here in A.D. 1100, just as the Normans "discovered" England, and that withered around A.D. 1300, not long after Marco Polo "discovered" China.

I "discovered" Chaco Canyon on my way back from the sixty-second Inter-Tribal Ceremonial at Red Rock State Park, outside Gallup, in August 1983. Tribes from all over the country were camped in permanent white concrete tepees during four days of parades, rodeos, frybread and dances. Every night the dancers paraded in a giant circle beneath a cliff of red rock silken as skin. When the circle was complete, they sat in the shadows cast by three pine fires burning in the center where the dancing began. There were a couple of thousand spectators, and those of us who had failed to adjust to ceremonial time were numbed by events like the Navaho Corn Dance, a boringly gentle pantomime of women grinding corn on their metates and brushing and braiding each other's hair. The final event, however, featuring "The Aztec Flyers" from Mexico City, made up for any languors. First a lone dancer climbed to the top of a dangerously tall pole and, while he played a flute, his feet beat out a rhythm on a platform small as a drum. Soon he was enclosed at the top by four feathered dancers, who swayed like a squash blossom until the blossom burst and each plumed body dove head first into space, spinning with ropes tied to their ankles in an ever-widening circle until they touched the ground.

I saw this circle carved in earth when I looked at Pueblo Bonito, the largest of the eight "Great Houses" of Chaco Canyon, where the Anasazi built a five-story apartment building of eight hundred rooms to house more than a thousand people. In the center of the crescent-shaped enclosure are nothing but circles, thirty-two of them, outlining the excavations of large and small kivas. The kivas began as pit houses dug into the earth for shelter, storage and burial, a practical cradle-to-grave womb, but their circular shape became potent as they evolved into ceremonial centers. For every kiva was and is today among descendant Pueblo Indians the vital link between the not yet born, whom we call the dead, and the undead, whom we call the living. The word "kiva" means "world below," and the ladder that men climb to reach the opening in the roof is also the ladder by which man emerged, with other forms of life, from the Earth Mother below—not a sudden fall from a heavenly garden but a slow ascent from a watery kingdom to one dry as sand.

Directly below the roof opening of the kiva is a sunken fire pit, for in the First of the Four Worlds, in the cosmogony of Mesoamerica and the Southwest, life begins with fire. Next to the pit is a small hole called by the Hopi *sipápuni,* "the path from the navel." This is the umbilical cord that attaches man in life and death to the Place of Beginning in the Underworld, in the earth's womb, even as he climbs toward the sky. For the Pueblo people, the center of the kiva is the navel of the universe, "the center of centers, the navel of navels," the sacred place from which the people of corn emerge and return.

What is now the American Southwest was once the northern edge of the Olmec corn circle as it spread slowly from Chihuaha into New Mexico through the Mogollon culture that emerged around 100 B.C., followed by the Hohokam and finally the Anasazi culture. By A.D. 400 the Anasazi were planting corn in the clefts of impossible canyons and dwelling in the overhang of improbable cliffs in the place where Colorado, Utah, Arizona and New Mexico now join to make "Four Corners." Here they developed irrigation systems based on seasonal rains and floods, covering an area as large as Ireland, to make the desert bloom at Mesa Verde, Aztec, Canyon de Chelly and Chaco Canyon. Builders as well as planters, they constructed massive buildings of fitted stone and dug in an ever-widening circle the vast underground chamber of the Great Kiva. At the end of the thirteenth century, suddenly, like the Maya at Palenque, they abandoned their settlements for reasons unknown and migrated to the high plateaus of Zuni and Hopi and to the valley of the Rio Grande.

Until a couple of decades ago, archaeologists believed that the climate at the time of the Anasazi must have been different for planters even to attempt to develop a canyon now as barren and waterless as Chaco. But recent studies have shown that the climate was the same; it's the farming that was different. The Anasazi, unlike the Hohokam of southern Arizona, had no perennial streams to tap for irrigation. But they turned disaster to advantage by a complex system of desert farming, in which they channeled flash floods as they poured over the cliff faces into a network of dams and diversion walls, canals and dikes, trenches and gates, and thereby distributed the water gradually into fields laid out in waffle patterns. The system we now call "flood farming" exhibits such sophisticated engineering that we are only now beginning to credit its intention.

At the time the Anasazi laid out their waffle fields, invading Athapaskan hunters from the Canadian Northwest swept down across the Plains and called these farmers *anasazi,* or "ancient enemy." The Zuni descendants of the Anasazi called the Athapaskan hunters *apache,* or "enemy." After a group of the nomadic hunters learned from the planters in the Pajarita Plateau in northern New Mexico how to plant corn, the Pueblo people began to call them the *apaches* of *navahu,* or "enemies of planted fields." While both Pueblos and Navahos plant cornfields today, the cultural tides are primordial and the enmity remains.

The myths of the Pueblo planters are divided between tales told as fiction and stories of The Beginning told as historical truth. "In The Beginning there were only two: Tawa, the Sun God, and Spider Woman, the Earth Goddess" is the way one Hopi creation story begins. From earth and spit, Spider Woman created twin boys whose job was to keep order in the world; next she created all plants, birds and animals; finally, from earth-balls mixed with the four colors—yellow, red, white and black—she created the First People of the First World. Here as in Maya creation, the First People emerge gradually, but now they emerge specifically from a circular center, from "Earth mother earth navel middle place." Their path is upward through the four womb worlds of Mother Earth, through the Second World, which froze into ice, through the Third, which was flooded with water, into the Fourth, which is the Middle World, the here and now of the four language groups of Tewa, Keresan, Hopi and Zuni, united as children of corn.

In his translation of Zuni creation stories, Frank Cushing began with the five elemental facts of Pueblo life—air, earth, water, fire and corn.

I once heard a Zuni priest say: "Five things alone are necessary to the sustenance and comfort of the dark ones among the children of earth.

> *"The sun, who is the Father of all.*
> *"The earth, who is the Mother of men.*
> *"The water, who is the Grandfather.*
> *"The fire, who is the Grandmother.*
> *"Our brothers and sisters the Corn, and seeds of growing things."*

So Cushing related what the Zuni priest told him in 1884 of The Beginning. In The Beginning was watery darkness from which the Sun Father rose to

"Grass thus became as milk to the creatures of the animal kingdom, and corn became the milk for mankind."
—FRANK WATERS,
Book of the Hopi
(1963)

give light and life. From his skin he rolled balls of flesh that became Earth Mother and Sky Father. When Earth and Sky embraced each other, Earth Mother conceived in her four cavernous wombs the first men and other creatures. When Sky Father spread out his hand, in the lines and wrinkles of his palm were yellow grains to guide their children. From a bowl of foam, Earth Mother created the boundaries of the Earth, but the parents were afraid to let their children go and so kept them in Earth Mother's womb. From foam Sun Father then created twin boys, warriors, whose bows were rainbows and whose arrows, thunderbolts. With their bolts they split the cave wombs of Earth Mother and gave the children of darkness a tall ladder, which they put against the cavern roof so that they might climb into the cave of twilight and finally into the light of the Sun. So bright was the light that "they fell grasping their eye-balls and moaning."

The priest-chiefs then taught them the sacred words and rituals, divided them into clans, and gave each clan a magic medicine. They were told they must wander for many generations until they reached the "Middle of the World." In their wanderings they came on "The Place of Misty Waters," and here their own seed clan found a rival group called Seed People, who challenged the clan to show its powers. The clan planted prayer plumes, and for eight days it rained and new earth washed into the valleys. Then for eight days the Seed People danced and sang and at the end the prayer plumes had turned into seven corn plants.

"These," said the Seed People, "are the severed flesh of seven maidens, our own sisters and children." They introduced their eldest sister, who was yellow corn, and so on down the line through blue, red, white, speckled and black, until the youngest, who was sweet corn. Each corn color came from a place, yellow from the wintry North, blue from the watery West, red from the summery South, white from the light-giving East, speckled from the cloudy heavens, black from the womb caves. And so the clans joined to form the one Corn-clan and their maidens danced the dance of the Beautiful Corn Wands.

As the Corn-clan continued to wander, they heard flute music from the Cave of the Rainbow and sent two chief warriors to investigate. In the cave, they found the God of Dew and Great Father of the medicine priests, *Pai'-a-tu-ma,* who showed them new dances to take back to their people. At night the God of Dew led his flute players to watch the corn maidens dance and, as they watched, the flute players lusted after the maidens of corn, "more beautiful than all human maidens," until the corn maidens passed their hands over their own bodies and vanished, "leaving only their flesh behind."

The people mourned and sent the eagle to look for them, then the sparrow hawk, then the crow, who had a sharp eye for the maidens' flesh, but even he could find no trace. The God of Dew found them at last in the Land of Everlasting Summer and brought them back, but they could stay only part of the year. "As a mother of her own blood and being gives life to her offspring," said the God of Dew, "so have these given of their own flesh to you." From the beginning of the new Sun each year, they should treasure their flesh; and when winter winds and water bring new soil, they should bury their flesh. Then when the corn maidens blew rain clouds from their homes in Summer-land, green corn plants would spring from the heart of the Earth Mother, the Land of the Zuni. Thus, said the priest, was born *Tâ'-a,* the Seed of Seeds.

Rain is the salvation and drought the enemy of these desert peoples, placed in the middle between the Spider Woman below and the Plumed Serpent above. Hopi creation myth and purification rites come together in stories that tell of famine, where a young hero must descend into the Underworld to find Spider Woman and by his bravery bring back the seeds of life. In one story, after the boy is aided by Spider Woman, he is tested by the God of All Life Germs, who whips him with yucca and willow, then gives him a prayer plume and a bundle of seeds. Finally, through a cleft in the deepest rock of the Underworld, the god reveals his splendor, haloed by his wives.

Upon their heads were terraced rain clouds; many kinds of flowers and jewels adorned them, besides every seed of corn such as they have sent us for food. There was white, red, yellow, blue and black; another kind was speckled red and yellow. Such colors! They were like precious stones.

The god commands the boy and others to serve as priests. They are to dip their hands in clay and make a print on the rock as a sign they will show no fear when flogged. After being whipped, each youth holds in his hand five different-colored grains of corn. "Plant one for the hot wind, one for the field rat, one for the kachina, and two for yourselves," the god tells them, as he departs, leaving his mask and robes. One day while they chant his prayers, a giant snake appears, crowned with feathers—Palulkon, the Great Plumed Serpent—who tells them that the bravest must return the mask and robes to the god. But the Death God has deceived them and stolen the mask. From now on, the Plumed Serpent commands, the bravest each year must don the god's mask at the feast of Powamu, the time of purification, when Hopi children even today are initiated by ceremonial whipping into the rites of the kachina, when men impersonate the Hopi gods.

For Anasazi descendants, Earth Mother and Corn Mother are exchangeable

masks, both represented by perfect ears of corn whose tips end in four kernels—"Corn Mothers." At the birth of a Hopi child, his Corn Mother is cradled beside him for twenty days while the house is kept dark. Before dawn on
the last day, the child's aunts arrive, each carrying a Corn Mother in her right
hand, to bless the child and present it to its Sun Father as he rises in the East.
The child has dawned in the earth, the child is sown in the sky, for earth-sky
are the parents of this child in spirit as well as in flesh. For the Zuni, the masked
impersonators of the Corn Mothers appear at the winter solstice six days before
the Fasting and six days after the night of Shalako, when the gods each year
return. Even in their seasonal absence, the Corn Mothers are always present,
either as sacred objects at the hearth or as masked dancers in the kiva.

Far to the north of the Olmec circle of corn, however, where the Iroquois
descendants of Woodland tribes once stretched from New York to Ohio and
from the Great Lakes to Canada's Georgian Bay, star
gods vied with corn gods wherever hunting vied
with planting. In a Senecan creation story (recorded
in 1883 by Jeremiah Curtin), the First People fell to
earth from the sky.

*Senecan artist Ernest Smith's
oil painting in 1936 of* Sky
Woman, *based on the Wood-
land creation story.* Rochester
Museum & Science Center,
Rochester, N.Y.

Originally, people lived above, in the center of
the Blue, and in the middle of their village grew
a tree with blossoms giving light. A woman
dreamed of a man who told her that that tree
should be uprooted. "A circle must be dug
around it," he said; "then a better light will
come." So the people cut around their tree and,
sinking, it disappeared. Darkness fell, and the
chief, becoming furious, ordered the woman
pushed into the hole. Down, down she fell.
Below there was only water, with waterfowl
and aquatic animals at play. Hell-diver, however, brought up mud, and Loon then sent all
the members of that tribe down for more. "Put
the mud on Turtle's back," he said. Beaver flattened it with his tail. Then Fishhawk brought
the woman down and, work continuing, the
earth increased; bushes presently appeared, and
soon the woman gave birth to a girl.

Very quickly the child grew. And when a

young woman, she was one day strolling, enjoying the animals and birds, when she met a nice young man. With their union, day and night came. At daybreak, she would go to meet him; at twilight, return home. One evening, she looked back and saw a big turtle walking where the man had just been. She thought: "A turtle has deceived me." At home, she told her mother and said, "I am going to die. You must bury me and cover me well. From my breasts will grow two stalks, on each of which an ear will appear. When ripe, give one to each of the boys I am to bear." She gave birth to twins, died, and was buried. And that was the origin of maize.

A better-known story of its origin, told by an Ojibway shaman of the Great Lakes to Henry Rowe Schoolcraft in the 1820s (and incorporated by Longfellow into *The Song of Hiawatha*), eliminated Earth Mother altogether in favor of a male named Mondawmin, who descends from the sky and wrestles with a young hunter named Wunzh, who is undergoing the ceremonial fast that will show him his spirit-guide. After the third day, the sky-youth Mondawmin surrenders, asking that his garments be stripped away so that he can be buried naked in the earth. He tells Wunzh to keep the spot clear of weeds and lay on fresh earth once a month. In secret the boy tends the grave and watches as green plumes come through the ground. When at last he brings his father to the spot, they see a tall, graceful plant with bright silken hair and golden arms. "It is my friend, Mondawmin," he says. "We need no longer rely on hunting alone. For this I fasted, and the Great Spirit heard."

Although the Ojibway became planters, they retained their hunting mythos. In this story of exclusively male struggle, triumph and expertise, a Father-Spirit, wrestler-athlete and farmer-chief displace Earth Mothers, pregnant women and corn maidens and make them irrelevant. In the Senecan story, by contrast, the dynamic of complementary creative powers, male and female, resembles the planting mythos of the Pueblo peoples. When Earth-woman mates with Turtle-man, their union generates day and night, birth and death, and sustenance. The corn that sprouts from the dying woman's breasts will furnish milk for her sons, for if wild grass is milk for animals, cultivated grass is milk for man. But still, the first woman falls out of the Blue into dark-

"All alone stood Hiawatha,
Panting with his wild exertion,
Palpitating with the struggle;
And before him, breathless, lifeless,
Lay the youth, with hair dishevelled,
Plumage torn, and garments tattered,
Dead he lay there in the sunset.
And victorious Hiawatha
Made the grave as he commanded,
Stripped the garments from Mondamin,
Stripped his tattered plumage from him,
Laid him in the earth and made it
Soft and loose and light above him. . . ."
—HENRY WADSWORTH LONGFELLOW,
Book V: "Hiawatha Fasting,"
The Song of Hiawatha (1855)

ness, is pushed down a hole and deceived by a turtle. Not a great role for an Earth Mother.

Longfellow's Hiawatha, on the other hand, so preempts all creative roles for himself that one suspects the Ojibway story has been polluted by patriarchal Victorian germs. Earth Mother Nokomis is reduced to a nanny, while Hiawatha and Mondawmin are transfigured into the sort of soft-focus image captioned, in my grandmother's Bible, as "The Light of the World." So Christ-like is Longfellow's Indian that my Uncle Roy could have presented him without qualm to the Brazilian heathen as a model of muscular Christianity that would put to scorn idolators of both the Corn Mother and the Virgin Mary.

Nonetheless, the boy who planted corn by the shores of Gitche Gumee is descended from the Young Maize Lords in the tropics of Copán, Palenque and Tula, just as the earth navel of the Pueblo peoples is connected to those earlier centers where civilization emerged. The Hopi tell of a legendary Red City of the South, a ceremonial center said to have been built by the original kachina people before a serpent destroyed the city and the hero-twins fled northward. Some Hopi who know Maya signs say that the Red City was Palenque and that here the clans were named.

At Chaco Canyon all the migrating clans of the ancestral Anasazi left their stories incised in stone, as well as in legends. On a cliff wall of pictographs you can see the clan signatures of Snake, Sun, Sand, Bear, Coyote, Lizard, Eagle, Water, Parrot, Spider and Bow. You can see the red handprints of the brave and the footprints of the wanderers. You can see the Guardian Snakes of the six directions and you can see too the Hump-backed Flute Player, who has left his mark from the bottom tip of South America to the top of Canada, bearing in the hump on his back the life-giving seeds of corn and bean and squash. It was the Flute Player who led the migrating bands to the ends of the earth in each of the four directions before they found their home in "Earth mother earth navel middle place," the sacred center of each kiva, of each village and of the universe. It was the Flute Player who led the feathered dancers of the Aztec Flyers at the Inter-tribal Dances at Red Rock. If red was the color of the seed of blood, flute music was the sound that set the feathered seed in motion.

Of all the marks at Chaco Canyon the most awesome figure of motion is a spiral carved into the cliff behind a pair of rock slabs weighing two tons each, positioned on top of a 480-foot butte that commands the full horizon. This is the spiral that a young artist, Anna Sofaer, began to puzzle over in 1977. It took her nineteen trips and an unprecedented melding of photography, archaeology, astronomy and physics to persuade specialists in each of these fields that she had discovered a unique sun-and-moon calendar for planting and ceremonies.

The three rock slabs of the Anasazi calendar at Chaco Canyon (A.D. 950 to 1150) are arranged to channel a dagger of light at summer solstice through the center of a spiral petroglyph, carved on the rock face behind the stones. Photos by Karl Kernberger, the Solstice Project

During the summer solstice, June 21, at high noon, the pair of behemoth rocks so control the sun's shadow that, as it moves, it bisects the spiral vertically, moving downward like a dagger from top to bottom. At the winter solstice, December 21, the arrangement of the stones divides the sun's shadow into two shadows that bracket the spiral, leaving its center empty of light. Sofaer was able to prove that the site of the Sun Dagger records not only the alternating positions of the solstices of the sun, but also the analogous positions of the moon. Her discovery brought to light the earliest known calendar in the New World that tracks both the twelve-month cycle of the sun and the nineteen-year cycle of the moon.

The site of the Sun Dagger would have been a spot as sacred as the kiva to the Anasazi because the spiral is a form of the circular maze that expresses in spatial terms the temporal myth of Emergence, compressing into one symbol both the birth from the earth-wombs and the migratory Path of Life. The Hopi call this circular maze *Tapu'at,* or Mother and Child, for the concentric spirals enfold the child just as the straight line at the entrance of the maze leads the child out through an umbilical cord. At the same time, the cross formed by the intersection of straight lines symbolizes the Sun and centers the four cardinal

The circular form of seasons and calendars shaped also kivas, cities and fortresses, linking the Americas north to south. Seen from above when it was excavated in 1917, the circle of the Great Kiva at Aztec, New Mexico (right), is echoed by the circular walls of the fortress of Sacsahuaman in Cuzco (opposite page, left), built 300 years later. Both echo the circularity of an ear of corn (opposite page, right), shown here in cross sections of two varieties: the 12-rowed is from the north, the 8-rowed is from Peru and named for Cuzco. (The Great Kiva) Neg. No. 119748, photo E. H. Morris; (Sacsahuaman) Neg. No. 288012, photo Charles H. Coles; Courtesy Department Library Services, American Museum of Natural History. (Corn) Courtesy Paul Mangelsdorf

points that will guide the unborn on his Path. At the site of the Sun Dagger in Chaco Canyon, the sun's shadow literally crosses the spiral, marking the place of Emergence from the literal earth. Circles within circles—calendar, kiva, corn. Maize within maze.

"For a people so intensely agrarian for so many centuries of their existence, all life does result from happenings within the earth, from the union of earth, water, and sun," explains Alfonso Ortiz, the noted Tewa anthropologist born at San Juan Pueblo, where his father taught him to throw a pinch of white cornmeal to the sun every morning upon awakening. A Tewa is at home in the universe because all its elements are members of his family and he of theirs. Family is the root metaphor that relates Pueblo man intimately both to the outer galactic fires of Father Sun and to the inner volcanic fires of Mother Earth. Wherever he is, he is at home. Earth navels are like airports, a Tewa once told Ortiz. No matter where airplanes fly off to, they always return. Emergence and return. "The word of mythology," as Levi-Strauss said, "is round."

The word of my own migrating clan was neither round nor square because my clan had long ago lost its sense of intimacy with the elements and with the music of the spheres that set them in motion. Earth roots we had left behind in our temporary encampments on the prairies, and "star light, star bright" was

not a guide but a child's wish-rhyme. The heavenly Father was not the sun that rose and set daily, but a stern avenger who damned without mercy and forever. My mother took it to heart. Uprooted and displaced, she lost her way in a maze unlit by the sun's path, pushed into darkness with no way out and no power on earth, or under the earth, to comfort her. Hers was a maze like the ones my father kept in his classroom laboratory for mice and rats.

On the darkest day of the year, by chance I visited another Anasazi site. Between blizzards, I had made my way with difficulty over ice-covered mesas to reach a small point on the map called Aztec, on the border of New Mexico and Colorado. I wanted to see the largest of all kiva navels, the Great Kiva, sunk in the center of the Anasazi ruins which, like those of Chaco Canyon, were once high-rise apartments. Excavated and now restored, the main altar room of the kiva is forty-eight feet in diameter and the ninety-ton roof is held by four elephantine pillars of masonry resting on four huge disks of stone. A raised stone altar in the center is flanked on either side by a stone-lined pit. These were used for the magic fire ceremony Hopis call the Ya Ya Ceremony. *"Yah-hi-hi! Yah-hi-hi!"* cried the chief of the Fog Clan when the god of the animals, Somaikoli, appeared, for Ya Ya gained its power from the animal world. The power was so great that men might jump naked into the fire-pits and come out unscathed. But some began to use the powers for evil, and now Ya Ya is practiced only by sorcerers and witches who kill others to prolong their own lives.

The Great Kiva was eerily dark and deserted, but it had been so fully restored that it seemed phony, and I was quite put out by the canned flute music and the amplified drums. I climbed back outside for a breath of reality and was hit by a bright sun that shot through a rent in the clouds. By its light a pair of archaeo-astronomers, armed with surveying instruments, were attempting to track the winter-solstice shadows across some vertical stones. That too disappointed. No spirals, no sun daggers. Noon passed and nothing happened. When I went back down into the kiva, however, for a final look, something had. The kiva was as empty as before, but this time the flute and drum got to me. There on the center of the altar was a freshly killed bird, its feathers still warm.

The Language of Science

SOLVING THE CORN MYSTERY

WHEN PAUL MANGELSDORF ASKED, "What is the corn?" he answered, "Corn is a mystery." For the scientist, mystery is not a condition but a prelude to action. "And mysteries are there to be solved," Mangelsdorf asserted, "as surely as mountains are there to be scaled." Corn's "mystery" has meant one thing to those who speak the discursive language of science and quite another to those who speak the symbolic language of myth.

My botanist father solved the conflict between science and myth by filing them in separate compartments. The Bible had solved one mystery of origin, and Darwin the other. My father was not a speculative man, and he took Darwin's *Origin of Species* with the same good faith with which he took God's Book of Genesis. God created and Darwin evolved. It was the scientist's job to describe and improve the plants and animals of God's garden, while measuring the mountain of knowledge that was there to be scaled. Although he was a Bible Belt fundamentalist, my father believed it was knowledge, not faith, that moved mountains, for in his world there was no mystery that a little midnight oil and mental elbow grease couldn't solve.

The first botanists to examine the mysterious plants of the New World, however, undertook their task with a fuller measure of wonder. "This Corne is a marvelous strange plant, nothing resembling any other kind of grayne," wrote Henry Lyte in *A New Herbal* of 1619, "for it bringeth forth his seede cleane contrarie from the place whereas the Floures grow, which is against the nature and kinds of all other plants." Corn was marvelous strange, that is, in its sex life, for the seeds of the plant grew at one place and the flowers at another. As we would now say, the ear was distant from the tassel. But to understand the implications of this sexual division, the first botanists had first to "discover" that plants in

The corn plant as imagined in the mid-16th century by an artist who has never seen one, for he improvises tassels, blossoms, symmetrical leaves and kerneled ears without husks.
Courtesy Paul Weatherwax

general had a sex life. Early in the seventeenth century, Camerarius in Germany, experimenting, as it happened, with the corn plant, determined that plants have sexual parts that correspond to the human sperm and egg.

Europe's discovery of the New World coincided with a new way of seeing the natural world, in which the medieval way of reading the world symbolically as God's poem was replaced in the Renaissance by a textual analysis of nature's prose. The new scientists began to apply human analogues to plants, as Indian myth makers had done, but for different ends. Where Indians had given corn gender and genetic relationship to make all God's creatures one, Europeans now used human analogies to separate the plant world from the human one and to reconstitute plants as an autonomous family. It was less the invention of new tools for observation, like the microscope, that led plant scientists to believe they were discovering "the thing in itself," than it was the growth of a new language in which to systematize their "discoveries" of new mountains to scale. To the question, "What is the Corn?" the Zuni who even today answers, "Our brothers and sisters," is worlds apart from the contemporary morphologist who answers, "A polystichous diploid with unisex inflorescences and rigid rachilla."

It was the Swedish botanist Linnaeus who, in the eighteenth century, determined to marshal plants into families labeled with the logic of Latin and Greek, but his names were as arbitrary as anthropologists' names for Maya gods. Linnaeus christened corn first with a Greco-Latin generic name, *Zea,* which means a wheatlike grain, and then with a Latinized specific name, *mays,* from its Taino original *mahiz,* which means "life-giver." For modern taxonomists, corn is a member of the grass family Gramineae, which divides into the tribe Andropogoneae (corn, sugar cane, sorghum and teosinte), then into the subtribe Maydeae (corn, teosinte and tripsacum) and finally into the clan *Zea,* which includes the species *Z. mays*, of which domesticated maize is a subspecies.

What was and is jabberwocky to me was a constant delight to my label-loving father, who was never happier than when he had a blackboard and chalk at his command. He would point out to his botany students that the seed of this grain called *mays* should more properly be called a fruit, in which the germ is embedded in nutrient flesh. Those nutrients he would itemize in the language of chemistry: for an average dried kernel of corn, 72 percent starch, 10 percent protein, 4.8 percent oil, 3 percent sugar, 8.5 percent fiber, 1.7 percent ash. Unlike most fruits, which convert starch to sugar, he explained, corn reverses the process and converts sugar to starch. The oil is in the germ and the rest of the nutrients are in the surrounding endosperm, composed of both hard (horny) starch and soft starch. Soft starch occupies the crown and central part, hard starch the sides and back. The ratio of hard to soft starch varies with each kind of corn, and we label them accordingly. Different pigments, such as blue, red, black, white, are literally only skin-deep, the pigmentation being limited to a thin layer (aleurone) covering the endosperm just within the thinner outer layer of the hull (pericarp). Yellow pigment is the only one that resides in the endosperm.

After thus anatomizing the kernel, my father would set up a laboratory experiment to show how corn grows. He would put a few kernels in a saucer of water in a warm room and in five or six days they would sprout. He would point to the shield, the scutellum, on the rim of the germ, which absorbs water into the germ's tip and channels it to the tiny shoot growing upward and the tiny shoot growing downward. Through a microscope he would point out the minuscule hairs covering the root, designed to adhere to soil and absorb water. Once you plant the kernel, he would explain, it will develop almost immediately a set of temporary (seminal) roots that branch sideways before the permanent roots develop underground to form a tight circle a foot or two in diameter. As the stalk grows, brace roots form another circle above ground, a kind of ballet dancer's tutu—a metaphor my father would not have used.

My father would quote straightforward texts like *Corn and Corn Growing* (1949), by Henry A. Wallace and Earl N. Bressman, who stated that corn grows primarily on air and water. While 97 percent of the elements in the kernel comes from air and only 3 percent from soil, corn demands a quantity of water because it sweats, or "transpires," as they said, heavily. They noted that a full-grown plant on a hot July day in an Iowa cornfield will transpire five to nineteen pounds of water, while an acre of plants will transpire 720 tons, or the equivalent of seven inches of rainfall. Wallace and Bressman used the metaphor of an unfolding telescope to explain how the stalk grows in nodes, about eight to twenty nodes per stalk. The section between nodes (the internode) is where growth takes place, one leaf for each node on alternate sides of the stalk. When the internode slides out of its leaf sheath, it makes a noise loud enough for farmers to swear that they can "hear the corn grow."

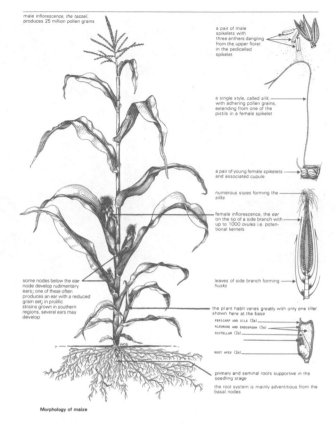

Morphology of maize

An anatomical drawing of a corn plant by contemporary geneticist Walton C. Galinat, detailing male and female parts. Courtesy Walton C. Galinat

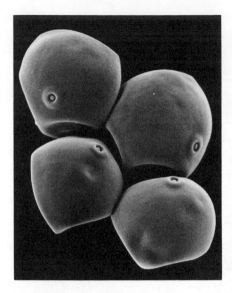

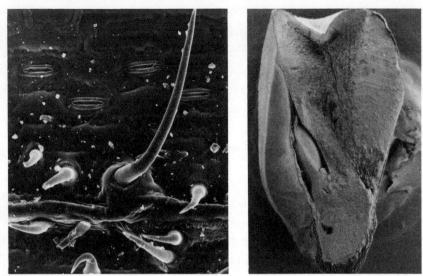

The electron micrograph reveals the sexuality of corn parts in a new perspective. Pollen grains (magnified x 1210), resemble mammaries. On a leaf's surface (magnified x 770), stomates look like mouths and spines like penile horns. The kernel, in cross section (magnified x 25) is a womb that cradles and feeds the embryonic germ. Pollen and leaf photos by Dennis Kunkel; kernel photo from the USDA Agricultural Research Service

During his own student days, my father would have read earlier textbooks like Frederick Sargent's *Corn Plants* (1899), in which Sargent charted the corn from infancy to old age. "For the baby leaves," he said, "a tube forms the snuggest sort of cradle." The upper part of the leaf unrolls as it grows, enclosing the rolled blade of a younger leaf, and because the edges of the blade grow more than the center, the edges get a wavy look. Through their green coloring matter (chlorophyll), the leaves suck up sunlight and carbon dioxide from the air and mix it with water to form sugar and starch.

When he took up the sex life of the plant, in a chapter titled with Victorian propriety "Provision for Offspring," Sargent explained that the flowers of the corn plant, divided into male and female, grow in spikelets on different parts of the plant, an unusual arrangement peculiar to the subtribe Maydeae. The male flowers grow in spikelets in a tassel (inflorescence) at the top of the stalk, where the spikelets are really miniature husks enclosing "the tender parts." These are a pair of flowers in each spikelet and in each flower a trio of anthers to hold and release the pollen, formerly called *farina fecundas*. Each tassel produces about two thousand grains per anther, or 14 to 18 million grains per plant. Like sperm, pollen production is supernumerary rather than cost-efficient. Since each kernel needs but one pollen grain to fertilize it, the plant overrun is about twenty thousand pollen grains per kernel. As Sargent said, "a very generous margin for mishaps has been allowed."

The female flowers, or "mother cells," he explained, are located in pairs (although only one will develop) along the tiny pubescent cobs that will turn into ears of corn. In Corn Belt corn, there are usually two ears per plant. Each cob grows within a leaf sheath at a node about halfway down the stalk. The flowers grow into kernels, four hundred to eight hundred or more per ear: one part of each flower encloses the ovary (pistil) and another part sends out a single strand of silk (style). In this remarkable arrangement, each single kernel must be fertilized separately by means of its single silk. Timing is everything, for the kernels at the base must send out silks from the tip of their leaf cocoon at the very moment the pollen is ready to drop. It usually takes the silks two to four growing days to emerge from the tip in a feathery green spray. The surface of each silk is hairy and sticky in order to catch that single but crucial dot of pollen dust. Once caught, each nuclear dot of sperm divides itself and becomes twins, as if following the plot of Maya myth. One twin forms a tube within the silk so that its brother twin can slide down the six- or eight-inch length of the silk to reach the virgin embryo sac at the base. While one twin fuses with the egg to create the embryo, which then becomes the kernel's germ, the other twin creates the endosperm. Corn mating takes place within twenty-four hours, and within a couple of days a farmer will know that conception has occurred, because the silks at the tip will then change color from green to reddish brown.

"By forming a judicious mixture with the gourdseed and the flinty corn, a variety may be introduced, yielding at least one third more per acre, on equal soil, than any of the solid [flint] corns are capable of producing, and equally usuable and saleable for export."

—JOHN LORAIN, in a letter to the Philadelphia Agricultural Society, dated July 21, 1812

Corn Belt corn takes about fifty days to mature after fertilization, Sargent said, ripening in five stages: milk, when the starch is still in fluid form; soft dough, when the starch is "soft and cheesy"; hard dough, when the starch is firm; glazed, when the hull is complete; and ripe, when the kernels are fully matured. Because kernels are attached to the cob in paired rows, corn rows on the ear are usually (there are a few variant types) even in number. A farmer running his hand over the outside of a green husk can tell whether an ear is ripe merely by the feel. If he feels separate rows, it's not fully ripe; if he feels separate kernels, it's over the hill; if he feels a smooth "heft," it's just right.

My father felt at home with the teleology of the scientific language of our founding fathers because it was based on utility. "What is not useful," said Cotton Mather in the late seventeenth century, "is vicious." Cotton Mather is important to the history of corn because he was one of the first of the preacher-scientists in this country to experiment with corn in the field. In 1716 he wrote from Boston to a friend to describe the effects of cross-pollination:

My friend planted a row of Indian corn that was colored red and blue; the rest of the field being planted with corn of the yellow which is the most usual color. To the windward side this red and blue row so infected three or four whole rows as to communicate the same color unto them; and part of ye fifth and some of ye sixth. But to the leeward side, no less than seven or eight rows had ye same color communicated unto them; and some small impressions were made on those that were yet further off.

Soon after, a personal enemy of Mather, Paul Dudley, made a similar observation, noting that a high fence could prevent the admixture of color resulting from this "wonderful copulation" of corn.

To a utilitarian like Benjamin Franklin, who conducted his own experiments in corn copulation, corn's sex life was precisely what made corn a most useful medium for studying and improving plants. Franklin was the man who produced the first commercial crop of broom corn (a distant relative of maize) and who founded the American Philosophical Society. One outgrowth of this Society is today's vast network of American agricultural societies that have, in effect, reinvented corn in our time.

Many pioneers of the new science in the colonies experimented with corn breeding, applying both Latin and colonial English to Indian corn in order to analyze principles of corn reproduction. Such was James Logan, secretary to William Penn, who wrote up his experiments in Latin in 1739 to validate the notion that male tassels were essential to female silks. Such was John Lorain, also of Pennsylvania, who saw the benefits of mixing different strains of corn from different parts of the country to improve yield. "They do not mix minutely like wine and water," he wrote in *Nature and Reason Harmonized in the Practice of Husbandry* (1825). "On the contrary like the mixed breeds of animals, a large portion of the valuable properties of any one of them . . . may be communicated to one plant, while the inferior of one or the whole may be nearly grown out."

From the beginning, what interested the newcomers to corn was mixing the breeds to further their utilitarian aims of providing the greatest number of ker-

Corn copulation sometimes produces deformities, like these multibranched cobs. Courtesy Paul Weatherwax

nels for the largest number of people. Instructive is Joseph Cooper's account in 1808, in the initial volume published by the Philadelphia Agricultural Society:

> In or about the year 1772 a friend sent me a few grains of a small kind of Indian corn, the grains of which were not larger than goose shot. . . . These grains I planted and found the production to answer the description, but the ears were small and few of them ripened before frost. I saved some of the largest and earliest and planted them between rows of the larger and earlier kinds of corn, which produced a mixture to advantage; then I saved seed from stalks that produced the greatest number of largest ears, and first ripe, which I planted the ensuing season, and was not a little gratified to find its production preferable, both in quantity and quality to that of any corn I had ever planted.

From the beginning, the language of the newcomers reflected different agricultural values from those of the natives, who were concerned less with productivity than with purity. Indian tribes had carefully selected seed to preserve purity of color and type, because each color had sacred meaning as well as food meaning. From each kind and from each crop, Indians selected perfect ears and saved these for seed, as their ancestors had done for thousands of years. A Hidatsa woman named Buffalo Bird Woman, born along the Knife River in North Dakota in 1839, described in detail the selecting methods of her tribe:

> When I selected seed corn, I chose only good, full, plump ears; and I looked carefully to see if the kernels on any of the ears had black hearts. When that part of a kernel of corn which joins the cob is black or dark colored, we say it has a black heart. This imperfection is caused by plucking the ear when too green. A kernel with a black heart will not grow. . . . When I came to plant corn, I used only the kernels in the center of the cob for seed, rejecting both the small and the large grains of the two ends.

She also described how they planted each variety separately, in fields away from each other. "We Indians understood perfectly the need of keeping the strains pure," she said. "We Indians knew that corn can travel." They knew that adjoining rows of yellow and white corn would produce mixed ears. "We Indians did not know what power it was that causes this," she said. "We only knew that it was so."

White men wanted to know what power it was because they wanted to control it. The white man's approach was founded on the principle that crossbreeding is better than inbreeding. Instead of a conservator of blooded lineage, the white man became a broker of mixed marriages, exercising control over every stage of the breeding process. As a result, he founded a new corn dynasty that was clean contrary to the native one. Over two centuries of experimentation, he developed a highly specialized method of crossing two sets of inbred strains, not once but twice, so that each hybrid seed today comes equipped with a pedigree of four named grandparents and two parents, in a listing that constitutes a kind of Debrett's Peerage of Hybrid Corn.

"Hybrid," however, is another term that breeds confusion. When my grandfathers began to farm as boys, they controlled pollination much as the Indians did, isolating different strains of corn in separate plots to prevent random crossings and to create inbred strains. Since the winds might blow from each and every corn tassel 14 million grains of pollen, some bastardy was inevitable and occasionally beneficial in open pollination. By the time my grandfathers were grown men, however, they had learned to cross the inbred strains of different kinds of corn deliberately, in order to get larger and hardier ears. These artificial hybrids they would keep pure by selecting and saving the best seed at each harvest. What they gained in genetic uniformity, however, they lost in reproductive vigor. To solve this problem, the modern corn breeder must return, at each planting, to seed produced from the first crossing of inbreds. Modern hybrid corn is generated not by the farmer but by the hybrid seed industry, a child of the industrial revolution of corn.

A remarkable figure who tried to mediate between the Indian's and white man's conflicting corn languages was a seedsman in the early decades of the century named George F. Will, who with his colleague George E. Hyde wrote *Corn Among the Indians of the Upper Missouri* (1917). Born in Bismarck, North Dakota, in 1884, George Will knew the Mandan, Arikara and Hidatsa at first hand, since they traded at his father's store and greenhouse. When his father put out a seed catalogue in 1887, the first seed corn he listed was a squaw flint named "Ree," short for Arikara. Father and son perceived the value of the early-maturing varieties that had been developed by the tribes of the upper Missouri, and the Wills experimented with them to provide good seed for their neighbor farmers in the northwest.

Trained at Harvard in archaeology, ethnology and botany, Will was uniquely equipped to recount Indian Corn Ceremonies and the Sacred Character of Corn at the same time he analyzed Indian agricultural methods and compiled a staggering list (with photographs) of the hundreds of corn varieties still grown in 1917 by tribes from the Northwestern Mandans to the Southwestern Pueblos. As one contemporary admirer put it, "He used what he

"The great scientific weakness of America today is that she tends to emphasize quantity at the expense of quality—statistics instead of genuine insight—immediate utilitarian application instead of genuine thought about fundamentals."

—HENRY A.
WALLACE AND
WILLIAM L.
BROWN,
Corn and Its Early Fathers (1956)

learned from the American Indian for the benefit of every Northern Plains citizen." Not every modern seedsman or scientist was as wise in seeing that the plant he took such pride in improving was one that was already highly bred. In the words of geneticist Walton Galinat, "The American Indians were not simply the first corn breeders. They created corn in the first place."

IN THE NAME OF DIVINE PROGRESS

"THE DESTINY of the nation is in the hands of the farmers," Edward Enfield wrote in 1866 in *Indian Corn: Its Value, Culture, and Uses*. This was at a time when farmers like my grandfathers governed the destiny and the imagery of the United States, not only by numbers—they outnumbered industrial workers by more than two to one and tradesmen by more than four to one—but by their sense of divine mission. When Enfield said farmers, he meant corn farmers, since the corn crop was five times greater than the crop of wheat and other cereals, and all other major vegetable crops, put together.

During the crisis of the Civil War, corn for the first time became big business, with a total of nearly 840 million bushels a year. At the end of the war, Enfield exhorted farmers to increase production so that the national *average* would be an unheard-of fifty bushels an acre instead of the usual twenty or thirty. Neither he nor my grandfathers could have imagined that exactly a century later, in 1966, the year Henry A. Wallace died, the national average per acre would be 120 bushels, producing a total of 9 billion bushels a year valued at $40 billion. My own family abandoned farming at the very moment Wallace staged the farming revolution that brought this about. In less than thirty years, from the 1920s to the 1950s, Wallace fulfilled the manifest destiny of American farmers by "industrializing" corn breeding and thus laying the foundations of modern American agribusiness. "No plant has changed so fast in so short a time as has corn," Wallace wrote, "in the hands of the white man."

Change, in the lexicon of the white man, was synonymous with improvement, and corn's natural variability made it a prime subject for "improvement" by human hands. It was corn, not wheat or potatoes, that became as crucial as oil to a nation hellbent on converting natural elements to mechanical ends. "Corn," boasted a contributor to the American Society of Agronomy's *Corn and Corn Improvement* (1979), "has achieved a higher level of industrial utilization than any other cereal grain."

More than a century ago, Enfield envisaged a New Jerusalem where agriculture and industry would march hand in hand to the sweet music of machinery. Of this new-age farmer he wrote,

> The discordant clatter of machinery that shocks the ears of other men is to him the sweetest of music; for it starts the long dormant corn from the crib, gives new activity and interest to butter and beef, and infallibly prognosticates a new top to the Sunday carriage, a silk gown for the wife, a suit of clothes for the little boy, and a new dress for the baby.

Enfield hailed the farmer as a closet manufacturer: "It may indeed be said that the farmer, in a broad and important sense, is himself a manufacturer, for, like the latter, he is essentially a creator of values."

The organic corn plant shared in this ennoblement by becoming an industrial plant. So Frederick Sargent in his *Corn Plants* (1901) praised corn: "The plant is like a factory, with the discouraging sign 'no admittance.'" From the way in which roots, stems and leaves are organized into "a singularly perfect system," he went on, "we may see that our self-building food-factory is governed by advanced business methods." Remember that this was a corn plant Sargent was describing:

> From the start, the policy pursued is to devote at once as much as possible of the product of manufacture to building additions to the establishment and to insuring its future safety. It is as if there were a wise and enterprising manager in charge of its affairs. This same spirit of enterprise which leads these plants to take fullest advantage of their opportunities appears also in the establishment of what we may call "branch factories" [or tillers].

Sargent's personification was as mythic as the *Popul Vuh,* but instead of a pair of enterprising twins in the Underworld we now had a factory foreman inside each cob.

The twin heroes of the new industrial myths were Energy and Power, generated in new form when agriculture, science, business and industry ganged up on Mother Corn. "Decade after decade, beginning in 1780," Wallace wrote in *Corn and Its Early Fathers* (1956), "the progress of American civilization was measured by the western expansion of the corn acreage." Progress and Civilization, another set of twins, were measured not just by plant expansion, that is, corn and factory acreage, but by increased efficiency of production. Since the industrial farmer produced his merchandise by employing the minimum amount of human labor to convert the maximum amount of solar energy, the rate of conversion was crucial. Where the Indian required twenty hours of hand labor for each bushel of corn, the Corn Belt farmer in 1956 required only six minutes. The story of the conversion of a native Indian corn into the world's most efficient industrial crop was, for Wallace, "one of the great and vital romances of all time."

This romance took its tone from evangelists in the latter half of the nineteenth century who preached Divine Progress through the medium of corn. One of the earliest preachers was Wallace's grandfather, "Uncle Henry" Wallace, a United Presbyterian minister in Iowa in 1862, about the time my own Great-Grandfather Harper, a minister of the same cloth, was preaching God and raising corn in the same neck of the woods. The spirit of these preacher-farmers still invests the corporate offices of Pioneer Hi-Bred International, in Des Moines, where I found three generations of hybrid seed growers. Pioneer is the company Henry Wallace founded in 1926 by selling forty-nine shares for $100 a share. Today, Pioneer sells 645 million pounds of seed corn a year, worth $500 million, from a complex of offices, laboratories, greenhouses, fields, processing plants and research stations operating in ninety countries around the world.

In 1914, tall corn was an index of progress and national destiny, accomplished here at the hands of Andrew Engstrom in Junction City, Kansas. Joseph J. Pennell Collection, Kansas Collection, University of Kansas Libraries

So recent is the hybrid-corn revolution that some of the founding members of Wallace's company are still there, still fired by the idea of doing the world some good. "The Idea," Wallace wrote in a 1932 booklet describing his original company, was to "improve corn by controlling its pollination." The possibilities seemed infinite: "The best hybrids of the future will be so much better than the best hybrids of today that there will be no comparison." When I spoke to James Wallace, Henry's brother, a modest, dignified man in his eighties, his belief in the Idea was undiminished. "I don't know how much more we can improve it," James said in his Iowan drawl, "but we spend several million dollars a year working at it and that ought to produce something." One thing it produces is seven to ten new hybrids each year, totaling more than five hundred now, which helps the company retain 35 percent of the U.S. market. But James is concerned with more than business. He worries that the Idea has not solved the problem of how to feed the world. Such worries, however, are mere static in the current of optimism that lights up the signs on his office wall: "The Three-Year Plan of Pioneer Overseas Corporation is not letting negativism creep into any of the operating units. WE CAN DO IT is the buzz word."

"We Can Do It" was the unofficial motto of *Wallace's Farmer,* the paper founded by James's father in 1895 under the rubric "Good Farming—Clear Thinking—Right Living." Not even the precepts of positive thinking, however, could blot out the boom-or-bust crisis after World War I, when in 1920 corn prices collapsed from $1.70 a bushel to 67 cents. The Depression that hit Wall Street later hit the farmers first. The early 1920s were such bad farm years, James recalled, that they may have hastened his father's death, in 1922, while he was serving as Secretary of Agriculture under Warren Harding. Certainly the farm depression hastened the departure of my family from their farms. When young Henry Wallace became Franklin D. Roosevelt's Secretary of Agriculture in the depths of the Depression, Kansas Republicans like my folks dubbed Wallace a Judas who had betrayed the farmer and sold his soul to a Democrat. And when, in the forties, he formed the Progressive Party, they knew he was the only thing worse than a Democrat—a Red.

Iconographic portrait of Henry A. Wallace with symbols of farming progress and prosperity: a twin-siloed barn loaded with corn and a jeep loaded with corn-fed chickens. Courtesy Pioneer Hi-Bred International, Inc.

From the beginning, Wallace's Idea was as radical as it was pragmatic. By applying the principles of mass production and marketing to the plant world, Wallace turned agriculture into business. George Mills, a reporter for *The Des Moines Register,* summed it up: "He looked like a sort of mystic, which he was, but he was a mystic who made an awful lot of money." That was part of the romance. As brother James explained him, "Henry was the first one to make a business out of the hybridization of corn."

Henry Wallace's curiosity about corn breeding had begun when, as a boy, he met George Washington Carver, the man who developed a more perfect peanut. From Carver, who believed that "God was in every plant and rock and tree and in every human being," Wallace learned to respect the way American Indians treated the plant world, even as he was altering that world forever.

In 1900, the revolution in plant breeding that was to make a businessman of Wallace and a botanist of my father was exploding. A trio of European botanists rediscovered Gregor Mendel's "laws" of inheritance, which he had drawn from genetic experiments in 1866. Mendel's "laws" were reinforced by Darwin's experiments with corn that led to his theory of "hybrid vigor," published in 1876 in *The Effects of Cross and Self Fertilization in the Vegetable Kingdom*. A year later, the United States produced its own revolutionist in William James Beal, whose systematic experiments with corn crossings caused one senator to accuse Beal of "pimping for the tassels."

After studying with Louis Agassiz at Harvard, Beal went on to Michigan Agricultural College and there produced the first controlled crosses of maize (scientists are wont to call corn "maize") by a technique of "castrating" the plant, or detasseling male spikelets, in order to "fix" the fathers. His first step was to create inbred strains by the process of "selfing," which was as cumbersome as safe sex and almost as simple. The breeder guaranteed corn chastity until the proper moment for copulation by slipping one paper bag over the tassel and another over the ear. At the right moment, he shook the pollen collected on top onto the ear below. His second step was to systematize the crossing of inbred strains by putting the pollen of one strain of corn on the silks of another strain. This was easy to control by making one row of corn female and the other male: that is, the breeder first detasseled a row of corn and then harvested the ears of that same row. His third step was to cross-breed the progeny yet again, for he discovered that doubling the crossings disproportionately increased yield, turning eight-rowed Indian corn into twenty-four-rowed hybrid corn. Beal's triumph was memorialized in a plaque erected by his successor at Michigan, P. G. Holden. "Near this spot in 1877, Beal became the first to cross-fertilize corn for the purpose of increasing yields through hybrid vigor," the plaque reads. "From his original experiment has come the Twentieth Century miracle—hybrid corn."

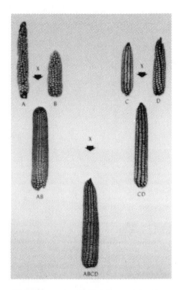

Double-cross hybrid corn is the offspring of four grandparents and two parents. From Wallace and Brown, *Corn and Its Early Fathers* (1956)

"Miracle" was the word an English botanist used in 1956 when he thanked American corn for saving Europe from starvation during and after the Second World War. From Beal's time throughout this century, the miracle workers were principally men like the Iowa teacher P. G. Holden, pragmatists who crossed theoretical science with applied agronomy in America's land-grant colleges.

Holden was a corn evangelist in the Wallace vein, and his mission was to educate Iowa farmers. First he motivated them to want to improve their corn crops and then he supplied them with the means to do it. To preach the gospel of longer, larger, smoother, more perfect ears, he sent out Seed Corn Gospel Trains, which would make seventeen stops a day. To spark the farmers' competitive spirit, he promoted the idea of the Corn Show, which was a county-fair beauty contest for corn. In 1893 at the World's Columbian Exposition in Chicago, he crowned the grand-prize winner "the world's most beautiful corn." This was the corn that changed the face of the American continent—Reid's Yellow Dent.

The Reid hybrid had begun accidentally in 1847, when an Ohio farmer named Robert Reid moved to Illinois and brought with him a reddish strain of corn which had been grown for generations in Virginia by the family of Gordon Hopkins. But when Reid planted this corn in Illinois, it did so poorly that he replanted some of his corn hills with a yellow flint from the Northeast, grown for centuries by the Indians. Over the years, Robert and his son James continually selected the best ears of this crossing of Gordon Hopkins Gourdseed corn and Little Yellow Flint to get the best qualities of each. They ended with their prize-winning beauty corn.

The romance of hybrid corn sometimes overlooks the evolution of the purebred strains that preceded the white man's "miracle." "One of the best things that happened for North America, and the world," wrote David Christensen in the 1989 *Seed Savers Exchange* was "the appearance in northwest Mexico about 700 AD of a soft flour starch which came in an eight-row strain." Because this strain proved to be highly productive, adaptable to cooler climates and easy to grind, it moved north through Anasazi territory and up the Missouri to

Reid's crossing of eight-rowed hard-starch northern flint (left) with many-rowed soft-starch southern gourdseed (right) produced Corn Belt dent, father of commercial corn around the world. From Wallace and Brown, *Corn and Its Early Fathers*, Michigan State University Press

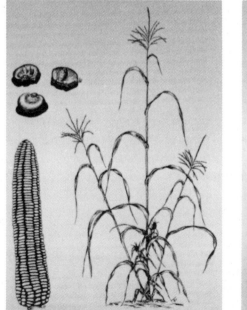

southern Canada. This Pueblo corn became the prototype of the many flint and flour corns of the upper Missouri tribes and, eastward, of New England Woodland tribes. Since the soft-flour starch component did not germinate well in cold climes, it took a few centuries of natural adaptation and selection for the strain to become the hard-starched Northern Flint that is "the more important of the two racial ancestors of today's Corn Belt Dents."

Ironically, one reason for the momentous success of Reid's Yellow Dent was that it came along soon after white settlers had taken over the major corn-growing territory of Indian tribes in the Northeast, at the end of the Black Hawk War in 1832. Further, the opening of the Erie Canal in 1825 had opened new lands for settlement and developed new markets for corn-on-the-hoof. In Cincinnati hogs were processed for oil in what became known as the "land whale" era, and then in Chicago, when railroads superseded canals, hogs were processed for every possible edible part. Increased corn production through Reid's Dent helped save the Union during the Civil War, and after the war a more perfect union of the industrial North and agricultural South was contained in the union of Northern flint and Southern gourdseed.

Reid's Yellow Dent was the medium through which Holden was determined to "carry the message of better farming, better living and better corn not merely to one hundred, one thousand, ten thousand, or even one hundred thousand farmers," as Wallace wrote, "but to all the farmers in the central Corn Belt." But Wallace, both a corn-show veteran and an ag-school graduate, wasn't buying it. He began his own backyard experiments in 1913 after reading one of the papers of George Harrison Shull, a farm boy from Indiana who was double-crossing inbred corn at the Carnegie Institution Station for Experimental Evolution at Cold Spring Harbor in Long Island (the place where Nobel Prize winner Barbara McClintock continues her work on corn today). Unbeknownst to Shull, another geneticist was working nearby, at the Connecticut Experiment Station, near New Haven, on the estate of Eli Whitney. In one of the buildings where Whitney had devised a method for the mass production of guns, as important to the North as his cotton gin to the South, Edward Murray East devised the first hybrid corn to retain full propagative vigor, known now as the Burr-Leaming double-cross. Shull and East did not meet until 1908 and then none too happily, but they are the twin heroes of modern factory hybrids.

In remembering Henry's unending experiments, James Wallace recalled watching him "in the early morning standing in his bare feet out in the small corn in his backyard reading his morning paper, just looking at the corn in between times and reading the paper in between times and observing how it

Saltzer Seed Catalogue of 1901. Courtesy Library of University of California at Davis

was doing." Henry was convinced that beauty in corn was only skin-deep. "Looks mean nothing to a hog," said Henry Wallace, who initiated the Iowa Corn Yield Contest and in 1924 won it with a misshapen red-kerneled hybrid of his own named Copper Cross. From then on, Wallace's mission was to sell Corn Belt farmers on the Idea that more is best and then sell them the seed. With James and a young corn breeder named Raymond "Bake" Baker, Henry founded a company to sell seed corn. From then on, corn farmers depended upon the specialized knowledge and equipment that characterize today's industrial farms.

Over lunch in Pioneer's corporate dining rooms, "Bake" Baker recalls how hard it was in the early days to persuade farmers whose fathers and grandfathers had grown open-pollinated corn to switch to hybrid seed. With hybrids each farmer had to detassel alternate rows of corn, which might involve five thousand to eight thousand tassels per acre. During the 1930s corn detasseling became as much a Corn Belt cultural ritual as the husking bee had been earlier. During the 1940s, women and girls took over the detasseling brigades as farm boys went to war, and after the war detasseling became as common a form of coed student employment as waiting tables elsewhere.

But if hybrid seed made planting more work, it made harvesting easier. For the first time corn ears could be harvested mechanically because breeding produced ears that stood up straight at a uniform height on each stalk, supplanting ears that bent with the weight of maturity. "The farmer was bent over all day picking up corn," Baker remembers. "He wasn't so sure about yield but he sure knew about bending over." Baker now concludes, "After fifty years there's no optimum ear, but we keep working to put more and more good characteristics together." His checklist includes Moisture, Stay Green, Test Weight, Seedling Vigor, Grain Quality, Ear Height, Plant Height, Early Stand Count, Number Stalk, Dropped Ears, Wind Resistance—to name a few.

Hybrids have changed the nature of farming, says Donald Duvick, head of the Plant Breeding Division, who has been with Pioneer for a mere thirty years. During this time the genetic capacity for grain yield has increased at the rate of one bushel per acre per year. Besides yield, plants have improved in root strength, resistance to stalk rot and stalk lodging, resistance to premature death, to barrenness, to the attack of the second-brood corn borer—Duvick runs out of breath. As a result, the factory farm has replaced the family farm, with every year fewer and fewer farmers working larger and larger farms.

Such displacement concerns William Brown, a geneticist and coauthor with Wallace of *Corn and Its Early Fathers,* but after forty-five years as a Pioneer executive Brown still brims with Pioneer spirit. "This is the most exciting time

A hybrid grown in Metropolis, Illinois, in 1917 to honor the Red Cross of World War I. The grower was Dr. J. T. Cummins, dentist. Lake County (Ill.) Museum, Curt Teich Postcard Archives

in the history of botany or biology," he says. "The reason is molecular genetics." Through the techniques of genetic engineering that were first developed in the 1940s, he explains, we can now move genes from one organism to another without carrying any extraneous materials. In other words, you don't have to back-cross corn to get rid of side effects you don't want. You can move genes at will, make up a high-lysine strain, or one resistant to drought or to saline soils or to pests like corn-ear worms. It's open-ended, he says, but we won't see major results until around the year 2000, a short time to wait in the life of "the amazing grass called corn."

Brown sustains Pioneer's zeal for improving corn breeds, but he too admits disappointment in improving men's lives: "Where the need is greatest, as in Africa, we've had least success." Elsewhere, they've had almost too much success. Supplied with American hybrid seed, China and other countries are now becoming competitive with the U.S. Corn Belt. In 1986, China produced 65,560,000 metric tons of corn, second only to America's 209,632,000. "We must improve productivity by reducing yield along with production costs," Brown says, "to get a greater net return." The Idea of ever-increasing yield has boomeranged, for we're now depleting our soils to grow ever greater surpluses that the government has to pay for. "We need programs to get out of production," Brown believes, "since the major income of farmers today is not what they sell but what they get from the government, and when the public learns that the big farms get close to a million a year for growing surplus, it will raise serious questions."

After the snazzy corporate headquarters of Pioneer, I visited the other end of the seed-corn scale in El Paso, Illinois, where the major buildings are a silo, the Corn Belt Motel, and the house and barns of Pfister Hybrid Corn. Here Lester Pfister, born in 1897 to tenant farmers, became the Horatio Alger of hybrid corn in the 1930s, in a story worthy of *Reader's Digest*, where it duly appeared. Young Lester had to quit school when his father died, but as a hired hand he began to test different strains of corn and record the results. He took samples to the agent at the County Poor Farm, where P. G. Holden had set up a system for testing and comparing the yields of local farmers. The agent was impressed with Pfister's records and asked him to do a three-year testing of Woodford County corn. In 1922 Wallace had awarded a prize to a high-yield Woodford strain brought in by an illiterate dirt farmer named George Krug. Krug had crossed a Nebraska strain of Reid corn with Iowa Gold Mine to make, as Wallace said, "the highest-yielding strain of old-fashioned nonhybrid yellow corn ever found in the Corn Belt." For the next five years Pfister worked to inbreed Krug corn, despite the ridicule of neighbors who laughed at

"For ten years, up until 1935, Lester Pfister's neighbors in El Paso, Illinois, were convinced that he wasn't quite right in the head. They couldn't understand why any sane individual should spend hours in a field under the boiling sun taping paper bags on corn tassels."

—GEORGE KENT, "A Farmer Bags a Million Dollars," *The Reader's Digest,* September 1938

Today, paper-bagged fields of corn to produce hybrid seed are commonplace. Courtesy Pioneer Hi-Bred International, Inc.

his fields of paper bags, covering row after row of corn tassels, and despite the painstaking selection that reduced 388 ears to 4. With these four he experimented for the next five years with crossings, going deeply into debt, feeding his family on cornmeal mush and fueling his stove with dried cobs.

Threatened with foreclosure in 1933, Pfister at last hit upon a double-crossed hybrid that outyielded the original Krug so substantially that word, and corn, began to spread. In another five years he was grossing $1 million a year, had invented a detasseling machine and was named "the outstanding corn breeder of the World" by *Reader's Digest* and *Life*. Selling most of the business in 1941, he kept the parent company and family farm, now run by his son Dan. "We're fifty years old," Dan says, as we talk in his backyard next to the shelling and drying shed, "but we've proved our quality." When I visit in September, they are working around the clock. "You've got to pick seed corn when the sun is shining and moisture is in the high thirties," Dan explains. He points to his new seed-corn harvester, an eight-row beauty with a special trailer that cost $128,000. "Look at that sucker go," he says, watching as it eats up the rows.

Dan's excitement comes from machinery, as he guides me through the shed where elevators take two hundred bushel loads of ears up to shellers (six hundred bushels an hour) and onto giant dryers with automatic temperature controls. I find the heavy, sweet smell of drying corn overpowering, but Dan is in full flush talking about the latest engineered product—Pfister's Kernoil. "Kernoil could revolutionize the feed industry," he says, since "feed efficiency" rises 4 or 5 percent with livestock fed on corn that contains 60 percent more oil in the germ. "My mind can't get away from the possibility of starting something like Dad did," Dan says. "You have a breakthrough, you're the only one doing it and pretty soon you establish a megatrend—you reinvent the world."

THE CORN WAR

To REINVENT THE WORLD is the dream of technologic man, but the question is—in which language? In the course of corn's reinvention in this century, war broke out among the second generation of plant breeders in whose hands the destiny of farmers lay, a war that accelerated as descriptive botanists like my father were displaced by geneticists who took giant leaps from taxonomy to morphology to cytology. The Corn War, as it has been called, is as much a product of post–World War II America as the Cold War, and springs in part from isolationist America's sudden discovery of the rest of the world. If in the first half of the century botanists quested for the Perfect Ear, in the second half they quested for the Primal Ear. The war over the origin of corn was part of the growing pains of the revolution in biology that gave us a new common language in DNA and of the revolution in outlook that gave Kansas a common corn language with Siberia and Peru. But not before shots were fired and opposing corn worlds reinvented.

After the Second World War, the two opposing generals in the burgeoning Corn War left their farms in Kansas and Nebraska to become world contenders. One became an internationally known geneticist at Harvard and the other won a Nobel Prize. The Nobel Prize went to George Wells Beadle, born in 1903 in Wahoo, Nebraska, and educated at the University of Nebraska's College of Agriculture, Cornell and Caltech. The Harvard prize went to Paul Christoph Mangelsdorf, born in 1899 in Atchison, Kansas, home of the famed corn carnivals at the century's turn, where buildings, streets and people were draped in husks, kernels and cobs.

Beadle was a new-wave geneticist concerned with how genes and chromosomes work within the cell. In researching the process of cell division (meiosis) in maize, he discovered that inherited defects in maize pollen were related to the behavior of chromosomes during cell division. Later he studied gene change in materials like the fruit fly and bread mold, becoming a co-winner of the 1958 Nobel Prize for Physiology or Medicine for his discovery that "genes act by regulating definite chemical events." Later still, he became president of the University of Chicago, but when he retired he returned to the corn trenches and remained there until his death in June 1989, just two months before Mangelsdorf's.

When Beadle began research in the 1930s, botanists agreed that corn was both the most productive of the grasses and the one least able to reproduce itself. No one agreed on how it had got that way. Beadle revived nineteenth-century speculation that corn might have evolved from a kindred grass, teosinte, when he began to experiment in his Stanford lab on teosinte seeds collected from Mexico and Central America, where annual teosinte was still found in the wild. When he heated the seeds, he found that their kernels "exploded out of their fruit cases indistinguishable from popped corn." The story of modern corn, he proposed in 1939, began with the *accidental popping* of

Paul Christoph Mangelsdorf in 1979, still plumbing the mysteries of corn in his garden at Carol Woods near Chapel Hill, North Carolina. Courtesy of his son Clark Mangelsdorf

such wild seeds. The problem with teosinte as a hypothetical ancestor of maize, however, was that it had twice as many chromosomes as cultivated maize, which would prevent direct crossbreeding.

In the same year, 1939, a fellow Midwestern farm boy, trained in taxonomy, fired the first shot in the Corn War from his post at the Agricultural Experiment Station of Texas A&M. Paul Christoph Mangelsdorf was destined for the ministry, his mother believed, and she joked that his initials stood for "Preach Christ Mangelsdorf." When I visited Mangelsdorf in his retirement home in Chapel Hill, North Carolina, in his eighty-fifth year of corn preachments, he joked that his initials stood for "Pod Corn Maize." Pod corn, in which each kernel on the ear is enclosed in its own tiny husk, is the earliest form of corn discovered in archaeological remains. And a wild pod corn, Mangelsdorf had declared in 1939 and continued to declare until his death in 1989, is the origin of cultivated corn.

Where Beadle had worked primarily in the laboratory, Mangelsdorf worked primarily in the field. After studies at Kansas State Agricultural College, the Connecticut Agricultural Experiment Station in New Haven, and Harvard, Mangelsdorf had continued the labors of earlier corn breeders like Edward East. At Texas A&M, Mangelsdorf gained fame for breeding a popular sweet corn named Honey June and for discovering a sterile strain of corn (named "T" for Texas) that seemed to be the answer to a hybrid-corn farmer's prayer because it ended the need for detasseling. Unfortunately, the strain was not resistant to the corn-leaf blight that in 1970 swept the Corn Belt and finally alerted farmers and breeders to the danger of reducing the wide world of corn to a handful of commercial types. Mangelsdorf did his most important field work, however, in the wilds of Mexico, Guatemala and Peru, collecting and organizing thousands of corn varieties into "races of corn," while he searched for the Primal Ear.

When I met him, Mangelsdorf was still a handsome man with a mane of white hair and an unabated mania for corn. Leaning on a walker, he still bred corn plants in his backyard and collected artifacts to add to the collection of almost five hundred corn objects he and his wife had donated to North Carolina State University at Raleigh. A glass case in the botany building there displayed the most valuable—a seventeenth-century Chinese corn ear carved from ivory, a Japanese corn netsuke, a Meissen pudding mold with indented ears, a Zapotec funerary urn with corn headdress. Stored unseen were box after box of majolica, 1930s pottery, carnival glass, British porcelain, tin molds, copper molds, ironstone and plastic—corn shapes cloned in the least likely materials. This was a form of corn madness I recognized.

Mangelsdorf's form of corn language, however, I did not. As a corn breeder, he had experimented with a third kindred grass, *Tripsacum*, and with his Texas colleague Robert Reeves had in 1939 formulated a "tripartite theory" to prove that "the ancestor of cultivated corn was corn." He speculated that there must once have been a wild corn, now extinct, and that a hybrid of this wild pod popcorn mated with *Tripsacum* to become the parents of teosinte. He concluded that a gene mix of these three related grasses evolved into our modern races of corn. Mangelsdorf preached his trinitarian gospel with such passion that after his comprehensive *Corn: Its Origin, Evolution, and Improvement* (1974), he became to the general public a Corn Father on the order of Henry Wallace.

Mangelsdorf's theory polarized the tight world of corn geneticists, seducing some and outraging others. Even today a Mangelsdorf loyalist such as Umesh Banerjee of North Carolina Central University will speak of conspiratorial enemies who know but refuse to acknowledge the *truth* for reasons of politics and revenge. From a Beadle loyalist, on the other hand, the mere mention of Mangelsdorf provokes gunfire. "It's all bombast, this crazy theory," shouts Hugh Iltis of the University of Wisconsin at Madison. "Mangelsdorf dominated the scene with it for forty years and almost all of it is *wrong!*"

What was right about Mangelsdorf and what gave juice to his theory was his pursuit after the Second World War of the connections between botany, archaeology and anthropology that a few adventurous botanists—like Junius Bird in Peru—had initiated in the decade before the war. The work of Edgar Anderson and of Paul Weatherwax, a botanist at Indiana University, explained to the layman what such crossovers could do. Studying Pre-Columbian ceramics in Central and South America, Weatherwax found that actual corn ears had often been used for the molds and thus early forms of corn were recorded in clay. Mangelsdorf too enlarged his experiments in the lab by encouraging archaeologists in the field, beginning with the pair of graduate students who discovered those prehistoric cobs of pod popcorn in Bat Cave in 1948.

Mangelsdorf was certain that he had won the Corn

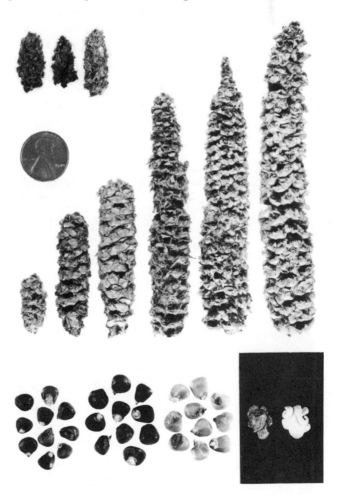

Cobs found in three levels at Bat Cave are shown next to a penny to indicate actual size. At bottom right, a prehistoric popped kernel (dark) is paired with a kernel from the same level that Mangelsdorf popped in 1948. Courtesy Paul Mangelsdorf

War when the first radio-carbon dating at Bat Cave suggested that the earliest layer of corn was seven to eight thousand years old. Although the date was revised, a discovery in 1949 supported botanists who thought the solution to corn's origins lay in archaeology. In that year, Richard MacNeish was digging for potsherds in the La Perra Cave in northeastern Mexico, near Tamaulipas, where he hoped to uncover some connection between the Moundbuilders of the lower Mississippi Valley and more ancient Mexican tribes. At La Perra he found eighty-seven cobs of cultivated prehistoric corn in a layer that he dated roughly between 250 B.C. and A.D. 150. The majority of cobs were primitive forms of a living Mexican race of popcorn called Nal-Tel, and some of the cobs had been charred, suggesting that the kernels had been popped on the ear. Some cobs showed evidence of battering and since stone mortars were also found in the cave, it seemed reasonable that its inhabitants ground meal from popped corn. Although this corn was not as old as the Bat Cave cobs, the find suggested that Mexico was the place to begin digging in earnest.

Mangelsdorf funded MacNeish to make further digs in the same area, particularly after he examined some grains of fossil pollen shown him in 1950 by a Yale botanist, Paul B. Sears. These came from two hundred feet below the present level of Mexico City, which had been built on the site of an ancient lake. (Sears had learned that engineers preparing for the city's first skyscraper had taken core samples in a couple of locations, and he got the cores for study.) When Mangelsdorf scrutinized nineteen "large" grains of pollen estimated to be sixty thousand years old, "as old as the early stages of the Iowan advance of the Wisconsin Ice Sheet" in the late Pleistocene era, he believed that he had found indisputable proof of the existence of wild corn. He was wrong. Nothing in the Corn War was beyond dispute.

The climactic discovery for MacNeish came in a different area of Mexico, in caves of the Tehuacán Valley south of Oaxaca, in a region dry as a desert but with seasonal rains and underground springs. In 1960, after digging through the debris in thirty-nine caves in the area, MacNeish came upon a big one, covered with a layer of goat dung. It took his workers four days, digging straight down, before they uncovered a single corncob—the size of a cigarette butt. When they uncovered more, MacNeish wired Mangelsdorf, "We've hit corn."

With new funding, Mangelsdorf and his wife joined the dig, which covered five caves and an unprecedented find of 24,186 specimens, dating from seven thousand to five hundred years ago. These remain the earliest cobs yet discovered, and Mangelsdorf was convinced that some of the cobs were wild. "Here was corn telling its own history," wrote Mangelsdorf, as he fell into a reverie that suggested Cortez discovering the Pacific:

As I stood with MacNeish in the San Marcos Cave looking down on the alluvial terraces I could see in my mind's eye wild corn plants growing here and there, never in thick stands but in favored spots. I could visualize the prehistoric cave-dweller, primarily a hunter of small game and a food-gatherer, bringing back small ears of wild corn to his shelter, picking off the small, flinty kernels, much too hard for him to chew even with his excellent teeth, and exposing them one by one to the glowing coals of his fire. After absorbing heat for several minutes, the kernels would have exploded, transforming the stony little grains into tender, tasty morsels. . . .

Like earlier corn evangelists, Mangelsdorf took to lecturing on "A Botanist's Dream Come True." The ears of wild maize, as he conjured them, were about an inch long and as thin as a pencil. The top half was a tassel and the bottom half a cob, enclosed by the leaves we now call husks, with eight rows of brown or orange kernels, seven kernels to a row, each kernel enclosed entirely by chaff. Here were all the distinctive characteristics, he said, of modern corn.

Rafael Guzman discovers a probable ancestor of corn, perennial teosinte, growing wild at La Ventana in the Sierra de Manantlan of south-western Mexico. Courtesy Hugh H. Iltis

In 1978, however, an extraordinary discovery in the enemy camp forced Mangelsdorf to capitulate on the tripartite theory. Only two years after Mangelsdorf published *Corn*, a young Mexican botany student at the University of Guadalajara, Rafael Guzman, spent his Christmas vacation looking for a form of wild teosinte thought to be extinct. He did so because of a Christmas card sent by Hugh Iltis of Wisconsin to young Guzman's botany professor in Guadalajara. Convinced that teosinte was the true ancestor of corn and hearing that a perennial teosinte had once been collected near Ciudad Guzman in 1910 but was now thought to be extinct, Iltis fantasized a *Zea perennis* on his greeting card and labeled it "extinct in the wild." Guzman's Guadalajara professor challenged her students to find the original.

In the heart of the mountains near Jalisco, not far from the earlier collection site, Guzman came on a large stand of grass and sent seeds to Iltis. Planting the seeds in his herbarium, Iltis found that the grown plants had half the number of chromosomes of annual teosinte. Instead of forty, these plants had twenty, the same number as corn. The student had discovered a new species, which Iltis labeled *diploperennis,* or perennial teosinte. Because they shared the same chromosome number, this teosinte could easily crossbreed with corn and produce fertile progeny. That reality made wild perennial teosinte, with its capacity to reseed itself, the primary candidate for the ancestor of corn. Iltis, not unnaturally, hailed perennial teosinte as "the botanical breakthrough of the twentieth century."

Mangelsdorf, not unnaturally, began to experiment with the seed as soon as he could get his hands on it, backcrossing it with primitive Mexican popcorns native to the same area. Earlier studies of pollen and chromosome structures had already ruled out *Tripsacum* as a progenitor, so the question now was how teosinte was related to corn. In the August 1986 issue of *Scientific American,* Mangelsdorf surrendered—but only halfway: "As I now see it both modern corn and annual teosinte are descended from the hybridization of perennial teosinte with a primitive pod-popcorn." From perennial teosinte, he concluded, modern corn got its good root system, strong stalks and disease resistance, while from primitive cultivated corn came modern corn's distinctive ear, tenacious cob and multiple paired rows of kernels. Because the chromosomes of the two parents were not perfectly aligned, new genes were exchanged through hundreds of thousands of crossings. "The ultimate result," Mangelsdorf wrote, "was a gene pool so extensive and so rich in variation that almost any kind of corn could evolve from it through natural and artificial selection."

Still, Mangelsdorf would not give up his faith that a hypothetical "wild corn" was the remote ancestor of all the Maydeae subtribe and their crossings, until wild corn was "eventually swamped by cultivated corn and became extinct." "The mystery of corn," he repeated, "has essentially been solved." "The domestication of corn is no mystery, and needs no mystique," countered Iltis. "The origin of corn is still a mess," sighed Richard Schultes of Harvard's Botanical Museum.

Actually the mystery of origin and domestication simply shifted ground. "Everybody agrees that domestic corn began about ten thousand years ago and that the place was Mexico and that present-day corn came, one way or another, from the interbreeding of teosinte and maize," says Garrison Wilkes at the Boston campus of the University of Massachusetts. The question is which way, rather than which one first—a question as problematic as the question of source; for as Paul Weatherwax determined thirty years ago, domestication is the real mystery of corn and whatever wild plant was ancestral, "domestication produced a sudden and profound change."

The nature of that change has drawn new battle lines, and while some allies have changed ground, others have changed sides. Walton Galinat, once a graduate student and collaborator of Mangelsdorf, now embraces Beadle's theory but remains loyal to Mangelsdorf the man. "He got mad on Mangelsdorf," Banerjee mutters, "and joined the Beadles in revenge." When I visited Galinat at the Waltham Cornfield Station attached to the University of Massachusetts, I found anything but a vengeful man. In his late sixties, Galinat has the shy, sly smile of Walter Mitty. He wears funny hats in his cornpatch, drives a rattletrap car with the license plate "CORN," and has gone corn-mad in his own fashion. "Corn is my religion," he says, "and this laboratory is my church."

His laboratory is also a cluttered fieldhouse stuffed with packets of seeds meticulously labeled to keep track of the two thousand pedigreed varieties planted in the adjoining two-acre plot. In the middle of the field he has painted a pair of giant eyes beneath Japanese balloons called Terror-Eyes, designed to scare off birds immune to the alarms that sound every three minutes. Near a greenhouse, an old meat locker serves as a germ plasm bank for some four thousand varieties, including the world's oldest viable corn seed. Upstairs in the "headhouse," his office door sports a brass cob-shaped knocker, his curtains are printed with gene gender signs, his desk bears a lusterware corn pitcher holding a bouquet of tiny real cobs and his walls are a gallery of corn productions, reinvented by his illustrative and breeding arts. He's bred corn two feet long, the world's largest. He's bred square ears of

Walton Galinat's monster eyes are designed to terrorize corn-eating birds.

corn—as airplane food, he jokes, because they won't roll off the plate. He's bred red-white-and-blue "Old Glory" corn for events like the Bicentennial, with blue-dotted kernels made to look like stars.

At home in nearby Waban, his wife, Betty, a weaver, covers her spindle with a corn-shaped cloth, knits him sweaters with corn motifs and dusts the clutter of corn artifacts in the china cabinet they call the Corn Morgue—which takes up where Mangelsdorf left off. Galinat shows me pictures of the Corn Tassel Lady, Miss Margo Cairns, who launched a campaign in 1955 to make the tassel our national floral emblem, but failed because it wasn't what most people call a flower. He shows me scrapbooks of corn postage stamps, corn wrapping paper, corn wallpaper. He points to bookshelves of works like Carl Sandburg's *How to Tell Corn Fairies When You See 'Em.* "I think Galinat would almost *be* corn," says a Harvard compeer, "if he wasn't chained to the animal kingdom." Galinat's wife says, "Sometimes I tell him I'm going out, and I put on his hat and coat just to see if he notices." It's tough playing second fiddle to corn.

When I ask him why corn scientists battle so fiercely about their theories, Galinat replies, "The corn plant and ear are so beautiful morphologically and so important economically that they arouse high feeling, not to mention ego systems. People are more indifferent to poison ivy or skunk cabbage." Galinat relates to corn like a citified Hopi. "It shows you everything," he says. "It's like watching TV." As he walks among his nurslings, he asks, "See the baby corn just coming up, saying hello to the world? They're having a chance to express their genes. We put questions to them and then they talk to us here in the field." He fingers a green shoot. "I like to touch a plant when I see it. It's like shaking hands with a person." He admits that his vegetable love has provoked some antagonists to accuse him of the "unfettered imagination" of poetry—or worse. "Galinat is completely stupid," Hugh Iltis explodes, "and Mangelsdorf is crazy like a fox."

"Iltis," warns another veteran of the Corn War, "is the most volatile man I've ever met." Hugh H. Iltis brought his volatility with him from Moravia, Czechoslovakia, when he escaped in 1939 with his botanist father, one step ahead of Hitler. Iltis is the Sir Richard Burton of the plant world, scaling the Andes

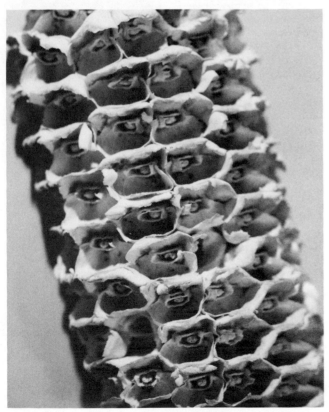

Enlarged closeup of a cob of sweet corn with kernels removed shows how rows of kernels are paired. To Iltis, a radical sex change transformed and condensed the paired male spikelets of a teosinte tassel into the paired female kernels of a corncob. Courtesy Hugh H. Iltis

in search of a wild potato and discovering a wild unknown tomato. As head of the University of Wisconsin's Herbarium, he is passionate about conserving what nature has put on the earth, especially the tropical rainforest of the Sierra de Manantlan, in southwestern Mexico, where perennial teosinte was discovered wild.

To explain how teosinte could have evolved by natural selection into corn, Iltis devised a theory as flamboyant as his person, the Catastrophic Sexual Transmutation Theory, better known as CSTT. To bridge the wide gap between plants as different as teosinte and corn, Iltis argued for an "evolutionary jump," one giant step or sudden transformation instead of gradual evolution. Perennial teosinte, he concluded in 1983, underwent a major sex change in the process of becoming corn. Essentially he argued that the male tassel spike at the end of a lateral branch of teosinte was transmuted into the female ear of corn attached to the central stem. A radically telescoped branch became the shank at the base of the corn ear, and the teosinte leaves became the

husks on the ear. By radical contraction and condensation, the double rows of kernels on a teosinte spike
were transformed into the several paired rows of
kernels on a corncob.

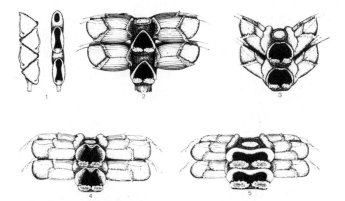

Galinat took issue with Iltis on the abruptness and
the means of change, arguing for a gradual transformation over one or two centuries in a three-phase
evolution controlled by man. In Galinat's view the
hard spike of teosinte was transmuted without sex
change into the soft cob of corn by condensation,
which "liberated" kernels from the separate pods of
the teosinte spike. This change was a simple inheritable gene trait that was then
"fixed" by human selection, so that what seemed to be a natural monstrosity
was actually the deliberate creation of man.

To Galinat, transformation was gradual as the process of condensation "liberated" paired kernels by forcing them outward from their coverings in the hard teosinte spike (figure 1 on the left). His drawing shows cross sections of different paired kernel rows. Courtesy of Walton C. Galinat

To Galinat, the argument stems from the opposing languages of taxonomy
and plant breeding. The taxonomist sees plant structures as discrete objects,
created through natural selection and ordered in vertical lineages, with a place
for every variant and every variant in its place. The plant breeder, on the other
hand, looks for relatedness in "horizontal" clusters, in a continual process
shaped by "the mind, hand and eye of man." What the taxonomist sees as a
honeycomb of niches the plant breeder sees as a meandering stream with trib-
utaries. Since a breeder can produce by whim or caprice objects that are non-
sense to the taxonomist, he calls them catastrophic. "Iltis," Galinat says with a
smile, "he's the catastrophe."

The catastrophe to Major Goodman, a botanist at North Carolina State University, is that both theories conflict with current archaeological and biosys-
tematic evidence, which suggests that "maize and teosinte were as different
seven thousand years ago" as they are today. While there is much evidence for
the early use of maize, there is none for teosinte. How corn came to be remains
a mystery, despite Edgar Anderson's fiat fifty years ago, "The history of corn is
now an exact science."

To Garrison Wilkes, the loss of national leadership now that Beadle and
Mangelsdorf are gone is the catastrophe. "We've lost the leadership in plant
breeding," he laments; "we've lost the edge." He lists the old who are winding
down and laments the young who have forsaken research for technologic
development in molecular biology. That was the field that gave Beadle a bright
vision of hope when he accepted his Nobel Prize. "Our rapidly growing
knowledge of the architecture of proteins and nucleic acids is making it possible, for the first time in the history of science," he said, "for geneticists, bio-

chemists, and biophysicists to discuss basic problems of biology in the common language of molecular structure." But in that common language new wars are stirring between those who would reinvent a brave new world of corn and those who would preserve what Henry Wallace called "the world of forgotten corns."

THE CORN RACE

THE WORLD of genetic manipulation, which followed mechanical manipulation, moved too fast for my father. Although he lived to be ninety-one, not dying until 1983, he never set foot in an airplane. He preferred to move more slowly. When he moved from Kansas to California, he had already lived through two rapid farm revolutions—one the change from horse to engine, the other the change from open-pollinated to hybrid seed—and that was quite enough. Subsequent revolutions in chemical and genetic engineering moved with such speed that, like the airplane, they were beyond his ken. He applauded Wallace's statement that the hybrid revolution was "as dramatic and important as the history of the automobile," but the genetic revolution of gene pools, germ banks, biotech protoplasts and opaque-2 mutants was as unthinkable as a trip to the moon. In only sixty years, the hybrid revolution that began with Reid's Yellow Dent in his childhood had spread so rapidly that by his death Reid's corn was not merely atavistic, but nearly extinct.

In that short span, corn became the substance and symbol of a new conflict between the prophets of divine progress and those of demonic decline. Science was discovering the diversity of corn's many races at the very moment it was eliminating most of them, so that the very notion of corn races suggested also a race against time. Even forty years ago the speed with which corn had moved from a plant of infinite variety to a "monoculture" hybrid alarmed the very men who had sped the change. Henry Wallace saw that in the first half of this century, man's exploitation of corn had altered the plant irrevocably and, in evolutionary lingo, more "catastrophically" than in all the millennia over which it had evolved. "When Reid's Yellow Dent swept the Corn Belt from 1890 to 1920, it destroyed thousands of [forgotten corns]," he

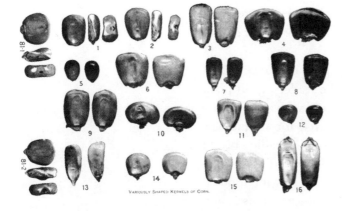

Problems of classification arise from the wide diversity of corn, revealed here in front and back views (and some cross sections) of corn kernels taken from a few major varieties of corn available in 1902. Yearbook U.S. Department of Agriculture, 1902

VARIOUSLY SHAPED KERNELS OF CORN.

wrote in 1956. "When hybrid corn swept the Corn Belt from 1930 to 1950, it destroyed most of what remained."

The Second World War, which sped genetic change through its need for high grain production, also alerted people, in the midst of waste and extinction, to the frailty of what already existed. In 1943, Wallace and a group of scientists including Paul Mangelsdorf met with representatives of the Mexican government and the Rockefeller Foundation to start a research program in corn and wheat that would help to solve Mexico's chronic food shortages. Scientists at the same time embarked on a vast inventory of existing corn varieties, first in Mexico and Central America and finally in the Western Hemisphere, the first time such a project had been undertaken anyplace in the world.

The ancient Peruvian and Mexican device of molding actual corn ears in clay has helped modern scientists to classify corn races. This Peruvian ceramic doubled ear (shown front and back), originally mistaken for a fossilized specimen, was classified by Mangelsdorf as a type of prehistoric pod corn. Courtesy Paul Mangelsdorf

The first problem was to create a new system of corn classification. The geneticists Edgar Anderson and Hugh Cutler had already started to revise Sturtevant's classification of corn by endosperm texture, the basis of the Big Six (pop, dent, flour, flint, sweet and waxy). They had decided to group varieties of corn by related genetic characteristics such as kernel shape, ear shape, row number. These groups they called "races." "Classifying the races of maize is comparable to classifying the races of man," Mangelsdorf wrote, "and the task is no less formidable and no less fraught with hazards."

For thirty years North and South American botanists took to the field to collect samples from every farm in every region under study. They grouped the samples into sets, planted together members of each set in order to eliminate strays, then saved the best ears with their seeds for future breeding. The list filled twelve encyclopedic volumes, beginning with *The Races of Maize in Mexico* in 1951–52. They arranged the thousands of varieties that they had found into roughly two hundred and eighty races, two hundred and ten of those unique to South America (most of them in Peru), forty to all of Europe, thirty to Mexico and twenty to the United States and Canada.

There were large problems of duplication, not to mention national pride. Mangelsdorf recalls that he was nearly lynched in Mexico City when he speculated aloud that maize might have originated in Peru, and was nearly lynched in Cuzco when he speculated that Peru's Gigante Race might have originated in Mexico. Since lineage is what interested the classifiers, they organized races into family trees. Peru and the upper Andes were especially valuable areas

Pop

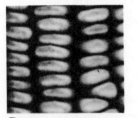

Flint

Dent

Flour

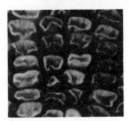

Sweet

Classification of corn by the type of starch in the kernels of each. From *Maize*, CIBA-GEIGY Agrochemicals Monograph (1979)

because corn strains there had not been hybridized. The result was "a virtually complete inventory of the corn of this hemisphere."

Since any classification is arbitrary, some geneticists now argue that corn races were caused as much by geographic isolation as by natural hybridization and that they should be called racial complexes. Revisionists like Bruce Benz have rearranged the earliest races (Ancient Indigenous, Precolumbian Exotics, Prehistoric Mestizos, Modern Incipient and Poorly Defined) into complexes divided by locales: for example, Mexican Narrow Ear Complex, which divides into Balsas-West Mexico Alliance, Isthmian Alliance, Mixe Alliance and Unaffiliated.

Whatever the linguistic manipulations whereby Poorly Defined becomes Unaffiliated, the achievement of the original fieldwork was unparalleled. The classification of races helped to explain the ancestral roots and routes of corn in the Americas and put them in the context of a world map. That map is based on the Big Seven: Northern Flints (found in the northern United States, southern Canada, central Europe), Corn Belt Dents (covering most of the temperate regions), Cateto Flints (southern South America, southern Europe), Mexican Dents, Cuban Flints, Caribbean Flints and Tusons (all found in tropical and semitropical regions). In Mangelsdorf's scheme, these races evolved from six major ancestral groups: Palomero Toluqueño and Chapalote-Nal-Tel (Mexico); Pira Naranja (Colombia); and Confite Morocho, Chullpi and Kculli (Peru).

The earliest corn to reach what is now the United States, according to Galinat, was a pre-Chapalote type. This was a twelve- to fourteen-rowed ear with brown kernels, each kernel enclosed in its own "weak pod" or husk. Because of longer days and shorter growing seasons north of Mexico, the spread of corn northward was delayed a few millennia until a combination of selection and irrigation helped to foster "day-neutral" varieties.

If we try to trace the ancestry of our own Corn Belt Dents, we find that they are composed of 25 percent Northern Flints (traced to a hybrid of Chapalote) and 75 percent Southern Dents (traced to Palomero Toluqueño). The key family name for Northern Flints is Maiz de Ocho, the soft-flour eight-rowed Mexican hybrid that appeared in the American Southwest around A.D. 700. The earliest Northern Flints, found in Ohio and upstate New York, date to A.D. 1040. By natural selection, their tight husks, which in desert climes protected the ears from ear worm and borer pests, evolved into looser husks to prevent kernels from molding in the rainy weather of the north. Southern Dents arrived later, since the earliest remains date only to A.D. 1500, and they probably arrived first in Florida, Virginia and Louisiana by sea routes from Mexico or the Caribbean. Two types of Southern Dents, Gourdseed and Shoepeg, are close kin to Pepitilla, all three derived from Palomero Toluqueño, of southern and coastal Mexico.

Sweet Corns

THE ANCESTRY and evolution of sweet corn tell a more complicated story. In ancient times, native Americans thought of two forms of corn as sweet. The most common was any type of corn that was young, or "green," and therefore sweet because the immature kernels had not yet converted their sugar to starch. The other type was ripe corn that was born sweet by genotype. This is the type that Galinat traces to the ancestral race from Peru called Chullpi. A descendant of this type, Confite Morocho, still grows in the high Andes, relatively unchanged from its appearance in ceramic replicas made one thousand years ago. The ear has a white cob with eighteen to thirty rows of deep-yellow kernels, which are extremely shriveled in their upper half.

The Andeans used this corn as a source of sugar before the post-Columbian introduction of sugarcane and honeybees. Peruvians today snack on parched and dried sweet-corn kernels (*kcancha*), just as we snack on the kernels of Cuzco flour corn we eat today as "corn nuts." Peruvians use descendant strains of Chullpi for their national drink, fermented and otherwise, called *chicha*. A Chullpi descendant arrived in Mexico several centuries before Columbus, and this Maiz Dulce made its way into the American Southwest by A.D. 1200 or 1300, the date of the earliest sugary kernels found in New Mexican caves.

Another type of sweet corn, called Papoon, reached New England from Mexico by way of the upper Missouri River. This one had a red cob (from the P1 gene named for "purple plant color"), which Indians used for dye. A letter written in 1779 in Plymouth, Massachusetts, by one "Plymoutheus" notes that "the core was a bright crimson, and after being boiled, and the corn taken off, if the core was laid in contact with any linen (the table cloth or napkin), it communicated an indelible stain." Papoon was the forerunner of hundreds of later varieties that crossed with types of Northern Flint, and one of the progeny was Darling's Early, born in Connecticut in 1844 and remembered now only as a parent of Golden Bantam.

The taste for sweet corn accelerated in the mid-nineteenth century "for culi-

"Corned Indian" and a "Corned Maid" from a catalogue for Parker and Wood Seeds and Tools. From the collection of Cynthia Elyce Rubin, photograph by Carleton Palmer

nary purposes," in the words of the *The Prairie Farmer* of May 22, 1856, at a time when that organ was still dividing all corn into two major types, yellow and white. A variety called Early Sweet Corn, *The Prairie Farmer* explained, had recently been introduced into Massachusetts from Virginia by a Captain Richard Bagnall and, when boiled green, this type could be preserved in hermetically sealed tin cans. "Preserved in this manner, you have apparently a fresh dish of corn at any season in the year." Another type which crossed northern Papoon with Southern Dent was called Old Colony, and this became a favorite variety for canning for the next fifty years. Ironically, the push to create new sweet corns, which today are synonymous with fresh corn-on-the-cob, began with the creation of the can.

Stowell's Evergreen, introduced in 1853 in New Jersey, was named for its ability to keep moist for nearly a year without a can—if the husks were tied at the ends with a piece of string and laid on shelves in a cool place. The desire to taste "green" corn year-round by developing and preserving sweet-corn types is revealed in the records of the U.S. Patent Office, which lists only six varieties of sweet corn in 1858, twelve in 1866, thirty-three in 1884 and sixty-three in 1899. The turn of the century ushered in the modern craze for sweet corn, although its cultivation was limited largely to the Northeast. Country Gentleman, a white sweet corn, became immensely popular after its introduction in 1890, but it was soon overtaken by a yellow sweet corn introduced commercially by the Burpee Company of Philadelphia in 1902 as Golden Bantam. By 1911 *Burpee's Annual* ("The Plain Truth about the Best Seeds that Grow") listed twenty-one "Select Strains of Sugar Corn," which included names like Black Mexican and Howling Mob. By 1953 the offering of sweet corns was so extensive it required subheads. But most of these would be irrelevant within the decade because of the takeover by the supersweets that began in the 1950s when J. R. Laughman, a geneticist at the University of Illinois, developed a mutant from a three-way cross and called it by the unlovely name of "shrunken 1." To botanists sweet corn is "a mutant defective" because its sweetness derives from a recessive gene, *su* (short for "sugary"). This gene prevents the full conversion of sugar into starch that occurs in other types as the endosperm develops. Because the endosperm of sweet corn contains many more sugars than starch grains, as the kernels dry they become wrinkled and somewhat translucent and appear shrunken or shriveled. In his *Garden Book* of 1810, Thomas Jefferson recorded entries at Monticello for "shriveled corn," which we would call sweet corn. Since their sugary condition reduces the total amount of food they can store, the kernels of sweet corn are more susceptible to mold than those of other kinds, and are therefore frailer and less productive. For that very reason, perhaps, their sweetness was all the more precious to native eaters and growers of corn.

In explaining the way corn genes work in relation to sweetness, Robert L. Johnston of *Johnny's Selected Seeds* in Albion, Maine (a good source of heirloom seeds), uses the metaphor of a "recipe." The nucleus of each corn cell, he explains, contains a recipe for all elements of its growth. The vocabulary consists of "words" or "sentences" that we call chromosomes, which are formed in turn of individual "letters," or genes. The chromosomes are made of chemical strands (DNA) that in corn form different combinations of four nitrogenous bases, plus a phosphate and a sugar. These are the basic ingredients of the recipe, and the genes spell out how much to add when, as in "add a pinch of salt," or in this case "add a teaspoon of sugar." The degree of sweetness depends upon how many teaspoons of sugar are added to each type.

Today's sweet corn genotypes are so sweet that seed catalogues classify them by sugar percentages: "Sweet" has 5 to 10 percent sugar, "Sugar-Enhanced" has 15 to 18 percent and "Supersweet" has 25 to 30 percent. Sweet (Su) types are bred for flavor and crispness, while Sugar-Enhanced (SE) types balance sweetness with juiciness, or good "poppy," as they say in the trade. So rapidly have the types multiplied that the trade has been left speechless: after Kandy Korn, Peaches and Cream, Sugar Buns and Snow Queen, they are reduced to names like Phenomenal and Incredible. Among supersweet (Sh) types, the mutant Sh2 is less vigorous than regular sweet corn, but may be five times as sweet and stay that way for two weeks longer because the sugar-to-starch conversion has been that long delayed.

Seed Movers and Savers

LIFE FOR GENETIC REVOLUTIONISTS is sweetened by any kind of corn. As a raw material, corn has always been at the forefront of genetic research because, like the fruit fly, its variability makes it a favorite medium for experimentation. As genetics became the message of modern botany and biology, corn became the medium.

What made corn so variable was its ability to take unpredictable leaps, as was shown in the molecular experiments of Barbara McClintock, once described as "the Greta Garbo of genetics" because she preferred to live and work alone. As a graduate student of botany at Cornell in the early 1920s, at the same time as George Beadle, McClintock devised a method for studying the morphology of

Corn varieties delineated by Matthieu Bonafous in his History Naturelle, Agricole et Economique de Maïs *(1836).* Courtesy Library of the University of California at Davis

maize chromosomes. For forty years she was a woman alone in a field of men, many of whom ridiculed her experiments at the Cold Spring Harbor Laboratory when she concluded that some genetic systems, such as those that control multiple colors in an ear of Indian corn, behave unpredictably rather than by Mendelian rules. She found that these genes were transposable and mobile— now called "jumping." But her theory so violated genetic dogma that she had to wait until 1983, when she was eighty-one, before the Nobel Prize validated her "jumping genes" and put them into the current mainstream of "evolutionary jumps" and genetic mobility.

Research, too is jumping. "Things we thought would take years to develop are taking months," said Virginia Walbot, a researcher at Stanford University, in 1986. "Everything is moving very quickly." She referred to a new high-speed method of altering corn cells by electric pulses. Her team had applied a technology of electricity (electroporation) to classic breeding techniques that was "100 times more efficient . . . for altering the genetic characteristics of plants" and that would soon "generate whole plants from single corn cells." A new breakthrough, wrote *The New York Times,* in custom-designed crops.

More than a century ago, the French botanist Matthieu Bonafous had threnodized corn's native ability to adapt to hostile climes: "One sees maize growing in the sandy plains of Nouvelle-Jersey; in the land of Carthagenes in Colombia, too humid for the *froment* and *orge* to succeed; upon the icy *ingrates* situated between Trevise and Bassan; in the schist terrain at the foot of the Apennines." Today the icy steppes of Russia grow an early-maturing, cold-resistant corn; the dry earth of Africa grows high-lysine, opaque-2 and QPM (quality protein maize); the humid jungles of Thailand grow downy-mildew–resistant corn; the insect-plagued fields of France grow corn-borer–resistant corn. Every month brings news of the newest biotech innovation: a gene-altered corn plant that grows its own pesticide to combat predators or one that grows its own antibiotic to combat disease.

Yet Henry Wallace in 1956 had warned corn breeders and researchers in their rush for the new to remember the Hopi: "For thousands of years, the Hopi or their ancestors have lived with corn with a depth of feeling which no white man can fully understand." That feeling is reflected in the language of mind and heart, he said, as well as in the ceremonies of daily life. The Hopi focus not on change but on "preparing," repeating what was in order to make ready for what will be. "The white man, on the contrary," Wallace observed, "rushes with maximum speed to change his machinery, his surroundings, his way of life and his attitudes, thereby creating obsolescence, waste and frustration, as well as rich, new values."

A catastrophe in 1970 lent credence to Wallace's view. Before that date, scientists had applauded the low annual disease rate in corn, ranging from 2 to 7 percent, and the localized nature of corn diseases. In 1970—the same year that brought a Nobel Peace Prize to Norman Borlaug for his development of a high-yield semidwarf high-lysine wheat that greened the world from Mexico to India—brought an epidemic to American corn that wiped out 13 to 25 percent of the crop. The genetic uniformity of commercial hybrid corn had made it susceptible to a new mutant strain of southern corn-leaf blight, *Helminthosporium maydis.* The ravages of the epidemic dramatized the dangers of sacrificing diversity to yield. Taxonomists and breeders alike now qualify "genetic improvement" with words like "genetic erosion" and "genetic vulnerability." More and more geneticists agree that the extinction of local corn varieties and primitive races in an effort to "improve" them is analogous, as Garrison Wilkes says, "to taking stones from the foundation to repair the roof."

In 1966, the same foundation that inventoried corn races organized an International Maize and Wheat Improvement Center. On a site just north of Mexico City, where Texcoco Indians had once created the garden capital of the Aztecs, the Center (CIMMYT) built a storage vault in which to preserve its seed collections and use them as a germplasm bank for both a global wheat and a global maize "improvement system." Currently the bank holds about 12,500 entries for maize, "more thoroughly collected than that of any other major food crop," grouped into thirty-seven gene pools, based on similar characteristics and environmental adaptations.

Originally the main idea was to help disseminate Latin American germplasm to Third World countries in order to end world hunger. More corn for more mouths. By 1971 the program was so large that a research consortium (CGIAR) was funded by the United Nations and the World Bank. Five centuries after the beginning of the Columbian Exchange, Iowa's massive Corn Belt has been cloned in southeastern Brazil, northeastern Argentina, the Danube Basin from Germany to the Black Sea, the Po Valley of northern Italy, eastern South Africa and the plains of Manchurian China. At the same time, improvement was redefined: conservation is now seen to be as important as change.

Within the United States, we now have a national network for distributing and preserving seed in the form of a twin storage program, both a checking and a savings bank. In 1954 the National Academy of Sciences and the National Research Council set up the Committee on the Preservation of Indigenous Strains of Maize to continue the collecting work begun in Mexico. This committee evolved into the National Seed Storage Laboratory in Fort Collins, Col-

"One of the major paradoxes of modern agriculture and particularly of corn production is that the short-term goal of high productivity runs directly counter to the long-term genetical health of the crop."
—"Irony and Paradox in the Corn Field," *Missouri Botanical Garden Bulletin* (July/August 1982)

orado. Ironically, it took over the function of what was previously called the Bureau of Plant Industry, organized in 1898 to regulate and encourage the introduction of new plants. By 1970 the Bureau's inventory listed three hundred and fifty thousand "introductions," but since there was no parallel system of preservation, 98 percent of those introductions were lost.

At Fort Collins, the National Plant Germplasm System houses, in addition to corn, other basic crops such as cotton, soybean, sorghum and tobacco. Today the bank holds about two hundred and fifty thousand genetically different samples from two thousand crop species, each sample containing around five thousand seeds, to total one and a quarter-billion seeds from every major world crop. The lab's director, Steve Eberhart, explains that seeds as they are received are tested for viability, then dried, hermetically sealed and stored in refrigerated vaults at zero degrees (Fahrenheit), where they retain viability for twenty to one hundred years. The next step is cryogenic storage, with temperatures at −196 degrees (Centigrade). Like animal breeds, seeds arrive with papers documenting their parentage, and these are stored in a data base with the acronym GRIN (Germplasm Resources Information Network), which keeps track of seed in all the U.S. gene banks.

Working seed collections, as opposed to storage collections, are located in four Regional Plant Introduction Stations, each specializing in a major crop. The place to go for corn is Ames, Iowa, at the North Central Plant Introduction Station sponsored jointly by the Department of Agriculture and Iowa State University. The station's job is to provide seeds for research and to keep track of the movement of germplasm in other countries that might affect what's going on in the States. Since the stations are geared to large-scale operations, domestic gardeners and others who want to grow a particular strain are encouraged to use networks like the Seed Savers Exchange.

The Seed Savers Exchange (SSE) at Heritage Farm in Decorah, Iowa, began in 1975 when Kent Whealy and his wife, Diane, heeded warnings by Garrison Wilkes and other breeders about genetic erosion. They began to look for gardeners who had continued to grow heirloom vegetables and fruits in their own gardens and then organized them into an annual seed exchange. What started as "a six-page newsletter to twenty-nine people copied on an unguarded Xerox machine at Boeing Aircraft in Wichita, Kansas," Kent explains, has become an annual *Winter Yearbook,* listing nearly eight hundred members and more than eleven thousand varieties of seeds. The organization is nonprofit and members must grow seeds to get seeds, since the notion is exchange: "We are making our seeds available to any gardener who will help us maintain them."

In the pages of *Seed Savers Exchange,* members exchange information on organic gardening, on hand-pollinating corn the old-fashioned way, on maintaining selected lines of corn, even on composing corn pictures of ducks and owls with kernels colored purple, pink and brown. In 1985 *SSE* compiled and published the first comprehensive inventory of the U.S. and Canadian garden seed industry since 1903. Overall, only 3 percent of vegetable varieties available then survive today in the Seed Storage Laboratory in Fort Collins. While in 1987 the number of newly recovered varieties increased, still there were fifty-four fewer seed companies than two years earlier. "Think what it would cost, in terms of time and energy and money, to develop this many outstanding varieties," Whealy has written. "But they already exist. All we have to do is save them."

Another seed savers' group evolved from a gardening and nutrition project labeled Meals for Millions, on the Tohono O'odham Indian Reservation southwest of Tucson, Arizona. Here Gary Nabhan, an ethnobotanist, and Mahina Drees, an extension agent, were working with tribal members to revitalize the land. In 1982 Nabhan and Drees, with their spouses, founded Native Seeds/SEARCH in order to collect, spread and save native seeds throughout the Southwest and northern Mexico. Although corn makes up much of their inventory, they also concentrate on corn's sister crops of beans, squashes, chilies, herbs and related wild plants that grow in these low desert and high semi-desert regions.

In their quarterly *Seedhead News,* you can learn of the Salt River Indian Community's restoration of native crops to fields long abandoned, of endangered monuments such as the eighteen prehistoric irrigation canals of the Hohokam that run through the Park of the Four Waters near Phoenix, and of current planting celebrations of the Pimas and O'odhams, described in the voices of celebrants. "When a man goes into a cornfield he feels he is in a holy place, that he is walking among Holy People, White Corn Boy, Yellow Corn Girl, Pollen Boy, Corn Bug Girl, Blue Corn Boy, and Variegated Corn Girl," a Navaho named Slim Curley said in 1938. "If your fields are in good shape you feel that the Holy People are with you, and you feel buoyed up in spirit when you get back home. If your field is dried up you are down-hearted because the Holy People are not helping you."

In the 1950s Carl and Karen Barnes of Turpin, Oklahoma, were ordinary farmers who saw the need to establish a living seed bank of open-pollinated varieties before they disappeared. Now the Barneses have developed a network of some three thousand corn growers in fifty states who work to maintain breed purity as Indian cultures have always done. In the 1990s the Garst & Thomas Hybrid Corn Company in Coon Rapids, Iowa, a town that boasts the

"We're like a society that's eating its seed corn instead of planting it."
—WALTER FRIEDMAN, Department of Economics, Harvard University (January 1989)

world's largest seed-corn processing plant, has started the Kernel Club to fund a Seed Corn Museum at the base of a five-story sculpture that will be the world's largest ear of corn. In 1927 Roswell "Bob" Garst had bought a bushel of hybrid seed corn from Wallace's new Hi-Bred Corn Company and parlayed it into today's multimillion-dollar seed-corn industry. Within sixty years hybrid corn has turned from monster prodigy to museum piece. "We have found that most people outside the seed-corn industry," a Kernel Club member explained, "have no idea what seed corn is, or why it is needed."

The corporate offices of Pioneer Hi-Bred International still display in a glass case an ear of Hopi Indian corn that is labeled "Grown from seed by Henry Wallace, gift of Hopi Indians, planted very dry." Henry Wallace's plea to save forgotten corns and to listen to forgotten voices has not gone unheeded. High-powered geneticists now speak of "plant sensitivity" and of the intimate "cultivator-to-plant relationship" among native growers of corn. Good thoughts are good for the plant, the Hopi believe, and bad thoughts are bad. That's a Hopi definition of maize improvement. "It is not scientifically feasible to demonstrate that *thought,* that *loving* a corn plant, will improve it or its progeny," Wallace wrote, but "all sincere plantbreeders use this very approach in some modified way." For the Hopi, time is not an antagonist, but rather a friend to the races of corn and men, who wax and wane together in the recurrent rhythm of the seasons.

The Daily Round

The Language of the Seasons

THE SACRED CORN OF INCA AND AZTEC

TIME IS OUT OF JOINT when you stand in the nave of the Church of Santo Domingo in Cuzco, high in the Andes of Peru, and imagine these massive slabs of Inca stone covered with sheets of gold. Where the cross of the Christian Son now stands you imagine the high altar surmounted with "the image of the Sun on a gold plate twice the thickness [of the other gold sheets]," as Garcilaso de la Vega described it, "with a round face and beams and flames of fire all in one piece . . . so large that it stretched over the whole of that side of the temple from wall to wall." In Santo Domingo, the crucified Son is shadowed by the blaze of the Sun that was.

The Temple of the Sun that dazzled the eyes and hardened the steel of Francisco Pizarro's swordsmen when they entered Cuzco in 1533 adjoined a garden of herbs and flowers, lizards and butterflies and birds, a small patch of quinoa and a great field of corn, in which every single natural thing was hammered from silver and gold, including the human figures of the gardeners and their spades and hoes. The corn was copied with exact realism, down to the "leaves, cob, stalk, roots, and flowers," Garcilaso has told us, as he described how "the beard of the maize husk was done in gold and the rest in silver, the two being soldered together."

The Inca called this entire temple and garden complex *Coricancha,* "the golden quarter." *Cancha,* meaning "enclosure," is also the Quechua name for toasted kernels of corn, each kernel a miniature garden of gold. The association of corn kernels with the globe of the sun and gardens of gold was natural to a people who called gold "the sun's sweat." And yet, while they honored gold, they were unable to understand the Spaniard's visceral hunger for it. An

This Inca figure of cast silver, holding five ears of corn and wearing a vegetative costume, may represent a harvest-festival dancer. Neg. No. 328548, photo Boltin, courtesy Department of Library Services, American Museum of Natural History

The cycle of planting, harvesting and storing, from Poma de Ayala's almanac.

old drawing shows an Inca handing a bowl of gold nuggets to a Spaniard and asking, "Do you eat this gold?" The Spaniard answers, "We eat this gold."

The misunderstanding was in their guts but deeper than hunger, for the Inca and Spaniard ordered their lives by different visions of the sacred, and the clash of Holy Sun with Son was as inevitable as it was bloody. In Peru as in Mexico, with the Inca as with their contemporaries, the Aztec, it was not gold but corn that was sacred as an emblem of the life-giving sun. The movement of the sun dictated the rhythms of daily life and organized the outposts of empire for the Inca, whose very name meant "Lords of the Sun." Although they had domesticated a few mountain animals, theirs was a planting culture and corn was its lifeblood.

Like the Aztec, the Inca inherited the agricultural wisdom of the many ancient planting cultures that had preceded them. Fifteen hundred years before the Inca empire commanded the Andes from Ecuador to Chile, corn was being cultivated in the highlands and on the coast. Potatoes were cultivated in the highlands at least eight thousand years ago, but the underground tuber lacked the cachet of sun-gilt corn. If gold was the sun's sweat, corn was the sun's gold, but exactly when Peru first domesticated corn is even more problematic than corn dates in Mexico, because archaeology in Peru is relatively young.

Darwin in 1859 became the first scientist to describe archaeologic corn there, when he found "heads of indian corn" mingled with shells on San Lorenzo Island near the port of Callao. In the 1860s, George Squier, then United States Commissioner to Peru, found corn in the contents of a tomb he uncovered in the ruins of the oracular shrine at Pachacamac, built in the first millennium after Christ on a headland five hundred feet above the sea. Buried with six mummies, including a fisherman with his lines and sinkers, a woman with spindle and thread, a girl with a makeup kit of pigments and cotton dabs and a baby with a seashell rattle of pebbles, were six earthenware pots of foodstuffs like peanuts and maize. Not until 1899 did Max Uhle uncover the ceramic corn pots at Huaca del Sol, buried between A.D. 300 and 600 in the Moche Valley south of Trujillo. Not until 1911 did an enterprising Yalie, Hiram Bingham, uncover the corn terraces of Machu Picchu. The story of corn in Peru has only begun to be told.

In 1989 a group of American archaeologists unearthed in the Casma Valley on the northern coast, at Pampa de las Llamas-Moxeke, a complex of storage chambers, stepped pyramids and temples ten feet high, built thirty-five hundred to thirty-eight hundred years ago, two thousand years before the great Mayan temples of Palenque, three thousand before the pyramids of the Aztec.

Pampa was as old as the great pyramids of Egypt. While corn was not found at Pampa, there was evidence of other cultivated crops such as peanuts, beans, sweet potatoes and manioc. So far, the earliest evidence of corn in Peru has been found in the highlands around Ayacucho, where Richard MacNeish discovered in the cave of Pikimachay (or Drunken Flea) corn remains that are three to four thousand years old and animal remains that may indicate aborigines hunted there sixteen thousand years ago. On the coast, where dry sands preserve well, the earliest evidence of corn has been the prehistoric cobs discovered at Huaca Prieta, a late pre-ceramic site of the Chavin culture at the mouth of the Chicama Valley, which dates from around 1050 B.C.

In the 1920s, Julio C. Tello, Peru's first native archaeologist, claimed that corn originated in Peru separately from Mexico, a claim Mangelsdorf welcomed to support his theory of wild corn. Evidence was sought in what appeared to be a petrified ear of corn found in Cuzco that botanists labeled *Zea antigua* until they discovered, on breaking it open, that it was made of clay and contained three small pellets—it was a child's rattle. Today the consensus of most archaeo-botanists is that corn migrated to South America from Mesoamerica along sea and land routes, but in Peru the extremes of the landscape, from coastal deserts to high sierras to Amazonian jungles, created a unique culture of corn.

Corn founded the culture that for three millennia dug irrigation canals and terraced the steep cliffs of the Andes, shaped and painted clay, wove fine cotton and alpaca, hammered gold and molded feathers, carved desert rock to chart the stars and morticed stone to "harness" the sun. During this time, not only did Peru evolve more diverse races of corn than any other country (Mangelsdorf distinguishes forty-eight), but its planters also evolved methods and rituals of agriculture in these formidable topographies that are still in effect today. While the Inca were but the last of Peru's rich civilizations, it was their awesome if fatal genius for organization that made permanent impress on the land, incorporating disparate ecologies into the "Land of the Four Quarters" and binding disparate peoples by chains of corn.

Francisco Pizarro's conquistadors reported corn plants "tall as soldiers' pikes" when they landed in 1528 at the Gulf of Guayaquil on the northern coast, but detailed knowledge of Peru's corn culture comes not only from Spanish chroniclers like Father Bernabé Cobo, but from two mestizos who knew Cuzco from the inside. One was Guaman Poma de Ayala, whose *El primer nueva corónica y buen gobierno,* written between 1583 and 1613 in a jumble of Indian dialects and queer Spanish, provides us with an Inca Farmer's Almanac. While his drawings melded mythic and historic time, juxtaposing Adam and

Photo Logan, courtesy Department of Library Services, American Museum of Natural History

A Moche stirrup-spout water jar in the shape of the fanged creator-god, Viracocha, whose fertility is figured in corn children miniatures of himself. The corn was molded from actual ears related to the highland race called Cuzco. Neg. No. 45663, photo J. D. Wheelock, courtesy Department of Library Services, American Museum of Natural History

Eve in the Garden with contemporary battles and earthquakes in Peru, his calendar showed clearly how the Inca organized his daily life around the seasons of the sun. Like the Christian calendar, the Inca calendar was based on a year of twelve months, and the word *quilla,* for month, suggests that the primary counting language of the Inca, the system of knotted cords called *quipu,* originated in an agricultural ordering of time, numbered by the recurrent cycles of planting, irrigating, weeding and harvesting corn.

The other mestizo was Garcilaso de la Vega, "El Inca," as he called himself proudly, son of a Spanish nobleman and an Inca princess. Born in Cuzco in 1539 and educated royally, Garcilaso left for Spain when he was twenty-one to claim his share of his father's estate. Denied it by reason of his bastardy, Garcilaso turned soldier and then scholar when he retired to Andalusia to finish his *Comentarios reales de los Incas,* four years before his death in 1616. In that same year Shakespeare died, and wrote no more royal commentaries on England and Rome. In that same year my ancestral Kennedys had already turned Presbyters in Scotland and my ancestral Culvers were plotting to set forth from England as the Children of Israel had done, in Exodus to the Wilderness. Even had Garcilaso's account been translated and made available to them, they would have spurned it. They had the new King James Bible for travel guide. Only in these latter, more secular days do we value the uniqueness of Garcilaso's early account of the New World, written in a European language, but by a native American.

When Garcilaso describes the farming of the Inca, he reveals in every sentence the Inca need for *system.* The Inca divided their empire into four quarters, each quarter into provinces, each province into communities, or *ayllus.* Their first act in conquering new territories was to make the land arable for corn. Their engineers dug irrigation channels and leveled fields to distribute the waters. They terraced impossibly steep mountains by a stair-step system of masonry walls filled with earth, "the platforms being flattened out like stairs in a staircase," diminishing in depth as they ascended. Once the land was arable, they divided it into thirds, one part for the Sun (or the Church, we would say), one for the king and one for the commoners. They planted corn in the fields each year without letting them lie fallow because they knew how to water and fertilize them. Along with corn, instead of planting beans they planted quinoa, an indigenous grain which Garcilaso called "a seed rather like rice," and which we know to be rich in protein.

The Inca monarchy was as absolute as the setting and rising of the sun, and the Inca believed that their emperors were direct descendants of the Sun and

His many brides—Mama Quilla (Mother Moon), Pacha Mama (Mother Earth), Mama Sara (Mother Corn). Commanded by the Sun, as they said, the first Inca left their island home in Lake Titicaca to travel through the high valleys of the altiplano until Manco Capa's golden staff should sink into the ground at the first blow. On the hill of Huanacauri above the Valley of Cuzco, the king's staff sank, and there they built the Temple of the Sun and planted fields of corn. "The keynote to all this activity was the search for good farmland," Paul Weatherwax commented, "and, at the dawn of modern history, the Valley of Cuzco was the center of the greatest diversity of maize types and the most highly specialized agriculture to be found anywhere in the New World."

It was also the most highly controlled. The Inca plowed in August, planted in September and harvested in May. After the proper planting ceremonies, sprinkling cornmeal and corn beer, the emperor himself would dig the first hole with a plow of gold, not unlike a city mayor in the States wielding his ceremonial shovel on Arbor Day. Garcilaso described the week of first planting as a time of great festivity, when the nobles strapped on their gold and silver breastplates, donned feather headdresses and sang songs of praise to the Sun and his Lords. Between the city of Cuzco and the hilltop fortress of Sacsahuaman was a terrace dedicated to the Sun and reverenced as the body of Mama Huaco (mother-sister-wife of Cuzco's founding Inca), reserved for exclusive tillage by those of royal blood. These lords set the rhythm of their plowing to songs that played with military and sexual puns on the word *hailli,* which was their victory cry when they crushed the enemy, furrowed the earth, ravished a woman. At harvest time they turned the maturing of corn into a puberty rite for their young knights, dressing them in parrot feathers and ear plugs, kilts and breechclouts, and allowing them alone to harvest this field of sacred corn and bring it to the temple, crying their version of hallelujah, "*Hailli, hailli!*"

Since this was a hieratic military society, the hierarchies were strict. At the bottom of the social order were the plowmen, *yanca ayllu,* or "worthless ones." These were the ones who worked the fields in common, but always in strict order: first the plots belonging to the Sun; then plots belonging to the king and state, which included land cultivated for the poor—widows, orphans, the disabled; finally their own communal plots. Their plow was a stick, the *taclla,* about two feet long and four fingers thick, with a flat front and a rounded back. Two sticks were lashed to the main shaft above the pointed end to serve as a footrest, and the other end was fashioned into a handle. A band of seven or eight men worked in a group, planting their plows in unison to the beat of the songs. A band of women followed them with clod-breakers or hoes; the *lampa* was a short-handled stick lashed to a doughnut-shaped stone or, later, to a broad blade of bronze.

The rhythm of the plowing was dictated by the rhythm of the songs. Garcilaso recalls that a choirmaster in the cathedral in Cuzco once composed a part-song for the feast of Corpus Christi in which eight of Garcilaso's mestizo schoolmates, plows in hand, mimed the action of plowing while singing a *hailli* in praise of God, the Spanish God that the converted Inca called Pachacamac, "He who gives life to the universe."

Each plowman was given a measure of land called a *tupu* for growing corn. If he had children, each boy was given a *tupu* and each girl half a *tupu.* Noblemen were given land in proportion to their retinue—wives, concubines, children, servants. In Cuzco and the highlands, they fertilized the soil with human manure, taking care first to dry and pulverize it. On the southern coast the manure used was "the dung of seabirds"; the offshore islands where birds flocked in great numbers seemed like "the snowy crests of a range of mountains," so thick was the guano. Each guano island was divided into village allotments, and trespassers were rigorously punished. In other parts of the coast they manured the land with the heads of sardines, which they would burn in small pits made by stakes and thereafter plant two or three grains of corn in each pit.

The system of storage was part of the system of tribute. Mixing clay with straw, they constructed *pirua,* or bins of different size, which they arranged in rows within the granary. They left alleys between the rows so that the bins could be emptied and filled as needed. By making a small hole in the front of each bin they could see at a glance how much grain remained. The harvests belonging to the Sun and to the king were stored in the same granaries but kept separate. The seed corn, *marca moho,* which they reserved for next year's crop, had its own special place in the granary and its own symbolic place in the heavens, in the constellation of the Pleiades, which they called "The Star of the Overflowing Grain Bins." These seeds were given out each year by the landowners to plowmen for their communal allotments.

In his *Historia del Nuevo Mundo,* the good Catholic Father Bernabé Cobo admires the totality of control the Inca emperor exerted over his subjects. Cobo's history, begun during his sojourn in Cuzco in 1609–13, was not finished until 1653 and not published until 1890, by which time other totalitarian empires had fallen and new ones were soon to be born. The acts of sowing, tilling and harvesting, Father Cobo assures us, were for the Inca acts of worship in which the entire community joined. The king and his nobles joyfully worked their plows of gold and only then did they sit down to the banquets and fiestas prepared for the celebration of the Sun on Field Planting Day. The commoners, of course, continued the job until the harvest was in, dividing their communal plots into sections where each laborer worked with his wives, children and hired hands if he could afford them. A poor man with no helpers simply took longer to work his allotment.

"When a field is to be broken up, they have a very loving, sociable, speedy way to dispatch it; all the neighbors, men and women, forty, fifty or a hundred, do joyne and come in to help freely; with friendly joyning they break up their fields and build their forts."

—ROGER WILLIAMS,
A Key into the Language of America (1643)

Cobo was struck by the communality of the farming. No man was granted any land except at the king's favor, and even that was divided equally among his kinsmen for sowing and harvesting in common. "When it was time to sow or cultivate the fields, all other tasks stopped," Cobo writes, and if there was a war on or some other emergency, "the other Indians of the community themselves worked the fields of the absent men without requesting or receiving any compensation beyond their food."

Marketing was also a communal exchange, since corn was the major unit of currency in the Inca barter system. In the central markets of village or town, Cobo explains, Indian women would exchange raw or cooked foods for corn-bread or for kernels of corn, which served as money:

The Indian women put all their goods, or part of them if they are fruits or things of this nature, in small piles arranged in a row; each little pile is worth about one-half to one real; if it is meat, it is cut up in pieces of equal value, and likewise with the rest of their goods. The Indian woman who comes to buy with her maize instead of money sits very slowly next to the one selling and makes a small pile of maize with which she plans to pay for what she is buying. This is done without exchanging a single word. The one who is selling looks at the maize, and if she thinks it is too little, she does not say a word or make any sign. She continues looking at it, and while she continues in this pose, it is understood that she is not satisfied with the price. The one buying has her eyes on the seller, and during the time she sees her uncommitted, she adds a few more grains to her pile of maize, but not many. If the seller remains inflexible, she adds again and again to the pile, but always in very small amounts, until the one selling is happy with the price and declares her approval—not with words, which from the beginning to the end are never spoken, even if the transaction lasts half an hour, but rather by deeds. The seller reaches with her hand

and brings the maize toward her. They never stop to think about whether or not these exchanges are in keeping with the principle of just and equitable commerce.

The tradition of assiduous bargaining did not end with the Inca, as any traveler to Peru today knows well. Nor did the ancient methods of farming. Anyone traveling along the Urubamba River through the Vilcanota Valley, once thick with runners and boatmen who carried jungle fruits from the Amazon to the banquet tables of the Cuzco lords, knows why it is called still the Sacred Valley of the Incas. To travel there in June, as I did, is to travel through a time warp lit by a harvest landscape golden with corn and wild Scotch broom. Warmed by the sun, protected from the snow-covered peaks that glitter against an ice-blue sky, the valley is fragrant with orange trees and lemon trees, red tomatoes and green peppers, geraniums and Pisonay trees that flame their color against hills of gold and ochre squares.

These are *tendales,* where rows of husked ears of corn have been laid flat on the fields in precise geometrical design to dry in the sun, squares of white alternating with red, deep yellow or startling purple. Drying ears poke from niches and corners of the squat adobe houses, some strung from a rafter, others heaped in baskets in a courtyard. Ahead of me by the side of the road three men run barefoot uphill, leaning forward against straps that bind their brows to the mountainous loads of cornstalks on their backs. On the hill behind them I glimpse a woman's red petticoated skirt and her tall felt hat, a boy tending his sheep, a pair of donkeys circling and circling a threshing floor, and in the distance a solitary man and woman bent unmoving in the field as if frozen in time.

Time is permanently out of whack in this rude land. Today's villagers still cultivate the steep terraces that mount the ruins of ancient Pisac, a place famed today as it was in the time of the Incas for the quality of its large-kerneled corn. And on the cliffside adjoining the sinister ruins of Pisac's fortress, you can see still a multi-leveled Inca granary covered so smoothly with yellow plaster that it looks like a modern urban high-rise. At Ollantaytambo, where the gorge narrows and the rapids begin, the village still conforms to the grid that Incas laid around a central square, each cobbled street cut down the center to channel water. At nearby Yucay, stone troughs still bring water down zigzag terraces from the glaciers of the Urubamba Cordillero far above to irrigate the valley below. High in the Cordillero, the terraces that crown ghostly Machu Picchu seem still to breathe with life from the smoke of little piles of burning grass and brush set afire by plowmen who now tend the ruins of this Sun Tem-

From this angle, Machu Picchu itself looks like a giant sundial clocked by the pointer of Huayna Picchu behind.
Neg. No. K10783, courtesy Department of Library Services, American Museum of Natural History

ple for tourists instead of for the Chosen Virgins of the Inca. Four centuries disappear in an eye-blink.

Armed with Garcilaso, on my first trip to Peru I came deliberately for the festivities at winter solstice, but I didn't expect ghosts to come to life at Machu Picchu the way they did on June 21, the day of the solstice itself. Having managed to climb, despite myself, the footholds carved by Inca in the vertiginous cliff of Huayna Picchu that thrusts above the site like a fang of the god Viracocha, I lay flat on a rock to peer over the edge. Across the central greensward of Machu Picchu far below, I saw a procession of white-robed figures, streaming banners of red and gold. They formed a circle, some four hundred of them, then moved slowly toward the great carved stone Intihuatana, the "Stone to which the Sun was Tied" on this day only, as the sun's rays crossed it at dawn. Later I learned from one of the white-robed sun worshippers that they come from around the world to meet here every twelve years at the solstice. "Thees ees magnetic center of earth where all forces converge," the man said in his distinctly East Indian accent. "Soon will end Age of Aquarius to begin Golden Age, when all will live in piss and hominy."

I knew what he meant, but I couldn't help thinking of why the emperor's virgins were chosen in the first place. They were commoners separated from their families as small girls, sequestered and trained in the domestic arts until

*"the Toltecs did not in
fact lack anything
no one was poor or had a
shabby house
and the smaller maize
ears they used as fuel
to heat their steam baths
with"*
—From the Florentine
Codex, Book 3,
Chapter 3

puberty, then presented to the emperor at the great solstice festival in Cuzco. He chose the beauties as servants or concubines for himself or as gifts to friends and reserved the rest for sacrifices to the Sun. Machu Picchu and Cuzco evoke such ghosts at every stone corner, but I preferred a quieter ghost, of a woman I had seen in the necropolis museum at Paracas on the southern coast, by the guano-coated islands of Ballestis, an ancient fertilizer factory. She was a mummy of leathery skin preserved for two thousand years, sitting cross-legged in a large ceramic bowl with the loom and spindles of her weaving. Next to her a tiny boy, who had, according to the sign, died of tuberculosis, lay curled around his little pipe, his pet cuy (guinea pig), four llama hooves, a bit of yucca and a few kernels of corn. I found considerable comfort in that corn.

LIKE THE INCA, the Aztec were empire builders, erecting in the swampy lagoons of the Valley of Mexico in 1345 the white city of Tenochtitlán, founded like Cuzco on sacred corn. Also like the Inca, the Aztec were cultural arrivistes, a tribe of barbarian Mexica (pronounced Me-*sheek*-a) from Aztlan, to the west, who wandered into the valley some thousand and a half years after the Olmec erected the metropolis of Teotihuacán in its cornfields and a thousand years after the Toltec raised in the same valley the powerful city of Tula with the help of the Plumed Serpent, Quetzalcoatl, who discovered the twin arts of agriculture and writing.

When I visited the National Museum of History in the castle of Chapultepec and looked east across the smog-filled bowl of Mexico City, built on the ruins of Tenochtitlán and Tlatelolco, toward Texcoco on the eastern perimeter where now lie hidden the world's accumulated seeds of corn, I found I was standing on the place where the last Toltec ruler hanged himself, where Aztec emperors carved their portraits in the rock and where only a century ago Maximilian set up house with Carlotta. Such are the palimpsests of history in Mexico, where corn was born and farming began.

The Aztec inherited an intensive method of agriculture, necessary to the Mesoamerican peoples who did not use domestic animals for planting and therefore used neither plow nor wheel for cultivating the soil extensively. While the hot wet jungles of the Yucatán favored the simple slash-and-burn method, the Valley of Mexico required different treatment because it was a swamp of fresh- and salt-water lakes. Planters there around 300 B.C. began to build artificial islands they called *chinampas* and we call "floating gardens." You can see their contemporary forms in the gardens of Xochimilco and their ghostly outlines in aerial photographs. The Franciscan Juan de Torquemada saw them in the sixteenth century and described how the Indians in their fresh-water lagoons "without much trouble plant and harvest their maize and greens, for all over are ridges called chinampas; these are strips built above water and surrounded by ditches, which obviates watering."

The Aztec like the Inca were masters of organization, and they elaborated the ridges into a system of dams, aqueducts and dikes to control the waters during their annual flooding as well as to provide for irrigation, cultivation and transport all at once. They divided the city into four quarters and each quarter into subdistricts based on clans, or *calpulli,* who tilled their land communally. Through the marshes, they dug a network of canals and built between them mounds of water plants covered with thick layers of lake-bottom mud. The mounds they held in place by hurdles of wickerwork, often three hundred feet long by fifteen or thirty feet wide, large enough to support reed houses and willow trees. They could grow crops year-round without the land lying fallow because they fertilized it with human dung, sold to farmers by city sanitation engineers, and renewed the land as needed with fresh mud. The mounds provided movable nurseries for seedlings of corn, which they transplanted as needed, and the canals provided transport for farmers and merchants alike.

The network was a marvel of city planning that at its peak in the fifteenth century supported an urban population of more than a million and a half people, three-fourths of whom were farmers. The first major public work of the Aztec was a broad raised-stone dike, which was both a highway and a dam to create reservoirs of fresh water for ever-increasing areas of cultivated land. How dependent the city of Tenochtitlán was on its gardens of corn is evident from records of successive years of frost and drought beginning in 1450, when famine was so severe that families sold their children for a basket of corn: four hundred cobs for a girl, five hundred for a boy.

The majority of farmers were hereditary clan members, with rights and duties to the state, but beneath them were *mayeques* who belonged to no clan and consequently became sharecroppers working for others. Each farm family paid tribute to church and state with goods and services, and when a neighborhood was required to supply firewood, say, to a god's temple, each family would share the cost by contributing "one large mantle, four small ones, a basket of shelled maize, and 100 cobs." So states a pre-Conquest tax list ordered by Moctezuma and recorded in pictures on thick sheets of maguey (since annotated in both Nahuatl and Spanish), whereby we have a fair notion of the annual tribute of corn paid to the imperial granaries. In this Tribute Roll, you can see two storage bins, or *troxes,* of wide planks or wicker plastered with mor-

Long before the Aztec, the Zapotec founded their civilization upon corn at Monte Albán, A.D. 300 to 900, near Oaxaca. Here a Zapotec funeral urn depicts the corn god, Pitao Cozobi, with stylized ears on his headdress. A cob with rows of kernels topped by a spike was typical of the prehistoric corn ears found in the Tehuacán Valley near Oaxaca. Courtesy Departamento de Arqueología, Museo Nacional de Antropología, Mexico City

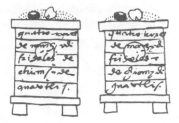

From the Codex Mendoza

tar, each topped with a bean and a kernel of corn. Each bin held eight thousand to ten thousand bushels, and the annual tribute due the state was twenty-eight *troxes* of maize, twenty-one of beans, the like number of a seed called *chian,* and eighteen of a mixture of greens and grain amaranth that they called *huauhtli.* Additional tribute was levied for the support of local temples, schools, garrisons and indigents.

Corn planting began in March and continued through May, depending on the breed, in time for the heavy rains of summer. Seed corn from the previous season, after its blessing by the goddess of maize, Chicome Couatl, was soaked in water while the farmer prepared the ground with his digging stick, which resembled the *taclla* of Peru. He hilled the earth in small hummocks in rows about a yard apart, made a small hole in the top of each and dropped in a few kernels from the cloth bag over his shoulder. He hoed the ground but two or three times during the growing season. Mid-July, when each stalk bore two or three young ears, he removed all ears but one that the green corn might be made into special cakes for the festival of Xilonen, the goddess of young corn. By mid-August he bent each stalk over just below the maturing ear and left it to dry. In September, after the harvest sacrifice to the god of ripe corn, Cinteotl (*cintli* means "maize" in Nahuatl; *teotl* means "god"), the farmer tied the ears in bundles, shelled some for his house and took the rest to the communal storage bins.

The Spanish calculated that the average yield per acre was sixteen bushels. As William Bray speculated in *Everyday Life of the Aztecs* (1968), an Aztec family of five would have needed to till three acres of land to provide enough food for themselves, apart from their tribute fields. The combination of a temperate climate and sophisticated farming methods ensured that a family could produce what they needed by working only half a year at farming. As a result, the Aztec had plenty of leisure for the arts, for building, for the festivals and ceremonies that punctuated their daily round, and for the rituals of war. "The material foundations for Aztec imperialism," one archaeologist has said, "were established by the farmers who had conquered the swamps."

We know details of Aztec farming, and other aspects of daily life, from the writings and drawings of Father Bernardino de Sahagún, a Franciscan who arrived in Mexico from Spain in 1529, learned the Nahuatl language and spent the rest of his life chronicling what he heard and saw in *La Historia general de las cosas de Nueva España,* not published until 1829. What he heard he transcribed with great care in both Nahuatl and Spanish—a lexicographer's method that created by mere accumulation a rhythm as incantatory as a planting song. Here is his account of the farmer in Book 10 of the Florentine Codex:

The farmer [is] strong, hardy, energetic, wiry, powerful. The good farmer, the [good] field worker [is] active, agile, diligent, industrious: a man careful of things, dedicated—dedicated to separate things; vigilant, penitent, contrite. [He goes] without his sleep, without his food; he keeps vigil at night; his heart breaks. He is bound to the soil; he works—works the soil, stirs the soil anew, prepares the soil; he weeds, breaks up the clods, hoes, levels the soil, makes furrows, makes separate furrows, breaks up the soil. He sets the landmarks, the separate landmarks; he sets the boundaries, the separate boundaries; he stirs the soil anew during the summer; he works [the soil] during the summer; he takes up the stones; he digs furrows; he makes holes; he plants, hills, waters, sprinkles; he broadcasts seed; he sows beans, provides holes for them—punches holes for them, fills in the holes; he hills [the maize plants], removes the undeveloped maize ears, discards the withered ears, breaks off the green maize stalks, thins out the green maize stalks, breaks off the undeveloped maize ears, breaks off the nubbins, harvests the maize stalks, gathers the stubble; he removes the tassels, gathers the green maize ears, breaks off the ripened ears, gathers the maize, shucks the ears, removes the leaves, binds the maize ears, binds the ears [by their shucks], forms clusters of maize ears, makes necklaces of maize ears. He hauls away [the maize ears]; he fills the maize bins; he scatters [the maize ears]; he spreads them, he places them where they can be reached. He cuts them, he dismembers them. He shells them, treads on them, cleans them, winnows them, throws them against the wind.

The bad farmer is a shirker, a lukewarm worker, a careless worker; one who drops his work, lazy, negligent, mad, wicked, noisy, coarse, decrepit, unfit—a field hand, nothing but a field hand; a glutton—one who gorges himself; nothing but a beggar—stingy, avaricious, greedy, niggardly, selfish. . . . He is lazy, negligent, listless; he works unwillingly; he does things listlessly.

Sahagún's doubled litanies of Nahuatl and Spanish are rendered by a voice and ear so tuned to the

This earliest recorded drawing of raised-field agriculture, from the Drake Manuscript, *or* Histoire Naturelle des Indes, *ca. 1586, shows a West Indian farmer using a pointed stick to plant seeds of different plants together. On the right, three corn stalks abut two bean stalks. The translated inscription reads: "The Indian making his garden sows several kinds of grain for his food to make it appear that he is working hard and also to please his fiancée and sufficient to feed his wife and children, the soil being so fertile as to bear fruit all the time."* Courtesy Pierpont Morgan Library

This sequence from the Florentine Codex shows farmers planting, cultivating, harvesting and storing corn. Negative Nos. 1738–40, 1743, courtesy Department of Library Services, American Museum of Natural History

high liturgical language of his own church that he makes even the most humdrum activities of growing and eating corn sound like corn crucifixion and resurrection: "For it was said that we brought much torment to it—that we ate it, we put chili on it, we mixed salt with it, we mixed saltpeter with it; it was mixed with lime. As we troubled our food to death, thus we revived it. Thus, it is said, the maize was given new youth when this was done."

Describing the many different kinds of corn that the Aztec farmer planted, Sahagún translates each as a particularized jewel. At the apex is white maize, a small ear "hard, like a copper bell—hard, like fruit pits," clear like a seashell, like a crystal, "an ear of metal, a green stone, a bracelet—precious, our flesh, our bones." This was the maize whose perfect seeds the farmer selected for planting, whose growth Sahagún turns into a planting primer and an ode:

Then it is gathering moisture; then it swells; then the grain of maize bursts; then it takes root. Then it sprouts; then it pushes up; then it reaches the surface; then it gathers moisture; it really flies. Then it forks, it lies dividing; it spreads out, it is spreading out. And they say it is pleasing. At this time it is hilled, the hollow is filled in, the crown is covered, the earth is well heaped up.

Also at this time beans are sown or cast. They say that at this time this [maize] once again begins to grow, also begins to branch out. Then it reaches outward; then it spreads out; then it becomes succulent. Once again at this time it is hilled. Then the corn silk develops; then the corn tassels form. At this time, once again it is hilled; it is, they say, the hatching of the green maize ear. Then an embryonic ear forms. Then the green maize ear begins to form; the green maize ear shines, glistens, spreads glistening.

[The kernels] spread forming little droplets; it is said that they spread taking form. Then [the kernels] form milk; they spread forming milk. Then the surface [of the kernels] become evened. Then it becomes the *nix-*

tamal flower; now it is called *chichipelotl.* Then [the milk] thickens, at which time it is called *elotl.* Then, at this time, it begins to harden; it turns yellow, whereupon it is called *cintli.*

Sahagún's minute attention to the naming of each moment in the birth, ripening and death of each corn plant conveys as powerfully as any transcription can the personal identification of ancient corn growers with their corn. His litanies are like prayers to Xilonen and Xochipilli, the green corn gods, to Cinteotl and Chicome Couatl, the ripe corn gods. Sahagún evokes as few others can the symbolic power of Chicome Couatl, "the Demeter of old Mexico, the Mother Goddess," as Erich Neumann has called her, whose son was the Sun. In the Aztec calendar which governed the daily round of Aztec life, chaos comes again every fifty-two years, when the Great Mother, Earth Mother, Terrible Goddess, Snake Woman, reasserts her power, swallowing all in darkness in order that her son, god of ripe corn, god of the heavens, may be born again. In the doubled columns of Sahagún's transcriptions we can hear the doubled rhythms of apocalypse and resurrection that underlie the metamorphic changes of both Sun and Son.

THE DESERT FARMERS OF THE SOUTHWEST

FARMING in the Southwest desert of what is now the United States was far more difficult than in the Sacred Valley of the Inca or in the marshes of Tenochtitlán. Yet for three centuries before Christ was born in a desert across the seas, the Hohokam were making their stretch of the Sonora desert bloom with squashes, lima and tepary beans, tobacco and, at the time of Christ's birth, corn. Although earlier desert cultures like the Mogollon had cultivated corn in the mountainous borderlands of southern Arizona and New Mexico, corn as a civilizer of the Southwest desert began with the new group called by their Pima descendants the *Huhugam O'odham,* or the Hohokam, meaning "the vanished ones," who developed in the first millennium after Christ the most diverse plantings of any of the tribes and one of the largest canal systems of North America.

The Hohokam were farmers, despite the fact that the desert climate was as hostile then as it is now. Besides the usual hazards of sandstorms and flash floods, temperatures ranged, then as now, from 7 degrees to 119 degrees Fahrenheit and rainfall averaged less than ten inches a year. Fortunately, there was the floodplain of the Gila River, formed by the Salt and Verde rivers flowing toward the Colorado. With stone hoes these farmers began to dig pit houses and wide shallow canals. If you visit Arizona's Park of the Four Waters today, you can see the remains of eighteen prehistoric irrigation canals, which run parallel to the modern canal that now waters downtown Phoenix. Phoenix itself is built over the ruins of 1,750 miles of Hohokam canals. Along the Gila south of Phoenix, you can see the extensive ruins of Snaketown, where the Hohokam flourished until A.D. 1450, covering 240 acres with their dwellings and irrigated fields.

"During the long Indian tenure the land remained undefiled save for scars no deeper than the scratches of cornfield clearings or the farming canals of the Hohokams on the Arizona desert."
—STEWART UDALL, *The Quiet Crisis* (1963)

As Mesoamerican cultures bred new strains of corn resistant to drought and found new ways of irrigating it, a Reventador popcorn, a Chapalote flint and the eight-rowed sixty-day flour corn we call Maiz de Ocho reached Mexico's northern frontier. Along with adaptive corn breeds came Mesoamerica's planting sticks and, no less importantly, their planting songs. In their many different languages, all the Southwestern peoples knew the power of corn song. "It is late July, the moon of rain," Ruth Underhill wrote in *Singing for Power: The Song Magic of the Papago Indians of Southern Arizona* (1938). "Now planting can begin." Every man, she explained, placed his field at the mouth of a wash where, after a torrent, the earth would be soft enough to puncture with his digging stick. In each hole he dropped four kernels and, kneeling, spoke to the seed so that there would be no misunderstanding: "Now I place you in the ground. You will grow tall. Then they shall eat, my children and my friends who come from afar." While the corn grew, night after night the farmer walked around his field, "singing up the corn." "There is a song for corn as high as his knee," Underhill explained, "for corn waist high, and for corn with the tassel forming."

> The corn comes up;
> It comes up green;
> Here upon our fields
> White tassels unfold.
>
> The corn comes up;
> It comes up green;
> Here upon our fields
> Green leaves blow in the breeze.

There was a song for the blue evening when the corn tassels trembled, for the wind when the corn leaves shook, for the fear the corn felt when the striped woodpecker struck at its heart, for the green time when the tassels waved for joy and for the harvest time when the corn was embraced lovingly by the harvester's arms. "Sometimes," Underhill said, "all the men of a village meet together and sing all night, not only for the corn but also for the beans, the squash, and the wild things." Songs and prayers were an essential part of cultivating wild things, and while no one has proved that loving a corn plant, as Henry Wallace said, will improve it or its progeny, the sense that corn was sacred did it no harm.

It was not lack of desert song but a disastrous series of droughts and floods that "stressed the Hohokam system," as Gary Nabhan puts it in *Enduring Seeds,* and depopulated their valleys a century before the first Europeans set foot in the Southwest. The first to come were three Spanish slave-catchers and a Moorish slave named Estevan de Dorantes, who had been shipwrecked on the Gulf coast of Texas in 1535. Before they worked their way back to Mexico, the Spaniards were told by the Indians they encountered of a kingdom of rich cities to the north. A later foray headed by Estevan and a Franciscan priest, Fray Marcos de Niza, got the slave killed for his trouble, but the priest's tales of imagined gold were enough for Francisco Vásquez de Coronado and his troops to saddle their horses and set out for the "Seven Cities of Cíbola." In 1540 they found, instead, the cornfields of the Zuni.

Zuni Pueblo is on the New Mexico side of the Arizona border, due south of Gallup and north of Bat Cave. Farther north the Navaho reservation straddles the two states, adjoining the Hopi to the west and the Pueblo group to the east. To reach Zuni Pueblo you must climb through rocky canyons and forests of piñon and juniper before hitting a barren plateau. Few Zuni grow corn here today, but theirs is the only one of the eighty pueblos conquered by Coronado that has retained its ancestral land, land they call the Middle Ant Hill of the World. When they do grow corn, largely for ceremonial purposes, they grow it as their ancestors did.

The corn of their ancestors impressed Pedro de Castañeda, who wrote about his trip with Coronado in *Relación de la jornada de Cíbola* (a copy of his original manuscript, made in 1596, rests in the New York Public Library). "The Indians plant in holes, and the corn does not grow tall, but each stalk bears three and four large and heavy ears with 800 hundred grains each," Castañeda wrote, "a thing never seen in these regions," by which he meant the regions around Mexico City. "In one year they harvest enough for seven years."

Even a century ago the methods of Zuni corn farming impressed another recorder, Frank Hamilton Cushing, who first led a Smithsonian expedition to the Pueblo in 1879 and discovered there a handful of Presbyterian missionaries working hard to cultivate a tribe of seventeen hundred unsaved souls. As an ethnographer and translator of the distinctive Zuni language, Cushing was as

This Mimbres pottery food bowl from New Mexico (c. A.D. 1000–1150) depicts six men with planting sticks, and a feline, in a cornfield. When a man died, a food bowl was inverted over his face like the domed sky of the Underworld, and a "kill hole" was punched in the center to allow his spirit to emerge, just as his ancestors had once emerged from the Underworld. Photo by John Bigelow Taylor, Within the Underworld Sky (1981)

remarkable as Sahagún had been among the Aztec. His Smithsonian bureau chiefs, however, found him remarkable in ways they did not approve. They thought he'd gone native, and he had. The Easterner who had come but to observe aboriginal ways remained four and a half years to become a Priest of the Bow and First War Chief, before his assimilation was cut short at the age of forty-three when he choked on a fishbone.

From Cushing we have learned in precise detail how Zuni and other desert farmers made the sand sprout corn. When a young Zuni wished to mark land as his own, Cushing told us, he looked for the mouth of an arroyo and carefully "lifted the sand" with his hoe—the nature of Southwest farming is condensed in the phrase. After lifting little mounds at intervals around his proposed field, he built them into embankments called "sand strings." At each corner he placed a rock to establish his claim to this land for his lifetime and, after his death, his clan's. Significantly, the first month of spring, the month of planting, was called the month of "Lesser Sand Storms."

Frank Hamilton Cushing in Zuni regalia around 1882.
National Anthropological Archives, Smithsonian Institution

Before he could plant, the farmer had to extend his flood control into an irrigation system. Upstream of his chosen arroyo, he drove forked cedar branches in a line across the dry streambed and built a dam with branches, rocks and earth. Downstream, he built more barriers on either side. Finally he looked for a ball of clay, which he buried at the side of the bed where he wanted rain freshets to flow, then packed earth over the clay to form a long embankment that angled into the arroyo. The buried ball of clay was important symbolically as well as practically, for the ball represented a wooden cylinder used in a Zuni game called *Ti'-kwa-we,* or Race of the Kicked Stick. Here two opposing teams, running at full speed, competed over a twenty-five-mile course by kicking ahead of them two small cylinders of wood. The clay ball provided a like cylinder for the water gods, encouraging them to race with the Kicked Stick and to push their waters ahead of them with like force and speed.

By this method of earth banking, the farmer built a network of smaller barriers across his field and created an irrigation system, directing any freshets that came and catching any rain that fell. To encourage the rain, he sought the

Corn-Priest of his clan to prepare a plumed prayer stick and a cane of wild tobacco. The priest knelt in the new field facing the east and implored the god-priests of earth, sky and cavern "not to withhold their mist-laden breaths, but to canopy the earth with cloud banners, and let fly their shafts little and mighty of rain, to send forth the fiery spirits of lightning, lift up the voice of thunder whose echoes shall step from mountain to mountain bidding the *mesas* shake down streamlets." That the streamlets might become torrents and feed the earth seeds, the priest "this day plants, standing in the trail of the waters, the smoke-cane and prayer-plume." Not quite the incantatory repetition of Sahagún, but Cushing's prose shares its Latinate root. Through the overlay of his romance-derived tongue, we glimpse the stone-hard reality of Zuni land.

The Zuni farmer had to allow a full year for the rains to deposit loam. Only then did he plant rows of sagebrush along the western boundaries of his field to catch the fine dust and sand blown during the month of the Crescent of the Greater Sand Storms. Usually there was but a single rainstorm in the spring and its waters, channeled by the embankments, helped redistribute and tamp down the soil until it was at last ready for the ceremonies of planting. In winter the seed had been blessed by the Corn-Matron, who had sprinkled a tray of selected kernels with the black powder of corn-soot (corn smut, we call it) and a mixture of yellow paint, yellow flowers and corn pollen, so that the grains became bright yellow in token of their strength. She then stored them in a pouch made from the whole skin of a fawn.

A cornfield laid out in waffle patterns and protected by corn-stalk hedges with the Zuni pueblo beyond, seen from the southwest. From Cushing's *Zuni Breadstuff,* reprinted 1974

A Zuni cornfield sports a network of traps to scare crows. In the foreground, a man-sized "watcher of corn sprouts" lolls his tongue at a caught crow. Neg. No. 273529, Courtesy Department of Library Services, American Museum of Natural History

On May 1, when the farmer heard the Sun Priest call from the housetops, he sharpened his planting stick of juniper. The base of his stick was forked with a branch stump that he could use as a brace for his foot. He brought with him to the fields a plumed prayer stick and, from a pouch, six different-colored kernels of corn, which a corn-matron sprinkled with water to bless with "rain." When the farmer arrived at the field, he dug four holes equidistant from the center, each of them a cardinal point, and in each planted a corn kernel of the right color—red for the South, white for the East, yellow for the North, blue for the West. He dug two more holes and planted a white kernel for the Sky regions and a black kernel for the world Below. In lines extending from each of the four directions, he planted rows of corn until all the kernels in his pouch were gone. After he returned home, he fasted and prayed for four days.

Now the farmer could plant his corn. Taking with him a lunch of piki bread and a seed bag, the planter dug holes four to seven inches deep, alongside last year's rows. A boy followed him and dropped in each hole twelve to twenty kernels, covering them with sand. Where the broken stalks of last year's rows were thin, the planter reinforced them with twigs of greasewood or sagebrush to catch drifting soil blown by the wind. The country was so dry, Cushing explained, that seeds had to be planted deep to gain protection from the underlying loam.

The planters made a network of crow traps. They erected a number of cedar poles, topped them with prickly leaves and strung between them ropes made from split yucca leaves. On these they hung rags, strips of hide, moss, old bones, anything that would sway in the wind. They also made small hair nooses in which a hair thread was baited at each end with a corn kernel, contrived to choke two crows at once. Boys were set to fashion human scarecrows with faces of painted rawhide, eyes of cornhusk-balls, teeth of cornstalk strips, hair of black horsetails and lolling tongues of red leather. These were the "watchers of corn sprouts," and soon they were joined by crows that had been caught and hung beak downward to warn their fellows off the corn.

When the kernels had sprouted, it was "leaf-lifting" time. The farmers pulled up all but four or five of the best shoots and killed the white grubs near the root. Then it was "hoeing time" or "staving time," when they dug out weeds with their ancient hard wood scythes or with the white man's hoe of hand-wrought iron. The work was hard and when the men went home at sunset, the women had prepared a feast with bowls of smoking stew red with chili and with baskets of waferbreads colored red, yellow, white and blue. After the second or third hoeing of the summer, the men hilled the corn with a pickaxe made from an elk's scapula or a broad stone and left the corn until harvest.

In autumn, they picked all the corn that was still too green to show signs of ripening and carried it to a hill. Here they dug a deep funnel-shaped pit, several feet in diameter at the base, and on the windward side a hole about two feet in diameter opening into the interior of the pit. Through the hole in the top, they threw in dried grass, leaves and wood until the pit was full, then fired the pit so that it would burn all night. When the coals were glowing, they threw in green cornstalks and all the unhusked ears of corn, plugging the top and the draft hole with green stalks, then mounding earth over the whole. After a day and night, the mound and the stalk plug were removed and steam shot hundreds of feet in the air like a geyser. By afternoon the mass had cooled and they could shovel out the corn through the draft hole and carry it into the village, where they husked the golden-brown ears and braided them, to hang from the rafters of their houses.

While the remaining corn in the field ripened, they built little huts in which children and old men would keep watch against coyotes and burros as well as crows. Any burro so foolhardy as to venture into a cornfield after its first beating regretted it. Cushing recalled a burro nicknamed "Short-horn," which had had its ears shaved, its tail and tongue cut short, some teeth pulled and its left eye put out. "The Zunis, and probably most other Indians," Cushing explained, "are touchy on the subject of their breadstuff."

When frost turned stalks to gold and shucks to feathers, the corn was picked and carried into town for husking. Women formed the husking bees, shucking the cobs in great numbers, selecting ears to string on threads of yucca fiber and carrying baskets of cobs to the roofs to dry next to heaps of chili peppers. Dried corn was stored in the corn room or granary of each house, in the center of which four sacred objects were kept: a perfect ear of yellow corn, a bifurcated ear of white corn, a bunch of black corn-soot and an ear blessed by a Seed-Priest in the sacred Salt Lake, "Las Salinas." The salt ear and the soot ear formed the couch or "resting place" of the "Father and Mother of corn-crops," the yellow ear for the Father and the white for the Mother. Each year the Corn-Matron presented the first new corn to its corn parents in a ceremony called "Meeting of the Children," reenacting the return of the lost corn maidens and their welcome by the Seed-Priests of the Zuni of former times. Each year repeated the cycle of the seasons and retold the narratives that gave them voice.

At Acoma Pueblo (visible on the clifftop in the distance), a farmer in 1945 harvests his corn with horse and wagon, but the corn stalks are planted as of old. Photo by Ferenz Fedor, courtesy Museum of New Mexico, Neg. No. 100471

Today Zuni and other Pueblos still farm by a version of the ancient system now called waffle gardens, in which they build mud walls four inches high to enclose small beds four feet wide by twelve to twenty feet long, dividing them into two-by-two-foot squares to hold rainwater and water they pour in by hand. Today as of old they plant in May, "under a waxing moon, so as to grow with the moon," as ethnobotanists reported in 1916, for "under a waning moon the seeds cease growing." And still they harvest in late September and early October, "after the watermelons have been taken." The day the Summer chief takes office, Alfonso Ortiz reports of contemporary Tewa, he begins the cycle anew by "bringing the buds to life," and then it is time for the medicine men to go to the sacred center of the village in dead of night to "reseed mother earth navel," to reach deep into the ground and waken her to life for the new year.

Still today the Zuni keep their varied strains of colored corn pure by cultivating them in fields isolated from each other, and still they keep back some seed year after year, to maintain the bloodlines of their own pueblo. "We could buy other seed, and perhaps better, from white people; or we could get seed from other pueblos; but the old men do not want that," a native of San Ildefonso told the 1916 ethnobotanists. "They want to keep the very corn of the pueblo, because the corn is the same as the people." Still they plant their corn with planting sticks and tend it by singing. "A planting stick is special," George Blue-eyes told some Navaho students in 1979 at Point Community School in

Chinle, Arizona. "You must finish your planting and put it away before the last quarter of the moon. . . . You should sing after planting in the first four holes."

There are more planting songs than cornfields now, for three centuries after Spanish adventurers brought horses and swords to the Southwest, white American engineers brought dams and similar improvements. The Salt River Project effectively ended Pima farming in 1920 when it diverted water from Pima lands. The pattern is familiar. At that date there were still more than forty-eight thousand native American farmers in the United States, half of whom owned the land they farmed. In 1982 the number had dropped to no more than seven thousand. Each year there are fewer to say with George Blue-eyes that "planting the old way is still best."

"Corn planted by tractor may take two weeks to come up," he explained. "Mine might be up in four days. Wind can blow tractor-planted corn right out the ground. Mine is strong. The plow rolls the ground over on itself across the whole field. Too much soil dries out. The stick digs just enough for each seed. The ground underneath stays wet." He might have added that the roar of a modern combine is nothing like a song, so how can it keep the corn from mis-understanding, how can it keep the tassels from trembling, keep the wind from its tender leaves, the woodpecker from its heart, until it is gobbled up by the ravening harvester?

BUFFALO BIRD WOMAN'S GARDEN

"OFTEN IN SUMMER I rise at daybreak and steal out to the cornfields; and as I hoe the corn I sing to it, as we did when I was young." So said Buffalo Bird Woman in *Waheenee: An Indian Girl's Story* (1921), after a long life devoted to the growing of corn. She'd been born in 1839 (just seventeen years before my grandfather Parks Ira Kennedy was born in Benton County, Iowa) to her father, Small Ankle, and her mother, Want-to-be-a-Woman, in one of the villages at Knife River, North Dakota. The year 1839 was one of grief for the Hidatsa, who had lost half their tribe two years earlier in the "smallpox year," so that they numbered but eight hundred. The Knife River region of the upper Missouri River had been the homeland of these Plains Villagers for more than a thousand years, beginning with the Mandan and later the Hidatsa and Arikara (known as the Three Affiliated Tribes), but their Northern Plains ancestors had cut a wide swath from Montana to Wisconsin for more than nine thousand years. Here around A.D. 900, about the time Monte Albán was being abandoned in western Mexico and the great city of Tula was rising in the east, the Plains Villagers of the barbaric north were beginning to plant seeds as well as to hunt wild game.

According to Sioux legend, it was Buffalo Cow Woman who first brought the Sacred Pipe to her people and the four different-colored grains of maize. These sprang from the milk that dropped from her udder when she kicked up her hind legs and departed, "so that maize and the buffalo were given together to be the food of all the red tribes." Cheyenne legend created a pair of culture heroes to express this dual culture. Corn was represented by Sweet Root Standing, whose other names were Rustling Leaf, Rustling Corn Leaf, Sweet Medicine. His twin was Standing on Ground, named also Erect Horns and Straight Horns.

But these legends are relatively recent, for corn rites among the tribes of the upper Missouri were older than buffalo rites. Long before the white man brought horses and guns to the Plains, the red tribes were far more dependent upon corn than buffalo meat. The Hopewells at the confluence of the Ohio, Mississippi and Illinois rivers had already come and gone, leaving behind them a continent-wide network of trade, fine ornaments of copper and mica, engravings of bone, magnificent pottery and the great earth circles of their ceremonial centers and burial mounds, all founded on a knowledge of agriculture. The Moundbuilders had planted corn up and down the Mississippi and Missouri rivers, and the myths of origin of the later Plains people reflected the ancientness of corn.

Here men were hunters and women were gardeners, and the Plains Villagers prospered as traders of both fur and corn, building prototypes of the sod houses of my grandfathers in their circular earth lodges, and farming the rich

In Florida as in Virginia, men used wooden "mattocks" to cultivate the ground while women used a "pecker" to make holes for planting. Jacques Le Moyne's version, as engraved by De Bry, gives the women Botticelli hair and the men Michelangelo muscles. From the Collections of the Library of Congress

river bottoms that snaked through the plains. To the east, the Woodland ancestors of Sioux, Algonquian and Iroquois from Minnesota to Maine were also planting the hardy flint corns as they adapted to snow and ice. To the southeast, corn supported the massive temple mounds of the Mississippians, the ritual fires and Great Sun king-priest of the Natchez. Wherever corn grew, north and south, it was planted with sticks and songs.

One of the best early descriptions of Indian corn planting was provided by Thomas Hariot in 1588, when he reported on the coastal Indians of the new-found land of Virginia, where land was easier to dig than in the frozen plains of the North or the desert of the Southwest. As a wheat grower, he puzzled over the lack of native plows:

> The ground they never fatten with muck, dung, or anything, neither plow or dig it as we in England but only prepare it in a sort as followeth: A few days before they sow or set the men with wooden instruments made almost in the form of mattocks or hoes with long handles, the women with short peckers or parers, because they use them sitting, of a foot long and five inches in breadth, do only break the upper part of the ground, to raise up the weeds grass and old stubs of cornstalks with their roots. The which after a day or two days drying in the sun, being scraped up into many small heaps, to save them the labor of carrying them away, they burn to ashes. . . . Then their setting or sowing is after this manner. First, for their corn, beginning in one corner of the plot with a pecker they make a hole wherein they put out four grains, with care that they touch not one another (about an inch asunder), and cover them with the mould again.

A few years later, Samuel de Champlain, reporting on the Iroquois along the St. Lawrence River, was also struck by the oddity of planting with sticks. "In place of ploughs, they use an instrument of hard wood, shaped like a spade," he wrote:

> Planting three or four kernels in one place they then heap up about it a quantity of earth with shells of the signoc. . . . Then three feet distant they plant as much more, and this in succession. With this corn they put in each hill three or four Brazilian beans which are of different colours. When they grow up they interlace with the corn which reaches to the height of from five to six feet; and they keep the ground very free from weeds.

Another early French traveler, Gabriel Sagard, noted in 1632 how Huron men began to prepare the ground a year ahead by girdling trees in the spring so that they would die over the winter, after which they burned the underbrush to make "oak openings" for planting. The women would then clean the ground and with a stick dig round holes at intervals, in each of which they sowed nine or ten grains of corn that had been soaked in water.

If in the Northeast clearing the fields was man's work, planting them was woman's work, unlike in the Southwest, where farming was largely a matter of hydrodynamics. Across the North, the survival of the tribe through corn was entrusted to the women, and the status of planting was equal to hunting.

"The quantity of corn destroyed, at a moderate computation, must amount to 160,000 bushels, with a vast quantity of vegetables of every kind. . . . I flatter myself that the orders with which I was entrusted are fully executed, as we have not left a single settlement or a field of corn in the country of the Five Nations."
—MAJOR GENERAL JOHN SULLIVAN, *Journals of the Military Expedition of Major General John Sullivan against the Six Nations* (1779, published 1887)

Among the Iroquois of New Hampshire the women of each settlement elected annually one of their number to direct their work. Her name meant literally "Corn Plant, Its Field Female Chief." "In the summer season we planted, tended and harvested our corn, and generally had our children with us," Mary Jemison, who had been taken captive by the Iroquois, later told James Seaver, who recounted it in *A narrative of the life of Mrs. Mary Jemison* (1862). The labor was not severe, she said, and they had "no masters to oversee or drive us, so that we could work as leisurely as we pleased."

The yeoman masters of wheatfields were unaccustomed to this division of labor and misunderstood the methods of planting along with their social meaning. "The women as is the custom with the Indians do all the drudgery," John Bradbury wrote of the Mandan in 1811, noting that the squaws were excellent cultivators despite the fact that they were so destitute of implements that they hoed their corn "with the blade bone of buffalo, ingeniously fixed to a stick for that purpose." Alexander Henry, traveling through the Mandan and Hidatsa settlements in the early nineteenth century, better understood the cultural differences when he wrote in his *Journal,* "Let it not be thought that this work was mere drudgery. Every woman had the company of some of the young girls, and the gardens were close enough together to permit of friendly intercourse. The women usually sang as they worked, and there are preserved great numbers of field-songs which were sung only in the gardens." Besides which, young men were always hanging about on the pretext of protecting the gardens from prowling war parties and that seemed "to detract in no way from the pleasure of the girls."

We know much about these gardens because of an unusual and invaluable collaboration between the Hidatsan Buffalo Bird Woman and the Presbyterian Gilbert L. Wilson, a minister who turned anthropologist after visiting Fort Berthold in 1906, when Buffalo Bird Woman was sixty-seven. Fifty years earlier, Buffalo Bird Woman had watched the construction of that fort next to her cornfields in a bend of the upper Missouri called Like-a-Fishhook. Here the small band of survivors of both smallpox and roving Dakota warriors had migrated, only to be rounded up in 1874 into the Fort Berthold Indian Reservation, where they were compelled to abandon the communal lands they held sacred in deference to the white man's consecration of private property. This was part of the United States government's reformist policy instituted by the Dawes Act of 1887, and formulated by the founder of the Carlisle School for Indians as: "Kill the Indian and save the man."

Buffalo Bird Woman refused to be saved. While her brother Wolf Chief learned English and became a storekeeper, Buffalo Bird Woman kept the

"The Mandans and Manitaries cultivate very fine maize without ever manuring the ground, but their fields are on the low banks of the river . . . where the soil is particularly fruitful. . . . They have extremely fine maize of different species."

—ALEXANDER PHILIP MAXIMILIAN, *Maximilian's Travels* (1833)

Buffalo Bird Woman appears on the right, with her son, Edward Goodbird, in the middle and her husband, Son of a Star, on the left. Photo by Gilbert Wilson in 1906. Minnesota Historical Society

Indian tongue and the gardening traditions practiced for centuries by Hidatsa women. Fortunately, Gilbert Wilson was as unusual in his way as Buffalo Bird Woman was in hers, for he wanted to learn about Indian life from the Indian point of view. Over the course of a decade and more, with Buffalo Bird Woman's son Edward Goodbird acting as interpreter, Wilson received from her a comprehensively detailed account of her life at Knife River Village beginning in 1846, about the time my grandfather's father, Roswell Kennedy, was applying the plow to the prairie sod of Indian territories south of the Dakotas and west of the Missouri. In 1917 Wilson published as a doctoral thesis the work now titled *Buffalo Bird Woman's Garden*—one of the most complete and articulate records we have of native agricultural life in the mid-1800s.

Buffalo Bird Woman, whose grandmother was Soft-white Corn, explained to Wilson how they had always scorned the hard and dry prairies for the bottomlands, which they worked with hoes instead of plows. "I think our old way of raising corn is better than the new way taught us by white men," she said. Just the year before, her corn had taken first prize at an agricultural county fair: "I raised it on new ground; the ground had been plowed, but aside from that, I cultivated the corn exactly as in old times, with a hoe."

Because her memory was sharp, Buffalo Bird Woman's descriptions of the old times were detailed and precise. When her grandmothers cleared a new

The seasonal round expressed in the corn language of the Senecans:

onä'o'	corn
waeeyŭnt'to'	she plants
ohwĕⁿo'dadyiĕ'	it is just forming sprouts
oga''hwäodaⁿ	it has sprouted
otgaä'häät	the blade begins to appear
otga'äähät	the blade has appeared
deyuähǎ'o	the blade is already out
ogwäⁿ'dääodyiĕ'	the stalk begins to appear
ogwäⁿ'dää'e'	the stalk is fully out
oge''odadyie'	it is beginning to silk
owäⁿ'dǎ'	the ears are out
o'geot	it has silked out
ogwäⁿdŭ'äe', ogwäⁿ'däⁿe'	the tassles are fully out
ono''gwaat	it is in the milk
dĕju'göⁿsäät	it is no longer in the milk
oweäⁿdäädyĕ', owĕⁿdādyĕ'	the ears are beginning to set
onĕ'oda'dyiē'	the kernels are setting on the cob
hadi'nonyoⁿcos	they are husking
yestä'änyoⁿnyano'	she is braiding
dŭstaⁿ'shoni	it is braided
gasdäⁿt'shudoho'	it is hung over a pole
ganoⁿ'gadi'	it is strung along a pole

field, they dug corn hills with digging sticks of ash and worked between the hills with hoes of bone lashed to wooden handles. At the time of Buffalo Bird Woman's girlhood, they worked with iron axes and hoes they bought from traders, although they still used rakes which they had fashioned from bent wood or from the antlers of black-tailed deer. Once the fields were cleared, they burned the dry grass, felled willows and brush and distributed the ash. This was the old method of slash-and-burn.

The old women knew it was time to begin planting when they saw wild gooseberry bushes leafing in the woods in May. First they loosened the soil of the old hills with their hoes, then planted six to eight seeds half an inch deep in a circular pattern in each hill. They planted the hills in rows about four feet apart and the same distance between hills, for if the hills were so close together

that the growing plants touched, "we called them 'smell-each-other,' " Buffalo
Bird Woman explained, "and we knew that the ears they bore would not be
plump nor large." In her family's garden, they planted nine rows of twelve-
hilled corn, alternating with beans and surrounded by squash, in an area 180
yards long and 90 yards wide. This garden was in the keeping of her grandmothers Turtle and Otter, and of their daughters Corn Sucker, Red Blossom,
Strikes-Many-Women and Want-to-be-a-Woman, all of whom were wives of
Small Ankle.

When the corn was about three inches high, they called it "Young-bird's
feather-tail corn," from the shape of its sprouting leaves. They weeded the hills
carefully with their hands and hoed between the hills. When the plants began
to blossom, they hilled the earth further by building it up around the roots to
protect them. They made stick-figure scarecrows, covered in buffalo robes to
ward off crows, and built a watching platform to protect the young corn from
thieves and to encourage it with "watch-garden songs." "We cared for our corn
in those days as we would care for a child," Buffalo Bird Woman said, "for we
Indian people loved our gardens, just as a mother loves her children; and we
thought that our growing corn liked to hear us sing, just as children like to hear
their mother sing to them."

Most of the watch-garden songs were love songs, she said, sung by the young
girls who sat on the platforms, doing their "needlework" with porcupine quills
and teasing passing boys with "love-boy" songs. When the girls were young,
around twelve, they sang,

> *You bad boys, you are all alike!*
> *Your bow is like a bent basket hoop;*
> *You poor boys, you have to run on the prairie barefoot;*
> *Your arrows are fit for nothing but to shoot up into the sky!*

Older girls elaborated on the theme for older boys:

> *You young man of the Dog society, you said to me,*
> *"When I go to the east on a war party, you will hear*
>   *news of me how brave I am!"*
> *I have heard news of you;*
> *When the fight was on, you ran and hid!*
> *And you think you are a brave young man!*
> *Behold you have joined the Dog society;*
> *Therefore, I call you just plain dog!*

Before their numbers were reduced, even settled agricultural tribes like the Hidatsa were accustomed to leave their villages and crops after the first hoeings for the summer buffalo hunt. According to George Will, in *Corn Among the Indians of the Upper Missouri* (1917), the hunt lasted through July for the Mandan, Hidatsa and Arikara, who returned to their villages in time for the green-corn harvest of August. This was a season of great feasting, said Buffalo Bird Woman. If they were working in the fields they ate whenever they got hungry, in little booths made of willow. They broiled buffalo meat on the coals and boiled green corn just shelled from the cob with freshly shelled beans and ate them with spoons made from the stems of squash leaves.

"The first corn was ready to be eaten green early in the harvest moon, when the blossoms of the prairie golden rod are all in full, bright yellow; or about the end of the first week in August," she said. Some of the corn they roasted and some they boiled in a pot "as white people do." She could tell by looking at the corn on the stalk if it was ripe enough to boil. "The blossoms on the top of the stalk were turned brown, the silk on the end of the ear was dry, and the husks on the ear were of a dark green color." Today, she lamented, young folks are not very good gardeners, for they have to open up the ears to look at the kernels. "In old times, when we went out to gather green ears, we did not have to open their faces to see if the grain was ripe enough to be plucked!"

Green-corn season lasted about ten days, she said, and every family dried and stored green corn for winter. When the later corn was fully ripened in September, the men went hunting to get buffalo meat for the husking feasts of the ripe-corn harvest. Now the whole community went to work, each family plucking the ears and piling them in a huge heap in the middle of their field. Next day the field's owner would notify the crier of some society like the Dog or Fox, and he would cry from the roof of the lodge, "All you of the Fox society come hither; they want you to husk." "As we approached the fields we began to sing, that the girls might hear us," Water Chief said, joining in Buffalo Bird Woman's recollections. "We knew that our sweethearts would take notice of our singing." The youths and their sweethearts would be dressed to the nines for the husking feast of a side of fresh buffalo roasted over the fire next to a steaming pot of meat and corn. The pile of unshucked ears might be four feet high and twenty feet long, but the young men worked fast, particularly near the pile of a pretty girl.

As they husked the smaller ears, they saved the best big ones to braid into strings of fifty to sixty ears. "A braid," Edward Goodbird remembered, "was long enough to reach from the thigh around under the foot and up again to the other side of the thigh." A husker tested a new braid with his foot by holding the ends in his hand. "Unless this was done a weak place in the string might escape notice and the braid break, and all the others would then laugh." There was a lot of laughter at husking season because it was courting season. "Boys and young men went to the husking bees because of the fun to be had; they wanted to see the girls!"

Ponies carried the braided corn and bags of ears to the family's drying stage, where the braided strings were hung "like dead snakes" over the railings. Loose corn was spread evenly over the stage, and after eleven days it was usually dry enough for threshing. Next spring, they selected their seed corn from the best ears of the many braided strings. Usually they took out five strings of soft white, half a string of soft yellow and ten ears of the type of sweet corn they called *ma'idadicake,* or "gummy" corn, for making cornballs. These were favorites among the Mandan and Hidatsa, George Will said, "made of pounded sugar corn mixed with grease" and tasting something like peanut butter.

Buffalo Bird Woman shelled her seed corn carefully, she said, using only the kernels in the center of the cob. Since the seed corn remained fertile for at least two years, in seasons when the crop was good her family would put up seed to last a second year and built up a good business of selling seed corn to less provident families. "The price was one tanned buffalo skin for one string of braided seed corn." When Buffalo Bird Woman recalled these events for Wilson in 1912, she still sold seed corn and seed beans, but the units of exchange had altered. "A handful of beans, enough for one planting, I sell for one calico," she said, "enough calico, that is, to make an Indian woman a dress, or about ten yards."

For threshing, they built an enclosed booth of buffalo-cow hides under the drying stage, removing some planks so that they could push the corn through. Three women, each with a flail of ash or cottonwood, would sit facing the pile of corn now in the booth and beat the dry cobs so that the kernels flew into the air but were caught by the walls of the booth. They spread a tent cover just outside the booth for the threshed cobs, and at the end of the day they shelled off every clinging grain, "for we wasted nothing." At sunset when the air was still, they carried the cobs outside the village, piled them up and fired them. Buffalo Bird Woman's job was to stay and watch the fire to prevent mischievous boys

"In my tribe in old times, some men helped their wives in their gardens. Others did not. Those who did not help their wives talked against those who did, saying, 'That man's wife makes him her servant!'

"And the others retorted, 'Look, that man puts all the hard work on his wife!'

"Men were not all alike; some did not like to work in the garden at all, and cared for nothing but to go around visiting or to be off on a hunt.

"My father, Small Ankle, liked to garden and often helped his wives. . . . My father said that that man lived best and had plenty to eat who helped his wife. One who did not help his wife was likely to have scanty stores of food."

—WOLF CHIEF, as told in 1910 to Gilbert L. Wilson, *Buffalo Bird Woman's Garden* (1917)

from playing mudballs. This was a game in which boys put a ball of wet mud on a green stick and stuck it into the fire so that some burning coals would stick to the mud. Then they would snap the fireballs through the air at each other, like snowballs. Next day Buffalo Bird Woman would squeeze pieces of the crusted corncob ash into little balls and carry them home, wrap them in dried buffalo-heart skins and store them in baskets to use as seasoning during the winter.

Each morning, they would winnow the grain from the previous day's threshing by holding their baskets aloft and pouring the grain into the wind. Then they would store the grain temporarily in round containers called "bull boats" within the lodge. In a good year the corn would last until the next harvest, and in a bad year there might be some left from the previous harvest. In any case "there were elk and buffalo and antelope to be had for the hunting."

Digging the cache pits for winter storage was also woman's work. The pit was shaped like a jug, wide at the bottom and narrow at the mouth. Big ones were deep enough to require a ladder. Once dug, the pit was lined with a bluish water grass that would not mold. Then they laid a floor of dry willow sticks on the bottom of the pit and covered it with a thickness of dried grass and then a circular skin. They next secured a thick layer of grass on the inside of the walls with willow sticks, against which they laid rows of braided ears with the tips of the ears pointed inward, the husk ends outward to protect against moisture.

When the braids were four rows deep, they pushed in enough shelled corn to make an even layer and then coiled a string of dried squash in the middle of it, covering it with corn to protect the squash from moisture. They continued layering until the pit was filled, storing at least four strings of squash and thirty or more strings of braided corn. On top they fitted a thick buffalo hide which had been cut to measure, and covered it with grass and puncheons split from small logs and laid flat side down in a trench so that they wouldn't roll. Over the puncheons, more grass, another hide and then earth topped with ashes and refuse to conceal it "from any enemy that might come prowling around." Small cache pits they dug just outside the lodge for family storage, one pit for yellow corn, another for white, another for dried squash and other vegetables, a fourth inside for dried berries and valuables.

Drawing by Edward Goodbird, in Buffalo Bird Woman's Garden *(1917)*

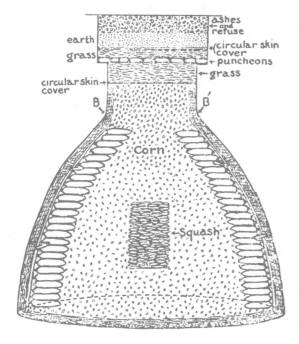

The first two crops planted on new ground were the best, Buffalo Bird Woman said, and when the yields grew less, they let the land lie fallow for two years, planting their crops elsewhere, since they never used all their fields at one time. Once the corn was husked, they let their horses eat the standing fodder and any husks left in the field, so that few vestiges of corn lingered until spring. They removed any dung the horses had dropped, for they found it attracted worms, insects and foreign weeds like sharp thistle and mustard with black seeds. "Now that the white men have come and put manure on their fields," she remarked, "these strange weeds have become common."

When Wilson asked if young men ever worked the fields, Buffalo Bird Woman laughed long and hard. "Certainly not! The young men should be off hunting, or on a war party," she said. "Also they spent a great deal of time dressing up to be seen of the village maidens." Buffalo Bird Woman had a strong sense of what was fitting and not fitting. It was not fitting for young men to help women in the fields. It was fitting only for old men, too old to hunt or go to war. While it was fitting for her son to learn new ways in the white man's school and read books and raise cattle, it was not fitting for her. "But for me, I cannot forget our old ways," she told Wilson.

Today you can visit the Knife River Indian Villages, north of Bismarck, North Dakota, as part of the National Park System, and catch glimpses of the old ways. You can examine reconstructed earth lodges and watch a historical pageant showing the arrival of Lewis and Clark in 1804, where they picked out Toussaint Charbonneau and the maiden Sacagawea to guide them farther west. You can learn from Gerard Baker, a National Park Ranger who is a Hidatsa, that the corn he plants in his garden grows from seeds planted for three hundred years and that every spring he asks a tribeswoman to come over from Fort Berthold to bless them. "That's the way it was done in the old culture," Baker says.

Today, there are white men too who are working to save some part of the old culture of the Mandan and Hidatsa. "One of the rarest of all corn," says seed-saver Charles Hanson, "is the 'Mandan little corn,' or midget blue flour corn." This corn, which produced the earliest roasting ears in green-corn season, had disappeared forever, he was told by an aged Indian near Fort Yates. Hanson persevered in his search and a decade later heard through an Indian trader of an old Oglala woman who had kept the gardening traditions of her mother. Hanson found the garden, the woman and one perfect little ear of midget blue. "It was enough," he reported in the *Seed Savers Exchange*; "today there is plenty of seed to keep the variety for posterity."

When the seed-saver Gary Nabhan visited the tribal headquarters of the

Mandan at New Town a few years ago and looked at the waters behind Garrison Dam which had swallowed the old tribal fields, he thought of John Bradbury's wonderment in 1811 at the elegance of Mandan cornfields: "I have not seen, even in the United States, any crop of Indian corn in finer order or better managed than the corn about the three villages." The old ways were extinct, Nabhan feared, until he saw a group of children eating cornballs and tracked them to a contemporary Mandan. "For cornballs, you need soft corn, flour corn, to make it," Vera Bracklin explained. "Mine is corn from my mother-in-law. I can't raise it here, but there's a white lady who gives me room to plant out at her place." Buffalo Bird Woman had said that in her time cornballs were a good present for a woman to give to her daughter to take to her husband and his parents and sisters. Today Vera Bracklin sells cornballs door-to-door to help support her family.

The old ways take new turns as the seasons come and go, but some ways do not come round again. "No one cares for our corn songs now," Buffalo Bird Woman lamented seventy years ago.

Sometimes at evening I sit, looking out on the big Missouri. The sun sets, and dusk steals over the water. In the shadow I seem again to see our Indian village, with smoke curling upward from the earth lodges; and in the river's roar I hear the yells of the warriors, the laughter of little children as of old. It is but an old woman's dream. Again I see but shadows and hear only the roar of the river; and tears come into my eyes. Our Indian life, I know, is gone forever.

The Language of the Machine

THE OCEAN-DESERT OF NEBRASKA

THE SONGS of the Oglala are gone forever from Beaver Valley near St.
Edward in Boone County, Nebraska, on the eastern edge of the Sandhills,
but the beavers are not. Even in the fall when the pin oaks are turning red, the
milo a deep rust and the cornfields ash-blond, the hills roll like green waves
above water hidden underground. Paradoxically, the prairies of Nebraska in
what was once called the Great American Desert are honeycombed with water
in the Oglala aquifer. This geologic core at the center of America was the alluvial tip of the Ice Age glacier that covered the top half of the globe and, when
it retreated, left Nebraska with the largest aquifer in the United States—good
for beavers, good for corn.

"Nebraska has no sublime scenery. No lake, cliff, cave or cataract," James
Butler wrote in 1873 when he addressed his pamphlet *Nebraska: Its Characteristics and Prospects* to "progressive, *calculating* men, who love nothing so well as
the logic of facts and figures, to prove how they can better their condition." As
if in compensation, unsublime Nebraska named its towns Harvard, Oxford,
Hebron, Cairo and Peru, in defiance of a landscape that suggested none of
these places. The rolling waves of corn that replaced a sea of grass in the prairie
center of America have a prospect and a rhythm of their own that defy more
civilized sites, as they defy the logic of facts and figures.

Prairie rhythms are better caught by America's poets than by its men of
calculation:

> *America was beavers,*
> *Buffalo in seas,*

Cornsilk and the johnnycake,
Song of scythes and bees.

So sang Robert Tristram Coffin in *Primer for America* (1943), evoking a pastoral like Buffalo Bird Woman's. Their corn songs, as it happened, bracketed the decade that wiped out the prairie center and turned green pastures and beaver valleys into the valley of the shadow of death. "As far as the eye could see in the Dust Bowl there was not a tree, or a blade of grass, or a field; not a flower or a stalk of corn, or a dog or a cow, or human being—nothing at all but gray raw earth and a few far houses and barns, sticking up like white cattle skeletons on the desert," Ernie Pyle wrote in *Home Country* (1947). "It was death, if ever I have seen death."

The rhythm of the prairies alternated between fecundity and drought, between heat blasts and blizzards, unmitigated by the communality of the Indians to whom this harsh and unforgiving land was native. The white man was there to go it alone, to challenge the wild and, if need be, the God who created it:

> You see them heat waves out there on the prairie? Them's the fires of hell, licking round your feet, burning your feet, burning your faces red as raw meat, drying up your crops, drawing the water out of your wells! You see them thunderheads, shining like mansions in the sky but sprouting fire and shaking the ground under your feet? God is mad, mad as hell!

Nebraska might lack sublime scenery, but ordinary farmers like this one quoted in the WPA volume on *Nebraska* in 1939 acknowledged the sublimity of its weathers, which tested faith and toughened hands and hearts.

In 1873 James Butler, as a man of his time, saw only heroic challenge in the white man's duty to transform the "vast ocean-desert" of Nebraska, as he called it, into "Nebraska the garden of the west." While the romantic ethos remains a century later, the economics have changed, and I had to work hard to locate a native Nebraskan who still wants to prove himself by running a family farm. Although every one of my Corn Belt cousins had been born on a farm, not a one of them was now a farmer. "I went to college so I wouldn't *have* to marry a farmer," laughs my cousin Eleanor, whose farm-born husband moved quickly into the petroleum business. Today the path to betterment leads straight off the farm because Nebraska's garden of the west, like other Corn Belt gardens, suffers from an excess of success.

The economic paradox was made clear when Duane Choat, one of St.

Edward's progressive native-son farmers, pointed to his corncribs stuffed to the bursting point with bumper harvests, three years in a row. Duane is both a progressive and a *calculating* man, and when he threw his arms wide as if to embrace with pride the three circular cribs by his barn, he groaned aloud. The logic of facts and figures, once the pride of the Nebraska farmer, is now his despair, for his farm like many another suffers from a mortal disease called "chronic excess capacity."

Duane is a heavyset farmer with a slow, deadpan sense of humor that takes some getting used to. He married his high-school sweetheart, Addis, a girl born on the far side of town on the farm of her parents and grandparents. It's not far to the far side of town, which consists of a barbershop, a beauty parlor, a gas station, a bank, a lumber company, a church, the City Cafe, the Bottle Barn Liquor Store and the St. Edward Beavers—a club. Addis worked in a factory for three years inspecting hypodermic needles, but now she raises Alida, Ann Marie and Wayne. Wayne at fifteen was raising prize-winning sheep and helping his father run the farm. When I spoke to Duane three years later, Wayne had won a regents' scholarship to the University of Nebraska to study agricultural engineering. "He's interested in farming," Duane said, "but he's going to want an income. He doesn't particularly want to work for nothing."

Duane and his three brothers farm the land they inherited from their father. "Where did your father come from?" I ask, looking for origins. "Four miles up the valley," Duane replies. Duane's portion was 560 acres, but to make an income he's pooled his land with his brothers' to total 3,000 acres. Duane's facts and figures are a litany of costs. First the pests—corn borers, red spiders, cornroot worm—"gotta be watchin' all the time." Then the chemicals. Duane and his brothers have their pesticide license but they must still hire a specialist to find out what chemicals they need before they hire an "aerial applicator" (an airplane, to the rest of us) to spray them at a cost of $8 to $10 an acre. Then the machines. The many machines they need to fertilize, cultivate and harvest their crop are costly to buy and costly to run. Duane's combine got a little rattle under the seat and repairs came to $1,369.12. He shows me the bill with the same mixture of pride and despair evoked by his bursting corncribs.

The rhythm of the prairies in 1987 created by the logic of physics and math.
Courtesy Pioneer Hi-Bred International, Inc.

A mechanical leviathan swallowing up the rows, six at a clip. Photo by David Plowden

His two combines condense a century of machine lingo and costs in their multiple parts: low-profile dividers, sloped gather sheets, individually mounted row units with long gathering chain lugs, center-pivot system, transversely mounted threshing cylinder, two-stage high-velocity air cleaner, cage sweep, distribution augers, trailing auger, center-mounted bin, swivel unloading tube. With the lingo I'm all at sea, but the sight and sound of one of these leviathans swallowing the rows in its steel-tusked jaws is, if not sublime, as awesome as an imagined herd of mastodon thundering across the glaciers.

Duane's planting year moves not to the songs of Buffalo Bird Woman but to the rhythmic clank of his machines. In November and December he fertilizes the ground with a "chisel" applicator mounted on a tractor, which injects anhydrous ammonia directly into the earth, three to fifteen rows at a time. He uses about two hundred pounds of fertilizer per acre, which costs 10 to 16 cents a pound and occupies five days on the tractor. He can't fertilize until the ground temperature has dropped to 50 degrees or below to prevent leaching into the groundwater. But he must fertilize in the fall rather than the spring because he doesn't want the tractor to compact the earth at planting time. After the "chisel" has done its work, a "shredder" pulled by a tractor on a PTO (power take-off) drive cuts up the stalks left from the harvest. Then a disk attachment mixes the top layer of soil with the stalk residue to make a compost four to five inches deep. "What we're doing," Duane explains, "is we're taking care of a big garden—if you helped your mother in her garden you'll know how to take care of your cornfield."

Last year he took care of 343 acres of cornfield because, under the government farm program, he's taken out between 10 and 50 percent of his crop base for the last ten years. He begins planting about April 25, but first he must turn the ground and weeds over with the disk, which is a cultivator "with a lot of little shovels on it." His planter does four rows at a time, but some planters can do up to sixteen. By a series of sprockets, the drive wheel controls how fast the seed is released into the furrows dug by the planter as it goes. A packer wheel then packs the ground over the seed. Duane's fields should be done within a week and a half, because if the corn isn't in by May 5, he says, "research shows that we'll lose a bushel of corn per day per acre."

At planting time he does his first spraying of herbicides and insecticides. The herbicide, a lasso-attrex mix, is sprayed by pressure through a nozzle attached to "saddle tanks" on the tractor. The insecticide—he uses about seven pounds per acre of a brand named Counter—goes on dry. He's used to defending his chemicals: "We're as much concerned as anyone about the chemicals, but if you have head lice you can get a chemical at the drugstore that is worse than anything we put on our fields." Like many traditional farmers, he believes that the big chemical companies are working with the EPA for the general good. "They're going hand in hand in the same direction," he says, and meantime he needs insecticides to fight the first broods of the root worm and root borer that attack root and stalk in May and June, then the second broods in August when the root worm becomes a beetle and when the borer attacks the shank of the ear so that it falls plumb off.

During the growing season, he continues to use the cultivator to throw dirt up around the plants for root protection and to make furrows for irrigation. He

"December 25: A lovely Christmas morning. The ground is frozen hard, yet the sun is shining nice. They are picking corn. I will read awhile in the Testament."
—From the diary of H. Greene, an Ohio farm woman in 1887 (a manuscript in the Schlesinger Library, Cambridge, Mass.)

irrigates by a gravity system that pumps well water at a cost of $10 to $30 an acre, depending on the rain. There's no outlay on scarecrow devices because there aren't enough birds to attack the corn, but there are plenty of other "maize thieves" to deplete the crop. The woods shelter marauding raccoons, squirrels and deer, and beavers will come up from the river to make a haul.

Duane's combines begin harvesting around September 20 when corn moisture is down to 25 percent. His pair of combines are twenty years old now, but a new one would cost him $100,000 or $150,000 for such added refinements as air-conditioned cabins and monitors that run like digital computers. When his corn yield is 150 to 200 bushels per acre, he can harvest ten thousand bushels, or about fifty acres a day. The combines run on diesel fuel, consuming four to eight gallons an hour, with fuel costs running from 60 cents to more than $1 a gallon. Annual upkeep on all his major machines—four tractors, two or three pickup trucks, two combines—begins at $4,000. "If an engine goes, just double the costs." Finally, Bahlen wagons and trucks haul the harvested corn into his series of grain bins, small ones that hold three thousand bushels and big ones that hold ten thousand.

The logic of facts and figures demonstrates that for today's farmer storing corn is as crucial as growing it. "High yield for high net income is the aim," Duane says. "Highest yield with the driest moisture gives you the net." Fourteen percent moisture is the key for his large reserves of corn, some three or

Ever-rising yield demands high-rise grain elevators that dwarf the small prairie towns that build them. Photo by Gregory Thorp

four years old, which he keeps in the glass-lined steel storage tanks that make his old-fashioned corncribs look like farm toys. These tanks are automatically monitored to balance temperature with humidity and keep it constant. New corn goes into a holding tank for wet grain, which starts at 35 percent moisture and is then air-dried for permanent storage. "Keep it dry to keep the insects out and clean to keep the rodents out and I suppose it would keep for ten years," Duane says, "but I wouldn't want to try it."

In his basement office a big computer taps into the head office of Pioneer Hi-Bred International in Ioway. In the Corn Belt, Iowa is always "Ioway." Pioneer devised its computer program principally for big-scale land managers who run farms for absentee landlords, Duane explains, but since he sows annually about nineteen kinds of seed corn, so that some will mature early and some late, he needs a computer to feed him the latest data on high-yield improvements. At the same time, organizations like the National Corn Growers Association encourage him with annual prizes to increase his yield to the maximum. He won a first in 1984 for 204 bushels, his best yield ever. Yield, however, is both the chief symptom and cause of the disease called "chronic excess capacity."

Duane is caught between loyalty to the old ethos and the illogic of the new economics. Chronic excess had not been envisaged by Nebraska's progressive pioneers, who were once so desperate simply to survive that they burned their crops for fuel. Today the government doesn't burn crops to support prices, but it puts them away. Duane supports the "grain reserve program," in which the government pays the farmer to store grain in his own bins. "The government does a good job," he says. "Our margins are so close we need a system to help control production, we need an organization and somebody has to pay the bill. We *all* do. We have tough times, but we're doing okay." Okay, however, may not be enough to keep farmers down on the farm. "As long as we have the land, we'll be growing corn—there's not much else you can do with it," he laughs, "but we'll have to grow our farmers too. With the present economy the young ones are in trouble and if they can't survive by farming, they'll leave for other jobs."

Around midnight, late for a farmer, he plays me a tape made by the American Agricultural Movement, a grass-roots group that protests corporate

October 13: *corn. Dig well.*

October 29: *I finished corn crib, sawed wood, moved pigs . . .*

November 2: *Went farm husked 17 shocks.*

November 3: *Clark—Adams and I husked corn. prayer meet.*

November 5: *cold. fix corn crib.*

[Undated]: *. . . Downs [?] and I husked 42 bu. corn.*

November 10: *144 bu. upstairs 172 bu. downstairs.*

November 18: *Warm and pleasant . . . wheat not thrashed corn not husked.*

—From Joseph Burt-Holt's diary when he homesteaded in Minnesota in 1859, part of the Holt-Messner Family file at Schlesinger Library, Cambridge, Mass.

Winslow Homer's The Last Days of the Corn Harvest *in* Harper's Weekly, *December 6, 1873.* Courtesy New-York Historical Society, New York City, Neg. No. 64980

takeover of the land. Only now, and in whispers, does Duane confess to frustration at what motivated the farmers to organize in the first place—the desire to control their own destinies. "We don't join the co-ops because we want to know who's controlling the co-ops," he says quietly. "We want to be self-sufficient, but you have to get cash to pay taxes on the land. You can't just go your own way and grow your own food the way we used to."

Those who took destiny in their hands in the 1930s and, like my cousins, left farming for good are not nostalgic about it. Having experienced the hardships, they welcomed the change. Change is still the Corn Belt credo as long as it can be made to suggest progress, prosperity and betterment in the spirit of the Optimist's Creed that hangs on Cousin Eleanor's bathroom wall: "Promise Yourself to talk health, happiness and prosperity to every person you meet, to wear a cheerful countenance at all times and give every living creature you meet a smile."

Even without her family farm in Hildreth, Cousin Eleanor kept the faith of our grandfathers and grandmothers who had invaded the land in order to change it. When Eleanor recalled her own farm days, she remembered the climactic moments of change, like the arrival of electricity in 1934. For the first time they had a water pump and a semi-attached bathroom and running water in the kitchen. "People who talk about the good old times forget the mother who died in childbirth, the babies' graves in the cemeteries, the stress and loneliness of pioneer women who came out here and might not see their husbands for weeks at a time," Eleanor says. She remembers how long it took the pair of horses to grind corn into meal between turning stones, how many jars of corn exploded because they hadn't been processed right, how often the cream wouldn't churn to butter because it wasn't cold enough. Today, her mother's butter churn sits in a corner of the parlor in Eleanor's neatly decorated house in Lincoln, holding a large-leafed houseplant.

But a new generation is questioning whether change is always an unmitigated good. Milan Moore, a young man in his thirties, uses words like "generational change" to describe what is happening today to Nebraska farmers. Milan, with his wide-set eyes and sincere voice, sitting with his quiet wife in their bungalow in Sutherland, himself exemplifies generational change. He is a farmer who doesn't farm at all. After graduating in animal science at the University in Lincoln, he found the demand by farmers for information on new chemicals and new equipment so large that he started his own consulting business.

"People come to me for information on federal regulations, environmental protection, chemical use, that sort of thing," Milan explains. "There are so many regulations—you have to be trained and licensed as a private applicator or commercial applicator to put any chemicals on the land. We have a chemical so toxic that one-sixteenth of an ounce per acre is enough to kill the weeds of the entire area, so it's critical that you make no mistake in how many drops to put in the tank. Farmers don't want to become chemical experts or business managers or lots of things they're required to be today. So they hire an animal nutritionist to formulate rations, a crop consultant to determine fertilizers, a chemical consultant to determine crop rotations, because all they want to do is *till the soil.*"

The big change for Nebraska farmers, he believes, began in the 1950s with the introduction of "center pivot irrigation." For the first time the aquifer of the Sandhills could be efficiently tapped by a sprinkling system in which a long mobile pipe, attached to a well in the center of a field, rotates in a half-mile-wide circle uphill and down to cover about 130 acres. With pivot irrigation, farmers could cultivate not only more land, but rolling land. Between the mid-1970s and 1980s, Nebraska increased its cropland by one million acres, to make corn by far the country's largest irrigated crop. Corn, Milan says, now occupies 19 percent of all irrigated acres in contrast to 4 percent for wheat and 4 percent for soy.

Banks were eager to lend money for land expansion, Milan continues, and the younger generation of farmers, unlike their fathers, were eager to borrow. Rapid expansion drove up land prices crazily in the 1970s and when they dropped by half in the 1980s, borrowers were in trouble. Farmers who'd borrowed heavily to buy more land had to buy more machines to produce more and more crops to pay the interest, but the more they produced the more they lowered their crop prices. Milan believes a major change must come in the economics of agriculture if any small farmers are to survive. It's the Catch-22 of the farmer, who needs, as Joel Garreau has said in his *Nine Nations of America*, "more and more land to pay for his machinery, the machinery that keeps on coming bigger and more expensive in order that one man can till more and more land." This is the rhythm Carl Sandburg caught in 1928 in "Good Morning, America":

> *"There are three great crops raised in Nebraska. One is a crop of corn, one a crop of freight rates, and one a crop of interest. One is produced by farmers who by sweat and toil farm the land. The other two are produced by men who sit in their offices and behind their bank counters and farm the farmers. The corn is less than half a crop. The freight rates will produce a full average crop. The interest crop, however, is the one that fully illustrates the boundless resources and prosperity of Nebraska."*
> —Farmer's Alliance Bulletin (ca. 1890)

We raise more corn
to feed more hogs
to buy more land
to raise more corn
to feed more hogs
to . . .

I heard an acceptance of change, without either the white man's optimism or his despair, in the talk of Frank and Alice Saunsoci on the Omaha reservation at Macy, up by Sioux City northeast of Beaver Valley. The Omaha were an agricultural tribe led by Big Elk and Iron Eye when they lost their territory in the Kansas-Nebraska Act of 1854 and the Homestead Act of 1862. "We used to have our big harvest festival, our big powwow, after the Buffalo Hunt," Alice says, "a hundred years ago." They still have an annual powwow in August, but there are only two hundred or so Omaha on the reservation to do the Gourd Dance and the War Dance and to protest the squatters' takeover of Black Bird Bend—a hundred years ago.

While looking for Alice, I decided to grab a bite in the corner grocery opposite the Umo Ha Ta'Paska school. I ate a pizza burrito heated in the Deli-Express microwave and then found Alice's husband, Frank, in front of the pinball machines watching some friends play Pac-Man. Frank took me to their house to see their cornfield because the Saunsocis are known hereabouts for their smoked corn, which they make every year from the deep-purple corn in their back lot. "It has no name," says Frank. "It's just the corn we grow, from seed handed down for generations." Some corn they parch, some they cook for hominy and some they smoke, to use in soups and stews for special occasions like the powwow. They build a fire with red elm—slow-burning, good for flavor—place a window screen over the coals and spread a couple of gallons of boiled sweet-corn kernels over the screen to smoke. Their four sons would like to keep on with the cornfields, Frank says, "to see every year the corn grow," and perhaps to acknowledge like their ancestors the blessings of Mother Corn. But change is afoot. Last year a French boy spent a month with them on a student exchange program, after their eldest son had spent a scholarship month in Nice. "Already the old things are being lost," the Pawnees' Eagle Chief had said almost a century ago. "It is well that they should be put down, so that our children, when they are like white people, can know what was their fathers' ways."

"Improvement in Illinois was snail-paced at first, for it came in on ox-teams," James Butler wrote in detailing Nebraska's "Progress of Settlement" after the Homestead Act. "It entered Iowa on steamboats, and was therefore long confined to the banks of navigable rivers. Its advent into Nebraska was on locomotives, which, plying on iron rivers, that render all prairies navigable, leave no corner of them untouched." Butler was so inspired by the muse of Nebraskan transport that only epic simile could express, in whatever fractured rhythms, his song of progressive betterment. "As much as steam is swifter than a steer, as much as railroads are more pervasive than rivers, so much more rapid and ubiquitous development than that of Illinois and Iowa may we expect to behold in Nebraska."

THE MARCH OF MECHANICAL TIME

IN THE 1990s we can behold in Nebraska the results of the radical changes that took place more than a century ago in the 1860s, at the close of the Civil War. The decade in which Nebraska achieved statehood was the decade that inaugurated America's industrial revolution of the farm. The prairies incited revolution because radical change was required to turn sod into corn, but revolution cut far deeper than sod in furrowing men's minds. Planting, harvesting and preserving—the organic cycle of agriculture plotted by seasonal change—were transformed by machinery that commandeered time and geared it to an ever swifter man-made clock. As homesteaders displaced Indians and penned them in reservations, the worship of technology displaced the worship of Father Sun and Mother Corn and organic myths and metaphors gave way before the newly deified Machine.

In that one decade, the Homestead Act and the Land Grant Act of 1862 both delivered land free to farmers, and the new agricultural colleges told them what to do with it. In that one decade the Indian Territory that was Nebraska was reorganized as a state (in 1867) and linked east to west by the completion of the transcontinental railroad (in 1869). In that one decade, a number of scientific theories proposed earlier in Europe confirmed America's faith that the laws of nature were ours to control and improve. Justus von Liebig's *Organic Chemistry in its Application to Agriculture and Physiology* (1840) became known to American farmers through journals such as the *Albany Cultivator,* and the farm chemical industry began. Darwin's *Origin of Species* (1859), together with Louis Pasteur's discovery of the germ (1861), brought the visible and invisible world of organisms to the attention of farm breeders, and the genetic industry began. By the 1860s German agricultural experiment stations had become the

"Attacking your opponent for being well educated is an old rube campaign tactic aimed at fetching the know-nothing vote, but to work successfully it has to come from a candidate who majored in corn at the state university. Coming from a Yale man, it is absurd."

—RUSSELL BAKER, on presidential candidate George Bush, in "The Ivy Hayseed," *The New York Times,* June 1988

model for newly founded land-grant colleges, and the union of agriculture, science and industry was cemented at the source.

It's small wonder that within that one decade the number of Nebraska farms grew from 2,789 to 12,301. But these were not subsistence farms, for from the beginning they were geared to industrial products. In 1844 Colgate & Company of New Jersey established a plant to extract starch from corn by the new method of steel-toothed rollers that Orlando Jones had introduced into England for wheat. The wet-milling industry began. After Isaac Winslow sold in 1843 a dozen tin cans of Maine corn to Samuel S. Pierce of Boston, he was finally issued Patent No. 35,346 in 1862 for an "Improved Process of Preserving Green Corn." The canning industry began.

And so began the industry of farm machinery. The *U.S. Patent Office Report of 1860* issued new patents for corn shellers, cornhuskers, corn cultivators, corn-shock binders, cornstalk shocking machines, cornstalk cutters, corn cleaners, corn and cob crushers, seed drills, corn harvesters, rotary harrows, corn and cob mills, smut machines and hundreds of corn planters. Nebraska farmers, on the cutting edge of the last frontier, turned sod into farmland in the heady atmosphere of industrialism expressed in the 1860 *Report*: "Agriculture is experiencing the truth taught in the history of all other manufactures—that machinery is, in the long run, the best friend of the laborer." The ruling metaphor for farmers for the next century and a half was manufacturing and the machine, and the Corn Belt farmer was unique in that he was the first to labor under its dominion.

In Nebraska as elsewhere in the Corn Belt, half of those laborers were German. In the 1850s the prairies had been swept by a second wave of immigrants from northern Europe. "To a bedrock of Anglo-Saxonism," as Garreau put it, "was added Germans, Swedes, Germans, Norwegians, Germans, Finns, Germans, Ukrainians, Germans, Poles, and Germans." With their ready cash and strong work ethic, Germans added scientific thoroughness to Yankee ingenuity. They brought new vigor to farmer-soldiers exhausted by civil war to help turn the prairies themselves into "vast armies . . . of gleaming corn." The military metaphor was current. "That so soon after turning their backs upon the field of battle, they should exhibit to the world a countless array of harvest fields stretching over a thousand hills and valleys, and covering a land redeemed by their valor and now embellished by their toil," wrote Edward Enfield of the citizen-soldiers of America in 1866 in *Indian Corn,* "—this indeed is a moral spectacle instructive to the world, and more to be prized than all the material prosperity and affluence which it indicates."

Material prosperity, however, was the trumpet and drum to which these

The Randall and Jones Double Hand Planter, popular in the 1850s. Smithsonian Institution, Photo No. 42113

Christian Soldiers marched, firm in their belief that, like religion, "science is an unfailing source of good," as James Dana said, in which "every new development is destined to bestow some universal blessing on mankind." In the last half of the century, four new languages of science fused—the languages of genetics, chemistry, mechanics and economics—to explode in a cannonade of technology that propelled pioneer farming into commercial farming and rocketed the family farm into corporate industry. The end of the century heralded the birth of modern American agribusiness.

That birth had to occur in the lowly mangers of the prairies because the prairies required the first major revolution of the plow since the time of the Pharaohs. On prairie sod iron plows were nearly as useless as wooden ones. "The prairie breaker," which had been developed in the 1820s from Jethro Wood's 1814 iron plow, weighed 125 pounds with the moldboard alone, and made slow, heavy and hard work for the three or four yoke of oxen required to pull it. In addition, its moldboard clogged in the dense loam and the farmer had to scrape it constantly with a paddle. In 1833 a blacksmith in Lockport, Illinois, named John Lane realized that highly polished iron or steel was needed to scour the furrows and prevent clogging, but he was unable to market his moldboard. Four years later, a more entrepreneurial blacksmith, John Deere of Grand Detour, Illinois, mounted a steel share from a broken band saw onto a wrought-iron moldboard and scoured the loam so cleanly it "sang." By the end of the 1840s, Deere had built a plant at Moline, Illinois, and a decade later was mass-producing ten thousand "singing plows" a year. By the 1860s, after a foundry in Wyandotte, Michigan, introduced the Bessemer prócess of converting pig iron to steel, Deere's improved steel plows had taken over the prairies, replacing popular cast-iron models like the Eagle and the Michigan Double-Plow. The same decade brought in specialty plows like the "rod breaker," the stirring, ditching or paring plows, rigs like the sulky or riding plows, and soon the American Rotary, or disk plow.

Harrows followed the same swift evolution. At first, the pioneer farmer used a hoe or a simple brush harrow, dragged by an animal across the fields. In the 1840s he replaced these with the giant rake called the Geddes, a triangular hinged harrow made of wood with iron teeth, and in the 1860s with one made of iron and steel. Soon the Geddes was overtaken by the Nishwitz rotary disk harrow, which first pulverized the soil and then with wooden rollers or clod-crushers packed it down.

The same period brought new developments in

John Deere's "singing plow" in 1837, with its steel share to scour the prairie loam. Courtesy Smithsonian Institution Photo No. 42647

corn planters. Until 1850, wrote R. Douglas Hurt in *American Farm Tools* (1982), American farmers planted corn as the Indians had first taught them, with a hoe or pointed "dibble stick." From the vantage point of New England, Thoreau could write as late as the 1840s, "This generation is very sure to plant corn and beans each year precisely as the Indians did centuries ago and taught the settlers to do, as if there were a fate in it." But Thoreau didn't reckon with Nebraska, where a pioneer required an axe to dig a hole in the sod. The first improvement on the Indian stick was a hand planter called the "stabber" or "jobber," which dropped seeds from a canister attached to a pair of boards hinged at the bottom like jaws and mounted on a pair of iron blades that were able to pierce the ground. The farmer now had only to jab the planter into the earth and open its jaws to deposit a few kernels of corn.

Improved tools for wheat farmers in America had developed half a century earlier, in conjunction with the wheat cultures of Britain and Europe. But the mechanical seed drill for planting wheat that was patented by Eliakim Spooner in 1799, for example, was of little use for corn. Corn could not be sown broadcast but had to be planted kernel by kernel. The first successful mechanical corn planter was not developed until the 1850s by George W. Brown at Galesburg, Illinois. His was a two-row horse-drawn vehicle which dropped seed from a mechanism attached to the wheels, but the mechanism was hand-operated. By the 1860s he had improved the rig by adding a pair of furrow openers or "shoes" in front and, at the rear, a "dropper seat" so that a boy could sit in front of the driver for more accurate dropping. As the farmer drove across the field at right angles to parallel lines previously marked, the boy worked the handle of the seed box to drop seed over each intersection.

Earlier pioneers had adapted the Indian method of planting their corn hills in a checkerboard pattern, or "check-rows," by dragging a four-runner sled over a field in first one direction and then another, so that they could cultivate between the rows. Thomas Jefferson described the method to his friend Charles Willson Peale when he wrote from Monticello on March 21, 1815, "We have had a method of planting corn suggested by a mr. Hall which dispenses with the plough entirely." Jefferson explained how the ground was marked off in squares and a grain of corn planted and manured at each intersection. Since Mr. Hall had taken a patent on the process, Jefferson was glad that he "has given me a right to use it, for I certainly should not have thought the right worth 50.D. the price of a licence."

Later farmers paid the price. In 1857 Martin Robbins of Cincinnati patented the first corn planter to drop seed automatically at the intersections of check-rows by the device of a chain that was fitted with iron buttons at regular inter-

Nancy Hendrickson planting corn with a "stabber" on her farm near Mandan, North Dakota. Photo courtesy State Historical Society of North Dakota

vals and was staked at each side of the field. In 1864 John Thompson and John Ramsay of Illinois substituted a knotted wire for the chain and thus created the standard check-row planter for the next forty years and beyond. Where the Western prairie bordered the Great Plains and was even harder to dig than in the Midwest, farmers developed the "lister planter," which dug deeper by means of a double moldboard plow to which a seed canister was attached.

By the 1880s the vision of material prosperity had altered the tone of America's moral spectacle, and lawsuits proliferated as fast as machines. George Brown sued Charles Deere and his partner Alvah Mansur for their version of the automated planter called the "Deere Rotary Drop." As Brown's threats flew, so did Deere's flyers:

> We shall continue to supply the trade with rotary drop planters, greatly improved, differing wholly from and therefore not infringing this old, abandoned and worthless device contained in Mr. Brown's reissued patent No. 6384, and continue as heretofore, to fully guarantee all parties who have bought or may buy, not only corn planters but any other implement from us, against all loss or damage, by reason of any claims or threats of Mr. Brown or any other man.

By 1885 Deere & Mansur had at least outblustered Mr. Brown sufficiently to add a fertilizer attachment, a stalk cutter and a sulky hay rake to their planter. A decade later they had developed the "edge drop," which regulated the number of kernels dropped in each hill by measuring a kernel's thickness rather than its length or breadth. Interestingly, the basic wire check-row system remained the chief method of planting corn until the advent of the corn combine in the 1930s revolutionized both planting and harvesting.

Still, planting large acreages had to await the evolution of cultivators, from a man wielding a hoe to one riding a sulky cultivator behind two or three horses that could till two rows at once. Usually, corn farmers hoed their crop four times during the growing season and, hoeing by hand, a farmer might have to spend six days per acre chopping out weeds. A one-shovel plow pulled by a horse was in common use by the 1840s, followed in 1856 by a "walking straddle-row cultivator," designed by George Esterly of Heart Prairie, Wisconsin, with movable shovels to cultivate two rows at a time. In the 1860s the sulky cultivator put the farmer on a seat behind a pair of horses, and he could now weed and ride with speed. Using three or four horses, he could weed fifteen acres a day with "as much ease and comfort as a day's journey in a buggy." With refinements—and in 1869 there were 1,900 patents issued for them—this cul-

"For reasons I never knew, perhaps it was nothing more complicated than pride of workmanship, farmers always associated crooked rows with sorry people. So much of farming was beyond a man's control, but at least he could have whatever nature allowed to grow laid off in straight rows. And the feeling was that a man who didn't care enough to keep his rows from being crooked couldn't be much of a man."

—HARRY CREWS,
A Childhood (1978)

The industrial evolution of corn harvesters, from the first one, labeled "primitive," to the latest progressive combine of 1892, published by the United States Patent Office. Courtesy Alfred A. Knopf, Inc.

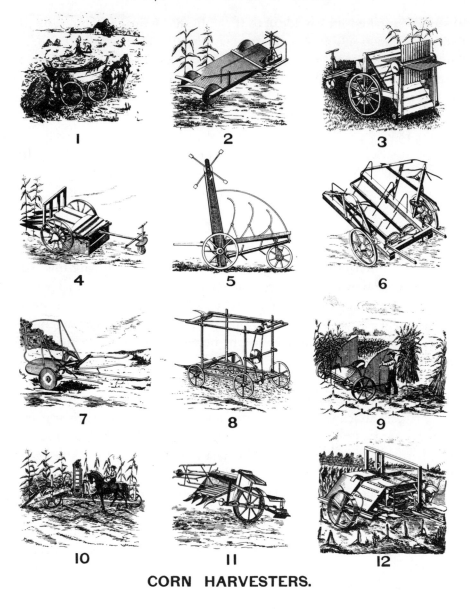

CORN HARVESTERS.

tivator remained standard until the International Harvester Company in 1924 changed plowing, planting and cultivating at once with a gasoline-powered tractor.

Although machinery for harvesting wheat appeared as early as 1831 with McCormick's Reaper, harvesting corn was another kettle of porridge. First the gasoline tractor had to be born and then corn had to be bred to produce only two ears per stalk and at a standardized height. Until then, corn continued to involve more hand labor than any other grain. Although the time required to produce one bushel of corn dropped from four and a half hours in 1855 to forty minutes in 1895, the only time-savers were in plowing and planting. Ears and stalks still had to be cut by hand. Where Indians had used cutters of stone and bone, colonists had at first used swords, sickles and knives. They then improvised a "corn knife" from a scythe blade (using an eighteen-inch blade and a six-inch handle), and eventually a knife manufacturer attached a knife-like blade to a boot so that the farmer could kick his cornstalk rather than bend to cut it. It was still back-breaking work.

One of the earliest methods of pioneer harvesting was the "corn sled," a wooden triangular platform with runners and blades extending on both sides to cut the stalks. Gleaners might follow to pick ears from the "down rows," or a couple of men might ride the platform to gather the stalks as they fell and bind them into shocks. With improvements like two-row cutters and chains to guide the stalks, two men could cut four and a half acres a day instead of one and a half with a corn knife.

While colonists learned from the Indians how to cut and bind stalks together to let the ears dry in the field, colonists had to devise new methods of harvesting to use green stalks and leaves for animal fodder. One of their earliest methods involved "fodder pulling" and "topping," in which a farmer cut off all the leaves just below the maturing ears and bundled them into fodder stacks. Next he topped the stalks just above the ears and added those to the stacks. He could then leave the ears to dry and harvest them when he was ready, but leaf removal tended to impede the full ripening of the ears and the method was abandoned early in the nineteenth century.

Corn "shocking" replaced "pulling" as the most efficient way to harvest, store and dry the ears, leaves and stalks in a single operation. As described by Nicholas Hardeman in *Shucks, Shocks and Hominy Blocks* (1981), a farmer would mark out a square of stalks for each shock, then twist the stalks from each of the four corners into a double-arched brace called a "horse," "gallows" or "gallus." With his heavy corn knife, he then cut and stacked corn in the openings around the brace, slanting the stalks from bottom to top to make a tepee. When the shock was five or six feet in diameter, he tied the "waist" with a band of twisted cornstalks or twine. Sometimes he used a wooden pole with cross-arms or a three-legged brace, some kind of "wooden horse," to help build his shocks.

The first successful mechanical binder didn't appear until 1892, when A. S. Peck of Geneva, Illinois, devised a horse-powered machine that passed down each side of a corn row and fed stalks into a pair of cutters. A chain carried the

A man shocking his corn into rows of tepees in a field in Kansas. Courtesy Kansas State Historical Society, Topeka

stalks back to a binder that bundled them with twine and dropped them in the fields for stacking. Increasingly, farmers used the binder to cut green corn for fodder, which they would run through a shredder or chopper and blow through an elevator into a silo. Since the binder could harvest seven to nine acres per day, two or three shockers were needed to keep up with it, which incited inventors to combine cutting, binding and shocking mechanically. In 1888 A. N. Hadley devised a mechanical "shocker" in the form of a rotating table behind the cutter that gathered the stalks vertically and enabled a binder to tie them on the platform.

The corn shock was a storage method designed to shed rain reasonably well and thus prevent spoilage among the ears of drying corn. When a farmer was ready to pick and shuck ears already dried on the stalks, his family would work as a team, each person removing a bundle of stalks. If, however, a farmer preferred to pick the ears before cutting and shocking the stalks, he would snap off the ears while walking behind a wagon equipped with a "bangboard." As a picker tossed his ears against the board, they would fall into the wagon. Inventors came up with various mechanical pickers—cutters, rollers, prongs—but nothing proved superior to the farmer's hands until the increased power of the gasoline tractor altered the entire sequence.

Until this century, farmers had improved on the husking pegs of the Indians only by substituting iron for bone. With metal pegs, a skilled husker could husk about an acre of shocked corn per day, or one and a half acres of unshocked corn rows. Still, husking was hard on the hands and those who didn't wear heavy husking gloves poured tallow on their cracked hands at night, or a patented cornhusker's lotion that is still sold today. Huskers were hopeful when Jonathan Cutler in Putney, Vermont, patented the first mechanical husker in 1837, which worked with a pair of rollers attached to a wagon, but his invention didn't take off. Fifty years later an inventor came up with a husker-shredder combination that stripped the ears and fed the husks, along with the stalks, through rotating shredding knives that pulverized them. The shredded fodder was then channeled through a funnel and onto a stack while the ears were carried by an elevator to a bin or wagon. This device could eat up to a thousand bushels a day, but it was too costly for the ordinary farmer.

Shelling by hand was as time-consuming as husking, and mechanical corn shellers, large and small, became standard household equipment during the nineteenth century. Colonists had at first simply imitated Indians in scraping kernels from their cobs with seashells or bones. But by the 1820s hand-turned shellers like the "Little Giant" had become popular. By turning a spiked wheel, a farmer could strip off the kernels and drop them into a basket or tray while the cobs fell through a separate opening. In the 1840s the cast-iron Burrall sheller became standard: this required one person to crank the wheel and another to feed ears into the spout. Soon the horse-powered "Cannon" could shell a hundred bushels a day and, when steam replaced horsepower, the Sandwich sheller could shell two hundred to three hundred bushels an hour.

As tools "improved," so did storage. From the beginning, colonists had favored "corn houses," "barnes," "cratches" or "cribbes" over the underground pits favored by many of the Indians, because the grains that Europeans knew were more subject to mold than corn was and were best preserved in dry lofts, sheds and barns. They noted, however, that tribes from Canada to Florida also built corn houses on poles above the ground, sometimes square and sometimes round, with thatched or bark roofs for protection. In the humid Southeast, Indians made corncribs of cane or saplings, which one of De Soto's companions in 1542 described by the Indian word *barbacoa:* "a house with wooden sides, like a room, raised aloft on four posts, and has a floor of cane." The corn within was thus "barbecued" by smoke from fires lit beneath the platform, which helped to dry the ears more quickly and to ward off insects.

Colonists likewise constructed V-shaped corn houses of rough slatted boards, spaced so that plenty of air could circulate between them for drying the ears stored within. These were the corncribs still seen in backwoods farms in rural America, cradling the corn like babies in a manger. While the origin of

the word is obscure, the first written reference to "corncrib," Keith Roe has told us in *Corncribs: In History, Folklife, and Architecture* (1988), comes from the town records of Brookhaven, Long Island, in June 6, 1681, and suggests that corncrib theft was as serious as cradle robbing: "I, Hannah Huls, through inadvertance and passion, defamed Nathanell Norten, of this towne, by saying he had stollen Indian corn out of my fatther daiton's [Samuel Dayton's] his corn cribb."

Even the round silos that have come to symbolize the Midwestern farm were adapted from Indian granaries. In the early seventeenth century the English explorer Henry Hudson reported seeing a great quantity of maize stored from the year before in a corn house "well constructed of oak bark and circular in shape with the appearance of being built with an arched roof." A century later, Father Joseph Lafitau found Senecan "granaries of bark in the form of towers, on high ground, and they pierce the bark on all sides, to allow the air to penetrate and prevent the grain from moulding."

The significant change in silos did not come until 1875, when America imported a French version for the large-scale use of green fodder, or ensilage. These silos, built of wood or brick, were made airtight, since their function was to ferment the green leaves and stalks, like pickles in a crock, in order to make the fodder easier for animals to eat and digest. The first silo in Nebraska was built as an experiment at the Agricultural College farm of the University in 1882. Ensilage on this scale demanded more efficient cutters than the old-fashioned "fodder sled" or the hand-operated stalk cutter that used a hinged knife like a paper cutter. But power cutters that could fill the silos had to wait for the advent of the gasoline engine.

The wait was short, for the turn of the century brought the internal combustion engine and a new revolution of power. Charles Hart and Charles Parr of Iowa built the first successful gasoline tractor in 1901, but it was Henry Ford's first tractor, the Fordson in 1917, that made the combustion engine available to the American farmer at a price most could afford—$397. International Harvester followed with the Farmall tractor in 1924, the first to be fitted with removable attachments to make an all-purpose machine that would outdo the steam-driven wheat combines for reaping and threshing in use since the 1880s. Once again, the more difficult process of harvesting and shelling corn delayed the advent of a practicable corn combine until the 1930s. In 1936 Allis Chalmers took the lead by adding a corn-head attachment to its Gleaner and calling it the ALL-CROP Harvester, but the onset of World War II delayed production until post-war peace.

After the war, corn "picker-shellers"—one homemade version in Ohio was called the "cornfield battleship"—came into vogue because they were far cheaper than combines with corn-head attachments, though combines were more versatile and efficient. Once artificial dryers and steel bins replaced the old-fashioned cribs, however, they demanded the mass harvesting of shelled corn that only combines could do. With the development of airtight Harvestore silos, those great blue towers that dot the land from Wisconsin to Mississippi, corn did not even require drying before storing because the silos prevented mold in high-moisture corn by replacing oxygen with nitrogen or carbon dioxide.

As silos multiplied, so did the need for corn to fill them, and the corn was now supplied by a combine that could devour four, six, eight, even twelve rows at a clip and thousands of bushels in a day. Like some fire-breathing dragon, the combine demanded an ever-greater supply of fodder, contributing mightily to the malaise of chronic excess supply. As the diesel power of the combine put an end to horsepower and steam power, the revolution of the Machine, like other revolutions, threatened to consume its perpetrators, displacing the family farmer as the pioneer had displaced the Indian.

In 1986, when I talked to farmers like Everett Johnson at the North Central Corn Husking Contest in Courtland, Kansas, where old-time huskers gathered to compete for sport, I found that the march of time had brought a change of tune. When Everett spoke of his machines, it sounded less like reveille than like taps:

A combine costs maybe a hundred and twenty thousand dollars to buy and has a life of probably six to eight years at the most. Then there's the cost to run it—burns up ten gallons an hour—plus labor, plus repairs. Now, thirty years ago, you could tear down and build up your own tractor, but today there's so much electronic stuff you don't dare touch it. They trade 'em in in a year to take the depreciation. The machines are rusting, the houses are gone. Pretty soon all we got to do is import some Indians.

"CORN SICK" LAND

WHEN COLONISTS, rather than Indians, were the imports, Captain John Smith at Jamestown in the spring of 1609—"this starving time," as he called it—wrote that "for one basket of corn they would have sold their souls." And so, without knowing it, they did. For two centuries they rationalized their territorial imperatives as God's will. "What is the right of a huntsman to the forest of a thousand miles over which he has accidentally ranged in quest of prey?" John Quincy Adams asked rhetorically in 1802. "Shall the fields and vallies, which a beneficent God has formed to teem with the life of innumerable multitudes, be condemned to everlasting barrenness?"

Toward the close of the third century after Jamestown, with the huntsman-planter now stripped of both forest and corn and enduring his own "starving time," economic imperatives were claiming dominion not just over fields and valleys but over minds and hearts as well. Addressing a conference of Friends of the Indians in 1896, the president of Amherst College, Merrill E. Gates, proclaimed:

> We have, to begin with, the absolute need of awakening in the savage Indian broader desires and ampler wants. To bring him out of savagery into citizenship we must make the Indian more intelligently selfish before we can make him unselfishly intelligent. We need to *awaken in him wants.* In his dull savagery he must be touched by the wings of the divine angel of discontent. . . . Discontent with the teepee and the starving rations of the Indian camp in winter is needed to get the Indian out of the blanket and into trousers,—and trousers with a pocket in them, and with a *pocket that aches to be filled with dollars!*

The nature of the white man's mission may have changed, but the moral zealotry of his language did not. The civilization of the intelligently selfish must convert the savage to the divinity of discontent. Corn, as always, was the catalyst in this divine alchemy, and the question, as always, was how many baskets of corn would it take to fill a pocket with the dollars it was aching for?

Despite a century tuned to ever-ampler wants by ever-louder choirs of discontent, there are small towns in America's corn country that do not ache for dollars. Some of the very small towns of Nebraska have slept so soundly that they seem to have awakened no wants at all. Wilcox is that kind of town—a Main Street, a grain elevator, a watertower and Dale's Cafe. My mother, Hazel Kennedy, was born in Wilcox on Christmas Eve, 1887, and I'm told that her father dug the town's first well. Today, Sunday dinner at Dale's Cafe is still served at noon and at century-old prices. You get a plate of crisp-fried chicken with mashed potatoes, boiled corn, white bread, iceberg lettuce and iced tea for $3. When I ask for the rest room, I am sent through the kitchen into a back room with a 1930s refrigerator and battered sofa, where an elderly man sits reading the funnies next to a hairy clump of dog asleep on the rug. The man points me to a clothes closet, and behind a door at the back of the clothes are a toilet and sink, flushed still, no doubt, by the water my grandfather dug. I would not have been surprised to see an Indian in his blanket and teepee out back.

Wilcox is one hundred miles west of Lincoln and next door to the equally small and unchanged crossroads of Hildreth, where Cousin Eleanor was born. Not far south is Red Cloud, where Willa Cather's upstairs bedroom is still papered in red and brown roses in the neat white frame house the Cathers lived in. After a century of land-shattering change elsewhere, Wilcox, Hildreth and Red Cloud stand like prehistoric prairie dolmens. To find a chunk of native prairie grass you have to go to a museum park like the Homestead National Monument near Beatrice, where little patches of big blue-stem, buffalo grass, blue gamma, Indian grass, switch grass and sand lovegrass have been "restored" for people who have never seen the like.

Not far north, at Grand Island on the Platte River, the changes of the land have been compacted in the Stuhr Museum of the Prairie Pioneer. Here an authentic steam engine and coach of the Nebraska Midland Railroad will take you by a real buffalo herd, a Pawnee Indian earth lodge, the log cabins of a pioneer settlement and the toy windmills and upright houses of Railroad Town, including the transported Grand Island cottage where Henry Fonda was born in 1905. Time has moved so fast on the prairie that one generation's wild is the next generation's Disney World and the ache of discontented pockets is at war with the ache of nostalgic hearts. In 1970 American nostalgia had produced so

"How beautiful to think of tough lean Yankee settlers, tough as gutta-percha, with a most unsuhduable fire in their belly, steering over the Western Mountains, to annihilate the jungle, and to bring bacon and corn out of it for the posterity of Adam."
—THOMAS CARLYLE

many local farm museums and "living history" farms that a national association was formed, ALHFAM (Association of Living Historical Farms and
Agricultural Museums), headquartered in the National Museum of American
History in Washington, D.C. Even twenty years ago the family farm was
ancient history.

"When the rich, black, prairie corn lands of the Central West were first broken up it was believed that these were naturally inexhaustible lands and would
never wear out," wrote C. B. Smith, from the Office of Farm Management,
Bureau of Plant Industry, in the *Yearbook of the U.S. Department of Agriculture*
for 1911. That belief was ill-founded, he said even then, for farmers had
planted crop after crop of corn on the same land year after year, and as a result
had decreased yield, increased insects and exhausted the land. "The land," he
said, "was 'corn sick.'" The remedy, he said, was to rotate corn with restorative
crops like clover or alfalfa and to fertilize it with barnyard manure.

"How much corn must be grown per acre to make it profitable?" he asked,
at a time when the average cost per acre was $14.63 and the price per bushel
42.4 cents. With a cost-and-profit chart he easily demonstrated that yield was
crucial to profit, since a yield of thirty-five bushels an acre would return a profit
of but 21 cents, where a yield of forty bushels would bring a profit of $2.33.
When the twentieth century began, government officials had to persuade
farmers that what mattered most was yield, rather than tall corn with beautiful ears. At the close of this century, government officials still urge greater and
greater yield, despite the farmers' consensus that overproduction is the enemy.
In the last half of the 1980s America's farmers produced the largest grain surplus in the world's history, and yet every one of the corn farmers I talked to
agreed that in one way or another the simplistic equation of yield with profit
has made the land corn sick.

*A bleak scene in the "corn sick"
land of Sherman County,
Kansas, around the turn of the
century.* Courtesy Kansas State
Historical Society, Topeka

"We got a billion bushels piled up in Ioway alone," George Mills tells me, as we look at a green wall of corn behind his house on the south fringe of Des Moines. "One hundred thirty-five bushels to the acre, finest corn we've ever had." I've driven from Nebraska to Iowa, reversing the western trail of my grandparents, because Iowa is still the Tall Corn State. Mills can recall a time when Iowa Shriners convening in 1912 in Los Angeles brandished cornstalks and sang, "We're from Iowa-y, Iowa-y, That's where the tall corn grows." Mills was not a farmer, but a political writer with *The Des Moines Register* for thirty years, before he retired to pay more attention to his backyard corn and to write a book on the decline of the Bible Belt from the 1930s to the 1980s.

"Iowa is in the middle of the biggest plain this side of Jupiter. Climb on to a roof-top almost anywhere in the state and you are confronted with a feature-less sweep of corn as far as the eye can see. It is 1,000 miles from the sea in any direction, 600 miles from the nearest mountain, 400 miles from skyscrapers and muggers and things of interest, 300 miles from people who do not habitually stick a finger in their ear and swivel it around as a preliminary to answering any question addressed to them by a stranger."

—BILL BRYSON, "Fat Girls in Des Moines" (1988)

Mills's reporting career coincided, as he sees it, with the rise and fall of the Bible Belt farm. "The old definition of a farmer was a man with one hundred and sixty acres who kept some hogs and some cows and whose wife kept chickens and sold eggs and took their milk to the milk station," he says. "Now the average farmer in Warren County tills eight hundred acres because you can barely make a living on three hundred. The land hasn't gone away but the farmer has." 1988 research figures show that although our national farm acreage has remained constant at 340 million acres, our average farm size has tripled while the number of farms has been halved, from 5.9 million in 1945 to 2.2 million in 1985. More significantly, farming today occupies only 2 percent of America's entire labor force.

Even at the dawn of the century, when enthusiasm for equating the farm home with a place of business was undimmed, there were warnings that profitability depended on size. "One of the first and most important factors having to do with profitable farming, as in all other lines of business, is the size of the enterprise," J. S. Cates, of the Office of Farm Management, wrote in the 1915 *Yearbook of the U.S. Department of Agriculture.* "Despite the much-talked of idea of 'a little farm well tilled,' actual records from thousands of farms covering pretty well the whole United States go to show that little farms do not often make big profits, and that as a rule the profits from farming vary directly with the size of the business."

Fifteen years later, at the onset of the Depression, little farms were going under wholesale, and the man who had done most to turn corn farming into a business, Henry Wallace, tried to save the small farmer by limiting production through the Agricultural Adjustment Act of 1933. After the act was declared unconstitutional, Wallace came up with the "Ever-Normal Granary Plan," which became the basis for government crop subsidies euphemistically called "government price-support loans." The government guaranteed the farmer a loan price and if the market price of corn fell below it, the farmer turned his corn over to the government for storage and the government paid him the difference.

Through this device, the government by controlling acreage could still encourage higher yields. The more the farmer produced, the larger his collateral. But at best it was a stopgap measure, conceived under the duress of the Depression and enlarged by the crisis of World War II. After the war, the benefits of Wallace's strategy were undone both by the unprecedented yields of his own hybrid corn and by the unprecedented use of chemical fertilizers. The herbicide 2,4-D, developed during the war as a chemical weapon for potential use against enemy soldiers, was introduced in 1947 as a weapon against enemy weeds. Since that time, America's average yield per farm acre has increased annually by 2 percent.

Wallace's device, of course, was also a political subterfuge by which capitalism's nominally free-market economy could be manipulated behind the scenes. Talking to Mills, I begin to understand why my farming family excoriated Roosevelt and Wallace as twin Antichrists. To my kinfolk, self-sufficiency was divine and anyone who interfered with that God-given right was doing the devil's work. George Mills's view, on the other hand, is more historical, and he sees Wallace as caught between wars. "You call upon your farmer to vastly increase production as part of national defense, but when the war's over it's hell to scale down." In 1920 after the First World War, Iowa land sold for $254 an acre and corn for $1.70 a bushel. Six months later, corn sold for 67 cents—a disastrous deflation that wasn't "corrected" until World War II. "Same damn thing happened after the Vietnam War in the 1970s—land prices tumbled and so did corn," Mills says. "When politicians get mixed up in farm economics, hold on to your hat."

But in Ioway the politics and economics of corn are one and the same, says Lauren Soth, another silver-haired *Register* man whose editorials on corn politics over the past forty years won him a Pulitzer prize. He recounted how overproduction after World War I had been increased by mechanization. With the advent of tractors, the need for oats to feed ten million horses and mules disappeared; so as more land was tilled, it was planted with corn. Soth had seen how overproduction after World War II was increased by commercial fertilizers, when specialization removed livestock and manure from the farms and

put cows and hogs into commercial feeding lots. By the 1960s he had seen how farmers had to turn their farms into cash crops in order to pay for the petroleum that ran their tractors and the anhydrous ammonia that increased the yields of a continuous corn crop. Today corn farming, he says, consumes 44 percent of all chemical fertilizers used in the States and half of all farm pesticides and herbicides. Now 95 percent of corn and soy acreage uses the synthetic chemicals that are demanded by intensive continuous cropping.

Smith in the 1911 USDA *Yearbook* warned, "Continuous corn culture has no place in progressive farming." Soth in a 1986 *Register* editorial uttered the same warning for opposite reasons: "The hard fact that the USDA top command and the Fertilizer Institute cannot face is that agriculture in this country is substantially overexpanded. So is the agribusiness superstructure that serves it." As one who remembers the Dust Bowl well, Soth wants the government and the farmer to retire eroded land and to restore it with grass and trees, to reduce the use of chemicals severely and to practice crop rotation, as Smith advised eighty years ago.

But Americans don't believe in what they can't see, and the superstructure of American agribusiness that controls the production of corn is as invisible and pervasive as the industrial products of corn. Measured by output per labor unit, the business of producing grain on farms is larger than any non-farm business in this country, and has been since the crop explosion at the end of the 1970s put America for the next five years in control of 70 percent of the world's trade in grain. Between the 1960s and 1980s, while inputs on American farms increased

A boy with his shovel contemplates the fruits of his labors in western Kansas, in a post–World War I economy where ever more corn brought ever less cash. Courtesy Kansas State Historical Society, Topeka

from $50 billion to $80 billion, gross outputs increased from $235 billion to $450 billion. But 80 percent of that output is produced by only 15 percent of all United States farms. In the heart of the Corn Belt itself, the average farm size is but 294 acres, so that three-quarters of its farm households must generate "outside" income off the farms in order to keep them.

The problem, Soth believes, lies in men's minds. The industrial model simply will not work for corn. "Growing corn is not like manufacturing automobiles," he says. "The small-enterprise farm is an industry, but it's also a living place, and they get in the way of each other." The free-enterprise market of supply and demand doesn't work for corn, because you can't control the supply side the way you can control it with cars or shoes—nature interferes. So, he continues, we have to rely on some kind of government program, which may suit the big corporations that are in it only for money, but not small farmers for whom farming is a way of life.

Today's government program for corn, already limited by the facts that it is voluntary and applies only to acreage, still operates on the basis of the antiquated loan system set up by Wallace in 1938, a half-century ago. Even the language is antiquated and obfuscatory. A farmer who goes into the program volunteers not to plant a certain percentage of his corn acres, which is called his "corn base." He gets a "loan," which is a government-guaranteed "target" price, for what he produces on the planted acres. "Congress picks the target price out of the air," says Soth. "That price is Congress's idea of what they think the farmer this year ought to get—it's a wholly political decision." The difference between the target price and the market price is the "deficiency payment" that the government pays the farmer that year. In 1986, for example, the target price was $3.03 while the market price was only $1.25, so that government subsidies for the year totaled $30 million. "It's ironic that Reagan, that luminous champion of the free-enterprise market and frugal federal budget," Soth says, "not only paid this sum but bragged about it."

Soth maintains, as my own family had vehemently confirmed, that small farmers don't like taking money from the government instead of from the market. Nor do they like government control. If the government would exert mandatory controls over both crop acreage and production, they could create a marketing quota. But more government control doesn't sit well with farming families who remember what brought their ancestors to the prairies in the first place. "I loved seeing things grow, being my own boss and working together as a family," says an Iowa farmer who recently lost his farm and is now a door-to-door salesman. "Farming is a calling," says another, "not a living."

Many ex-farmers like my cousin Don still believe that the farmers who are losing out today are those incapable of making the change to total mechanization and computerized farming. "We don't need farmers, we need businessmen," Don says with the fervor of his youth. Milan Moore, on the other hand, speaks for a younger generation when he says that the small farmer has simply been squeezed out by corporate business. Big corporations mean absentee landlords, managerial companies and ever-more-specialized factory functions that manipulate and displace organic ones, like industrial feedlots for cattle and hogs. Size is the determinant. "I think there'll have to be a major change in the economics of agriculture before it's all controlled by large companies who have to get a large return on their money or they won't get involved," says Milan. Farmers with small acreage would be satisfied with smaller profit, he believes, in order to be more self-sufficient. The remedy as he sees it lies in price control, where the government would initiate a reverse graduated price to decrease production: "Say four dollars a bushel for the first ten thousand bushels, then three for the next ten thousand, and so on down the line."

In the 1980s other voices began to question the rigid logic of facts and figures outlined a century ago. In 1989 specialists gathered by Wes Jackson of the Land Institute met in Salinas, Kansas, for a symposium on "The Marriage of Ecology and Agriculture." They assessed the costs of industrial farming in a larger context than crop economics, including the costs of land erosion and groundwater loss and of the pollution of both elements. "The pioneers who ripped away the virgin sod of the prairie to plant wheat and corn committed sacrileges for which man has yet to atone," Jackson said, "and the penalties have been erosion, droughts and dust bowls."

In November 1989, Richard Rhodes, in a *New York Times* editorial, voiced the concerns of all those who have adopted the term "sustainable agriculture" to replace the "chemical agriculture" of agribusiness. "We ought to place the blame for chemically intensive agriculture where it belongs: in Washington, with the politics of farm subsidies," Rhodes wrote. Collectively, agribusiness, the largest industry in America, has redefined a farmer as "someone who launders money for a chemical company." He cited as typical a farming family near Kansas City, Missouri, who grossed $152,090 in 1986. After the chief expense— feed for their cattle and hogs—they paid $22,345 for fertilizers and pesticides and $17,910 for machines and fuel. With the government subsidy of $11,000 to idle 10 percent of their land, they cleared $19,000. In short, more than $41,000 of their gross went to agribusiness. Rhodes's plea was for a federal farm program that would limit production, encourage crop rotation and biological controls, and remove dependence on chemicals.

The Summer-Autumn 1989 issue of *The Journal of Gastronomy* contained a

"A corn plant is a little
factory out there, work-
ing to convert carbon
dioxide to starch and
cellulose . . . forming
leaves and flowers and
ears. Under the stressed
circumstances we have
now, the factory just isn't
working as well."

—D. E. ALEXANDER,
professor of plant
genetics at the
University of Illinois,
quoted in *The New
York Times,* July 12,
1988

number of articles by different writers addressing the costs to food and consumers of current methods of farming. "Farming isn't manufacturing," said
the noted restaurateur Alice Waters of Chez Panisse. "If our food has lacked
flavor . . . that may be because it was treated as dead even while it was being
grown." We are a nation of industrial eaters, warned the noted essayist Wen-
dell Berry. "The industrial eater is, in fact, one who does not know that eating
is an agricultural act, who no longer knows or imagines the connections
between eating and the land, and who is therefore necessarily passive and
uncritical—in short, a victim." Most tellingly, Frances Moore Lappé was concerned that we have no democratic language of agriculture, but rather only the
"free-market" economic language of industry, which assumes that crops are
commodities, based on private property and the accumulation of resources, on
a division between labor and ownership and on control over processing and
distribution. "Cheap food has been made possible at the farmer's expense, not
at the expense of the food processor or distributor, who receives 75 percent of
every dollar spent on food," she wrote. "The economic miracle of today's cheap
American food has involved a colossal transfer of income and capital from producers to middlemen—to the agricultural equivalents of Wall Street arbi-
trageurs and bond sellers."

In 1989 the Board on Agriculture of the National Research Council for the
first time in its history put out a volume called *Alternative Agriculture,* which
applied the logic of facts and figures to the costs of our shortsighted farm policies since the 1930s. "In effect, a high target price subsidizes the inefficient,
potentially damaging use of inputs [fertilizers, pesticides, and irrigation]," the
Council concluded. "It also encourages surplus production of the same crops
that the commodity programs are in part designed to control, thus increasing
government expenditures."

At the same time, the National Research Council was aware that any significant decrease in American corn production will have not just a national but a
global effect. In 1988 the United States, with 4.1 billion bushels of corn in storage, held 73 percent of the world's supply. Meanwhile the world's demand for
corn has been rising by about 200 million bushels a year. Oddly enough, China
has become the world's second largest supplier of that demand and in China
today one can see more visibly than elsewhere the political effect of corn. In
China one can see how closely the alarming increase in the world's population
is tied to the increased production of corn.

When I went to China in October 1987, the moment I shook the city dust of
Beijing from my heels, I was in corn country. Corn was everywhere. The bike
paths, where kernels were laid to dry, were calligraphic strokes of yellow.

Tile rooftops, eaves, ledges were looped with corn. Golden-red ears were stacked like logs against walls, hung in bunches from trees, strung from poles like laundry, heaped in mountains walled by drying stalks. I might have been in Mexico or Peru. Not a tractor in sight, just men, women, burros and donkeys, toiling under their golden burden as they have done for four centuries, ever since corn found its way to China along the trade routes, sometime between the 1520s and 1560s.

Bouquets of corn carpet a village square in China in the 1970s. From *Scenes of China,* Hong Kong Beauty View Publications

The introduction of corn revolutionized the agricultural life of China and helped produce a population explosion that began in the seventeenth century, quadrupled between the eighteenth and nineteenth centuries and is now out of sight. To the Chinese, corn was and remains poor man's food because it can be grown where their favored crops of rice and wheat cannot. "We think of corn as an auxiliary staple," said a young country-faced woman named Ren Rui, a crop researcher with the Chinese Academy of Agricultural Sciences in Beijing. Ren Rui, whose husband is a physicist, studied for a year at Ames, Iowa, and knows well the wide world of corn. Corn now forms 22 percent of China's staple crops, she tells me, yielding 14.3 kilograms per *mou* (a *mou* is one-sixth of an acre). China's commercial crop, which began in the 1950s with seed imported from the United States, is grown in Heilongjiang province in the northeast, in Manchuria, which with its Corn Belt climate is now the second home of Corn Belt Dent.

Corn has been important historically to China; it helped to extend and sustain the power of the Manchu invaders who overthrew the last of the Ming emperors in the mid-seventeenth century. Corn enabled the overcrowded Yangtze delta farmers to cultivate inland hills where other crops would not grow, as it enabled laborers in the mountains of Yunnan and Szechwan to become full-scale farmers for the first time. By the end of the eighteenth century, corn was the primary food crop in southwest China and today it still provides a goodly portion of the food energy for north-central China, although those who can afford rice or wheat eat corn only when desperate. "We once *had* to eat corn," Ren Rui says, "so we don't want to eat it anymore." Today, from a

"Let there be more corn and more meat and let there be no hydrogen bombs at all."

—PREMIER NIKITA KHRUSHCHEV, on his first visit to Roswell Garst's farm in Coon Rapids, Iowa, in September 1959. After Khrushchev was deposed, he devoted himself to writing his memoirs, puttering in his garden, and growing corn.

crop yield of 65,560,000 metric tons (in 1986), they can afford to feed 60 percent of their corn to their animals and export most of the rest to Russia and Japan.

As American farmers have learned that corn in Kansas is tied to the weather in Siberia, so they know that their corn dollars are tied to the value of the yuan in Manchuria. The language of agriculture, like the language of economics and ecology, is worldwide no matter what the national politics of its constituencies. While Chinese farmers have been sowing more land with corn, American farmers have been sowing more cornfields with soybeans. In 1987 the dollar value of American exports of soy topped both corn and wheat by $1 billion—a new variation on the post-Columbian Exchange. After a century and a half of exporting the Industrial Ideal along with our industrialized crops, the United States is beginning to look not only outward but inward, seeing perhaps for the first time that the cure for a corn-sick land begins at home.

At long last we are listening to the native huntsman-planter, who has never lost his sense that man belongs to the land, not the land to man, and that a nation's health as well as a planet's requires that earth, sky, plant, animal and man be treated as one. Such are the complexities that, near the dawn of a new century, are altering our corn politics and our corn-pone opinions, as in Mark Twain's pronouncement, "You tell me whar a man gits his corn pone, en I'll tell you what his 'pinions is." I doubt that Twain knew the Chinese had been eating corn pone for as long as our colonists had, but he knew a thing or two about cultural arrogance and humility, as he knew the savagery of those who would mistake their corn-pone opinions for God's will and their greed, in this or any other starving time, for divine discontent.

One of fifty houses of sun-dried corn in a village in the Erlang Mountains in Sichuan Province in 1985. Photo by Harald Sund

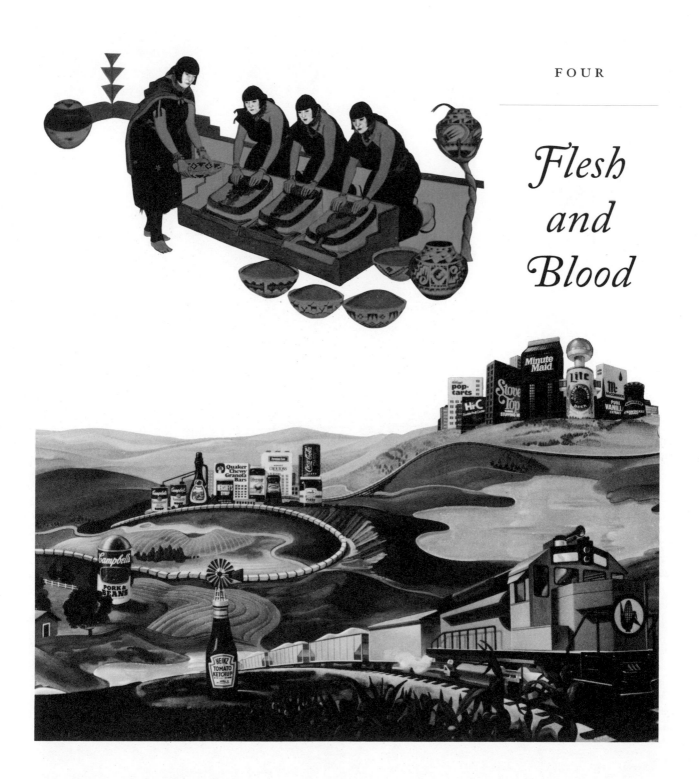

FOUR

Flesh and Blood

(overleaf) Pueblo women at San Ildefonso grind corn from coarse meal to fine on a triple metate, to drumbeat and song, in this painting by Gilbert Atencio in 1962. From the Dale Bullock Collection, New Mexico State Records Center
A corn commodities train speeds through a rural landscape of villages, silos and windmills, embodied in products using corn sugars. Corn Refiners Association, Inc. booklet, 1980s

The Language of Food

FROM PIKI TO CORNFLAKES

"CORN IS LIFE," said Don Talayesva, Sun Chief of the Hopi in 1942, "and piki is the perfect food." Most of America has never heard of the fast finger-food called piki, but all the world has heard of cornflakes. "Piki are the original cornflakes," the Hopi matriarch Helen Sekaquaptewa told me, and indeed, the more I learned about North American native cooking, the more I saw that cornflakes are the white man's piki. They are also the white man's aboriginal fast food—"In two jiffies a flavory meal to satisfy the hungriest man," read a Kellogg's ad in the 1930s. "In a bowl, flakes race with milk to the finish, beyond which the food turns and collapses to paper, to the cardboard, soaked, from which it had been poured," wrote the food critic Jeff Weinstein in *The Village Voice*. "A bowl of cornflakes ignited by milk is a meal automatically clocked, constructed to speed you up and out." Cornflakes speed our racing engines, and therein lies the difference between the Hopi's view of corn as life and the white man's view of corn as high-octane fuel.

From the start, the food languages of native and colonial America were as disparate as the cultures from which they came. Any organic food culture is rooted in the place where it was born and bred, but white Americans are all transplants, migrating to this place, these weathers, this ecology, with a load of culinary baggage packed elsewhere. The subtlety and sophistication of native corn cooking was integral with corn, life and language on this continent. "The terms in Zuni for every phenomenon connected with corn and its growth are so numerous and technical," Frank Cushing wrote a century ago, "that it is as difficult to render them into English as it would be to translate into Zuni the terminology of an exact science." Because the primary language of corn, in its thousands of dialects, was more often spoken than written, was performed rather than abstracted, the language of wheat subdued the language of corn as quickly as swords subdued arrows. Many of corn's secrets were misunderstood and lost, literally and figuratively, in translation. Like the forgotten seeds from which it sprang, however, native corn cuisine did not die but evolved and hybridized. While much of it dwindled into a few standardized forms, much remained hidden, like the prehistoric cobs in Bat Cave, awaiting rediscovery.

For more than eleven centuries, piki sustained and still sustains life in Old Oraibi on Second Mesa, the oldest continuously inhabited village in the United States, as old as the earliest settlement of Aztec or Inca and the center of the ten thousand Hopi who occupy the small chunk of northeast Arizona called Hopiland—the land of "the people of peace." Old Oraibi, however, is barely visible, so fully does it blend into the pink wrinkled skin of the mesas, as the mesas themselves blend into the desert horizon of sand and sky.

In contrast, Battle Creek, named for the people of war, in central Michigan near the kingdom of Ford in Dearborn, shouts from the rooftops its name and cereal number. On the side of his four-story factory of 1906, William Keith Kellogg, the father of cornflakes, had "THIS IS BATTLE CREEK" painted in block letters to make "Kellogg's of Battle Creek" a chivalric vaunt like "William of Burgundy" or "Timon of Athens." If the original stone Sanitarium of his brother, Dr. John Harvey Kellogg, the father of health zealots, is now "just a heap of rubble—passed away, dead," as a local Battle Creekian put it, the grandiose "San" of 1904 (now the Federal Center) still proclaims its glory fifteen stories tall and twenty Ionic pillars wide.

The difference in language is not just a matter of style but of organic substance. Although the Hopi language was officially outlawed in the 1910s and the Hopi land officially shrunk to 501,501 acres in the 1940s, even today the Hopi are the American natives who continue to speak most fully the ancient language of corn, because their daily lives are still intimate with the growing, cooking and ceremonies of corn that gave meaning to the lives of their ancestors. Theirs is also the last place on the continent where the art of transforming blue corn into the tra-

Dr. John Harvey Kellogg, with his brother Will K., applied Barnum hoopla to "health" and sold the world on flaked corn. Courtesy Battle Creek Sanitarium, Battle Creek, Michigan

ditional blue wafer bread is still handed down by the grandmothers to the mothers and daughters of the clan.

Helen Sekaquaptewa, born in Old Oraibi ninety-three years ago, is one of the honored grandmothers and the reigning matriarch of the Eagle clan, whom everyone calls "Grandma." Her life, like the life of every Hopi from cradle to grave, has been shaped by corn. For nineteen days after childbirth, her mother fasted, while Helen's paternal grandmother placed beside the new baby two perfect corn ears, a long one to represent the mother and a smaller one for the baby. Each day for twenty days her mother marked each of the four walls of her room with white cornmeal in five horizontal lines to prepare for the naming ceremony. Then both mother and baby were washed with soapweed and the baby's face rubbed with white cornmeal. As the grandmother blessed the baby with the pair of corn ears, she put a pinch of cornmeal in the baby's mouth and said, "This is your food, which the earth mother will give you all your life."

When Grandma dies, her kinsmen will dust her face with cornmeal and cover it with a cotton mask in which holes have been cut for eyes and mouth. They will fold her body in a fetal curve, wrap it in a blanket, tie it with yucca strips and bury it deep in the earth. They will cover her grave with a slab of sandstone and rocks, in which a greasewood stick will provide a way out for the spirit to depart on the third day to the spirit world. At the far end of Second Mesa you can see the rocks and sticks of Hopi graves clustered at the foot of Corn Rock, which juts from the flat mesa like a thick and phallic double ear of corn, symbolic of eternal as well as daily life.

Grandma's earliest memory was of her mother taking her to the "training rocks" beyond the village, where she and her playmates were each given a few kernels of corn and a stone to grind them with in the small hollows of the rock. Now I could see the shallow depressions where the girls ground corn next to grooves where boys learned simultaneously to file the shafts of arrows and to flirt with girls. "Grinding is good for you," Grandma said, since grinding was for girls what running and hunting were for boys, a form of exercise as well as a way to get food. At puberty, girls had to grind corn ceremonially for four days, just as boys had to run all night to place cornmeal and prayer sticks on distant shrines and return before the rise of the morning star.

Even today when a Hopi girl is betrothed she takes, as Grandma did seventy-three years ago, a pan "full of fine white cornmeal" and a basket of blue piki bread to the house of her groom-to-be. From then until the day of her wedding, the women of the village grind corn for the wedding feast while the men weave the bride's wedding robes from white cotton, which formerly they both grew

"The Navaho chose the long ear of yellow corn because it was soft and easy to shell and easy to grind, but the Hopi, he chose the shortest, hardest ear. It was tough. It would survive."

—George Nasoftie, in "The Hopi Migrations" by Tony Hillerman, in *Arizona Highways* (September 1980)

A Hopi woman lifts a sheet of piki from the hot stone. The bowl of batter sits next to the row of folded wafers on the mat. Courtesy Arizona State Museum, the University of Arizona, Helen Teiwes, photographer

and spun. The last four days before the wedding, the bride grinds corn in the house of the groom in a room set apart, shades drawn, talking to no one. Each day her husband's kinswomen bring her a quart of corn, white the first day, blue the second and third. "After the first grinding I handed the corn out and waited while it was roasted and passed back to me to be ground real fine," Grandma remembered. On the fourth day she ground unparched blue corn for the special wedding cake called *someviki.* After the wedding, the bride returned to her mother's home to grind more corn to "pay" for the weaving of her wedding robes, and only then would the groom move into her home.

Grandma's son Eugene took me to the village of Shipaulovi to watch a group of women in the house of Frieda Youhoena make piki in preparation for the "payback" feast of a recent bride. I had read many accounts of the sacred piki stone, of how the men would quarry a two-foot granite slab two to three inches thick, how their wives would rub and polish it with fine pebbles until it was smooth as glass, how they would season it with watermelon seeds, ground and roasted until black, which they would then rub over the surface of the stone until its blackness shone like a mirror. So I was startled to find a young woman in jeans and harlequin glasses, kneeling against a piece of foam rubber over a smoky fire in the back shed that served as Frieda's piki room.

"I'm just a novice," laughed the daughter of Rex Pooyouna, a famous moccasin maker, as she chatted with her husband. He sat on a low bench while she fed a small but intense wood fire beneath the stone placed on a foot-high hearth. She dipped her right hand into a large plastic bowl of blue batter, rubbed off excess batter along the rim, then smeared her hand quickly over the top of the stone, from the far edge to the near in successive arcs, dip and smear, dip and smear, until the stone was completely covered. On top she put a sheet of already cooked piki in order to soften and fold it. She folded both sides into the middle and then folded the wafer in thirds from the bottom up. She added the folded piki to a pile of wafers at her side before she stripped the new layer from the stone. Every now and then she cleaned the stone with a rag of soft leather and greased it from a bowl of fat rendered from sheep brains.

"Piki's so expensive now," she said. "I wanted to learn to make it because it costs so much and because I thought it was time. I have three girls and I want them to learn." At first, she burned her fingers constantly on the stone, which is heated to 400 degrees, but she had learned to use the heel of her hand and her fingertips had toughened as she had picked up speed. "I'm still so slow," she groaned. "It will take me two or three hours to finish this amount of batter." Although Frieda had already stored four boxes, she would need hundreds more piki wafers for the ceremony and the women in her kitchen were making tubfuls of silky blue batter.

Because of the way the corn has been prepared before the batter, piki will keep indefinitely if properly stored. First the corn is cracked, then ground coarsely, then roasted, then ground fine. It's the roasting that preserves, as Indians learned in ancient times when making their "traveling" bread or "journeying" cake, the little bag of parched meal they carried with them on their hunts and migrations. In Grandma's home they always kept plenty of piki on hand for guests, she told me, some white, some blue, some lavender—the color blue-corn meal turns when heated without any alkali. But the alkaline of wood ash not only keeps the color true blue but also lends flavor, leavening and nutritional value to the meal. Ash cooking, as we shall see later, begins the alphabet of America's corn cuisine.

The Hopi make many other blue-corn dishes—boiled dumplings called *mumuozpiki,* pancakes called *saquavikavike,* fried grits called *huzrusuki,* which any traveler can eat in the restaurant at the Hopi Center—but piki remains their quintessential food. "No man will marry a girl unless she can make piki," they said in Grandma's day, but that was then. Now Hopi girls buy hand mills and electric blenders to grind most of their corn, and many a fine finger will never have touched a piki stone. But if a Zuni or Pueblo girl wants to learn to make wafer bread, she must go to Hopiland and begin by grinding meal by hand as fine as the powdered corn Grandma's mother taught her to put on her face to make her skin as smooth and silky as a piki stone.

Such wafer breads were once a staple among the Pueblo people, called *mowa* by the Tewa, *buwa* by the Rio Grande Tewa and *he'-we* by the Zuni, for whom a *he'-we* stone was "the rock's flesh," to be anointed with hot piñon gum and cactus juice. In *Zuni Breadstuff* (1920), Frank Cushing devoted a chapter to the wafer's many colors and kinds: a salty one flavored with lime yeast; a rich one made with milk, tasting like "cream biscuits"; a red one of red-corn kernels, leaves and shoots, sweetened like "London sugar wafers"; a delicious fermented one sweetened by saliva, baked in layers between hot stones, called "buried-bread broad *he'-we.*" Stored wafers which became dry and flaky they might turn into a batter and cook again as "double-done *he'-we*," like zwie-back, or they might eat them as chips or flakes. Grandma said that the Hopi liked to crumble piki and eat it with milk and sugar as a breakfast cereal. Like cornflakes.

Cornflakes! The Kellogg brothers no more invented cornflakes in Battle Creek in 1898 than the Hopi invented corn in Oraibi in 898. The century that invented the adman has been conned by its own hokum. We believed our tribal chiefs who said, "Publicity is life and cornflakes the perfect food." In 1986 I participated in a cornflake ritual that condensed the personal breakfast lives of four generations, a ritual performed over the last eighty years by six and a half million people from around the world at the sacred fount of the Kellogg Company and which on April 11 ended forever. It was, as Jeff Weinstein put it, The Last Cornflake Show.

There had been thirty thousand of us that week waiting to tour the cornflake plant, waiting in the anteroom beneath a world map that flagged twenty-two Kellogg's plants in seventeen countries and fifteen languages, from Japanese to Finnish. We stood by the thirty-pound silver National Corn Trophy that bore an enamel portrait of the "Sweetheart of the Corn," the original cornflake girl of 1907, whose image evolved along with the art and science of advertising to put Kellogg's factory version of piki into the mouths of babes in Rangoon and Patagonia. We stood in our hairnets, whole families of us, including bearded men encircled in hairnets from chin to eyebrows, waiting by posters that reca-pitulated a century's myths of pep, health and digestion, waiting to be touched by the magic of machines that, among the 6 million cereal packages they produced each day, turned 48,700 bushels of corn grits into 70,000 cartons of corn-flakes.

My interest was personal. The culinary rites of my family table sprang directly from Battle Creek at the turn of the century, which had enshrined Clean Colons, Purity and Postum, sanctified Horace Fletcher's "thirty-two chews per bite" and elevated colonic irrigation to lustration and atonement. My grandparents rejoiced in the Bible Belt union of health foods and high colonics that paved the way for the union of engineer, preacher and adman in the Kel-logg boys. While Dr. John sold health cures at the "San," brother Will sold health food at the factory. They appealed to the puritan need to convert flesh, and the grain that fed it, into the transparent wafer of the Eucharist. Or into Elijah's Manna, as C. W. Post first christened his rival brand of cornflakes before he renamed them Post Toasties.

Fabricating their own myths of origin, the new breed of zealots believed they were inventing what they were simply industrializing. Processing corn grits by

"It is highly necessary that the bowels move freely. If they do not completely evacuate at least two or three times a day you are constipated. It is wise to clean them once or twice a week with an herb enema."

—JETHRO KLOSS,
Back to Eden (1939)

roasting, drying, tempering, flavoring, flaking and retoasting to make a form of transportable, long-keeping and instantly digestible finger-food, in both powdered and wafer form, was of course ancient cooking history. What the industrialists contributed, along with their machines, was not culinary methods but techniques of marketing—the Big Sell.

Since mid-century, health moralists had been pounding cereal grains into granules on their kitchen tables to make them digestible as water. Dr. James Jackson had cracked wheat into "Granula" (made from water mixed with toasted graham flour), which C. W. Post would promote as "Grape Nuts" and Dr. John Kellogg as "Granola." Dr. John had ground wheat into finer granules for his coffee substitute "Caramel Cereal," which Post labeled first "Monk's Brew" and then "Postum." Soon the Kelloggs began to crank a gummy mess of boiled wheat through a pair of rollers on their kitchen table in an attempt to rival Henry Perky's newly patented shredded wheat. In the lucky accident endemic to myths of origin, the Kelloggs "invented" flaking when they forgot a batch of boiled wheat for a couple of days and found that the "tempering," despite mold, resulted in a perfect flake.

Local myths ignored the facts that England had introduced the roller mill to America after the Civil War and that the brewing industry had already been rolling raw corn grits into flakes (Cerealine or Crystal Malt Flakes) to use for malt. When the Kelloggs turned to corn, their homemade flakes were at first thick, tasteless and rancid, until they decided to flake hulled corn with commercial rollers and to flavor it with salted and sugared brewer's malt. In 1898 their Sanitas Toasted Corn Flakes had the edge, but within a decade a cornflake boom had generated 108 rivals, who leapt to exploit the milling industry's "improved" rollers, which automatically degermed corn to remove the oil.

In 1906, after the first of many court battles with his brother, W. K. Kellogg set up his own company and began to exploit the new century's appetite for sugar and showbiz. W. K. was nothing if not a showman. He threw his signature cornflakes onto streetcar signs, shop windows, billboards. He fashioned nine-foot ears of corn and giant cornflake boxes into walking ads. He sent canvassers door-to-door with cases of free samples, snared shopping housewives with gimmicks like "Wink Day" when a wink brought a prize from their local grocer, dazzled the jaded in Broadway's Times Square with the world's largest electric sign, in which a smiling boy declared, "I want KELLOGG'S." In downtown Chicago, he improved the sign when a change of lights on the word "KELLOGG'S" changed a boy crying "I want" to a boy smiling "I got." With the same Barnum hoopla, the current Kellogg Company ended its family tours with brass bands, a cavorting Tony the Tiger and a costumed Rice Krispies trio

A typical Kellogg's ad in 1913. The box displays the Kellogg logo, "The sweetheart of the corn," and advises the consumer to heat before serving. Courtesy Historical Pictures Service, Chicago

handing out balloons in the guise of Snap! Crackle! and Pop! Despite the death of both brothers at ninety-one, still locked in litigation and brotherly hate, the Kellogg name, branded on $3 billion worth of products each year, lives on.

By harnessing mechanized power to old-fashioned flaked corn, the Kelloggs introduced cornflakes to a world that, five centuries after Columbus, still identifies corn with field corn, the food of pigs and peasants but not of civilized tables. "The hardest part of selling corn to Europeans is getting them to taste it," Peter Schubeline said recently. An Americanized Swiss, Schubeline retired from nuclear physics to found the Unicorn Sweetcorn Company in Strasbourg, France, in order "to colonize Europe with sweet corn." Europe is a few centuries late. The reports of early French explorers like Dumont de Montigny fell on deaf ears. Navigating the Mississippi in 1753, Montigny was impressed by the high degree of Indian culture evidenced in their corn cookery: "forty-two styles, each of which has its special name." A century later, however, genteel snobs like Harriet Martineau and Frances Trollope set the European tone of contempt. "Everything eats corn from slave to chick," Martineau complained of the American South. "They eat Indian corn in a great variety of forms," Trollope acknowledged of the American North, "but in my opinion, all bad."

Early colonists in North America struggled to translate corn into wheat because their lives depended on it; but while wheat was simple, corn was complex. Not only was corn both cereal and vegetable, but there were many different kinds of corn, each demanding different preparation, whether raw or cooked, fresh or dried, pureed or popped. A modern European encyclopedia of *The Food of the Modern World* still divides all corn into two parts, *indentata* and *saccarahata:* the first is "maize or Indian corn," used for a cereal, and the latter is sweet corn, used for a vegetable.

Today we know that different Indian tribes grew many different varieties of corn and varied their cooking methods according to type. The Chickasaw named corn types by their cooking uses; the Tewa in the Southwest organized their universe and their palates by corn color; Buffalo Bird Woman, like all Woodland peoples, distinguished corn types by both color and texture, discriminating hard and soft white, hard and soft yellow, and gummy. Roger Williams, searching for *A Key into the Language of America* in 1643, found it in the culinary language of the Narragansett, who used different nouns for dozens of differently prepared corns, not to mention verbs for grinding and parching. Trying to grind Zuni words into English, Frank Cushing noted different terms for corn on the ear, in the grain, cracked, skinned, rubbed, broken into coarse meal, reduced to fine meal, ground to exceedingly fine flour— naming hundreds of corn dishes.

While modern Americans divide corn roughly between sweet corn and cornmeal—between a fresh vegetable and a dried cereal—ancient Americans divided corn by season and ceremony. Their basic distinction was between early-ripe and late-ripe, between corn harvested at the beginning and at the end of the growing season, between the green-corn harvest of early summer and the ripe-corn harvest of the fall. Beyond the realm of season was their ash cooking, which might be called lye or lime cooking.

There is virtually no corn preparation today that doesn't have some ancient analogue. Indians, after all, have a recipe backlog of a few thousand years. They roasted, steamed, parched, dried and pickled fresh corn on the cob. They cut kernels from the cob for succotash, soups and stews, just as they "milked" fresh cobs by scraping, grating and pureeing the kernels to make puddings, dumplings and breads. They dried fresh kernels to preserve them whole or parched them to eat as snacks or ground them to make what they called cold meal. Their subsistence crop, however, was ripe corn as a cereal grain, preserved for winter feeding until spring came around again. Their ancient methods of milling corn produced degrees of refinement from coarsely cracked grain to meal ground fine as powder; their methods of preserving produced diversity from roasting to toasting, smoking and parching.

Ash cookery, which was once the major building block of ripe-corn cookery, evolved differently in North America than in Mesoamerica. Just as the first corn plant required man's help in planting, so corn as a staple food required man's help in processing, because unprocessed corn lacks certain nutrients essential to man. Early planters instinctively made up for the protein deficiencies of both corn and beans by planting and cooking them together. Then they discovered "how to unlock the nutritional potential of maize," as Solomon Katz of the University of Pennsylvania describes it, by processing the grain with alkali. The great civilizations of Mesoamerica with their large populations, Katz asserts, could not have been built or sustained without the knowledge of alkali-processed corn.

In Mexico, divided between jungle and desert, the Indians processed corn chiefly with slaked lime. The processed kernels they called *nixtamal,* which they ground wet to make what the Spaniards called *masa* or dried to make *masa harina. Masa* was the dough they turned into their staple breadstuffs of tortillas and tamales. North of Mexico, however, where forests were deep, Indians pro-

"I ought here to describe to my English readers what this same Indian Corn *is. . . . It is eaten by man and beast in all the various shapes of whole corn, meal, cracked, and every other way that can be imagined. It is tossed down to hogs, sheep, cattle, in the whole ear. The former two thresh for themselves, and the latter eat* cob *and all. It is eaten, and is a very delicious thing, in its half-ripe, or* milky *state."*

—WILLIAM COBBETT, *A Year's Residence in the United States of America* (1819)

cessed corn chiefly with lye made from wood ashes, to make what we generally call whole-kernel hominy and what our Southwest called posole. Because the North American colonists tended to look on corn as deformed wheat, they misunderstood the nutritional function of ash cooking and saw it only as a form of milling, since the ash bath removed the hulls. In America hulled corn, or hominy, became a minor branch of corn cooking and today is nearly extinct. As soon as they could, our colonists imported their own wheat-milling devices to remove the hulls of corn and did not think to apply chemical processing until they wanted to turn corn into commercial starch.

Their misunderstanding was no different from the rest of the world's. After Columbus, in countries where corn was imported to become a major staple, men suffered the disease we now know as pellagra, because they did not import a knowledge of alkali processing along with the corn. Recently Professor Katz, a "biocultural evolutionist," studied fifty-one Indian societies in the Americas and concluded that all of them that were dependent upon corn had devised some form of alkali processing, to compensate for corn's lack of niacin. Certainly such processing was as ancient as the lime-soaking pots of 100 B.C. discovered at Teotihuacán, a discovery which has led many to believe that corn is the oldest chemically processed grain in the world.

Cooking is by definition an ephemeral language, but we have many witnesses in the past to the glories of the urban cuisines created by Aztec and Inca and to the country cuisines of those farther north. We also have witnesses in the present, women like Grandma Helen Sekaquaptewa and her friend Louise Udall (mother of Congressman Morris Udall) who have tried to bridge the gap between languages and cultures by mutual respect: "I am talking," Grandma said. "She is writing." Even if our texts are garbled, there is still a tie that binds Grandma's piki to Kellogg's cornflakes, Tex-Mex tortillas to New England johnnycakes, popcorn to Cracker Jack and metates to General Mills in a biocultural evolutionary succotash that could have happened nowhere else but here.

GREEN-CORN COOKING

"PEOPLE HAVE TRIED and they have tried," says our *Prairie Home Companion,* Garrison Keillor, "but sex is not better than sweet corn." For the Indians "sweet" meant the first tender cobs that were "green" and "in the milk," rather than a specific sugary breed, and the sexiness of sweet corn was sung and danced at the fertility feasts called Green Corn Busks. The types of corn that were planted to be harvested young, or "early-ripe," varied by tribe and ecology. In the climes of North Dakota, the Hidatsa planted two crops of corn to be harvested green, one that would be ready by the first week of August and another that would be ready in late September when the other corn was getting hard. In far warmer Virginia, the early-ripe corn, as described by Robert Beverley, was of two types: a smaller ear, about the size of "the Handle of a Case Knife," which was ready to eat by mid-May, and the larger ear, "thick as a Child's Leg," ready a fortnight later. Down in Florida among the Chickasaw and Choctaw, the earliest corn harvested was "little corn" or "six weeks' corn," which was a popcorn; then came the soft dent corns, harvested in time for the Green Corn Dance, and finally the flint or hominy corns for late harvesting. In general, each stage of ripeness of each type of corn—which controlled all those variables of size, texture, flavor, hardness, softness, sweetness and starchiness—dictated the way the particular corn was cooked. Buffalo Bird Woman found that hard yellow corn and soft yellow corn made the best "green roasting ears," but she was less choosy about green boiling ears. "For green corn, boiled and eaten fresh, we used all varieties except the gummy," she said, "for when green they tasted alike." (The gummy, ironically, was a type of sugar corn—or sweet corn—that the Hidatsa used exclusively for making "sweet cornballs.")

Benjamin Franklin in the spring of 1785 neatly summarized the differences between green- and ripe-corn cookery when he outlined for the French, suffering famine at the time, the virtues of importing and planting Indian corn. Franklin noted that when English farmers first reached America they were wont to "despise & neglect the Culture of Mayz" because they were Wheat farmers, but that they inevitably turned to Mayz when they observed "the Advantage it affords to their Neighbours, the older Inhabitants":

1. The Family can begin to make use of it before the time of full Harvest; for the tender green Ears stript of their Leaves and roasted by a quick Fire till the Grain is brown, and eaten with a little Salt or Butter, are a Delicacy. 2. When the Grain is riper and harder the Ears boil'd in their Leaves, and eaten with Butter are also good & agreable Food. The green tender Grains, dried [may] be kept all the Year; and mixed with green Haricots also dried, make at any time a pleasing Dish, being first soak'd some hours in Water, and then boil'd.

He was right thus to summarize the three basic ways green corn was prepared by Indians and settlers alike until our own century: roasting, boiling and

"Corn balls *were a favorite article of food among the Mandans and Hidatsas. . . . One was made of pounded sugar corn mixed with grease. . . . Another kind of corn ball was made of pounded corn, pounded sunflower seed, and boiled beans. It tasted like peanut butter and was called* opata *by the Mandans.*"

—GEORGE F. WILL, *Corn Among the Indians of the Upper Missouri* (1917)

drying. Although drying was eventually replaced by canning, it was once the chief means of preserving green corn. "Sweet corn is gathered before it is ripe, and dried in the sun," John Bradbury wrote in 1811 to explain the food ways of the Arikara to the English. "It is called by the Americans green corn or corn in the milk." Roasting and boiling, on the other hand, were the ways to enjoy fresh corn-on-the-cob, and even the odd wheat lover was occasionally seduced by its erotic mystique. "Roasting Ears," William Cobbett averred in *A Treatise on Indian Corn* in 1828, "are certainly the greatest delicacy that ever came in contact with the palate of man." If the older inhabitants had the edge on emollients—"When boiled green with rich buffalo marrow spread on it," an English traveler reported, "it is very sweet and truly delicious"—colonists decided that butter was no more a bad substitute for marrow than sweet corn for sex.

Corn-on-the-Cob

"FIRES ARE BLAZING in all directions around which gather merry groups to feast on boiled and roasted ears," Henry Boller wrote of North Dakota tribes feasting at Green Corn time in the 1860s. Whether the ears were steam-baked in an underground pit lined with green husks, or boiled in a bark pot or roasted in the embers, what Indians prized was sweetness. When they roasted green ears they usually husked them first so that the kernels acquired a caramel taste and color in the embers. Buffalo Bird Woman said they would lay a "fresh

Georgia O'Keeffe: A Portrait—Eating Corn, *1920/1922, by Alfred Stieglitz, 1864–1946.* National Gallery of Art, Washington, D.C., Alfred Stieglitz Collection

ear on the coals with the husk removed" and roll the ear back and forth to roast it evenly. If any kernels popped with a loud noise, they would joke that it was corn stolen from a neighbor's garden. They would roast ripe corn as well as green until frost, when it lost its freshness, she said, but they had a trick to restore it: "We would take the green corn silk of the same plucked ear and rub the silk well into the kernels of the ear as they stood in the cob."

Settlers adapted the Indian method of roasting corn, husks off, in their hearth fires. Even as late as 1847, Mrs. T. J. Crowen in her *American Lady's Cookery Book* instructed the housewife: "Strip off all the husk from green corn, and roast it on a gridiron, over a bright fire of coals, turning it as one side is done. Or, if a wood fire is used, make a place clean in the front of the fire; lay the corn down, turn it when one side is done; serve with salt and butter." Long after gas and electric broilers had replaced wood hearths, Irma Rombauer followed the same ancient tradition in her 1943 *Joy of Cooking*. To roast corn, husk the ears, she said, spread them with melted butter and turn them under a heated broiler to brown.

Roasting green corn in the shuck, however, had its own traditions. The Iroquois roasted corn in quantity with the husk on, digging a trench for the fire and placing a stick lengthwise over the embers. "The ears of green corn were then leaned against the stick on both sides and turned from time to time until they were roasted," F. W. Waugh observed in 1916, adding that children were warned to eat green corn from the whole cob rather than break it in pieces, lest they be gobbled up by a woodland monster made entirely of legs.

Our modern practices of roasting with or without husks vary from one man's grill to another man's microwave and from one ethnic pocket to another. In

Settlers in Emmons County, North Dakota, in 1915 roast corn in hot coals "Indian style" by rolling the ears back and forth. Courtesy State Historical Society of North Dakota

Roast Corn Man, *Orchard and Hester Streets, May 3, 1938.* Berenice Abbott, photographer. Museum of the City of New York

Alabama, A. L. Tommie Bass, an Appalachian herbalist, prefers to roast his corn not only in the shuck but inside foil as well: "I generally cut off the part that fits to the stalk and one inch off the silk end and wrap it up in foil. You put it in the oven or in ashes. Of course, if you don't use foil, the ashes don't get through the shuck. Most folks boil the corn on the cob, but I can't eat it on account of having no teeth. I takes the corn off." I know a lot of city folk who soak their corn in the shuck for ten to twenty minutes in cold water before putting them on their grills to prevent the husks from burning and imparting a scorched taste. I know other folk like Juanita Tiger Kavena who, Hopi-style, deliberately scorch their husked ears over live coals or a gas-stove flame to make *twoitsie,* or Scorched Corn Stew.

Street vendors around the world husk corn to flavor it before grilling. Iranians soak their charcoal-roasted corn in heavy brine and call it *balal; balal* vendors, I'm told, are as popular in Iranian towns as pretzel vendors in New York or chestnut vendors in Paris. Southeast Asians brush their grilled corn with salted coconut milk, which they call *kao pot ping.* Chinese shake on soy sauce and Mexicans chili pepper. Best of all, Peruvians grill the big-kerneled corn they call *choclo* over roadside braziers, then wrap it in grilled cheese.

Nowadays all this happy diversity goes for naught when it comes to *boiling* fresh corn-on-the-cob. Here even cultural relativists become shrill with authority, myself included, in dictating the One True Way. Dictation begins, as in John Doerper's *Eating Well* (1984), with the demand for speed: "Make sure to have as little distance as possible between the corn patch and the kettle." Indians solved the timing problem by putting the kettle, or earth oven, *in* the cornpatch. Because we learned decades ago that corn sugar begins to convert to starch the moment the ear is plucked, and because the cornpatch for city folk may be a state or a continent away from the kettle, our primary sweet-corn ritual is a mad dash to the kitchen with whatever corn we've found.

Our ancestors were far more particular. A Wisconsin friend remembers that her farming grandmother first stripped back the husk at the top to test the kernels with her thumbnail. If milk oozed out, she threw that corn to the pigs because it was already too *old*. Today, even with supersweet corns, each breed and batch will differ in its ripeness and sweetness. It's wise to nibble a few kernels raw to determine precise cooking times. If there's no starchy taste at all, the less heat the better to retain sweetness and crispness. With the supersweets we've even learned to eat corn raw.

Still, the full erotic thrust of corn-on-the-cob comes only when the corn is at least as warm as human flesh, so a dip into a hot bath will do it no harm if the dip is quick. The formulaic three-minute bath, which has been standard in cookbooks for twenty years, is as antediluvian for modern sweet corn as the hand plow. Worse is the prescription for a three-minute boil *after* the kettle of water has returned to the boil. Worst of all is the advice, from no less an authority than James Beard, to start corn in a skillet of *cold* water and then bring it to the boil. Since heat speeds the conversion of corn sugar to starch, the longer the cooking time the tougher, starchier and soggier the corn. Jasper White, of Jasper's restaurant in Boston, who grew up with corn on a New Jersey farm, recommends no more than a second for the youngest, most sugary ear and no more than a minute for a slightly riper one.

The cooking times for our elders were much longer because their corn was very different. In nineteenth-century cookbooks, twenty-five or thirty-five minutes was standard for flint and dent corns that had a high degree of starch and tough hulls. But cooks of that time followed an Indian precedent for retaining sweetness which we have abandoned: boiling corn in the husk. As usual, Eliza Leslie's *Directions for Cookery in Its Various Branches* (1837) was exact in explaining how to boil Indian corn with the inner husks on:

> Corn for boiling should be full grown but young and tender. When the grains become yellow it is too old. Strip it of the outside leaves and the silk, but let the inner leaves remain, as they will keep in the sweetness. Put it into a large pot with plenty of water, and boil it rather fast for half an hour. When done, drain off the water, and remove the leaves.

Not until the turn of the century did our cookbooks advise housewives to remove all the leaves before boiling. In her 1878 *Dinner Year-Book*, Marion Harland suggested tying the inner leaves with thread around the tip of each ear to present a smooth appearance, but by 1903 she said simply in her *Complete Cook Book:* "Strip husk and silk from the ear and put over the fire in plenty of boiling water, slightly salted." *The White House Cook Book* (1902) explained why the new practice of denuding corn before boiling caught on: "The corn is

"Hot corn here's your nice hot corn
Come boys and girls now quickly come,
And buy my hot corn nice;
Two pence an ear is all I charge,
A treat of no great price."
—"The Cries of New York" (1830)

The Hot Corn Seller, *1840/1844, a watercolor drawing by Nicolino Calyo, 1799–1884.* Museum of the City of New York, Gift of Mrs. Francis P. Garvin in memory of Francis P. Garvin

Jules Starbuck Bourquin, eating corn in Horton, Kansas, 1910. Kansas Collection, University of Kansas Libraries

much sweeter when cooked with the husks on, but requires a longer time to boil." Since corn is also sweeter when cooked without salt (salt toughens the kernels), many cookbooks advised housewives to add, instead of salt, a little sugar and milk to the water.

The English, for whom Indian green corn remained an exotic novelty, wavered between husking and not husking, but their concerns were often as extra-culinary as William Cobbett's in the voluntaries he performed as Peter Porcupine in *A Treatise on Indian Corn* (1828). To prepare green ears for cooking, he observed,

> there are none of those cullings and pickings and choosings and rejectings and washings and dabblings and old women putting on their spectacles to save the caterpillars from being boiled alive; there are none of those peelings and washings as in the case of potatoes and turnips, and digging into the sides with the knife for the eyes, the maggots and the worms, and flinging away about half the root, in order to secure the *worst* part of it, which is in the middle; none of those squeezings and mashings and choppings before the worthless mess can be got upon the table. . . . Nature has furnished this valuable production with so complete a covering, that washings from the purest water cannot add to its cleanness.

Nature, he assumed, had devised this covering for the sole purpose of sanitation, for he concluded: "The husk being stripped off, it is at once ready for the pot."

In her recipe for "Boiled Indian Wheat or Maize" in her *Book of Household Management* (1861), Mrs. Isabella Beeton called "the ears of young and green Indian wheat" "one of the most delicious dishes brought to table," but her concern was more for the growing than the cooking of it. She regretted that it was so rarely seen in Britain and wondered that it was not invariably cultivated in the gardens of the wealthy. She followed Eliza Leslie in directing that "the outside sheath" and "waving fibres" be removed, but since Beeton mentioned no inner leaves, it's hard to know whether she stripped or retained them. We do know that Eliza Acton stripped them all in her *Modern Cookery* of the same date, asserting without truth that Americans picked and ate their corn "at a less sweet and delicate stage" and therefore needed to retain the inner leaves.

Significantly, it was the French or French-trained who first halved the customary half-hour boil and who exploited the husk for both cooking and serving. "If it seems desirable to strip off the inner husk just before sending to the table," Oscar Tschirky of the Waldorf wrote in 1896, "this must be done very quickly and the corn covered with a clean napkin or cloth to prevent the escape of heat." Escoffier was more explicit in his 1921 *Guide culinaire:* "Take the corn when it is quite fresh and still milky, and cook it in either steam or salted water; taking care to leave the husks on. When cooked, the husks are drawn back so as to represent stems, and the ears are bared if served whole. This done, set the ears on a napkin, and send a hors-d'oeuvre dish of fresh butter to the table with them." By the time an American edition of Escoffier's *Guide* came out, however, in 1941, American practice had so changed that the editor noted, "In the United States, the silk and husks are removed, and corn-holders are sent to the table with the ears of corn."

The proper way to eat corn had been a subject of dispute from the mid-nineteenth century on. Sam Beeton had noted in his wife's original *Household Management* that he had been introduced to green Indian wheat when visiting America and "found it to combine the excellences of the young green pea and the finest asparagus." That may be why Mrs. Beeton directed that it be "sent to table with a piece of toast underneath, as one might serve asparagus, to absorb any drops of water." Sam, however, had further worries. He confessed that "he felt at first slightly awkward in holding the large ear with one hand, whilst the other had to be employed in cutting off with a knife the delicate green grains." To simply gnaw the cob with one's teeth was unthinkable, and Americans worried the subject according to their pretensions to refinement.

Corn holders for the cob were a late refinement that appeared after Frederick Stokes in 1890 had given a full account in *Good Form: Dinners Ceremonious and Unceremonious* of how and how not to eat corn-on-the-cob:

> Corn may be eaten from the cob. Etiquette permits this method, but does not allow one to butter the entire length of an ear of corn and then gnaw it from end to end. To hold an ear of corn, if it be a short one, by the end, with the right hand, and bite from the ear is good form. A little doily, or very small napkin, is sometimes served with corn to fold about the end of a cob that is to be grasped by the hand, but this arrangement is as inconvenient as it is unnecessary. Good form disallows it.

Whether good form would have disallowed the corn holders Sarah Tyson Rorer recommended in her *New Cook Book* (1902) we do not know, since her concern was less with manners than digestion: "To eat, score each row of grains right through the centre. Then spread the corn on the cob lightly with butter, dust it with salt, and with the teeth press out the centre of the grains, leaving the hulls on the cob. Fresh, carefully cooked corn, eaten in this way, will not

"Some people take the whole stem and gnaw [the kernels] out with their teeth . . . it really troubles me to see how their wide mouths . . . ravenously grind up the beautiful white, pearly maize ears."
—FREDERICK BREMER, visiting America in 1850

produce indigestion." As an afterthought, she mentioned corn holders in the form of small wooden or silver handles, which were pressed into the cob ends, and also wire frames for the same purpose, "rather clumsy, but convenient." Even at that date she warned cooks not to remove husks, for they "prevent the sweetness from being drawn out in the water."

Corn holders were not sufficient to satisfy Emily Post in her *Etiquette: The Blue Book of Social Usage* (1928). "Corn on the cob could be eliminated so far as ever having to eat it in formal company is concerned, since it is never served at a luncheon or a dinner," she warned, "but, if you insist on eating it at home or in a restaurant, to attack it with as little ferocity as possible is perhaps the only direction to be given, since at best it is an ungraceful performance and to eat it greedily or smearingly is a horrible sight."

The original drawing by John White (in 1585–87) for Thomas Hariot's Briefe and True Report of the New Found Land of Virginia *shows a native couple eating corn. "Their meate is Mayz sodden . . . of verye good taste, deers flesche, or of some other beaste, and fishe. They are verye sober in their eatinge, and trinkinge, and consequentlye verye longe liued because they doe not oppress nature." The only visible ingredients here are kernels of cut corn and perhaps beans.* Courtesy of the Collections of the Library of Congress

Milking the Cob

R AW KERNELS cut from the cob and mixed with a variety of ingredients was the basis of Indian succotash (from the Narragansett word *m'sick-quatash,* with variants *sukquttahash* and *msakwitash*). The word meant "fragments," or the jumble of ingredients that the Spanish call *olla podrida* and American-Chinese call chop suey. The Indian jumble always included corn, for Roger Williams tells us that the Narragansett word also meant "boild corne whole."

Green corn and green beans were natural partners for the pot because they were planted and plucked together, so that succotash suggested spring feasts.

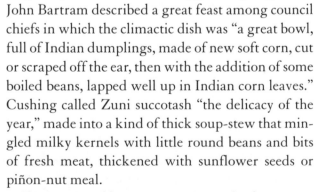

John Bartram described a great feast among council chiefs in which the climactic dish was "a great bowl, full of Indian dumplings, made of new soft corn, cut or scraped off the ear, then with the addition of some boiled beans, lapped well up in Indian corn leaves." Cushing called Zuni succotash "the delicacy of the year," made into a kind of thick soup-stew that mingled milky kernels with little round beans and bits of fresh meat, thickened with sunflower seeds or piñon-nut meal.

Since corn and beans were twin staples for reasons of nutrition as well as of taste, succotash became an important American one-dish meal, to which

colonists added salt pork when venison or other game was unavailable. By the mid-nineteenth century, salt pork was the third staple ingredient, evidenced in "How to Make Succotash" from the *Western Farmer and Gardener,* a recipe which D. J. Browne included in his *Memoir on Maize or Indian Corn* (1846). Instead of sunflower-seed thickening, the Western Farmer boiled the cobs.

> To about half a pound of salt pork, add 3 quarts of cold water, and set it to boil. Now cut off 3 quarts of green corn from the cobs; set the corn aside, and put the *cobs* to boil with the pork, as they will add much to the richness of the mixture. When the pork has boiled, say half an hour, remove the cobs and put in 1 quart of freshly-gathered, green, shelled beans; boil again for fifteen minutes; then add 3 quarts of corn and let it boil another fifteen minutes.

By the turn of the century the dish had declined into a mixture of salt pork, dried beans and dried corn for winter, seasoned with sugar and thickened with flour. Charles Murphy in *American Indian Corn* (1917), commented without irony: "This old Indian dish was probably served originally without the seasoning or thickening that is used by modern cooks." Fortunately, some of our own modern cooks have resuscitated the dish by returning to fresh ingredients, seasoned with interesting new possibilities like caraway seeds and yogurt.

Wherever corn grows around the world, each locale has added its own particularized fragments to the pot, so that in West Africa we find an "okra-corn mix-up" seasoned with hot Guinea peppers, in East Africa a "coconut corn curry" flavored with poppyseeds and peanuts. A French succotash, sampled in Giverny, mixed sweet corn with grated onion and—hold on to your hats—caviar. A Peruvian one mixed corn with onions and red chilies, thickened with evaporated milk and garnished with hard-cooked eggs. As for sweet kernels raw, I have found them sprinkled over everything from broiled oysters to chicken breasts; I have found them folded into whipped cream as a garnish for fish, layered into salads from lentils to seafood, mixed into crunchy salsas of chilies and tomatillos or into creamy sauces of mustard and mayonnaise. Unexpectedly I even found them, on a hot summer's day in Umbria, mixed into angel-hair pasta in a cream sauce flavored with lemon rind.

The pride of Indian green-corn cooking, however, was neither whole sweet kernels nor whole cobs, but pounded kernels and milked cobs: Indian milk came not from cows or sheep, but from corn. Indians used mussel or oyster shells, or "the half of a deer's jaw with the articular portion or ramus broken off," as Waugh detailed it, to scrape the milky kernels from the cob before they

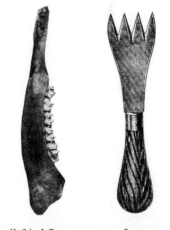

(left) A Seneca scraper for green corn fashioned from the jawbone of a deer. New York State Museum, Albany
(right) A nineteenth-century corn scraper fashioned from iron and wood. The Bettmann Archive

pounded them into liquid. The Senecan name for a deer-jaw scraper of this sort was "green corn," and using it a Senecan housewife would say, "I am letting the deer chew the corn first for me."

"Ripening green corn, with the grain still soft, was shelled off the cob with the tip of the thumb or with the thumbnail, so as not to break open the kernels," Buffalo Bird Woman said. They then pounded the kernels in a mortar to make such delicacies as *naktsi',* or "buried-in-the-ashes-and-baked corn bread." They would enclose the pulp an inch or two thick in green husks "overlapping like shingles," then bake the loaf in the ashes. For this bread, no fat or seasoning was added, she said, "the pounded green corn pulp was all that entered into it."

The Seneca called a similar bread "green corn leaf bread," Chief Gibson said, in which the corn might be pounded with beans, berries, apples, chestnuts or venison and enclosed in an "envelope" of corn leaves tied with basswood bark. The Cherokee called it "dogheads," or *di-ga-nu-li.* Two recipes for it appeared as late as 1933 in the brief *Indian Cook Book* put out by the Indian Women's Club of Tulsa, Oklahoma. Despite echoes of "hush puppies," the name "dogheads" seems to come from the squared shape of bread wrapped like tamales in green husks. The Zuni made a similar green-corn dish, mixing the pulp with pounded green squash and sunflower seeds, then boiling the mixture until "thick and gelatinous like curdled milk." However unappetizing Cushing's description, he declared that "no green-corn cookery of civilization can boast anything more delicious."

Such were the native origins of colonial creamed corn and green-corn pudding, which *The Genesee Farmer* of 1838 acknowledged were "derived from the tawny natives among whom our ancestors squatted down two hundred years ago." To enrich their green-corn "milk" from pounded corn, colonists added cow's milk, just as Indians had added "hickory cream" from pounded nuts. ("It is as sweet and rich as fresh cream," William Bartram had reported, "and is an ingredient in most of their cookery, especially homony and corn cakes.") For proper milking of the cob, instructions were exacting, as in the *The Buckeye Cookbook* (1883): "Cut with a sharp knife through the center of every row of grains, and cut off the outer edge; then with the back of the blade push out the yellow eye [the germ], with the rich, creamy center of the grain, leaving the hull on the cob." For "stewed corn" the *Buckeye* author added to a quart of this corn "milk" a cup of rich cow's milk, seasoned with salt, pepper and butter, and then steamed in a covered tin pail inside a kettle one-third full of boiling water.

Housewives soon found that grating corn was much quicker than slicing and squeezing, and corn graters became a standard kitchen item, for a grater could be made simply by pounding nails through a board in even rows. A friend from

Norfolk, Connecticut, John Barstow, tells me that his family has been grating corn this way for three generations, replacing graters as needed in high corn season. They found that plunging the cobs first into boiling water and then into cold water helps to set the milk and make the kernels easier to grate.

For settlers accustomed to the puddings, custards and thick sauces created by their wheat and dairy products, corn pulp had the advantage of being both thickener and liquid at once, with the added kicker that it was naturally sweet. Sophisticated urbanites like Eliza Leslie in 1837 turned the basic green-corn pudding into a rich baked custard, adding to twelve grated ears of corn a quart of rich milk, a quarter-pound fresh butter with sugar and eggs, and served with a sauce of whipped butter, sugar and nutmeg. As the century proceeded, the pudding was converted into "a veritable soufflé and incomparable," as Marion Harland said in 1903, but by the 1920s canned creamed corn had replaced freshly grated in Fannie Farmer's *Boston Cooking-School Cook Book,* and her soufflé was thickened with flour. Even Escoffier, in his 1934 *Ma Cuisine,* made corn soufflé with a can of creamed corn, noting, "If fresh corn is not on hand, excellent canned or frozen kinds are to be found on the market."

Southerners had their own ways with creamed corn. What they called fried corn was simply "young, tender green corn" that is "milked" from the cob, as *The Picayune's Creole Cook Book* (1901) said, and mixed Creole-style with browned minced onions or country-style with ham fat or butter and cooked in a skillet until thickened. Sarah Rutledge in *The Carolina Housewife* (1847) showed how readily colonists turned Indian green-corn "breads" into English "pies." One of her favorites was "green-corn pie with shrimp," in which she lined a baking dish with a batter of corn pureed with eggs and tomato pulp, then filled it with shrimp—or stewed chicken, veal, ham "or whatever you choose to make your pie of"—and topped it with another layer of batter.

Southerners were especially fond of turning green corn and eggs into a batter to make fritters, frequently called "corn oysters" because of their shape. "Grate the corn while green and tender," Sarah Rutledge advised, before adding egg yolks and whites beaten separately, thickened slightly with butter and flour, seasoned well and shaped into "oysters" with a spoon to fry in hot butter. New Englanders, on the other hand, chopped real oysters into their batter, mixing them with pureed kernels in "Pagataw pancakes." Texans didn't bother cutting off the kernels. They simply battered the cob whole and deep-fried it like chicken-fried steak.

There were dozens of variations on the fritter theme of battered corn, sometimes sweetened for dessert and sometimes peppered as a savory accompaniment to meat. Their continuing popularity inspired Irma Rombauer in her

"I remember my mother's fried corn. She cut it off the cob real thin, and she'd put her some butter in one of those old iron skillets and put the corn in that hot butter and just stir it till it thickened. Lots of times she'd put it in the oven and it would brown on the top and the bottom. There's nobody could cook it like she did."
—INEZ TAYLOR, quoted in *The Foxfire Book of Appalachian Cookery* (1984)

1943 *Joy of Cooking* to include an account written by a man whose father had told his children "of a fritter tree he was going to plant on the banks of a small lake filled with molasses, maple syrup or honey, to be located in our back yard. When one of us children felt the urge for the most delectable repast, all we had to do was to shake the tree, the fritters would drop into the lake and we could fish them out and eat fritters to our hearts' content." Today corn fritters fall from fritter trees in most countries of the world, flavored with cumin and coconut in India to make *makai nu shaak,* with minced leeks and carrots in Korea to make *kwang-ju,* and with chilies and ground shrimp in Indonesia to make *perkedel djagung.*

Corn soups and chowders also exploit the double blessing of green corn as both vegetable and thickener. The simplest green-corn soup was furnished by the Westminster Presbyterian Church ladies of Minneapolis in *Valuable Recipes* (1877): "Two quarts of milk, ten ears of corn scraped down, season highly." Today the same simple formula of liquid, scraped corn and seasoning appears in the sophisticated bowls of Alice Waters's Chez Panisse as "corn soup with garlic butter," or of Stephan Pyles's Routh Street Cafe as "grilled corn soup with ancho chile and cilantro creams." As for chowders, corn appears in an astonishing number of them, including seafood and shellfish chowders of New England and chile and tomato chowders of the Southwest.

The classic continuum in green-corn cookery was what was called inter-changeably creamed corn and stewed corn, and here the white man reversed Indian tradition. Since Midwesterners canned whole-kernel and creamed corn as soon as they were farmed, cookbooks extolled the can. In recommending "stewed corn" for the month of October in her *Dinner Year-Book* (1878), Marion Harland advised, "Green corn, even in city markets is both indifferent and dear at this season. We do better, therefore, to fall back upon the invaluable canned vegetables that have made American housewives almost independent of changing seasons." Not independent, however, of rituals more appropriate to fine wines than canned corn: "Open a can of corn one hour before it is to be cooked," Harland said, even though she proceeded to cook the contents, in hot water to cover, for thirty minutes before adding milk, butter and flour and cooking fifteen minutes more.

Although French exponents like Ranhofer and Escoffier enriched with béchamel sauce their "corn stewed with cream," their *"crême de maïs, dit Washington,"* their "cream of green corn à la Hermann" (fancified with chicken forcemeat, egg yolk and butter) and their "cream of green corn à la Mendocino (with crawfish butter and shrimps), they did not eschew the can. Nor did Irma

Corn canners in New England scrape raw kernels from ears of green corn picked on the site. The Bettmann Archive

Rombauer, who used canned and fresh corn interchangeably in *Joy of Cooking*, giving preference to the No. 2 can. The craft of making a fresh green-corn pudding "a luscious dish" is not lost but made difficult, she said, "because corn differs with the season." Picked early, what the Indians called early-ripe, the corn may be so watery as to require flour; picked late, what the Indians called late-ripe, additional cream may be needed. When corn is just right it should look, after grating, "like thick curdled cream." Buffalo Bird Woman herself could not have been more precise.

Contemporary logo of John Cope, driers of sweet corn in Rheems, Pennsylvania.

Corn Dried, Pickled and Parched

CANNED CORN must have been a boon to prairie households longing for the sweetness of summer in mid-December. Indians had assuaged this longing by the art of drying, an art that lingered into the twentieth century but finally succumbed to the can. Today, sweet corn is dried in quantity only in the Southwest and in Pennsylvania Dutch country. In Rheems, Pennsylvania, four generations of the Cope family have been drying corn, first over wood-burning stoves and now in high-tech dehydrators, but John Cope's Food Products is the only supplier of any size left in the States. And that's a pity, for drying intensifies corn's sweetness and lends it a delicious caramel taste.

"Every Hidatsa family put up a store of dried green corn for winter," Buffalo Bird Woman said, and the first step was to pick the corn when the husks were a particular shade of dark green. "Sometimes I even broke open the husks to see if the ear was just right; but this was seldom, as I could tell very well by the color and other signs I have described. . . . Green corn for drying was always plucked in the evening, just before sunset; and the newly plucked ears were let lie in the pile all night, in the open air." In the morning she brought them to the lodge, where kettles of water boiled over the coals of the fire. After husking the ears—"a pretty sight; some of them were big, fine ones, and all had plump, shiny kernels"—she dropped them into the kettles and, when the corn was half cooked, lifted the ears onto the green husks "with a mountain sheep horn spoon" and then laid them in rows on the drying stage to dry overnight.

The second morning, she laid a skin tent cover on the floor of the lodge and began to shell the corn. "I had a small, pointed stick; and this I ran, point forward, down between two rows of kernels, thus loosening the grains." She shelled the rows one at a time with her thumb or loosened them with the stick to "shell them off with smart, quick strokes of a mussel shell held in my right hand." The kernels were spread on the drying stage outside, covered at night with old tent skins, and left about four days until they were fully dried. Finally she winnowed out the chaff and put the kernels in sacks for the winter.

The Hidatsa word for dried corn meant "treated-by-fire-but-not-cooked." The method of half cooking the corn by boiling or roasting was practiced everywhere; Arikara and Huron women also roasted their green ears before a fire, or in sand heated by fire, as Gabriel Sagard noted in *Le Grand Voyage du Pays des Hurons* (1632). They shelled and dried the kernels on bark sheets, then stored the corn with a quarter-portion of dried beans, ready to boil in the caldron with a little fresh or dried fish. As open fires evolved into kitchen stoves, tribes roasted and dried their corn indoors. Shawnee tradition held as late as 1932, when Roberta Lawson in *The Indian Cookbook* explained how she dried a pan of scraped kernels in a slow oven and baked them for an hour before crumbling the mass on a "drying board in the sun" to complete the drying.

The best corn for drying was late-ripe sweet corn, rather than early-ripe. Juanita Tiger Kavena, in *Hopi Cookery* (1980), specified that "the later crop" of sweet corn is the one to bake and dry on the cobs for winter use. Baking helps the corn retain its nitrogen, potassium and minerals, she claimed, while storing the whole cob helps protect it from insects. That settlers struggled to learn the right stages of early- and late-ripe is clear from Peter Kalm's journal of November 4, 1749, while he was traveling in New York state: "From Mrs. Vischer with whom I had lodgings, I learned one way of preparing corn. . . . They take the corn before it is ripe, boil it in a little water, allow it to dry in the sun and preserve it for future use. . . . The younger the corn is when picked, the better it is provided, however, that it is not too young."

In the Southwest, Spanish settlers called dried green corn *chicos.* Cleofas Jaramillo recalled how they made chicos at her family hacienda in Arroyo Hondo, New Mexico, almost a century ago: first they roasted white unhusked

Drying corn in Bismarck, Dakota Territories. Photo by D. F. Berry, State Historical Society, North Dakota

corn in the oven, then shelled and cracked the kernels on a metate and finally tossed them in a basket "to allow the air to blow away the skin." When ready to eat the corn, they would soften it and mix it with onions, garlic and red chilies fried in lard, or add it to stews with beef or venison jerky. In Peru, Spaniards developed one of the glories of criollo cooking from the dried purple corn that gives its name to the dish *mazamorra morada*. Boiled in water until the liquid is as royally purple as the corn, the corn is discarded and replaced with a variety of dried fruits, while the liquid is thickened with sweet-potato starch, sweetened with the dark sugar called *chancaca* and flavored with cinnamon, clove and lemon.

As late as 1908 drying corn was still so commonplace in American farm households that when Sidney Morse compiled his *Household Discoveries* he listed four different ways "To Dry Corn":

Cut the corn raw from the cob and dry it thoroughly in pans in an oven. This gives a finer flavor than when it is partly boiled.

Or dip green corn on the ear in boiling water, remove, and hang up the ears until dry in a room where there is a free circulation of air.

Or . . . place the ears in a colander over a kettle of steaming water, and steam a half hour or more. Split the kernels with a sharp knife, scrape out the pulp and dry it on clean tines or earthenware platters. . . .

Or shave off the kernels with a sharp knife, scrape the remaining pulp from the cobs, and lay on earthenware platters. Sprinkle ¹/₂ teacupful of sugar to each 3 quarts of corn, stir well and place in a medium hot oven for ten minutes, but do not scorch or brown it. . . .

It should be dried as quickly as possible as it deteriorates with exposure. Store in tight jars or boxes in a dry place. When required for use soak it in lukewarm water.

Morse gave equally detailed instructions for canning corn, but they are so tedious as to suggest why the commercial product was popular. Clearly both the new-fashioned canning methods and old-fashioned drying methods were practiced simultaneously for some time.

Methods of preserving other sorts of vegetables and fruit were also applied to corn. Charles Murphy in his *American Indian Corn* (1917) suggested smoking whole cobs in a tight wooden box with sulphur, as one smoked apricots to preserve their color, before immersing the cobs in a large crock of water and sealing. A more common practice was to pickle corn in layers of salt in a stone jar as one might put up cabbage to make sauerkraut. A nice recipe for pickled

At the end of Prohibition, the parched dried corn now called "Corn Nuts" was originally sold as "Brown Jug," the proper snack to go with beer.

corn, collected in *Pioneer Cookery Around Oklahoma* (1978), affords a glimpse of the pioneer life of one Annie Henthorn, born in 1864, who advised her fellow corn picklers to keep "the crock jar" in a cool place like "the back bedroom," where in winter you can "push the ice off it" to dip out corn as needed.

A curious combination of pickling and canning appears in *The Picayune's Creole Cook Book* under the heading "canned corn," or *Du Maïs en Conserve.* First boil the corn on the cob "until no milk will exude if the grains are pricked with a needle." Then cut the kernels off and pack them in cans or jars in two-inch layers of corn alternating with one-inch layers of salt. Pour melted lard over each can and heat the cans to 80 to 100 degrees in a bain-marie, hermetically sealed.

Everywhere ladies pickled corn in the vinegar-sugar preservative characteristic of the sweet-sour relishes labeled "chowchow," in which corn kernels mingled with many other vegetables. Typical is a relish found in the Official Recipe Book of the *Patriotic Food Show* held in St. Louis, Missouri, in 1918, which called for twelve ears of corn, four cups cabbage, four green bell peppers, three cups chopped onions, one cup sugar, two cups white vinegar and one cup flour, seasoned with salt, turmeric, Tabasco, celery and mustard seed, the whole boiled together.

Parched dried corn was a branch of cooking unto itself and one of the most important for the Indian because parching cooked, flavored and preserved corn simultaneously. Most Americans today know parched corn only through whole-kernel snacks like "corn nuts" or popcorn, but Indians pounded the parched kernels into a fine powder to make their all-important "journeying" bread or "traveling food." The high culinary art by which they created "a highly concentrated and nutritious substance, capable alone of sustaining life throughout extended journeys," as Frank Cushing said, as easy to transport as it was quick and easy to prepare, might give pause to those who identify high cuisine or high culture exclusively with their own time and arts.

Both early- and late-ripe corn were used, but especially favored was "the little corn of the nature of popcorn, which was the first to mature." Benjamin Franklin in explaining parched corn in his "Mayz" pamphlet was clearly describing a popcorn of this type:

An Iron Pot is fill'd with Sand, and set on the Fire till the sand is very hot. Two or three Pounds of the Grain are then thrown in and well mix'd with the Sand by stirring. Each Grain bursts and throws out a white substance of twice its bigness. The Sand is separated by a Wire Sieve, and return'd into the Pot, to be again heated and repeat the Operation with fresh grain.

That which is parch'd is pounded to a Powder in Mortars. This being sifted will keep long fit for Use. An Indian will travel far, and subsist long on a small Bag of it, taking only 6 or 8 Ounces of it per day, mix'd with water."

This is the meal the Narragansetts called *nokehick,* of which Roger Williams had personal experience denied to the urban and urbane Franklin:

Nokehick: Parch'd meal, which is a readie very wholesome food, which they eate with a little water, hot or cold; I have travelled with neere 200 of them at once, neere 100 miles through the woods, every man carrying a *little Basket* of this at his *back,* and sometimes in a hollow *Leather Girdle* about his middle, sufficient for a man for three or four daies.

With this readie provision, and their *Bows* and *Arrowes,* are they ready for *War,* and *travell* at an *houres* warning. With a *spoonfull* of this *meale* and a *spoonfull* of water from the *Brooke,* have I made a good dinner and supper.

The Seneca called it "burnt corn" and the Natchez "scorched corn." Antoine Le Page Du Pratz in his 1758 *Histoire de la Louisiane* reported in detail how the grain was ground and then "scorched in a dish made expressly for the purpose," where it was mixed with ashes and shaken until it attained "the red color which is proper." Once the ashes were removed, it was pounded in a mortar with the ashes of dried beans until reduced to a coarse meal. The meal was then crushed finer and dried in the sun. To help preserve it, they exposed the meal to the sun from time to time, and when they ate it, they mixed it with twice the amount of water.

Parching corn in a vessel made for the purpose was the earliest form of pot cooking in the Americas. Pre-Inca Peruvians devised a pot with a small opening on one side and a handle on the other to shake over the fire so that the kernels would pop but not pop out. When iron replaced pottery, the Zuni used a black shallow roaster, according to Cushing, which they filled with dry sand and heated over the fire. They stirred corn kernels in with a bundle of hardwood sprigs until "a judicious shaking of the toasting vessel brought all the kernels to the top, whence they were easily separated from the sand." The hot sand

"Americans have never taken a proper pride in this great native cereal Indian corn. . . . I can personally speak of the sustaining power of Indian corn, for in the early days of our war of the rebellion I was a prisoner of war in Richmond, being captured at the battle of Bull Run. I was fortunate enough to be one of the first three officers who escaped from that prison. . . . We were eleven days reaching the Potomac River, and during all that long and dreary tramp through the woods and swamps of Virginia, subject to intense excitement, we had nothing to eat but raw corn, gathered at long intervals, which fortified us in our race for liberty."

—CHARLES MURPHY,
American Indian Corn (1917)

both cooked the kernels evenly and prevented them from popping out. (The use of such vessels was not limited to the Americas. A modern anthropologist in Upper Burma found Chin tribes there in the 1940s parching corn in a *pei-bung,* "the traditional grain-roasting pot, shaped rather like a beer pot but with a hole in one side." From this they made a type of "journeying corn" from grain that had been dried and soaked, then roasted and pounded with salt or honey to carry on hunting parties.)

While parching in itself imparted a deliciously sweet and nutty flavor, often other seasonings were added. Sometimes the Zuni parched their corn in heated salt rather than sand, Cushing said, and sometimes they flavored the ground meal with pounded and fermented licorice root to make a sweet gruel that was "ever the favorite at the Zuni evening feast." The Iroquois similarly flavored their parched meal with maple sugar or dried cherries, and we know that the Inca flavored their journeying corn with pounded dried vegetables and hot peppers. So tasty was journeying corn that J.G.E. Heckewelder, reporting in 1822 the *History, manners, and customs of the Indian nations which formerly inhabited Pennsylvania and the neighbouring states,* issued a warning: "Persons who are unacquainted with this diet ought to be careful not to take too much at a time, and not to suffer themselves to be tempted too far by its flavor; more than one or two spoonfuls at most at any one time or at one meal is dangerous; for it is apt to swell in the stomach or bowels, as when heated over a fire."

Akin to parched corn was the smoked corn Dumont de Montigny found among the Natchez of Louisiana in 1753. But the Natchez favorite was dried green corn that was parched and pounded to make *farine froide,* as Montigny called it, cold meal. The Indians called it *boota copassa* and its purpose was clear from the names they gave their lunar months: the third moon (May) was "Little Corn," the seventh moon (August) "Great Corn" and the eleventh moon (January) "Cold Meal."

Dehydrated powdered corn was for the Indians both food and drink. *"Sagamite"* was the word the Iroquois used, recorded by a French Jesuit father in 1638–39: "As for drinks, they do not know what these are—the sagamite serving as meat and drink." *"Pinole"* was the Aztec word as recorded by Bishop Diego de Landa in 1566: "They also toast the maize and then grind and mix it with water into a very refreshing drink, putting into it a little Indian pepper or cacao." Since they weren't accustomed to drinking water straight, he noted, they added water to maize as it was being ground, cooked and flavored in various ways during the day, and so had food and drink at once.

Such drinks are still common today throughout Central and South America and in our own Southwest, generally under the names *pinole* and *atole.* Cleofas

Jaramillo gave a typical recipe for *pinole,* saying it tasted something like malted milk: "Toast to golden brown a cup of *maiz concho,* dry sweet corn. Grind into fine powder. Dissolve in fresh milk, sweeten with maple sugar, and mix." Phyllis Hughes, in her *Pueblo Indian Cookbook* (1977), mixed toasted and ground blue or white corn with cinnamon and sugar in hot milk. Richard and Wendy Condon, in *!Ole Mole!* (1988), recorded an exotic variant made with toasted cocoa, dark-brown sugar and dried jasmine flowers, all beaten into cold water until foamy, the foam then scooped off and mixed with hot corn *atole.* In the Southwest, *atole* more often than not refers to toasted and finely ground blue-corn meal, whether it is dissolved in water to make a mush or a beverage. Because it is easily digestible, it has remained a favored nourishment for invalids, and was once prescribed as a "very light and nutritious" drink for the sick by a New Englander, Maria Parloa, who called it "corn tea."

ASH COOKING

Hominy

Hom-in-y man, hom-in-y man,
Com-in' around on time!
Hom-in-y man, hom-in-y man,
Com-in down the line!
Two quarts for fif-teen cents,
One quart for a dime!
Hominy! Beautiful hominy!

EARLY IN THE CENTURY, the hominy man sang his cantos of mutability throughout the land. From the days of his youth in Portland, Oregon, James Beard remembered how "the hominy man passed through our neighborhood in his little horse-drawn cart twice a week," selling horseradish as well as hominy. Near Portland, Maine, Arnold Weeks remembered the hominy man in "his horse-drawn wagon driving through Town selling his hulled corn to the housewives by the quart." In New Orleans, the *Picayune* remembered him as the "Grits man," who was "as common a figure in the streets of the old French quarter as the 'ring man,' the 'bottle man,' or the 'Cala woman.'" He had a great tin horn, nearly three feet long, the *Picayune* recounted, at which sound housekeepers rushed to their doors to bargain for their dainty breakfast cereal. But even in 1901 the Grits man, like the Cala woman, was "fast becoming a memory of other days."

Certainly few Americans today under the age of thirty have any memory of hominy, either in the form of Southern grits or Southwestern *posole* or in the canned form that was a staple of the Depression 1930s but is now a supermarket rarity. The kernels of the hominy we bought were always white, about the size of chickpeas but slightly softer, packed in water turned chalky from starch. We heated them in their liquid with butter and salt and served them instead of rice or potatoes or canned creamed corn. To a family of Fletcherizers they were a boon. They were firm but tender and a snap to chew and swallow since the kernels had no skins. In those days skins were thought to offend delicate constitutions.

When corn was the year-round staple for the Indians, no corn was referred to so often as hominy, nor so confusingly. Each Indian tribe called it by a different name, or by several names: what was *rockahomonie* and *sagamite* to the

A farm family and hired hands in Illinois fill up on a bowl of hominy or grits. Photo by Grant Heilman, Agricultural Photography

Algonquian was *atole* to the Mexica, *sofki* to the Creek, *tanlubo* and *tafala* to the Choctaw. English colonists muddled words and meanings when they lumped under the single word "hominy" any number of preparations made from the fully mature kernels of any late-ripe corns but principally of the thick-skinned flints that Northern tribes called "hommony corn." ("Iroquois Hominy Corn" was eight-rowed, fourteen inches long by $1\frac{1}{2}$ inches round, and creamy white in color.) Perversely, French colonists preferred the word "sagamite," which Louisiana Creoles transmuted into *la saccamité,* so beloved in Creole households that grandmothers would say to the young and restless, "Tempi, pour toi! La Saccamité te ram…nera!"—"Never mind! Hominy will bring you back!"

Colonists of all languages struggled mightily to translate the Indian dishes made with this corn into the thick wheat gruels, pottages or puddings they called frumenty, loblolly and hasty pudding. What wheat-conditioned colonists failed to see was that how the corn was hulled was as important as how it was cooked. Indians distinguished between two kinds of hulled corn: one was made of kernels broken into coarse pieces in a mortar, then cleared of skins by winnowing; the other was cleared of skins by boiling the kernels in lye. Traveling in Virginia in 1849, William Strachey detailed the first process of winnowing and described the resulting pottage: "The growtes and broken pieces of the corne remayning, they likewise preserve, and by fannying away the branne or huskes in a platter or in the wynd, they lett boyle in an earthen pott three or four howres, and thereof make a straung thick pottage." The method was unchanged a half century later when the anthropologist Alanson Skinner took "Notes on the Florida Seminole" (1913):

> The meal [once taken from the mortar] is first sifted through an open-mesh basket and then winnowed by being tossed into the air, the breeze carrying away the chaff, while the heavier, edible portion of the corn falls back into the flat receiving basket. In this condition the meal is mixed with water and boiled to make sofki.

The second method was what settlers eventually called lye hominy, in which the hull was loosened and removed by the chemical action of wood ash or some other alkali. Anthropologists were no wiser than colonists in assuming that the ashes were there principally for flavoring or for softening the hulls to make them easier to remove. "The ripe corn is usually hulled for cookery purposes," Waugh wrote of Iroquois hominy in explaining the function of lye. "The first step in hulling is to add sifted hardwood ashes to a pot of water in the proportion of about one double handful to three quarts of water." Once the lye is dissolved by boiling and is strong enough "to bite the tongue when tasted," the corn is boiled until it swells and the skin can be slipped off when pressed between the fingers. The corn is then drained in a washing basket and washed in several tubs of water or under a running stream until the hulls are all removed, "a process which is assisted by friction against the twilled sides of the basket and by rubbing with the hands."

*"Ginny cracked corn and
I don't care
Ginny cracked corn and I
don't care
Ginny cracked corn and I
don't care
My master's gone away."*
—American folk song
from the South

Eastern settlers hulled corn by both methods after cracking and pounding their corn in the hollowed log mortars and wooden pestles they called interchangeably "hominy blocks" and "samp mills." But throughout the nineteenth century, American cooks north and south labored valiantly, and hopelessly, to squeeze the rich nomenclature of native corn dishes into the narrow confines of hominy, samp and—worst of all—grits. Anglo-Saxon *grytt* for bran and *greot* for ground had melded in "grist," which colonists applied generically to dried, ground and hulled grain. The New Orleans *Picayune* only confused matters when it called hominy "the older sister of grits," since it was the Indians who taught Creoles to thresh the hulls from dried yellow corn until the

"My squaws have fine mat, big wigwam, soft samp."

—JOHN GREENLEAF WHITTIER, *Passaconaway* (1866)

"Grits is grits. There's not a whole lot of range to them."

—ROY BLOUNT, JR.

grains were white. Grits might be yellow if the hull was left on, the *Picayune* specified, but "the daintier preparation" was white with the hull off. Plain hulled corn was "big hominy"; grits ground superfine were "small hominy," "without which no breakfast in Louisiana is considered complete." Lye hominy, on the other hand, was identical with samp as "an old-fashioned Creole way of preparing hulled corn," that is, with the lye from wood ashes. The virtue of lye hominy, the *Picayune* claimed, was that the alkali reduced the oil in the corn and therefore made samp in hot Louisiana summers "a splendid summer food."

In the North, samp (from the Narragansett *nasaump,* or unparched corn, beaten and boiled) came to be identified with coarsely ground corn however it was hulled. Thomas Hazard, already nostalgic in the 1870s for the hasty puddings and pottages of his Rhode Island childhood, wrote lovingly of "the samp—coarse hominy pounded in a mortar—and the great and little hominy, all Indian dishes fit to be set before princes and gods." And best of all, the hulled corn of old—"None of your modern tasteless western corn, hulled with potash, but the real, genuine ambrosia, hulled in the nice sweet lye made from fresh hard oak and maplewood ashes."

Grits for many reasons became strongly identified, as they are today, with the South. When Eliza Leslie of Philadelphia confronted corn terms in her *New Receipts for Cooking* (c. 1854), she defined samp as skinned corn pounded fine, hominy as "perfectly white" corn skinned with lye, and Carolina grits as "small-grained hominy," sometimes called "pearl hominy." This apparently was the white grits ground superfine that the *Picayune* called small hominy and that the rest of the country began to call hominy grits—everywhere but in Charleston, South Carolina, that is, where the phrase *hominy* grits can still provoke otherwise sweet-mouthed ladies to profanity. There grits are grits, or as a recent cookbook title has it, *Grits R Us.*

In the backwoods South, in the bayou Deltas, in the hills of Appalachia, in the garden patches of former slaves, the rural poor continued to grow and cook corn in Indian ways. "Transforming dried corn into hominy seemed a most miraculous process" to Edna Lewis, growing up in Freetown, Virginia, watching her Aunt Jennie Hailstalk make hominy in the big iron pot on the back of the cookstove. "In the old days two-thirds of the people were raised on hominy," Tommie Bass remembers of Appalachian Alabama. The best hominy was made with Hickory King corn and hickory ashes. "The hominy was actually healthy for you because lye," Tommie said, "would clean your liver off, and your stomach." You had to be careful, however, with your wood ash. "Mother wouldn't let Daddy around the fireplace when she was fixing to make lye, because she was afraid he would spit in the fire when he was smoking!" You had also to be careful with store-bought lye. "Folks began to use Red Devil lye instead of ash. Once the Red Devil people told you how to make hominy, but not now. The Red Devil lye is a poison. It will kill you right dead, if you take too much."

A favorite Southern dish was hog and hominy, a colonized version of the universal Indian dish described by William Biggs when he was captured by the Kickapoos in 1788: adopted by the tribe, Biggs was given an Indian bride who made a wedding dish of *"hominy,* beat in a mortar, as white as snow, and handsome as I ever saw, and very well cooked. She fried some dried meat, pounded very fine in a mortar, in oil, and sprinkled it with sugar." Gentrified, the dish became New Orleans' grillades and grits (pounded smothered steak, fried with onion and tomato and served with grits on the side) and Charleston's grits and liver pudding, a favorite Sunday-night supper of calf's liver with grits on the side. Liver pudding is a name hung over from the days when women made scrapple of cornmeal mush and "the head, liver and feet of a hog," as Lettie Gay said in *200 Years of Charleston Cooking* (1930). Gay put grits or hominy with everything, including a delectable recipe for butter-sautéed shrimp and hominy recommended by "a charming old gentleman seventy-eight years old [who] avers that as far back as he could remember he has eaten shrimp with hominy for breakfast every morning during the shrimp season and shrimp salad for supper every Sunday night."

Outside the South, the status of hominy and grits steadily declined, except for a brief resurgence in the 1890s. Recently hog and hominy has acquired new chic in the form of pozole (or posole), a Mexican version of Indian corn and game still so popular south of the border that every region has its own specialty. In Guerrero, from Acapulco through Taxco, Thursday is "green *pozole* day," Rick and Deann Bayless have told us in *Authentic Mexican* (1987). They define pozole as "half-cooked hominy" made from dried white field corn, boiled in slaked lime, washed and then "deflowered" by picking out the small, hard, pointed germ at the bottom of each kernel so that the kernel will splay out, or "flower," as it cooks. Green pozole is green from a sauce of pumpkin seeds, tomatillos, green chilies and herbs. Pozole Guadalajara-style is one familiar to our own Southwest, made with hominy, pork and chicken, flavored with garlic and ancho chilies and garnished with salsa and

Advertisement for State Fair. Photo by Holmboe Studio, State Historical Society, Bismarck, North Dakota

cheese. While ideally this dish is as hearty as a French *pot-au-feu,* I have had many a pozole best described by Herb Walker's "Indian Rock Soup," which calls for hominy plus vegetables and three or four smooth clean rocks the size of potatoes to be boiled in a kettle, the rocks later washed and saved for future use.

One Indian hominy use that has almost completely disappeared is a baked hominy bread. Curiously, this is the one corn dish of which Mrs. Frances Trollope approved: she wrote that hominy flour (by which she meant white hulled corn finely ground) "mixed in the proportion of one-third, with fine wheat, makes by far the best bread I ever tasted." Southern recipes often mixed wheat and rice flours with boiled hominy and eggs to make a "custard-bread" they called "owendaw." In *The Carolina Housewife,* Sarah Rutledge mixed "two teacups of hot hommony" with butter or lard, eggs, milk and cornmeal; when cooked, she said, it looked like "a baked batter pudding" and tasted like a delicate custard. A century later the recipe resurfaced in the Junior League's *Charleston Receipts* (1950) as "Mrs. Ralph Izard's Awendaw," but during the interval many mixtures of hominy and grits with other corn and wheat meals appeared in such works as Célestine Eustis's *Fifty Valuable and Delicious Recipes Made with Corn Meal for 50 Cents* (1917)—"Pour les Pauvres." The ancient ancestry of Eustis's recipes might suggest that Indian palates were no less discriminating than the palates of the poor.

Nixtamal

H OWEVER COMPLEX the hominy cooking of the North, it was rough country cooking compared to the cuisine of Mexico that reached its apex in Moctezuma's court. The very name Moctezuma means "elite Aztec food," and the lords of Moctezuma, whatever else they did, ate royally. If sauce was the root of France's royal cuisine, bread was the root of the Aztec's, the twice-cooked bread of myriad shapes and kinds made from the highly processed corn called *nixtamal.* In Nahuatl, the language of the Aztec, *nextamalli* meant tamales of maize softened in wood ashes and *tenextamalli* meant tamales of maize softened in lime. Of both kinds there was a plenitude that put the northern world of hominy, samp and grits to shame.

Ordinary folk survived frugally on a diet of maize gruel, with the plainest of tortillas and tamales mixed with chili and beans, but the noble and rich feasted with an extravagance that the Sun King at Versailles might have envied. Every day, Bernardino de Sahagún wrote in his *History,* the majordomo set out for his king two thousand dishes, and when the king had eaten, the food was divided among the lords and then the various ranks of ambassadors, princes, high priests, warriors, courtiers, artisans and multiple hangers-on. That every meal was a feast was confirmed by Bernal Díaz del Castillo in *The True History of the Conquest of Mexico.* What with the "cooked fowls, turkeys, pheasant, native partridges, quail, tame and wild ducks, venison, wild boar, reed birds, pigeons, hares and rabbits, and many sorts of birds," Díaz wrote, what with the fruits of all kinds and the two thousand jugs of frothed-up cacao, and what with the numbers of servants and bread makers and cacao makers, Moctezuma's expenses, Díaz calculated, "must have been very great."

To illustrate the quality of the king's personal service, Díaz wrote,

> while Moctezuma was at table . . . there were waiting on him two other graceful women to bring him tortillas, kneaded with eggs and other sustaining ingredients, and these tortillas were very white, and they were brought on plates covered with clean napkins, and they also brought him another kind of bread, like long balls kneaded with other kinds of sustaining food, and 'pan pachol' for so they call it in this country, which is a sort of wafer.

They also placed before him three gilded tubes of *liquidambar* mixed with the herbs they called *tabaco,* and after the music and dancing, he took a brief smoke and fell asleep.

In the midst of this dazzlement, Díaz mentioned rumors that Moctezuma was fond of eating "the flesh of young boys," but the chronicler assured us that once Cortez censured the practice, Moctezuma readily gave it up since he had so much else to eat. The Aztec were not hungry for flesh but for maize, for they regarded everything other than maize, as Sophie Coe explained in her article "Aztec Cuisine" (1985) as a sauce or an auxiliary to maize. The Aztec were able to construct an entire food chain on maize because they processed it with ashes or lime and thereby compensated for the lack of game or domesticated animals more abundant to the north and south. As Sophie Coe showed, the high art to which the Aztec developed ash or lye cookery, and its nutritional significance, should disarm any who claim that human sacrifice was the means by which "the protein-starved Aztec higher classes got their minimum daily requirement." The assumption that the lords of Moctezuma were protein-starved because they lived chiefly on corn restates the earliest colonial prejudices against Indian grain.

One need but listen to the music of Sahagún when he lists what the Tortilla Seller does with tamales in the marketplace:

[He sells] salted wide tamales, pointed tamales, white tamales, fast foods, roll-shaped tamales, tamales with beans forming a seashell on top, [with] grains of maize thrown in; crumbled, pounded tamales; spotted tamales, white fruit tamales, red fruit tamales, turkey egg tamales; turkey eggs with grains of maize; tamales of tender maize, tamales of green maize, adobe-shaped tamales, braised ones; unleavened tamales, honey tamales, beeswax tamales, tamales with grains of maize, gourd tamales, crumbled tamales, maize flower tamales.

Quite distinct from tamales, and even more varied, were the little cakes called *tlaxcalli*, or, as the Spaniards called them, tortillas.

All this baroque splendor went for naught to those convinced of the cultural barbarism of the Indian. That attitude prevented the true gift of the Aztec, the akaline processing of corn, from being understood. Only in the last three decades has modern science discovered its biochemical function, and only recently have we come to value a process described by Francisco Hernández as early as 1651, when he reported on the uses of plants found in Nueva España. *Atolli,* he said, was made by combining eight parts water with six parts maize, plus lime, cooked together until soft, the maize then ground and cooked until thick. In the language of biochemistry, the addition of slaked lime, or calcium hydroxide, altered radically the protein potential of corn. Nonetheless, the bad name corn had with the first colonists was extended in the eighteenth century in Europe and elsewhere when corn became increasingly the fodder of the poor and an apparent source of disease. Peasants who lived on corn throughout the winter came down with "corn sickness," as it was called, until an Italian in 1771 named it the disease of "rough skin," or pellagra.

By the end of the nineteenth century, Egypt and other African lands were suffering this sickness in epidemic proportions, but it was little reported in the United States until an epidemic broke out in 1906 in a black insane asylum in Alabama. "The characteristic symptoms are very raw rashes and skin sores, sore mouths, sore joints and muscles, accompanied by dizziness, nervousness, and not infrequently, insanity," C. C. and S. M. Furnas wrote in *Man, Bread and Destiny* (1937). In 1915 the U.S. National Institute of Health appointed Dr. Joseph Goldberger to investigate the sickness that had a name but no proven cause. For a century it had been medical opinion that corn contaminated with

An Aztec education manual lists the tasks a father should teach his son, and a mother her daughter. The age of the child and difficulty of the task are graded by the number of tortillas, from half a tortilla for a child of three to six years, to two tortillas for a child over ten (continued on opposite page).

ergotic rot or a similar plant disease was the probable cause of pellagra. Then once Louis Pasteur's discovery of the infectious nature of bacteria took hold, scientists looked for the cause of pellagra in contagion from animals such as sheep. Goldberger tested the theory of an infectious cause by scratching his skin with pus from pellagra sores. No results. Finally he experimented with the diet of eleven prisoners at the Rankin Prison Farm of the Mississippi State Penitentiary. He fed six on cornbread, grits and sow-back. To the diets of five, he added milk, butter, lean meat and eggs. None of the five got pellagra, but the other six did. Later he experimented with dogs and found that "dog pellagra" could be prevented with yeast extract and liver.

Perhaps because the discovery of vitamins was as recent as 1911, or because the belief that man could live on corn and salt pork alone was as old as the slave trade, Goldberger failed to convince fellow scientists that pellagra was caused by a deficient diet. Even long after Goldberger's death in 1929, champions like the Furnases of the new science of nutrition had to shout to be heard: "There is no doubt that an adequate diet is a sure-fire preventive. Good food—no pellagra; Goldberger proved it." Fortunately, Goldberger had proved it to the American Red Cross, who distributed yeast to Southern sharecroppers during the Depression and encouraged them to grow vegetables. By 1933 pellagra deaths had dropped by a third.

While early nutritionists were concerned with "digestibility" and "dyspepsia," nutritionists now began to speak of "biological value" and "protein balance." They were discovering that proteins in our bodies were rebuilt from proteins in our foods, but that plant proteins were incomplete. Ranking the biologic or protein value of cereals in descending order of merit, the Furnases put wheat first, then barley, rye, rice, corn and oats. Conclusion? "Corn-eating peoples are definitely more susceptible to [pellagra] than those who do not have access to this gift of the Aztecs." They still could not explain why the Aztecs themselves, and other corn peoples, did not suffer from pellagra.

The proteins needed in the human diet are made up of amino acids, and one of them, the acid called niacin, is "crucial to the metabolic processes of every cell in the body," as Harold McGee wrote in *On Food and Cooking* (1984), for without it "our tissues begin to degenerate." Corn lacks niacin, and while the human body can synthesize niacin from an amino acid named tryptophan, corn also lacks tryptophan; anyone living on corn needs compensatory amino acids from another source, such as beans, which happen to be rich in the three acids corn lacks—niacin, tryptophan and lysine. But Indians did not have to rely wholly on an external supplement for their corn, for the necessary amino

At bottom a girl grinding corn on a metate with a griddle (comal) in front of her is now old enough to make the two tortillas appropriate to her task. Codex Mendoza, Neg. Nos. 120209/10, 2 10321, Courtesy Department of Library Services, American Museum of Natural History

A nineteenth-century engraving of natives selling corn in the streets of Cape Coast Castle, Ghana, at a time when pellagra was common. North Wind Picture Archives

acids are not so much absent in corn as locked in and therefore unavailable as nutrients. The protein in corn is of four kinds—albumins, globulins, glutelin and zein. Adding an alkali changes the balance among these, decreasing the zein (which has the least lysine and tryptophan) and increasing the availability of these two acids in the glutelin. At the same time, alkali aids the conversion of tryptophan to niacin and thereby releases niacin for the body's use. In their study of fifty-one Indian societies in the Americas, Solomon Katz and his colleagues observed that no matter which alkali they used (lime yields calcium hydroxide, wood ash potassium hydroxide, and lye sodium hydroxide), there was nearly a "one-to-one relationship between those societies that both consume and cultivate large amounts of maize and those that use alkali treatment." The Indians who used lime in processing corn—all of them in Mesoamerica and the American Southwest—had the additional nutrient benefit of the calcium in lime.

In our Southwest the secrets of processing were inherited and transmitted by the blue-corn cuisine of the Anasazi and their descendants, the Tewa, Zuni and Hopi. Rather than first cooking corn in lime and then washing it off, the Tewa method was to mix wood ashes or finely ground lime directly into their ground meal. In this way they retained the sacred color of the blue corn. Because this corn is rich in anthocyanin dye, Katz explained, it is highly sensitive to color changes that occur with heat or with any changes in the acid content (measured by pH). The lower the pH of the corn, the pinker it turns; the higher, the bluer it remains. Anyone who has cooked with blue-corn meal knows that sometimes the meal will turn pink by the mere addition of water, or lavender, brown or gray in a hot pan, or greenish blue with the addition of baking soda. Baking soda, however, has neither the flavor nor the mineral content of the wood ash used by the Indians. "Culinary ashes," Juanita Tiger Kavena called them: Creek and Seminole favored hickory, the Navaho juniper and the Hopi the four-winged saltbush, or *chamisa,* especially when green. When burned, green chamisa has an unusually high mineral content of potassium, magnesium and sodium. The Hopi chop down chamisa bushes, which grow in clumps like sagebrush, then stack them in a pyre and fire them until they've burned to ash. Once the ashes are collected in tubs, sifted, and stored in airtight containers, they are ready to do three things at once: improve nutrition, heighten flavor and preserve the sacramental color blue.

Frank Cushing also observed that when the Zuni fermented this ash-meal, preferably by chewing the grain and then spitting it out, they produced a leavening that he called "lime-yeast": "The most prized leaven was chewed *sa'-ko-we* mixed with moderately fine meal and warm water and placed in little narrow-necked pots over or near the hearth until fermentation took place, when lime flour and a little salt were added. Thus a yeast, in nowise inferior to some of our own, was compounded." Although this yeast had the remarkable property of changing the color of the flour during cooking to a beautiful green or blue, color was secondary in Cushing's view to the yeast's remarkable power of leavening. To this yeast he attributes not only a "greater variety and nicety of cookery," but also a host of cooking appliances—a *batterie de cuisine* of yucca sieves, meal trays, bread plaques, enormous earthenware cooking pots, pygmy water boilers with round stone covers, polished baking stones, bread bowls, carved pudding sticks—and even a separate place in which to use them, "which we may without exaggeration term the kitchen."

In the Zuni kitchen, lime-yeast leavened cornbreads from the rudest to the finest. Shaped into thick cakes and set to rise, "fire loaves" (*mui-a-ti-we*) were baked over hot coals, and "ash-bread" (*lu-pan-mu'-lo-ko-na*) was buried under hot ashes. The Zuni's finest delicacy, "salty buried-bread" (*k'os-he-pa-lo-kia*), made of a sticky paste spread on husks between layers of stones, was buried in the hearth floor, sealed with mud and baked overnight. Often it was flavored with "dried flowers, licorice-root, wild honey, or more frequently than any of these, masticated and fermented meal." Made this way as "sweet buried-bread" (*tchik-k'we'-pa-lo-kia*), it was usually cooked in an earthenware mush-pot lined with husks and was "sweet like our own Indian pudding, which it exactly resembled in taste." Boiled very thick and placed between stones laid out in the cold, it resembled a much-prized if "exceedingly coarse ice-cream."

As we know from Hopi wedding breads, the Zuni were not alone in prizing saliva-fermented meal. Major Powell, exploring Hopi villages in 1875, found

(Below left): Women mixed corn with saliva to start fermentation for both beer and bread. Girolamo Benzoni, traveling in Central and South America in 1541–55, shows three steps in the making of corn liquor.
(Below right): Benzoni shows three stages of breadmaking: boiling corn with lime, grinding the husked corn to make fresh dough, patting the dough into small cakes to cook on the comal, or griddle. Courtesy Special Collections, New York Public Library

their daintiest dish to be "virgin hash." "This is made by chewing morsels of meat and bread, rolling them in the mouth into little lumps about the size of a horse-chestnut, and then tying them up in bits of corn husk" to be boiled like dumplings. He found it curious that "the tongue and palate kneading must be done by a virgin" and that anyone bent on settling an old score might do so by offering to his enemy a "virgin hash" that had been secretly "made by a lewd woman."

Many explorers had commented on the Indian practice of fermenting corn in different forms. Champlain had noted "corn rendered putrid in pools or puddles," which Waugh explained as "stinking corn," left to rot for a couple of months in stagnant water before important feasts. Sagard was notably appalled: "They also eat it roasted under the hot cinders, licking their fingers while handling these stinking ears, as though they were bits of sugar cane, notwithstanding that the taste and odor are vile, and more infectious than the filthiest gutters."

But the practice was as ancient as it was honorable. Garcilaso had observed it in Cuzco, as Sahagún had in Tenochtitlán, where the Aztec soured gruel as we sour milk for yogurt. Lime-water helped preserve *masa* and prevent it from souring, but sometimes the Indians deliberately fermented their dough until it developed "an agreeable sourness," wrote Hernández, and this they mixed with a double portion of fresh corn flour (as we would mix in a sour-dough "starter") and cooked it with salt and chili to make a bread they called *xocoatolli*.

A contemporary tortilla maker in Mexico, using a trough metate and a comal on the open fire. From *El Maíz*, Museo Nacional de Culturas Populares (1987 ed.)

We now know that in addition to its agreeable taste, fermented dough or gruel provided the same nutritional advantages as alkali, by increasing lysine and niacin through the production of yeast cells. Masticating the grain first sped fermentation just as malting does in making beer; since an enzyme in saliva (ptyalin) will digest starch and turn it into malt sugar (maltose), adding chewed corn to meal was like adding mash to a brew. Chewed corn started the enzymatic action that would not only sweeten but leaven the meal with carbon dioxide as maltose fed the yeast. Cushing was accurate in his discovery of "lime-yeast."

Such were the sophistications that made the world of Aztec breads the wonder of the New World. Tamales were more notable for their fillings, while tortillas were praised for the variety and wit of their shapes. Spanish commentators were as awestruck by their configurations as Americans today by the contents of a Paris boulangerie. Thus Francisco Hernández described tortillas:

> They make with the palms of their hands thin tortillas of medium circumference, which are immediately cooked in a *comal* placed over the coals. This is the most common and frequent way to prepare maize bread. There are those who make the tortillas three or four times larger and also thicker, they also make of the dough balls like melons, putting them to cook in a pot over the fire and at times mixing in beans; they eat this with pleasure, as they are very smooth, easily digestible and taste good. Some make these breads a palm long, and four fingers thick, mixed with beans and roast them on a *comal*. But for the important Indians they prepare tortillas of sifted maize, so thin and clean they are almost translucent and like paper, also little balls of sifted maize, which despite their thickness are quite transparent, but these things are only for the rich and for princes.

Not even the princes of imperial China could have been displeased with tortillas thin as paper or little balls translucent as dim sum. Such seventeenth-century descriptions balanced more moderate nineteenth-century ones, after the post-Columbian conquest had taken its toll. Here is John Stephens writing of a village in Guatemala near the Honduran border, in his *Incidents of Travel in Central America, Chiapas & Yucatán* (1841):

> The whole family was engaged in making tortillas. . . . At one end of the *cucinera* was an elevation, on which stood a comal or griddle, resting on three stones, with a fire blazing under it. The daughter-in-law had before her an earthen vessel containing Indian corn soaked in lime-water to remove the husk; and, placing a handful on an oblong stone curving inward, mashed it with a stone roller into a thick paste. The girls took it as it was mashed, and patting it with their hands into flat cakes, laid them on the griddle to bake. This was repeated for every meal, and a great part of the business of the women consists in making tortillas.

Even a century later, a great part of the business of the women of Mesoamerica was to make tortillas, but few do so today. The culture in which tortilla-making was held in high esteem as an art worthy of princes and potentates went the way of Louis XIV's *pièces montées*. In Mexico today the remotest village has its long line of women waiting with plastic bags to take home their daily supply from the local tortilla "factory-shop." Regional differences, however, still abound. Oaxaca, known for Mexico's finest and thinnest tortillas,

Corn kernels boiled with slaked lime, ready to have their skins removed (for nixtamal*) and then ground to make the dough (*masa*) for tortillas. This bucketful is enough to supply a Mexican family of six to eight with tortillas for a single day.* Courtesy Centro Internacional de Mejoramiento de Maíz y Trigo, Mexico City

boasts thirty different kinds. There are thick yellow ones in Guadalajara and platter-sized ones topped with garlic in Tabasco and blue and red ones in the central highlands.

To gain some insight into what the business of women must once have been in making tortillas, three times a day, every day, one can consult Diana Kennedy's fifteen-page instruction in *The Art of Mexican Cooking* (1989). Here a few paragraphs must serve: You must begin by slaking lime. In the market buy a lump of *cal* (calcium oxide), break off a piece the size of a golf ball, crush it, pour on enough cold water to make it sizzle like Alka Seltzer. When it stops, strain the liquid into your pot of dried corn and water. The water should taste just acrid enough to "grab your tongue." (You can buy slaked lime in powdered form in hardware or gardening stores, but only in formidable quantities. For two pounds of dough you'll need as little as a tablespoon of lime.)

Simmer your pot of corn about fifteen minutes and as the mixture heats, the kernel hulls will turn yellow. Let the kernels stand in the liquid overnight, then drain, rinse, and rub off the skins between your fingers so that the kernels are snowy white. Cook the kernels too long and your dough will be "tacky"; use too much lime and your tortillas will be bitter.

Now send the wet corn to your local mill to be ground, and if you don't have one, grind the corn yourself through a plate-style grain mill (*molino de maiz*), or dry it with paper towels and grind it in a food processor. Tortilla dough must be used as soon as made, so now work in water to get a very smooth dough, softer than Play-Doh but not sticky. Of course your tortilla press is ready and your griddle, a heavy black cast-iron *comal,* hot. Place one end of the griddle over a burner with medium high heat and the other over a burner with medium low heat (or on a single burner, know where the hot spot is in the center and the cooler spots around the edge).

Without proper temperatures, the tortilla will be tough and won't puff properly (the puff is from moisture evaporating). Put the pressed tortilla on the cooler part of the griddle and in fifteen or twenty seconds, after its edges have loosened, flip it over onto the hotter part of the griddle. After twenty to thirty seconds more, when the underside shows a few brown spots, flip the tortilla back and let the top puff and the bottom speckle for another fifteen to twenty seconds. Remove it and wrap it in a towel to keep it from drying out. You have now made a single tortilla.

Once you have made many tortillas, you can wrap them around almost anything—in Mexico, high-protein items that go back to pre-Hispanic days: fish eyes (*tortillas de ojos*); crisply fried maguey worms (*gusanos de maguey*); the dried and toasted egg skeins of water bugs (*moscos de pajaro*); toasted locusts doused in chili; salamanders, iguanas, rattlesnake meat; the lake algae or slime that the Aztec called *tecuitlatl* and the Spaniards "cheese of the earth." Or, instead of using tortillas as wrappers, you can layer them in casseroles and pies, or grind them up and reshape them into dumplings.

Fry them as chips and you have Fritos. Fritos are to tortillas what cornflakes are to piki, and the founding of the commercial Frito company is a comic echo of the Kelloggs' blare. In San Antonio in 1932, a man named Elmer Doolin bought a five-cent package of corn chips at a small cafe, liked what he ate and tracked down the Mexican who made them. For $100, Doolin bought the Mexican's "recipe" for *tortillos fritos* and his manufacturing equipment, an old potato ricer. Doolin handed over both to his mother, whereupon Mrs. Daisy Dean Doolin and son began to turn out ten pounds of fritos a day until they could afford to move to Dallas and expand. Expand they did through World War II, when they joined with H. W. Lay potato chips to fill America's eternal hunger for the salty, the crisp and the portable.

Should you wish to turn your *masa* into a tamale, more work is at hand. To get a spongier dough, you must boil the corn in a larger quantity of lime-water and grind the hulled kernels less fine. You may want to dry the hulled kernels and then grind them to fine grits for the *tamales cernidos* of central Mexico. Or you may want to whip in quantities of melted lard for the *tamales colados* of Yucatán. You may want to add beaten eggs and herbs, or chili-sprinkled frogs, wild cherries, peanuts, black olives, pork rind and hot or sweet peppers, sour orange juice and shredded chicken; or sweeten them with honey, cinnamon, raisins and *manjar blanco* candy, or dried prunes, chocolate and pumpkin seeds. "To sum up," Diana Kennedy wrote, "the cooking of corn in Mexico with all its elaborations and ramifications is, and always has been, within the realm of the highest culinary art, beyond that of any other country." I don't know any country cousin foolhardy enough to dispute that.

CORNMEAL COOKING

Murder at the Mill

THE CORNMEAL of my youth came from the supermarket in a round cardboard box with a smiling Quaker on the outside. It would keep forever, like baking soda, like Kool-Aid, like soap powder. My family of ex-farmers numbered the supermarket and the grains therein as evidence of God's grace, for which we thanked Him thrice daily in the blessings before each meal. Only much, much later did I realize I'd been accessory to a crime.

Even though my family had raised corn with their hands, like the rest of the nation they had wheat in their heads, and the American conflict between an invading wheat culture and a native corn culture was most clearly expressed in the process by which Americans turned grain into meal. The mother wheat culture had been emotionally combusted in 1851 by what Lewis Mumford called the machine age's "cock-crow of triumph," the Crystal Palace Exhibition of London, where Queen Victoria brooded like a mother hen over her new mechanical chicks. Among her brood were iron roller mills that were to revolutionize the milling of wheat in the motherland and therefore the milling of corn in the "colonies." Although England had lost her colonial land in America, she still ruled the minds of colonial descendants forever determined to transform the crude native stuff into British wheat. Now the alchemy was to be done by milling.

"The improvement in corn milling is by the adoption of the roller reduction process similar to that used in wheat milling, but requiring much greater power, and by this process a flour is produced quite as impalpable as the best grades of wheat flour," wrote the authors of *The Book of Corn* in 1904. They were largely professors of agriculture at land-grant colleges, and they rejoiced in the promise of the new when "corn will yet be the spinal column of the nation's agriculture." That corn had been the flesh and bone of native agriculture for several millennia went unnoticed. At the dawn of the new century, machinery would do the trick:

> Through the use of very ingenious machinery the chit, or germ, is mechanically removed from each grain of corn before it passes into the rolls, by this means removing all but a trace of oil from the meal or flour. The product by this process loses some of the distinctive corn flavor, but the loss is more than offset by the gain in keeping quality, and corn flour can now be used or shipped under the same conditions as wheat flour.

The milling history of wheat had been very different from that of corn because for two thousand years wheat had been ground by wheel. Rotary mills, which first appeared in the Middle East around 800 B.C., worked by crushing grains between a pair of thick round stones. Around the first century B.C., the Romans "improved" their mills by attaching a horizontal millstone with gears

Preparation for "a wedding" in the Drake Manuscript, or Histoire Naturelle des Indes (ca. 1586), shows a woman pounding or grinding corn in a basin metate or mortar, a hunter with a hare, and a basket of tortillas. The inscription reads, in part: "This woman beats the wheat kernel in a wooden mortar and produces a very white flour from which they make very good and very nourishing bread." Courtesy Pierpont Morgan Library

to a vertical wheel, so that the stones could be turned "mechanically" by the power of slave, animal, water or wind. From then on, there was no essential change in milling for almost two millennia.

Before the rotary mill, the Old World had crushed and pounded its grains with mortar and stone just as New World inhabitants had done. The stone saddle quern of ancient Egypt was the same saddle-shaped stone with a stone rolling pin used in ancient Mesoamerica, but the New World kept to the principle of the mortar and pestle and evolved its own "improvements" on hand-powered mills. Around the time of Christ, the "basin" metate—a vessel shaped like a bowl in which corn was ground by rotating a simple round stone, or "one-handed mano"—was replaced by the "trough" metate, open at one or both ends so that the grinder could push back and forth the "two-handed mano." In the eleventh century, with the flowering of Toltec and Anasazi, the "trough" was replaced by "slab" metates, set at an angle within a "metate bin," a slab-lined box designed to catch the flour as it was ground. The bins were set three in a row in a grinding room, where the grinders had devised a cornmeal production line, the first woman crushing the meal coarsely and passing it on for successively finer grindings.

Such milling refinements worked more easily with the soft-flour varieties of corn grown in Mexico and the Southwest than with the hard flints of the North. These demanded pounding, rather than grinding, with wood mortars and pestles. "Each house had its permanent wood mortar, set firmly into the earth floor, with a heavy wooden pestle fitting into it," Will and Hyde reported

A trough metate, found in Argentina, is shaped like a fanged and double-headed beast. Catalogue No. 233636, National Anthropological Archives, Smithsonian Institution

of the Indians in the upper Missouri. Small stone mortars, they noted, were used only for seasonal migrations when mobile mortars were essential. "Hominy blocks" were still a household fixture when F. W. Waugh reported on the Iroquois in 1916. They made a block of black or red oak and placed it upside down just outside the door, next to a pestle sometimes six feet long of maple, ironwood, ash or hickory. To make a block, they felled a tree and, selecting a section of trunk with uniform diameter, cut it to a height convenient to the pounder. Next they hollowed out the top, about a foot deep, by burning the wood and then scraping out the ash. To make the pestle, they rounded it on the bottom end and cut it broader at the top to act as a weight and give it more force. One to four women might pound at once, bringing "the pestles down smartly one after the other," and they often made the task into a competitive game.

Whether the mortar was of stone or wood, it had the social and religious significance of corn itself. The mortar was an object of reverence as the act of grinding was an act of worship and of social bonding. The Aztec buried the umbilical cord of a newborn girl under the metate, as they buried a boy's cord under a shield and arrows. Even in 1909, when Frank Speck reported on the Yuchi Indians of the Southeast, he noted that the dooryard mortar seemed to be "an important domestic fetish," for "the navel string of a female child" was laid beneath it "in the belief that the presiding spirit will guide the growing girl in the path of domestic efficiency."

"Domestic efficiency," however, was not an Indian but a colonial term. Men geared to efficiency would have trouble understanding a modern Pueblo woman who can say that a woman never tires of grinding corn. "She can grind it for three or four hours straight, because while she grinds, the men come and sing," explains Agnes Dill of Isleta Pueblo. "And in the grinding songs they tell you almost what to do. And you have to grind to the beat, to the rhythm of the songs." An efficiency expert might mistake this for a method of improved milling by controlling motion and morale. Not so the Tewa. Corn grinding like corn dancing is a way of getting in tune with the primal energy of life. "The grinding song may tell you first of all that what you're handling is very sacred," says Paul Enciso of Taos Pueblo, "and that you've got to put yourself in tune with that spirit of what you're doing, so it doesn't become a chore to you, but it becomes part of you."

How much a part of you, and how much the sacred was part of the secular, are evident in Frank Cushing's account of the "crooning feast" of the Zuni, which was a kind of milling bee. A gaggle of young girls and boys met at a large house, Cushing said, to grind and sing and dance to "sounding drum, shrieking flute, clanging rattles, and the wailing, weird measures of the chant." About eight girls at a time would step to the milling trough and pass the toasted kernels from right to left, reducing the coarse meal to flour as fine as pollen: "Not only did they move their molinas up and down in exact time, but at certain periods in the song—shifting the stone from one hand to the other—passed the meal from trough to trough in perfect unison." The crooning party continued late into the night, Cushing added, "as it usually does in the well-to-do families of Zuni."

The well-to-do families of colonial settlers, on the other hand, would have seen in such grindings cause not for singing but for groaning. Any descendant of those settlers who has tried to grind corn on a metate with a mano knows why Hopi grandmothers say that grinding makes women strong. She quickly learns that grinding is an exact and exacting skill, and knows with what relief her own ancestral grandmothers in the East watched the crew unloading from the hold of the *Fama* at Fort Christina in New Amsterdam in 1644, "3 large saws for Saw Mill, 8 grindstones, 1 pr. stones for Hand Mill, 1 pr. large stones for Grist Mill."

At first our colonial grandmothers made do with native mortars, but they soon "improved" the efficiency of the hominy block of the woodland Indians by attaching the pestle to a tree limb, or "sweep," to make a "sweep-and-mortar mill." By the eighteenth century, every cabin and clearing had a samp mill or two, said Nicholas Hardeman, and sailors traveling along Eastern shores in a heavy fog could locate land by the "thump, thump, thump" of the mills. Imported stones for gristmills were a luxury limited to settlements like New Amsterdam. At the gristmill, women could transfer their domestic grinding efficiency to a professional miller, who used water instead of woman power.

Toward the end of the eighteenth century, the women learned of a new "improvement": a Londoner in Blackfriars had substituted steam for river

In 1902, a pair of Hopi women, Ruth and Mabel Honani, grind their corn on slab metates set within metate bins in a grinding room. The grass brush in the left bin is used to sweep the meal together. Photo by J. H. Bratley, National Anthropological Archives, Smithsonian Institution

Mrs. Little Crow pounds corn in a hominy block in North Dakota. Courtesy State Historical Society of North Dakota

power to drive his wheat mill. Still, the principle of crushing grain between rotary stone wheels held firm until the first iron rollers were devised in Switzerland in 1834 and until Henry Simon in England built the first complete roller-mill plant in 1878. This change was far more radical because, combined with more efficient bolting, it promoted in the name of industrial efficiency the genocide of the living germ. Modern industrial roller mills for corn are grooved in such a way that when the rollers mesh they first fragment and then process the parts: they shear open the kernel, scrape out the starch and crush the germ for oil. Thus developed the first "ingenious machinery" lauded by the 1904 *Book of Corn* for its ability to remove the germ and therefore "all but a trace of oil from the meal or flour."

While the progressivists of *The Book of Corn* admitted some loss of "distinctive corn flavor" in the process, the loss was minor in comparison to "the gain in keeping quality," which would make corn flour as mobile as wheat. The future was theirs: "The economic possibilities of the corn crop are only beginning to be understood." No sounding drum or shrieking flute for this milling bee, but certainly the sound of money. What was not understood by the wheat thinkers, however, was the far greater loss to corn than to wheat when the germ was removed. Today we know that a typical wheat berry is roughly 85 percent endosperm to 2 percent germ, whereas a typical dent corn kernel is about 82 percent endosperm to 11.5 percent germ. Of the total oil in the corn kernel, 83.5 percent is in the germ. The taste is in the oil: remove the germ and you remove the taste. Anyone who samples freshly ground whole-kernel cornmeal can tell first by smell and then by tongue the difference between dead and living corn.

In mainstream America, my grandparents' generation was the last to know, without conscious effort, the taste of meal ground from living corn, which they took for granted and never missed when it was gone. In their farming days they had hauled corn to a local mill by wagon, but they were as happy to trade their sacks of meal for Quaker boxes as they were to exchange Kansas mules for Ford V-8's. For a family of cornflake Fletcherizers, the sweetly nutty flavors and varied crunchy textures of freshly ground cornmeal were quite beside the point. The point for mainstream America was not corn, but wheat.

Even in the midst of our current gastronomic and health-food revolutions, American eaters remain faithful to wheat. In 1982 Americans consumed an average per capita of 114 pounds of wheat flour, plus 2.9 pounds of wheat cereal, in contrast to 11.1 pounds of corn flour and grits, and 2.3 pounds of corn cereal. While the number of people who search out local mills that sell freshly ground cornmeals has increased since the whole-food generation of the 1960s, such mills are even rarer than organic farms. Consumers can scarcely demand what they have never known, and the majority of Americans outside the South and Southwest are as innocent of newly ground cornmeal as of newly laid eggs.

Fortunately, however, Americans are quirky and there's usually a rebel around the bend. Today, just as there's a new crop of farmers rescuing endangered corn species, so there's a new crop of millers rescuing cornmeal flavor along with the moribund milling art. "We're not just selling flour and cornmeal," says Tim McTague at Gray's Gristmill in Adamsville, Rhode Island. "We're selling history." Young McTague learned his milling arts from John Hart, eighty-eight, who with his father kept Gray's Mill going for a century; it is now the oldest continually operating mill in the nation, with the original building dating back to 1675. The current 1870s building looks like a gray-shingled garage, but that's appropriate to the power source that replaced the old millrace of the Westport River with the drive shaft of a 1946 Dodge truck.

Gray's Gristmill is just down the road from Paul Pieri's farm, which grows the same type of white flint corn—called White Cap today—that was cultivated originally by the Narragansett. Though this type of corn was once common throughout Rhode Island, today in all of New England there are but thirty acres of White Cap, and twenty of these are Paul's. Some of the others are Robert Wakefield's at the University of Rhode Island, where Wakefield has long championed the purity and preservation of the breed. This is a matter of some moment to the Society for the Propagation of the Jonnycake Tradition in Rhode Island, loyal promoters of stone-ground Rhode Island White Cap

In the age of the motorcar, a man grinds corn between a pair of stones in a handmill.
Courtesy Utah State Historical Society

Flint corn and producers for twenty years of the *Jonnycake Journal* (spelled their way).

These minutemen have marshaled three local gristmills to carry on the Jonnycake Tradition, one of them at Uskepaugh in West Kingston, where Paul Drumm, father and son, are selling history at Kenyon's Grist Mill, in operation since 1886. Son Paul first alerted me to the importance of millstones made of Narragansett granite, so hard that it flakes the grain paper-thin instead of crushing it, and to the importance of the bible of Rhode Island millers and jonnycake makers, *The Jonny-Cake Papers of 'Shepherd Tom,'* written by Thomas Robinson Hazard for *The Providence Journal* in the 1870s.

Hazard (1797–1886), in chapters called First, Second and Third Bakings, was a practitioner of what I call the Cornmeal Lament, a subgenre of English pastoral. He was blowing his pipes at a time when imported French burrstones were in vogue: between 1877 and 1900, America imported three thousand a year. French burrstones, made of a porous quartz from La-Ferté-sous-Jouarre on the Marne River, were thought to be the finest stones for wheat because the cut faces of the stones kept their edge and seldom needed dressing. Some, but not Shepherd Tom, believed that burrstones were also best for corn because they did not expel the oil but left it in the meal. These were fighting words to Tom:

The 32-foot overshot waterwheel at Falls Mill, built in 1873 in Belvidere, Tennessee, to power a cotton and wool factory has been restored by John and Jane Lovett to grind corn and other grains. Courtesy John and Jane Lovett

The idea that a burr stone can grind meal even out of the best of Rhode Island white corn, that an old-fashioned Narragansett pig would not have turned up his nose at in disgust, is perfectly preposterous. Rushed through the stones in a stream from the hopper as big as your arm, and rolled over and over in its passage, the coarse, uneven, half-ground stuff falls into the meal box below, hot as ashes and as tasteless as sawdust.

Since jonnycake meal should feel soft and flat rather than harsh and round, Tom stated, the only millstones fit to grind it were the fine-grained stones of Narragansett granite found at Hammond's Mill, on the site of the elder Gilbert Stuart's snuff mill, above the head of Pettaquamscutt pond. Here the beloved miller tends his meal as some Raphael his palette or Canova his chisel:

See the white-coated old man now first rub the meal, as it falls, carefully and thoughtfully between his fingers and thumb, then graduate the feed and raise or lower the upper stone, with that nice sense of adjustment, observance, and discretion that a Raphael might be supposed to exercise in the mixing and grinding of his colors for a Madonna, or a Canova in putting the last touch of his chisel to the statue of a god, until, by repeated handling, he had found the ambrosia to have acquired exactly the desired coolness and flatness—the result of its being cut into fine slivers by the nicely balanced revolving stones—rather than rolled, re-rolled, tumbled, and mumbled over and over again, until all its life and sweetness had been vitiated or dispelled.

Milling is so much a lost art that a brief explanation of how a gristmill works may help: the miller feeds grain through a hopper (by means of a leather "shoe," agitated by a device called the "noisy damsel") into a hole in the center of a flat "runner" stone that rests on a lower "bed" stone. As the grain falls into the hole, only the upper stone turns. The grain is ground between the faces of both stones, which have been cut, or "dressed," in radiating grooves, or "furrows," that act like scissor blades when they come together. The cut grain, funneled through the furrows to the outer edges of the stones, is then channeled down a spout to a bin below. How closely the stones fit together and how fast they are turned determines how much friction is generated and how much heat. "If you get the rocks too close together, it'll burn. You can smell it," says George Oswald, who has restored a gristmill in Lexington County, South Carolina. "When the rocks are dull, or you grind too close, it heats up."

The first enemy of finely milled corn is heat and the second is quantity milling. Shepherd Tom's was not the only Cornmeal Lament for the days of yore before the huge burr millstones, driven by steam, were geared to mass production. In his *American Indian Corn* Charles Murphy complained of how little the manner of grinding corn was understood and how much it mattered: "The steam-mill with its huge burr mill-stones, in the hands of a miller whose ambition is quantity, and who knows nothing of quality, cuts and burns all the life out of the meal, and leaves it a heavy, dead mass. The cook may use all the customary appliances for making light and palatable bread, but all in vain." The capacity of the old horse-driven millstones was about three bushels an hour, he explained, and in the hands of a miller whose ambition was quality, the "meal came cool and lively, with a 'grain' perceptible to the touch."

Millers and farmers knew that the oil in corn rendered it more liable than wheat to spoilage, so they milled corn in small quantities to avoid long storage. Indians had avoided spoilage by parching or toasting the meal they stored for winter, but they were

An interior view at Falls Mill of the wheels and belts that transmit power from the turning waterwheel to the runner and bed grinding stones. Courtesy John and Jane Lovett

also skilled in applying the right amount of heat to each kind and grind of corn. When commercial roller mills were first introduced in order to grind corn in previously unimagined quantities, millers began to dry corn in commercial kilns to speed the drying. That brought new Laments, among them Maria Parloa's in her *Kitchen Companion* (1887). She regretted that the sweet-flavored meal of old had passed away: ". . . the time for drying has been reduced more and more, until now the grains of the corn meal are as hard as the grains of hominy. . . . Then, too, the meal is ground much finer than formerly. All these changes in the meal have damaged it considerably, and it is almost impossible to get the moist, sweet corn-bread of years gone by." Since the finer grind alters proportions, Parloa suggested reducing the quantity of "modern" cornmeal by an eighth when following old recipes for cornbreads.

A favorite villain of current Laments is the heat presumed to be generated by steel roller mills as opposed to cool stones. Edward Behr, however, in a recent investigation of wheat mills, discovered that the temperatures of steel roller-milled flour were apt to be lower than those produced by electric-powered millstones. The major difference, Behr concluded, lay not in the mechanical process but in the miller—his knowledge, skill and care. The older miller was more apt to begin with a high-quality flavorful grain that had been locally grown and dried, and he was more apt to treat it with care in the milling because he knew the meal would be eaten fresh. "There is no substitute," Behr stated, "for freshly stone-ground corn."

Dedicated to that proposition is the Society for the Preservation of Old Mills, run by Fred Beals in Mishawaka, Indiana. In the hope of restoring and preserving "old mills and other Americana now passing from the present scene," the society's quarterly, *Old Mill News,* is a mine of practical and historical information on gristmills past and present in Canada and the United States. As "Keeper of the Computerized Mill List," Beals compiled a representative list of about 114 working mills that produce stone-ground cornmeal today, most of them in the South.

Old mills, like other anthropological relics, condense social as well as milling history. Such is the mill at Philipsburg Manor, one of the Sleepy Hollow Restorations, at Upper Mills on the Hudson River above Tarrytown, New York. The mill was built in 1682 for the manor of Frederick Flypse, about forty years after the *Fama* had unloaded its grist stones in New Amsterdam and after Flypse struck it rich by shipping goods and marrying wealthy widows. Such is the War Eagle Mill on the banks of the War Eagle River southwest of Eureka Springs, Arkansas. Built in the 1830s, it was burned to prevent capture by the Union Army during the Civil War, rebuilt, burned again in the 1920s, then restored in 1973 by the Medlin family as the only working undershot waterwheel in the United States.

Thanks to a few history buffs and milling rebels, I have a better chance today of tasting the ambrosial meal of Shepherd Tom or the moist, sweet cornbread of Maria Parloa than I did in my youth. Even my supermarket offers an alternative to the smiling Quaker in the profile of a sober Indian. Since 1960 an Indian head has stamped the meal of Arrowhead Mills in Hereford, Texas, where Frank Ford set up a thirty-inch stone grinder in an abandoned railroad car in order to grind organically grown whole-grain wheat and corn. Although Ford now uses a "hammer mill" instead of stone, the function of the rotating hammers is to shatter the grains into flour without generating heat. "It has been an interesting struggle," Ford says, "against the flow of junk-food madness in this nation."

No matter how good the original grain nor how careful the milling, the problem of freshness remains. Whole-grain cornmeal must be kept in a cold place, refrigerated or frozen, to keep fresh. Costly stone-ground meals on the

Chef Louis Romain, at the stove of the Anthony Wayne Hotel in Hamilton, Ohio, in 1927, shows Princess Dawn Mist of the Blackfoot tribe "how to create American hominy out of Indian cornmeal."
The Bettmann Archive

shelves of gourmet or health-food stores are no better than the storekeeper's awareness of the frailty of living grains. No matter how it's been ground, stale meal is stale. Not until we learn to treat milled corn as if it were as perishable as fresh sweet corn, or butter, or eggs, will we give corn the respect that is its due as "the spinal column of our nation's agriculture." If we can resurrect the dead art of milling, we may give new life to a murdered grain.

Sad Paste and Ash Powders

ONCE THE CORN was ground to meal, the question was what to do with it. For wheat eaters, corn was a punishment. Rebecca Burlend, who emigrated to Pike County, Illinois, in the frontier days of 1848, complained when she was reduced to making bread out of corn:

> As our money was growing scarce, [my husband] bought a bushel of ground Indian corn, which was only one-third the price of wheaten flour. . . . Its taste is not pleasant to persons unaccustomed to it; but as it is wholesome food, it is much used for making bread. We had now some meal, but no yeast, nor an oven; we were therefore obliged to make sad paste, and bake it in our frying pan on some hot ashes.

In frontier America, as in colonial America, any form of bread made with corn instead of wheat was the sad paste of despair. How sad is reflected in the lowliness of the names—pone, ashcakes, hoe-cakes, journey-cakes, johnnycakes, slapjacks, spoonbreads, dodgers—all improvised in the scramble to translate one culture's tongue and palate into another's. Names got muddled by region and recipe as much as samp, hominy and grits and for the same reason: the desperate attempt of a wheat culture to order by its own canon the enormous variety of pastes, batters and doughs cooked by native grinders of corn.

From the start, colonists put interchangeable labels on the generic native ashcake, baked in an open fire, which seemed to the people of iron griddles and pots an appalling reversion to Stonehenge. Words slithered in the mud of translation, Narragansett *nokehick* becoming "no-cake" and "hoe-cake"; "journeying cake," "Shawnee cake" or "every John's no-cake" becoming "jonny" or "johnnycake." At the same time, these Anglicizations of hoe-cake and johnnycake took hold early and hung on late as symbols, like Yankee Doodle, of rebel identity. In 1766, just after the Stamp Act, Benjamin Franklin fought back when *The London Gazetteer* opined that "Americans, should they resolve to drink no more tea, can by no means keep that Resolution, their Indian corn not affording an agreeable or easy digestible breakfast":

> Pray, let me, an American, inform the gentleman, who seems ignorant of the matter, that Indian corn, take it for all in all, is one of the most agreeable and wholesome grains in the world; that its green leaves roasted are a delicacy beyond expression; that samp, hominy, succatash, and nokehock, made of it, are so many pleasing varieties; and that johny or hoecake, hot from the fire, is better than a Yorkshire muffin.

A century later, Joel Chandler Harris dubbed cornmeal the cause of America's political greatness: "Real democracy and real republicanism, and the aspirations to which they give rise, are among the most potent results of corn meal, whether in the shape of the brown pone or the more delicate ashcake, or the dripping and juicy dumplings."

Still, for those who actually cooked the stuff, cornmeal was hard going. Not only was corn obdurately hard to pound even to coarse meal, but the meal refused to respond to yeast. No matter how they cooked it, in iron or on bark or stone, corn paste lay flat as mud pies, which particularly saddened the Dutch. With their tile stoves, the Dutch were better bakers than the hearth-cooking British and were the more frustrated by the incapacity of Indian wheat to make the light noodles, dumplings, cookies and doughnuts in which they took pride. In New Netherlands in the seventeenth century, refined wheat flour was so scarce and so valuable that authorities prohibited Indians from bartering pelts for Dutch-baked breads and cookies. Records show that a baker was fined a considerable sum after "a certain savage" was seen leaving his bakery "carrying an oblong sugar bun."

Feinschmeckers fond of sugar buns understandably had trouble with pone. Pone, like samp, was stamped Indian by its name (from Algonquin *oppone* and Narragansett *suppawn*) and ashcake origin. Isaack deRasieres, a Dutchman visiting Plymouth Colony, was more generous than most colonists in describing Indian bread as "good but heavy." Heaviness was a constant colonial complaint, which cooks sought to remedy by mixing cornmeal with the more finely ground flours of rye or wheat—when they could get them. In the first American cookbook of 1796, Amelia Simmons typically mixed wheat flour with Indian meal in her batters and cooked her Indian pudding in a British pudding bag. "Some think the nicest of all bread is one third Indian, one third rye, and one third flour," said Lydia Child in *The Frugal Housewife* (1829), of what was usually called "thirded bread." Typical again was her use of a British name, "bannock," for her flat cake of Indian corn.

Names were as hybrid as the pastes and doughs, as one can see just by skimming the dozens of names Eliza Leslie gave her recipes in *The Indian Meal Book* (1847). We can learn more about mid-nineteenth-century Eastern establishment cookery from Leslie than from anyone else because no one was more detailed or more discriminating than she, but we can also learn how impossible names are and how little they matter. Her "common hoe-cake" was baked on a griddle, her "plain and nice johnny cakes" on a board and her "Indian pone" in an oven. The hoe-cake was a stiff dough of coarse meal, patted into cakes the size of a saucer and laid on a hot griddle over the fire. "Where griddles are not," she hastened to explain, the cakes may be baked "on a board standing nearly upright before the fire, and supported by a smoothing-iron or a stone placed against the back." With a wood fire, she continued, the cakes could be wrapped in paper and laid on the hearth, covering the paper with red-hot ashes. This was what our early settlers did, and "the custom is still continued by those who cannot yet obtain the means of cooking them more conveniently." The dough for "plain johnny cake" she also smoothed onto a stout, flat board (such as a piece of the head of a flour barrel), placed "nearly (but not quite) upright" on a smoothing-iron before the fire, an improvement over the hoe that "in some parts of America it was customary to bake it on." "The cake must be very well baked," she warned, "taking care that the surface does not burn while the inside is soft and raw." To make a "plain" one into a "nice" one, she added a little molasses, butter and ginger to the batter and greased the board with fresh butter.

Terms, ingredients and methods remained in flux for two centuries and should make cautious any naïve epistemologists who seek the "definitive" and "authentic." *Mrs. Curtis's Cookbook* (1909) contained an encyclopedic number of johnnycakes and hoe-cakes, including Southern hoe cake No. 1 (which called for a greased hoe) and a "genuine johnny cake" distinct from a "Rhode Island johnny cake." Fighting words to the Society for the Propagation of the Jonnycake Tradition, for whom "genuine" can mean only Rhode Island. Fighting words to the residents of Newport County, Rhode Island, for whom "genuine" can mean only Newport County. Fighting words, stoves and fists to the Rhode Island Legislature in the 1890s, which fixed by law the spelling of "jonnycake" and would have legislated the recipe as well, had Newport County on the west of Narragansett Bay not deadlocked with South County on the east.

Thirty years later they were still at it. Representative Benjamin Boyd cudgeled his opponents with rhyme: "South County mush, stick the coffee in it and a pig would think it slush." Representative James Caswell of South County took it in snuff: "I did not come here to be insulted—especially by anyone who has been reared on Newport County hick feed." The issue of the cornmeal war was texture. Newport County added milk to meal to make a thin, crisp griddlecake about five inches in diameter; South County scalded the meal in boiling water to make a thick cake about three inches in diameter. "We don't scald all the pep out of it, and we never wash the griddle," said Boyd. Caswell refused to negotiate: "Over my way, we scald the meal and we wash the griddle." The fight itself is now part of the Jonnycake Tradition, celebrated twice annually in Rhode Island with May and October jonnycake cookoffs.

I had had my own battle with johnnycakes and lost handily. I followed Sarah Rutledge's recipe for "corn journey or johnny cake" in *The Carolina Housewife*: two tablespoons "cold hommony" mixed with one tablespoon butter, one egg, one cup milk and enough corn flour to make a batter "just so stiff as to be spread upon a board, about quarter of an inch thick." I had just such a board, twelve by fourteen inches, which I propped against an iron trivet in front of an open fire, as directed: "Put the board before the fire, brown the cake, then pass a coarse thread under it, and turn it upon another board, and brown the other side in the same way." Simple? No. The batter must be just so moist that it sticks to the board, and the board must be just so close that the batter will not burn or dry out and slide into the ashes. Forget the coarse thread; the problem was to keep the batter on the board. The first cake slid off whole into the ashes. The next cake stuck to the board in patches, some burned, some gummily raw. Choked with smoke, front red with heat and back blue with cold and stiff from bending, I had new respect for my ancestral grandmothers and sympathy for their corn complaints.

Like "johnnycake," the word "corn-dodger" was another compound neologism, as H. L. Mencken says, that colonists invented as a way of coping with "an entirely new mode of life." "Dodger" suggests that artful bakers took to substituting corn for honest wheat buns. Nineteenth-century cookbooks suggest that it was simply one more cornmeal dough made "just so stiff" that it could be shaped by hand and baked on tin sheets in a Dutch oven. Eventually dodgers took on a particularized shape, detailed by Harriett Ross Colquitt in *The Savannah Cook Book* (1933), in which she told the cook to form the dough "into long, round dodgers with the hand (about four or five inches long and one inch in diameter)." Corn sticks molded in cast-iron pans with corn-ear depressions replaced the dodger in common parlance, after Wagner Ware in the 1880s began to manufacture Tea-size, Junior-size and Senior-size "Krusty Korn Kobs Baking Molds."

"Come, all young girls, pay attention to my noise; Don't fall in love with the Kansas boys, For if you do, your portion it will be, Johnnycake and antelope is all you'll see." —From "Kansas Boys," in A Treasury of Nebraska Pioneer Folklore (1966)

The Southern hush puppy is simply a latter-day dodger, despite the regional mystique that puppies and dodgers are to ordinary corn bread what brandy is to wine. Because the puppy batter adds minced onions, French-style, some have attributed its origin to the Croquettes de Maïs cooked by the Ursuline nuns at the founding of their New Orleans convent in 1727, but there's no record of the word before 1918. And the thing itself is no more than a corn fritter fried with fish in the happy cafe style of Little Pigs in Asheville, North Carolina, whose customers every day consume a thousand puppies, shaped by an ice cream scoop.

These are the cornmeal civilities that Thoreau abjured when he baked unleavened corn loaves in the fire at Walden Pond. Publishing *Walden* in 1854, around the same time as Eliza Leslie's *Receipts*, he exulted in his return to culinary innocence, to the "primitive days and first invention of the unleavened kind"—the primal ashcake, the original staff of life. Even so, he encountered problems with pure corn:

> Bread I at first made of pure Indian meal and salt, genuine hoecakes, which I baked before my fire out of doors on a shingle or the end of a stick of timber sawed off in building my house; but it was wont to get smoked and to have a piny flavor. I tried flour also; but have at last found a mixture of rye and Indian meal most convenient and agreeable.

"... so Jim he got out some corn-dodgers and buttermilk, and pork and cabbage and greens— there ain't nothing in the world so good when it's cooked right...."
—MARK TWAIN,
The Adventures of Huckleberry Finn
(1885)

Thoreau's city knowledge was evident not only in his mixture of meals but in his preserving methods, when he acknowledged that he kept his ashcakes "as long as possible by wrapping them in cloths." Such urban adhesions in no way inhibited his pastoral Lament that "fresh and sweet meal is rarely sold in the shops, and hominy and corn in a still coarser form are hardly used by any." For primitive purity, he decided to eschew not only leaven but salt: "I do not learn that the Indians ever troubled themselves to go after it." Nor did they trouble themselves to go after rye. Thoreau was a native not of Walden but of Concord, and that made all the difference.

The distinctions between wheat and corn continued to make all the difference in the South, where it was wheat biscuits for the gentry and corn pone for the slaves. Wheat meant "baker's bread," as Huckleberry Finn said, "what the quality eat—none of your low-down corn-pone." A contemporary descendant of freed slaves recalls that on weekdays her Mammy made ashcakes in the fireplace "outen meal, water and a little pinch of lard," but on Sundays they were special, "on Sundays day wuz made outen flour, buttermilk an' lard." Sharecroppers black and white limited the distinction to breakfast, William Bradford Huie said in a collection of reminiscences, *Mud on the Stars* (1942), but it was absolute because biscuit for breakfast meant dignity. "A Garth Negro or white cropper would relish corn pone for dinner or supper, but to have had to eat it for breakfast would have broken his spirit," Huie said. "Corn pone for breakfast among croppers is like a patch on the seat of the britches for a man, or drawers made of flour sacks for a woman among the landowning whites."

Native corn eaters of the Southwest, whose caste status did not depend upon wheat, nonetheless incorporated wheat into their cornmeal pastes as they incorporated the Madonna into their Corn Mothers. A recipe for a contemporary Navaho cake, in *Traditional Navajo Foods and Cooking* (1983), is a true child of the hybrid cuisine engendered when wheat met corn. It is a ceremonial cake baked by the entire community of women at "the Fourth Dawn of the Kinaada," and they bake it as of old in an earth oven fired by piñon and juniper.

A nineteenth-century engraving after the painting by Alfred Kappes, Hoe-cake and Clabber *(thickened sour milk).* North Wind Picture Archives

They mix fifty pounds of yellow corn, roasted and ground to the consistency of "Cream of Wheat," with fifty pounds of stone-ground whole-wheat flour and twelve pounds of sprouted wheat, dried and ground. After sweetening the mixture with brown sugar and raisins, they pour it onto the bottom layer of cornhusks that line the pit, then draw a sacred pattern with the pollen of the four corn colors before covering the whole with a layer of husks. Next they shovel on a layer of sand and hot coals and let the cake bake overnight. When they uncover it, they cut it into eight giant pieces until only the center, the heart, remains. This they cut in four pieces, to represent the cardinal directions, and these they put back in the ground to feed Mother Earth. "Steamed and moist, slightly sweet, chewy, with the full flavor of the grains, nothing could taste as good on a cold, sleepy dawn," the community of Navaho women agree, four centuries after the community of women at Plymouth struggled to feed their men with a sad paste baked in the irons and ashes of hearths far distant from their native ground.

WHAT DISMAYED Plymouth women most about cornbread was that no matter how much you kneaded it, or how much yeast you added, the loaf would not rise to any baking occasion. Wheat, in contrast, was king of the mountain because, more than any other grain, wheat was made for yeast. A wheat dough kneaded with yeast would rise slowly like a balloon and stay there under fire. Because of the high gluten content of its proteins, wheat dough could be made so elastic that as the yeast slowly produced carbon dioxide bubbles, each bubble could be trapped within a gluten parachute to make a light and airy dough. Not so corn. The low gluten content of its proteins kept the dough from absorbing the bubbles of fermenting yeast, which simply dissipated into thin air. If corn dough were to be made lighter, it would have to work quickly to trap bubbles—like the air bubbles of whipped eggs or the gas bubbles of a carbonate that could be produced chemically by combining an acid with an alkali.

Wood ash, lime and lye, all the alkalis employed in Indian ash cookery, furnished just such a leavening, as Cushing saw, for their cakes and breads of corn. Colonists, improvising their cooking over campfire and hearth, learned to adapt and refine the ash powders of Indian meal for use with their own wheat and rye. When they leached wood ashes in a pot, the colonists appropriately called the liquid "pot-ash" (a potassium carbonate), which they mixed with fat to make soap, or with an acid like sour milk or molasses to make a quick leavening for dough. Potash they soon refined in both word and substance into "pearlash," and then into the more easily prepared aerated salt they named "saleratus," a sodium bicarbonate known today as baking soda.

The evolution was speedy, but because these were wheat bakers they first applied the quick source of bubbles to wheat. In 1796 Amelia Simmons used pearlash for her gingerbread cakes of wheat, leavened with "three small spoons of pearlash dissolved in cream." In 1805 J. B. Bordley, in his *Essays and Notes on Husbandry and Rural Affairs,* prescribed "a tea spoonful of salt of tartar heaped, or any other form of pot or pearl ash" for a "handy-cake," a bread made with soured milk and wheat. In 1825, by the time of her second edition of *The Virginia Housewife,* Virginia Randolph called the quick bread she made of soda and wheat flour "soda cakes."

A new world of quick wheat breads was opened by Indian ash powders meant for corn. We can see a strange crossbreeding of Old World yeast and New World ash powder in Eliza Leslie's "Indian Meal Preparations, &c." in *New Receipts* (1854), where mixed batters of wheat and corn got mixed leavenings of yeast and pearlash or some other powder. Leslie's batter for "Indian slap-jacks" of yellow meal mixed with flour she leavened with "three large table-spoonfuls of strong fresh yeast" and "a level teaspoonful of pearlash, soda, or sal-eratus, dissolved in warm water." After the dough had risen from the yeast, the cook was to "add the dissolved pearlash to puff it still more."

The refinement of ash powders led directly to a cosmos of cakes, the glory of the American kitchen in the second half of the nineteenth century. The "Madison cake" proposed by Eliza Leslie, however, was a bewildering hybrid of a traditional British spice cake, made of wheat flour enriched with the usual butter, eggs, raisins and brandy, *and* an American mush cake, made of yellow cornmeal stirred with "a hickory spaddle," which she explained is "like a short mush-stick, only broader at the flattened end." In addition to eggs, she leavened the cake batter with "a large salt-spoon of saleratus, or a small tea-spoonful of soda" combined with half a pint of sour milk, and she explained to the housewife how the new powder worked: "For this cake the milk must be sour, that the saleratus or soda may act more powerfully by coming in contact with an acid. The acidity will then be entirely removed by the effervescence, and the cake will be rendered very light, and perfectly sweet."

"Lightness" and "sweetness" were Cushing's words for Zuni cakes made with the addition of "lime-yeast" added to meal mixed with acid saliva. Sahagún applied the same words to Aztec cakes made with lime and fermented meal and other combinations of alkali and acid. Ironically, although acid-alkali compounds were as native to corn cookery as yeast fermentation to wheat, Britain rather than the colonies was the first to commercialize ash powders for both grains. Between 1835 and 1850, Britain began to manufacture bakingpowder compounds on a large scale and they quickly caught on, not just for the baker's ease and speed but from a new general distrust of yeast. Louis Pasteur's discovery in 1857 that yeast was full of living organisms meant to the popular imagination that yeast was full of germs and therefore harmful. Scientists as respectable as Professor Eben Horsford of Harvard warned that yeast organisms were poisonous molds and suggested that a baker avoid these poisons and speed his work by premixing bread flour with sodium bicarbonate and "dry phosphate of lime" (extracted from bones) to make a "self-raising flour." At the same time, extremists in the American health movement that produced Sylvester Graham and the Kellogg brothers were fulminating, like Thoreau, against leavening of any kind as a corruption of the staff of life. "Rotted by fermentation or poisoned with acids and alkalis," the staff of life had well nigh become "the staff of death," gloomed the proponents of the Boston Water Cure in 1858. By 1872 Boston purists like S. D. Farrar had narrowed their focus to devil "saleratus, that abomination of the household, or cream-of-tartar, its companion in guilt."

Americans who wanted flat pones to be light as wheaten cakes had to do something and typically overdid it. If one leavening was good, three were better, as in the cornmeal cakes offered in *The Genesee Farmer* (1847): "Mix two quarts of corn meal, at night, with water, and a little yeast and salt, and make it just thin enough to stir easy. In the morning stir in three or four eggs, a little saleratus and a cup of sour milk . . . bake three-quarters of an hour, and you will have light, rich honeycomb cakes." Without wheat, the yeast would do nothing for the meal overnight, but American nineteenth-century cookbooks

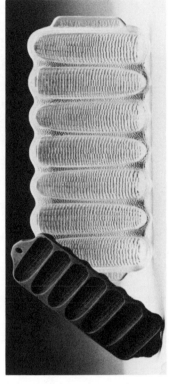

The ceramic corn molds used anciently in Mexico and Peru to cast corn ears in clay for sculpture are the ancestors of these modern pans used to shape corn batter into edible "corn sticks." The castiron pan is labeled Griswold Krispy Cornorwheat Stick Pan #262 from Erie, Pennsylvania. The glass one is Wagner Ware. From the collection of Meryle Evans, photo by David Arky

"A very common mode of aerating bread in America is by the effervescence of an acid and an alkali in the flour. The carbonic acid gas thus formed produces minute air-cells in the bread, or, as the cook says, makes it light. When this process is performed with exact attention to chemical laws, so that the acid and alkali completely neutralize each other, leaving no overplus of either, the result is often very palatable. The difficulty is, that this is a happy conjunction of circumstances which seldom occurs."

—CATHARINE BEECHER and HARRIET BEECHER STOWE, *The American Woman's Home* (1869)

are full of recipes that mash one culture's cookery with another's. Perhaps no bread tasted like bread to wheat eaters unless flavored by yeast.

By the turn of the century, an improved understanding of the chemistry of foods eliminated yeast for corn and demonstrated why cornmeal was better suited to quick-acting acid-soda mixtures and to small forms like biscuits and muffins. In *Fifty Recipes,* Célestine Eustis included a great variety of breads, cakes, biscuits and muffins leavened entirely with saleratus, soda, baking powders and eggs. Not a word about yeast.

Until baking powders were readily available and understood, housewives and especially Southern ones leavened their corn batters primarily with eggs. Just as they turned green-corn puddings into fritters and soufflés, so they turned puddings and breads into spoonbreads. Mrs. Bliss of Boston offered what we now call spoonbread in her *Practical Cook Book* (1850) under the name "Indian puffs." Her proportion of one quart of milk to eight tablespoons of meal and six eggs, "beaten as light as possible," suggests how much more easily Americans turned their corn in the direction of British puddings than British breads.

Americans were not alone in redeeming sad paste with mixed flours and leavenings. After the post-Columbian Exchange, Europe developed a wide range of baked corn goods that Britain knew nothing of. The Basques developed a huge cornmeal cuisine, with fine breads like *gâteau au maïs* (a sweetened bread with eggs and butter) and *méture au potiron basquais* (a pumpkin cornbread), cookies like *biscuits au maïs* (with wheat and corn flour mixed), and muffins like *taloa* (shaped flat and split open). In Agen they made deep-fried cornsticks to serve with oxtails and prunes in a dish called *queue de boeuf à l'agenaise et au milhas,* an echo from the time corn supplanted millet (*milhas*) by deed if not by word. Lombardy made a *pan Giallo* or *pan di Mais* of wheat and corn flavored with olive oil and shaped into wheels weighing two kilos. Ireland made a cornmeal soda bread called *paca, pike, yalla male* bread, said to be named for the ship *Alpaca* which brought cornmeal to Ireland during the potato famine of 1846. Romania made a cornbread with sour milk and dill called *alivence,* baked in cabbage leaves and served with sour cream.

England alone remained cut off from the possibilities of corn, for reasons that had more to do with its caste system than its agriculture. Indian paste was too base for the high monarchy of wheat. Franklin knew what he was about when he challenged Yorkshire muffins with Yankee hoe-cakes, and Joel Chandler Harris when he saw democracy rise from pone.

You Say Polenta, I Say Mush

WHEN I WAS A CHILD, I said *mush*. On a winter night when frost whitened the oranges outside our house and smudge blackened the curtains within, I said *mush*. Of all the belly-warming, heart-soothing, mind-comforting pottages, puddings, pablums and purees that I spooned down my childhood gullet, mush was the most. Mush was the heritage of our prairie past, the prerogative of a family palate honed to reduce all textures to mush. Mush, in our household, was the Platonic form to which all food aspired, and my mouth was ever open to it.

I little dreamed that halfway around the globe little Bantu children in Africa were comforted with *putu,* Venetian bambinas with *polenta,* petites filles in Gascony with *armottes,* junior Romanians with *mamaliga,* pocitas madrileñas with *milha* and tiny Transylvanians with *puliszka.* All these were names for cornmeal mush, and because mush was comfort food wherever eaten, each nation claimed it for its own.

Even now that I have put away childish things, I have never put away mush. I have simply incorporated a lifetime's travels within its wide and comforting embrace, adding Mexican jalapeños, Italian Parmesan, Danish butter, Ceylonese cinnamon, French crème fraîche. I don't mean at different times to different servings of mush, I mean all at once. I mean muddling peppery-hot, salty, sour, sweet and creamy all together in the same mush bowl to make one ambrosial pap.

The classic way to eat mush, of course, is with milk. Milk and mush was one of the earliest yokings in the hybrid cuisine of the colonials and remained one of the most cherished. A British army doctor during the War of 1812, tending captured soldiers in the prison hospital at Halifax, remembered how the prisoners cried incessantly for *"mush and milk,"* and since none was to be had, "their lamentations took the tone of despair."

A Dutch artist, Rufus A. Grider, who had emigrated to New York, remembered in his memoirs of 1888 the "Mush & Milk Dish" of his childhood which the Hollanders called "Mush Sapahn." Mush and Milk symbolized togetherness, not just the cold ingredients in the bowl, but the whole family eating communally from a large pewter dish:

> MUSH was prepared in the fall & winter of the year.—it was boiled in the afternoon & about one hour before meal time poured from the Iron Pot into the Pewter Dish & set in a cold place, cooling stiffens it. Near meal time the House Wife made as many excavations as there were guests—piling or heaping up the Centre, & filling the hollows with COLD MILK ... as many PEWTER Table Spoons as milk Ponds were supplied. After Grace was said by the head of the family—Every one began to diminish the bank & increase the size of his White Lake by feeding on its banks and Centre—but there were limits beyond those no one could go—if for instance any one tapped his neighbors MILK POND it was ill manners—if children did so—the penalty was FINGER CLIPS.

A nineteenth-century engraving of a colonial gentleman, Eating Hasty Pudding.
The Bettmann Archive

Once the starving times of the seventeenth century were past, the manner and manners of eating mush and milk took on the significance of art and ritual. In New Amsterdam, Grider painted a Dutch genre scene with a landscape of mush hills and milk ponds at the center, surrounded by squalling children in finger clips. In New England, Shepherd Tom in his *Jonny-Cake Papers* saw the mush-and-milk ritual of his childhood in the early nineteenth century as an index of class:

> Curious enough, I can remember when the eating of no-cake and milk was considered somewhat a test in Narragansett of good breeding. To be eaten gracefully, no-cake must be placed very carefully on the top of the milk, so as to float, and a novice, in taking a spoonful of it to his mouth, is very liable to draw his breath, when the semivolatile substance enters his throat in advance of the milk and causes violent strangling or sneezing.

For pioneers, tested by survival rather than breeding, the dish called "Dry Mush and Milk," in an 1861 issue of *The Nebraska Farmer,* was recommended to adults and children alike as a cure-all better than snake oil: the paper cited a student who, suffering from poor health, for a term of eleven weeks "ate *only* mush and milk for breakfast, dinner, and supper," and became first in his class.

Wherever mush was eaten, the mush mystique was sustained by associating the gruel with British pudding or Italian polenta. On March 26, 1722, the phrase "Indian Pudding" appeared in print for the first time in Boston's *New England Courant,* where Benjamin Franklin was working for the editor, his brother James, and noted with amusement "that at a certain House in Edgar Town, a Plain Indian Pudding, being put into the Pot and boiled the usual Time, it came out a blood-red Colour, to the great Surprise of the whole Family."

The name "Indian pudding" evoked the world of British pottages and gruels that had been upgraded in the seventeenth- and eighteenth-century homeland to puddings and pies. The staple cereal or milk pottage of medieval times, stirred with a stick in a pot over the fire, underwent radical change during the century when yeomen and bondsmen left for the colonies. For a "modern" British cook like Hannah Glasse in 1747, pottages were *hors de combat*. She preferred enlightened puddings, baked in a crust or boiled in a bag, at once avoiding the tedium of stirring and encouraging the pleasure of enrichments. For the colonies, suffering from the usual cultural lag, the term "hasty pudding" was a wheat-culture euphemism intended to redeem mush made of barbarous corn.

For Joel Barlow, hasty pudding was "A name, a sound to every Yankee dear," because it came to symbolize Yankee rebellion. A New Englander, Barlow was traveling through the Savoy in 1793 as Minister Plenipotentiary to France when he came on a steaming bowl of *polente au baton* in a small inn at Chambéry and was straightway seized by homesickness and the muse. Given to writing epics like *The Vision of Columbus,* he now tore off several hundred mock-epic lines on the subject of mush. Although Barlow was so avid a revolutionist that John Adams thought not even Tom Paine "a more worthless fellow," Barlow reveals his British heritage in a burlesque indebted to Alexander Pope's *Rape of the Lock.* "The soft nations round the warm Levant" call it *Polenta* Barlow said approvingly, "the French, of course, *Polente."* But his fellow Americans embarrassed him by the vulgarity of their tongue: "Ev'n in thy native regions, how I blush/ To hear the Pennsylvanians call thee *Mush!"* Its true name, Barlow explained, came from the haste with which the pudding was cooked, served and eaten, which proves he'd never actually stirred mush in a pot, because the one fact about mush is that you can't hurry it. The ladies of Deerfield, Massachusetts, aptly described "slow mush" in their recipe for "hasty pudding" in *The Pocumtuc Housewife* (1805): first you soften sifted meal in cold water, then add it to boiling water until thickened. "Then stand over the kettle and sprinkle in meal, handful after handful, stirring it thoroughly all the time. When it is so thick the pudding stick stands up in it, it is about right." Or, as *Ye Gentlewoman's Housewifery* put it as late as 1896, "beat like Mad with the Pudding Stick."

The stick was as essential as the iron pot to colonial and later kitchens. *Prac-*

"Father and I went up to camp,
Along with Captain Goodwin;
And there we saw the men and boys,
As thick as hasty pudding."
—A verse of "Yankee Doodle" used in 1767 in the ballad opera by Andrew Barton *The Disappointment; or, The Force of Credulity*

A wooden paddle (21 inches long) for stirring corn was carved by Iroquois in western New York in 1918. Milwaukee Public Museum

tical Housekeeping (1884) specified "a hard wood paddle, two feet long, with a blade two inches wide and seven inches long to stir with," and "stir-about" was the name the Irish gave to the pudding when England shoveled cornmeal into Ireland during the potato famine. Meanwhile American natives used two kinds of sticks for their mush. Among the Iroquois, one was a long narrow stick, often carved the length of the handle to exploit phallic suggestions. The other was a wide paddle, often carved with a heart-shaped hole in the center of the blade, to drain water from breads boiled in bark pots like dumplings. Even in this century, F. W. Waugh found that stirring paddles were in frequent use by Iroquois housewives for their "puddings" of beans, pumpkin, acorns, chestnuts and other native ingredients mixed with corn.

As soon as she could, the American housewife left behind the rustic stir-about pudding to make the batter pudding in vogue in the Age of Enlightenment. Comically, Indian pudding came to mean mush cooked *with* milk, either baked or boiled *English*-style in a pudding bag. While Amelia Simmons offered no hasty pudding recipe, she gave a trio of recipes for making "a nice Indian pudding." The simplest was softened with milk, sweetened with sugar and boiled in the strong cloth of a pudding bag for twelve hours. The nicer one was baked with eggs and butter, sugar or molasses, and spice. The nicest of all was baked like a custard, in which a small proportion of fine meal thickens the milk, along with a quantity of eggs, molasses, spice and a half pound of raisins.

Eliza Leslie went to town on Indian Puddings, from her first *Seventy-Five Receipts* (1828), when she elaborated the nicest Indian above with cinnamon, nutmeg, lemon and the finely chopped suet traditional in British mincemeat, to make a boiled pudding served with a drawn butter sauce of nutmeg and wine. In her *New Receipts* (1854) she offered a sumptuous "baked corn meal pudding," substituting butter for suet and emphasizing the rind "of a large fresh orange or lemon grated," plus a pound of Zante currants or sultana raisins, which suggests a British plum pudding. She patriotically balanced this one, however, with a "pumpkin Indian pudding," adding stewed pumpkin to much the same ingredients, all to be boiled in the bag.

In contrast to the urbane Leslie of Philadelphia, New Englanders remained apostles of austerity on the order of Lydia Child, who counseled that a hasty pudding made of rye grain and West India molasses would benefit any whose "system is in a restricted state" from dyspepsia. Both Catharine Beecher and Marion Harland provided recipes for "An Excellent Indian Pudding without Eggs (A Cheap Dish)," and Fannie Farmer's Indian pudding in 1896 was a strict survival mush of milk, meal and molasses, from which "ginger may be omitted." The same pudding without eggs and stiffened with rye flour became

Boston brown bread, steamed in a pot or mold (a one-pound baking-powder box or a five-pound lard pail "answers the purpose," said Farmer) instead of in a pudding bag.

Not that baking batters in an oven or steaming them in a pot was a British invention. Cushing described the Zuni version of a double-boiler used when a kind of steamed mush-bread was made from little balls of dough spread over a yucca sieve:

> A large pot half-filled with water was set over the fire, inside of which a smaller vessel, partially filled with water and weighted with pebbles to keep it steady, was placed. Upon this smaller part was laid the sieve or screen holding the balls of dough, the larger pot then being covered with a slab of stone and kept boiling until the dumplings were thoroughly cooked by steaming.

Fortunately today, many American chefs who are rediscovering native ingredients are also restoring sensuous pleasures to the minimalist version of Indian pudding purveyed by Fannie Farmer. One of my favorites is offered by a contemporary native Indian in a form that would have done no discredit to the luxurious palate of Eliza Leslie. The cornmeal dessert contributed by Ella Thomas Sekatau of the Narragansetts to Barrie Kavasch's *Native Harvests* (1979) puts cheap dishes to shame. She poured into her white cornmeal thick cream, maple syrup, berry juice and fresh berries, nutmeg and nut butter and enriched it with three lightly beaten eggs.

The other way colonists conferred dignity on mush was to call it polenta. Virginia Randolph's directions in her *Virginia Housewife* (1824) "To Make Polenta" were similar to the *Pocumtuc's* "hasty pudding," except that Randolph sliced the cooked mush when cold, layered it with butter and cheese in a deep dish and baked it in a quick oven—Italian-style. We know that she thought of it as Italian because she follows it with recipes for "macaroni" and "vermicelli." Fifty years later, Marion Harland included polenta in her *Dinner Year-Book,* turning it out on a plate to cool, then cutting it into squares and frying them yellow-brown. "This is a favorite dish with the Italian peasantry," she explained, "who generally eat it without frying." At the turn of the century, Célestine Eustis outlined four polenta recipes, including "alla Toscana," which initiated *les pauvres* in the polenta mystique taught today to rich Americans by expensive Italian cooking teachers. Here was the ritual pouring of the meal in a slow trickle into boiling water, the constant stirring, then the holding of the saucepan over the hottest part of the fire until the meal was detached from the

"I sing of food by British nurse designed
To make the stripling brave and maiden kind,
Let Pudding's dish most wholesome be thy theme,
And dip they swelling plumes in fragrant cream."
—BENJAMIN FRANKLIN KING, JR., *Hasty Pudding* (ca. 1875)

bottom so that it would turn out easily onto a board, then the cutting of it into slices with a wire or string. Eustis's *pauvres* may not have the cachet of Italian peasants in the American imagination, but the mush is the same.

So is the cornmeal, for there are even fewer stone-ground mills in Italy than in the United States. One of the last is the picturesque mill of the Scotti family outside Bergamo; the family grow heritage strains of corn for a mill that has been grinding since the early 1500s. As for continuous stirring in the traditional copper polenta pot, most Italian housewives I know buy blocks of packaged precooked polenta from their supermarkets. Busy American housewives, following British tradition, long ago displaced stir-about mushes with steamed ones, which were not only easier on the cook, but made a smoother, moister and more evenly cooked mush. Today the double-boiler (and microwave) has displaced both stirring sticks and pudding bags, so that the busiest housewife can make lump-free polenta, suppawn or mush: just moisten the meal first with cold water in the top of a double boiler, stir it until it comes to the boil over direct heat, add boiling water to the mush, place the top over the bottom of the boiler, clap on the lid and steam it for an hour.

A good reason for the polenta mystique, apart from the chic of copper pots and peasant cooking, is that Italians during four hundred years developed a fine corn cuisine of their own. When Columbus first brought corn to the continent, Italy was as suspicious as France or England of the grain they called *granoturco*. But since it was the cheapest of all grains to grow, they soon called corn by the ancient Roman name for pottage, *puls,* or *pulmentum,* and thus polenta. By the eighteenth century, corn had become a hedge against famine for the peasants of the northern provinces and, for the nobility, a version of

Nineteenth-century farmers in Middle Europe shelldried corn by "threshing" it as if it were wheat. Courtesy Library, University of California at Davis

pastoral. Among the Palladian villas a "polenta cult" developed, the subject of songs, poems and Manzoni's famous nineteenth-century romance *I Promessi Sposi.*

"Polenta is indeed a very simple food—cornmeal mush," Waverley Root wrote in *The Food of Italy* (1971), but like the simple wheat food called pasta, Italy subjected it to a multitude of regional spins. "Traviata," the wits called it, because of its ability to couple with any condiment. Since Italians knew nothing of Indian ash cooking, the condiments were important for nutrition and may be one reason that polenta was so often mixed with cheese, as in Piedmont's *polenta grassa,* in which polenta is layered with fontina, or Lombardy's *polenta cunscia,* in which it is mixed with Parmesan and garlic butter.

If Emilia-Romagna became the province of pasta, as Waverley Root said, Lombardy became the province of polenta. Here bowls or squares of polenta were sprinkled with truffles, flavored with lemon peel or orange water, accented with dried figs and walnuts, smoothed with roasted garlic and olive oil. In Trentino a black corn made "moorish polenta," enhanced with sausage, wild mushrooms, salt cod and cheese. It was the Veneto, however, which took polenta to new culinary heights in *polenta pastizzada,* layering the mush with minced veal, mushrooms and cockscombs in a wine-tomato-butter sauce seasoned with salt pork. Or in a sweetened *smejassa,* in which polenta was dried and crumbled with cookies, then baked like an Indian pudding with milk and molasses, raisins, pine nuts and candied citron.

The pride of the Veneto, however, was its famed *polenta con osei*—"fresh polenta, migratory birds, wine from the cellar and joyful folk," in the words of an ancient proverb. The birds were tiny grilled songbirds, wrapped in a baby blanket of crisp fat, each cradled in its juices on a square of polenta. Or sometimes the entire spit was brought to the table, Root said, "the chaplet of little birds skewered together on it, their beady eyes fixed reproachfully on the diner, a sight which has been known to indispose Anglo-Saxons." Venetians were more apt to be indisposed by *not* seeing beady eyes, and so gave a joke name to plain polenta, *polenta e osetiti scapai,* meaning "polenta and the little birds that got away." Cornmeal not only made mush, but also strengthened pastas, pizza crusts, soups, gnocchi, breads, cookies and cakes, among them a delicate confection flavored with maraschino liqueur and romantically titled *amor polenta.*

The French too developed a rustic cornmeal cuisine, but one far less familiar to Americans because each region gave its own vernacular twist to the mush theme. Perigord called it *las pous,* Paula Wolfert has said, because the porridge as it cooks sputters like a person softly sputtering in his sleep. The Savoy, where Barlow had his homesick meal, became the heart of French cornmeal cooking during the last years of the eighteenth century, when the French Revolution put peasant fare on the overturned tables of noblemen. Because Savoy mush (now called polenta) is stirred with a long stick for a long time, it is *polenta au baton.* The Savoyards serve it like the Italians with game and cheese, dress it in sauces, turn

While a woman in the foreground stirs her pot of mush (mamaliga, puliszka, polenta) *with a mush paddle, a woman at the rear prepares to cut with a string the mush turned out on the table.* Courtesy Library, University of California at Davis

it into soups and pastas and into an unusual *polenta en pilaf.* This treats coarse grits like rice, adding the grits to sautéed onions, steaming them in chicken broth and garnishing them with prunes and bacon or snails and hazelnuts.

Romania was so taken by cornmeal that it included the comforting sound of "mama" in the mush it called *mamaliga.* This was the mush that made its way to delis like Ratner's on Manhattan's Lower East Side, where it had "somehow crossed an ocean and a continent to become a staple for generations of Romanian peasants and their Jewish neighbors," wrote a Romanian descendant in *The New Yorker* (January 15, 1990). "Mamaliga, which I had always thought of as quintessentially Rumanian, was, of course, sweet corn, maize—the New World's gift to the Old."

Cornmeal is still a country staple of Romania and Hungary, beloved especially by the gypsy tinsmiths who called themselves *kalderash,* the name given to little corn cakes flavored with cumin and coriander. Northern Hungary and Transylvania lived on the mush they call *puliszka,* whether made into simple mush-and-milk puddings or stuffed with ricotta or beat into sweetened cakes. "Poor people made it with water instead of milk," George Lang told us in *The Cuisine of Hungary* (1971), "and they drank the milk with it, making an entire meal of it."

Cornmeal mush became a staple too in Africa, wherever the sixteenth-century Portuguese landed their ships. Corn spread also from the north to the interior along Arab trade routes, but after 1517 it was grown principally around the slave-trade ports of the West in order to supply cheap fodder for slaves during transport. " 'Tis generally observ'd, that *Indian* corn rises from a crown to twenty shillings betwixt February and harvest, which I suppose is chiefly occasion'd by the great number of *European* slave ships yearly resorting to the coast," wrote John Barbot, traveling between Ghana and Dahomey in the late seventeenth century. In eastern Africa the maize meal called *posho* in

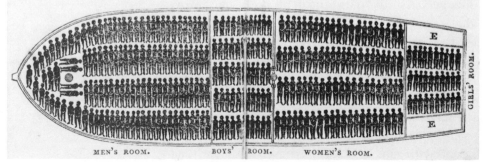

In the corn–slave conjunction, Thomas Branagan's plan for a slave ship in his 1807 The Penitential Tyrant *seems to disclose a giant ear of corn with paired rows of slaves for kernels.* Rare Book Room, Library of Congress

Plan of an African Ship's lower Deck, with ‍Negroes in the proportion of not quite one to a Ton.

MEN'S ROOM.   BOYS' ROOM.   WOMEN'S ROOM.   GIRLS' ROOM.

Swahili was so common by the end of the nineteenth century that colonials used it as a verb: an accountant for the Imperial British East Africa Company in 1895 wrote that they had so many stores between Lake Victoria and the coast he was "in a position therefore to 'posho' caravans right through," meaning to supply them with meal. But not until this century did cornmeal become a staple of the eastern and central regions of Africa and so essential today throughout Africa, Laurens Van der Post has written, that "millions of Africans now eat it in the belief that it is something inherited from their own earliest beginnings."

Africans continued to grind corn, as Amerindians did, between flat stones and stone rollers or pounded it in wooden mortars. They too celebrated ripe-corn harvest festivals, such as Ghana's "Hooting at Hunger," celebrated today with the dish *kpekple,* a mush stew with fish and palm nuts. In South Africa mealie-meal has become the national porridge, despite the fact that when boiled simply with water, as Copeland Marks complained, "it comes out tasting like old inner tubes."

A Ghanaian woman uses a wooden paddle to mix her corn-meal dough of sofki. *Courtesy Centro Internacional de Mejoramiento de Maíz y Trigo, Mexico City*

The cornmeal belt was a two-way stretch along the slave-trade routes that crossed the Atlantic: the Caribbean got its own back in an African form. Barbadian cornmeal mixed with okra in a dish called *coo coo* is African *frou frou.* West Indian *konkies* of coconut and sweet potatoes, a treat for Guy Fawkes Day, is African *kenkey.* West Indian *fungie* comes from Zaire, where they dump mush into a bowl, shape it into a smooth ball with the fingers, flip it against the side of the bowl to make it round, then tear off a small chunk and indent it with the thumb to use as a spoon for sauce. Where the cornmeal belt stretched north from the Caribbean into our Southern states, the African connection surfaces in the memories of slave descendants. One woman recalled the "meat tit" which they hung in their cabin to put meat skins in until they got enough for the mush pot, just as their African ancestors had done:

> I would put some of my meat skins in that pot and boil them and go out to that garden and crop some of them onion. I would make that pot of soup good and put some corn meal in. I had to feed all them children with that stuff. I'm like towards eleven or twelve years old. And I had to see that the children get something to eat or they would perish to death.

In America, a Southerner's meat tit was a Northerner's scrapple, and what bonded the childhood mush memories of one race to another, whether they had come as farmers from Saxony or slaves from Zaire, was the comfort of mush to empty guts. The Pennsylvania Dutch mixed it with scraps left over from butchering and called it "poor-do." In Germany and Holland they had mixed such scraps with buckwheat, and immigrants at first substituted cornmeal with reluctance until mush-and-hog scrapple became a dish as cherished as mush-and-milk. For the poor of the rural South, mush and hog offal had always been a special treat, like the "meat tit." A country woman in Appalachia today, a Mrs. Mann Norton, remembered for *Foxfire* how they cooked the scrapple of her youth:

> Take th' head, an' take th' eyeballs out, an' th' ears, an' cut down in there. Then y'got all th' hairs off of it. Y' put it in a big pot an' cooked it til th' meat just turned loose of th' main big bone.
>
> Y' lifted them bones out, an' laid your meat over in there an' felt of it with your hands t' see if they wasn't no bones in it. Then y' strain yer liquid through a strainer so th' little bones'd come out. Put'cher liquid back in a pot, and put that mashed meat back in that liquid. Put'cher sage an' pepper in there. Then y'stir it til it got t' boilin'. Then y' stick plain corn meal in there til its just plumb thick. Then y' pour it up in a mold, an' cut it off 'n fry it, an' brown it. Tastes just like fish.

And I remember the mush my Grandmother Harper made during the Depression for Sunday supper. She poured it hot into my Orphan Annie bowl and I made a well in the center with my Mickey Mouse spoon and filled it with a large pat of melting butter, then sprinkled the top with cinnamon and sugar and baptized it with cold milk. Hot mush, cold milk. The drama was there. I never asked for seconds because even before I'd finished my bowl I was dreaming of breakfast—thick slices of cold mush fried crisp on both sides in hot butter and slathered in syrup which, when my grandmother wasn't looking, I would lick from the plate with my tongue. Mush is still my favorite four-letter word.

One Man's Smut Is Another Man's Truffle

PERHAPS NO FOOD PLANT has ever been utilized more fully for edible, drinkable, inedible and unthinkable uses than corn, but all these uses depend upon language and the potency of names. What is "devil's corn" to a New Jersey farmer is *huitlacoche* (pronounced wheat-la-COH-chay) to a Mexican and *nanha* to a Hopi. These three terms name the common but visually monstrous smoky black-blue fungus, akin to a mushroom, that grows on corn and that American farmers call "corn smut." The Hopi thought it a delicacy and gathered it when young and tender for fried nanha; the fungus was parboiled for ten minutes, then sautéed in butter until crisp. Although older Hopi savored the fungus, few younger ones have tasted it, and today children use it to blacken faces in a game of tag.

Cushing said that for the Zuni corn-soot symbolized the "generation of life." In the Zuni granary, "a bunch of unbroken corn-soot" was laid each year next to a perfect ear of corn, dipped by a Seed-Priest in the sacred salt lake, Las Salinas. During the ceremony of the "Meeting of the Children," commemorating the return of the lost Corn Maidens, the Corn-Matron dusted the kernels of newly gathered and shelled corn with the old bunch of soot so that the seed might grow and reproduce. For the Zuni, Cushing added, such ceremonies were "testaments of faith, proving the infallibility of his 'medicine,' or fetishism, and of his practice of religion." By its very deformity, corn-soot was endowed with medicinal and miraculous powers.

For the typical American farmer, on the other hand, corn smut was and remains a disease to be eradicated, and it is seldom distinguished from the aflatoxin that attacks field corn in the form of a mold invisible to the eye and is wholly destructive to corn. Corn smut, on the contrary, is a highly visible spore, *Ustilago maydis,* that grows only on sweet corn and has been eaten for centuries, just as truffles have. But one man's medicine is another man's poison. Listen to the language of Edward Enfield in his *Indian Corn* (1866):

> The principal disease of this cereal appears in the form of a dark spongy growth, sometimes of a blue black or purple tinge, that occasionally shows itself on the stalk or leaves, but is more apt to take the place of the blighted ear. This substance increases gradually in size, sometimes reaching six or seven inches in diameter, and is generally regarded as a rank and luxuriant species of fungus [caused by bruises inflicted on the young plant by careless cultivation]. The bleeding that occurs from these wounds results in the formation of the dark morbid substance above described.

The modern scientific language of Paul Weatherwax doesn't carry the jolt of Enfield's bleeding wounds, but still presents a formidable obstacle to appetite: "The galls, which consist of hypertrophied host tissue mixed with fungal filaments, are at first greenish white in color throughout, but they darken from the inside outward and finally turn into sooty masses of black spores held together by remnants of the host tissue." The French called this *goitre du maïs,* Matthieu Bonafous reported in his *Histoire Naturelle, Agricole et Économique du Maïs* (1836), noting that most botanists considered it a form of mushroom. "I have tasted this substance several times without harm," he added. "I have seen cows eat a considerable quantity with impunity."

Soot, smut, goiter—none of them pretty names, least of all *huitlacoche,* which means "raven's shit." A story about Corn Soot Woman, translated by Ruth Benedict in her *Tales of the Cochiti Indians* (1931), deals with the name problem:

> One of the women [in the grinding house] heard somebody crying. She said, "Listen, somebody is crying." Just then the door opened and Corn Soot Woman came in crying. She said, "Nobody likes me to be with the corn they are to grind. I am fat but nobody has any use for me." The head woman of the [corn grinding] society said to Corn Soot Woman, "Why are you crying?" "I am crying because they don't ever put me among the good ears. I am not rotten." The head woman of the society said, "Don't ever separate her from the good corn. She is fat; that is why she is what she is. She is the mother of the corn soot and you must put her in with the good corn whenever you shell it, in order that they too may be fat, as she is." They gave her a new name, *Ioashknake* (shuck), and they gave the soot a ceremonial name, *Wesa.*

Bonafous's accurately baroque drawing of a corn "mushroom" in 1836 belies its less attractive names of corn soot, smut, goiter, raven's shit. Courtesy Library, University of California at Davis

If the Aztec gave her an irreverent name in *huitlacoche,* they relished the substance, as Mexicans do today in every kind of preparation from a hearty peasant soup to French-style crepes. When *huitlacoche* is renamed "Mexican truffle," even Americans become attentive, just as when fish eggs are called caviar. Since corn truffles grow only seasonally on unsprayed sweet corn, regrettably few Americans have had a chance to taste them outside Mexico. But Mexican farmers cultivate *huitlacoche* in special plots, so that it can be sold fresh in season and canned or frozen when not.

To give Americans a tasting and corn smut a new name, the James Beard House in New York City presented in 1989 an all-*huitlacoche* dinner of seven courses, conceived by Josefina Howard of Rosa

Mexicano restaurant. *Huitlacoche* appetizers were followed by *huitlacoche* soup, crepes, tortilla torte, salad and a startling but triumphant ice cream. Sautéed simply in butter, the corn truffle tastes delicately earthy and smoky like a mushroom, but because it is always attached to small kernels, it has also the sweetness and crunch of fresh corn. For mushroom and truffle lovers, corn truffles are a gastronomic joy. To American corn farmers, smut is smut.

Americans have, however, embraced without cavil other traditional uses of the corn plant that the ingenuity of native growers wrested from it. One was a major use of cornstalks, before the introduction of sugarcane, as corn sugar. Ben Franklin, pitching the sweetness of corn in his spiel to the French, focused on the juice in the stalk:

> The Stalks pressed like Sugar-Canes yield a sweet Juice, which being fermented and distill'd yields an excellent Spirit, boiled without Fermentation it affords a pleasant Syrop. In Mexico, Fields are sown with it thick, that multitudes of small Stalks may arise, which being cut from time to time like Asparagus are serv'd in Deserts, and their sweet Juice extracted in the Mouth, by chewing them.

Mexican bottled fruit drinks use corncobs for corks. Photograph © 1986 by Ignacio Urquiza, from *The Taste of Mexico* by Patricia Quintana; Stewart, Tabori & Chang, New York

Many early explorers mentioned cornstalk sugar, including Ralph Lane in Roanoke in 1585: "And within these few days we have found here maize, or Guinea wheat, whose ear yieldeth corn for bread, four hundred upon one ear; and the cane maketh very good and perfect sugar."

For both natives and invaders the uses of corn for food and drink overlapped with medicinal and household uses. The Iroquois, after extracting juice from the stalk, turned the juice into a medicinal lotion for wounds and the stalk into a medicine bottle to contain it, plugging the cut section at both ends. The pith they made into a sponge to absorb liquids, and from the dried stalks they cut floats for fishing lines, while boys used the stalks for playtime spears. Colonists were quick to absorb corn into their own traditions of herbal medicine, as John Josselyn did in 1672, citing the uses of "Indian wheat": *"To ripen any Impostume or Swelling. For sore Mouths. The New Englands Standing Dish. . . .* It is hotter than our

Wheat and clammy, excellent in *Cataplasm* to ripen any Swelling or impostume," he explained. "The decoction of the blew Corn, is good to wash sore Mouths with." Roger Williams recommended it as a laxative: "If the use of it were knowne and received in England (it is the opinion of some skillfull in physic) it might save many thousand lives in England, occasioned by the binding nature of the English wheat, the Indian Corne keeping the body in a constant moderate loosenesse." English opinion, on the contrary, complained of the binding nature of Indian corn, along with its general indigestibility. This was a prejudice revived by lady nutritionists like Mrs. Mary Lincoln, who warned in 1887 that corn "is heating for persons with weak digestion, and should not be given to scrofulous children, or to invalids when there is any inflammatory condition of the system."

Corn silks brewed into tea, on the other hand, was a colonial medicine that remained in good standing. Herbalist Tommie Bass recommends it today to fellow Appalachians as a good kidney medicine. "If you just want to make a dose, you know, right quick, take about as many silks as on a good ear of corn and put it in a tea cup and run hot water over it and let it sit about ten or fifteen minutes and then drink it." Corn parched and ground as a substitute for coffee was once almost as common as corn tea, for both health and economy. "Dyspepsia Coffee," Libbie Thompson called it in the *Kansas Home Cook-Book* (1874); she diluted regular coffee with a mixture of cornmeal browned with molasses in the oven. During the Great War, corn coffee was a patriotic sacrifice of the home front, served up by Charles Murphy as "War Coffee":

> Mix together, thoroughly rubbing with the hands until the mixture resembles soft brown sugar, two quarts of bran, one quart of corn meal, and a large cup of molasses. Spread the mixture in a large dripping pan, brown it in a slow oven, stirring it often with a long-handled spoon until it is a rich seal brown. Do not let it scorch or burn. When done, put in jars like regular coffee.

Anthropologists were always keen to cite the medicinal uses of corn among their studied tribes and were often struck by the way in which every part of the corn plant was made a specific medicine against some ailment. Among the Tewa at Santa Clara, rubbing a warmed ear of corn with the foot was said to help swollen glands in the neck. At San Ildefonso Pueblo, corn pollen was recommended for palpitations of the heart and corn smut for women suffering from irregular menstruation. The Oklahoma Cherokee practiced preventive medicine with new corn silk in order to ward off green-corn fever: after wading into a stream at dawn, the medicine man filled a container of green ears and corn silk with water, stirred the contents counterclockwise while chanting four times, then presented the liquid to the patient for drinking or bathing.

Among Nebraska pioneers corn was used in ritual ways to prevent or cure warts, an alarming number of them summarized in *A Treasury of Nebraska Pioneer Folklore:*

> Steal a grain of corn and destroy it so that its owner will never have it again, and your warts will leave.
>
> Rub the warts with a kernel of corn and feed the corn to a rooster. Be sure the rooster gets it and your warts will disappear.
>
> Touch seventeen different kernels of corn to each wart, then feed the corn to the chickens. If they eat the corn, the warts will disappear.
>
> Bury a small bag of corn. When the corn decays, the warts will leave. Cut a corn cob crosswise and take out the white pulp center. Put this on the wart. Then fill the inside of the cob with soda and add a drop of vinegar to boil the soda away. Hold this over the warts. Repeat two or three times a day until cured.

The number of variants would suggest that warts were as common in Nebraska as corn, and as hard to get rid of.

For the Indian household, no part of the corn plant went to waste: leaves, stalks, husks and cobs were transformed into mats, trays, cushions, hammocks, scrub brushes, moccasins, feather holders, bottle stoppers, combs and back scratchers. Settlers followed aboriginal example in contriving their own uses, such as cornshuck mattresses. After the Civil War, these were a sign of hard times, wrote Elizabeth Woolsey Spruce (1873–1969) in a "corn memoir" telling how her grandmother prepared dowries for her daughters in south Texas:

> Since cotton was too expensive to use for mattresses, they used cornshucks instead. The hard end of the shuck was cut off. In one hand a thin layer of shuck was held and split all the way down with a table fork. . . . When they had sufficient for a bed it was placed in a bed tick without tacking. Of course it took days and days but what was time for, in those reconstruction days, except for hard work by every one? This mattress was always placed under the feather bed. There were no bedsprings.

The discomfort of cornhusk mattresses figured in a great deal of American humor, as in Josh Billings's description of a "modern slat bottom" bed with two

Cornhusk dolls made by Indians of the Six Nations. Milwaukee Public Museum, Neg. No. 425333

mattresses, "one cotton, and one husk, and both harder, and about az thick az a sea biskitt. Yu enter the bed sideways and kan feel every slat at once, az eazy az yu could the ribs ov a grid iron."

A more unusual use for cornhusks was that described by Mattie Huffman, one of the voices from the Kansas frontier collected by Joanna Stratton in *Pioneer Women* (1981). Mattie remembered how her aunt gathered cornshucks, cut them crosswise and wound her knitting yarn on them, twelve inches thick on each one, in order to dye the yarn: "When it was taken out, if the dye was red, for instance, next to the shuck would be the natural white color of the yarn, next to that a pink shade, and next or on the outside it would be red. This was the manner of making what they called clouded yarn." Clouded-yarn knitters in Kansas echoed weavers in Mexico, who primed the threads of their loomsin corn gruel. Because of the corn, they kept their children away while weaving, explained a contemporary Maya woman in Chiapas: "If they put their heads in our loom, they will be big eaters and will want to drink a lot of corn gruel."

Indian craftsmen relied on corn products in even more unusual ways. In pre-Columbian Peru, south coast Indians ground corn kernels to make a glue for their feather masks: they first covered a human skull with finely woven cotton and then glued feathers to the cotton. In post-Columbian Mexico, artists ground up the inner core of cornstalks and mixed the stuff with a natural glue to make a material, like papier-mâché, for sculpting figures. After covering the sculpted paste with cloth, they painted it to make realistic saints and crucified Christs which, because they were light, were favored for carrying in religious processions.

For Indian and colonist alike, dried corncobs furnished a natural supply of fuel, but a new-fashioned twist is the invention of the Dovetec Corn Heater by Carroll Buckner of North Carolina, to replace wood. His corn stove holds seventy pounds of cobs, fed into the fire by an auger. "It takes years to grow a tree," Buckner says, "and only four months to grow a crop of corn." More than a century ago, *The Prairie Farmer* of March 20, 1869, advised its readers to burn corncobs to make "cob coal," not as a fuel but as a medicine for hog cholera:

> Collect your cobs in a pile and burn them until they are thoroughly charred, then wet them out. Sprinkle brine or salt on the coals and let your hogs eat all they want. . . . Last winter I neglected to give my hogs cob coal and the result was, in the spring, they took the cholera; ten of them had it bad. I raked up the cobs in the lot and charred them well, then salted the coal freely. They all ate of the coal but three that were too far gone to get up. They died; the rest got well.

A more usual use of cob coal was to "cure" hogs another way, smoking their slaughtered parts to flavor and preserve them for food. New Englander Amelia Simmons recommended corncobs for smoking bacon, and the tradition continues in the cob-smoked maple-cured hams from Enosberg Falls, Vermont, where "Puffer's Cob-Smoked Ham" has made Puffer Lumbra a household name.

Country folk everywhere remember one use of the corncob that was later supplanted by store-bought paper. "All the farmers, black and white, kept dried corncobs beside their double-seated thrones," Harry Crews wrote in *A Childhood* (1978), "and the cobs served the purpose for which they were put there with all possible efficiency and comfort."

A more public use of the American corncob was for pipes. The corncob-pipe center of the world is Washington, Missouri, where the Buescher Corn Cob Pipe Company turns out twelve thousand to eighteen thousand pipes a day to sell in seven thousand outlets in fifty-seven countries around the world. Today they cost $1.95; twenty years ago they cost 10 cents, and more than a century ago, when Henrick Tibbe of Holland started the company, they cost but a penny a pipe. Tibbe was an emigrant woodworker in 1869 when he decided to adapt his native Dutch pipe to corn country by shaping a cob on his lathe and applying a plaster-of-paris mixture to the outside. Today, his grandchildren

Interior of corncob ("meerschaum") pipe factory, Washington, Missouri, July 26, 1926. Photo Pierce W. Hangge, courtesy Missouri Historical Society

run the company and grow a special hard-cob hybrid for their pipes made according to family tradition: The cobs are aged for two years before they are sawed into "pipe bowl blanks"; then a "cob boring bit" drills a hole in the center of the blank and the blank is turned and shaped on a lathe; the indentations are filled with plaster of paris, which is finally sanded and shellacked "to produce a high luster while still preserving the texture and appearance of the corn cob."

If corncobs turned into pipes are as American as General MacArthur, striding through the waters of Manila Bay with a smoking cob clamped in his teeth, corncobs and cornshuck mattresses symbolize other unforgettable, if less heroic, moments in the American imagination. What reader of William Faulkner's *Sanctuary* can forget the way Temple lay in bed the night before her rape in the corncrib?

> There was no linen, no pillow, and when she touched the mattress it gave forth a faint dry whisper of shucks. . . . in the silence Tommy could hear a faint, steady chatter of the shucks inside the mattress where Temple lay, her hands crossed on her breast and her legs straight and close and decorous, like an effigy on an ancient tomb.

Faulkner cuts from the cornshuck innocence of Temple to the trial of Popeye, at which the district attorney offers as criminal evidence a corncob that appears to have been dipped in dark brownish paint. "You have just heard the testimony of the chemist and the gynecologist. . . . this is no longer a matter for the hangman, but for a bonfire of gasoline."

If a corncob in a psychopath's hand could be an instrument of dark defilement, so cornmeal, in a housewife's hand, could be an instrument of cleansing. Sidney Morse's *Household Discoveries* (1908) counted the ways: Rub cornmeal on calcimined walls to clean them, spread a cornmeal and oxalic-acid paste on straw goods to clean them, clean Panama hats with dampened cornmeal applied with a stiff nailbrush, clean white kid gloves by rubbing your gloved hands together in fine cornmeal, improve the luster of furs by browning cornmeal and while still hot rubbing it through the fur with a flannel cloth, clean wallpaper by making a dough of rye flour dipped in cornmeal to use as a rubbing cloth, clean blood or mud stains with cornstarch, make hand soap from cornmeal and powdered borax.

Just plain corn kernels were also used in extraordinary ways. If the French learned to force-feed geese with kernels poured through a funnel down the throat, to make their livers fat (or their *foies gras*), so the Spanish learned to force-feed heretics with dried raw kernels and water, and made them sit naked in the sun until their bellies burst. So Americans learned to tempt fish with kernels as bait. Louis de Gouy records an old Oregon game law that permitted fishermen the use of corn kernels but made it a misdemeanor to use canned corn. Corn fishing and hunting were part of the tradition of the West, as described by Richard Ford in a story named for Great Falls, Montana, in which the narrator tells how his father baited his lines with corn to catch fish in springtime: "He used yellow corn kernels stacked onto a #4 snelled hook, and he would rattle this rig-up along the bottom of a deep pool below a split-shot sinker, and catch fish." In the fall, they used corn as a "hunger-line" to catch ducks: "We would set out his decoys to the leeward side of our blind, and he would sprinkle corn on a hunger-line from the decoys to where we were. . . . And after a while, sometimes it would be an hour and full dark, the ducks would find the corn, and the whole raft of them—sixty sometimes—would swim in to us." Corn is used as bait even in Eastern cities, where poisoned corn kernels are strewn along city roofs to diminish the encroaching population of pigeons. Even in the animal kingdom, one bird's meat is another one's poison.

The totemic power of corn, for good or evil, has survived wherever people live close to the earth. A Southern black woman, who contributed an oral history to *When I Was Comin' Up* (1982), saw death in a cornshuck: "I seen a token, a great big, black bear, reachin' his mouth into a shuck of corn—and then my momma passed in three days. That was a token." In Haiti, corn retains demonic power, and the cornmeal that is ritual medicine is also ritual poison of a particularly potent kind. A recipe devised by the *voudon* La Bonte was outlined by Wade Davis in *Serpent and Rainbow* (1985): Take wood ground from a particular healing tree, leg-bone shavings and other decayed matter from a human cadaver, add white sugar, basil leaves, seven drops of rum, seven drops of claïrin and a small amount of cornmeal and mix well. Cornmeal and corn kernels figure not just in concoctions and incantations, as when the *mambo* traces a cabalistic design with meal on a coffin or gravel, but in rites of possession, as in Davis's powerful evocation of a woman possessed by the spirit of corn:

Then, on the steps of the church, the scene turned into an epiphany. A healthy peasant woman, dressed in the bright-blue-and-red solid block colors of Ogoun, the spirit of fire and war, swirled through the beggars possessed by her spirit. Over her shoulder was slung a brilliant red bag filled with dry kernels of golden corn. She twirled and pranced in divine grace, and with one arm stretching out like the neck of a swan she placed a small pile of corn into each of the begging bowls. When she was finished, her bag empty, she spun around to the delight of all and with a great cry flung herself from the steps of the church.

The power of the corn spirit that possessed Aztec priests as they once twirled and pranced on the steps of their temples resides still in the kernels of corn with which contemporary "daykeepers" of the Quiché Maya in Guatemala divine the future. The daykeeper passes his hands over the kernels and divides them into lots, then finds his auguries by counting the day numbers and names of the 260-day cycle of the ancient calendar. The Zuni too measured time, past and future, by kernels of corn. They measured lifetimes by "generations of corn," counting from the time a boy received from his father his first planting seed to the time he in turn gave seed to his son to plant. To number our seven ages of man, they counted seven ages of corn. In the numberless generations of corn possessed by the corn spirit, even the darkly monstrous corn-soot could take its place as a maker of miracles, when it was called "generator of life."

The Language of Drink

CHICHA IN PERU, MOONSHINE IN ARKANSAS

WHEN I STOOD in the great cathedral on the Plaza de Armas in Cuzco, my eye was seized not by the altar of beaten silver and the monstrance of solid gold, but by a large canvas of the Last Supper painted by an Indian converted in the seventeenth century to the white man's gods. Here the Inca Jesus and his twelve attendant lords sat before a table laden with the two chief elements of an Inca feast: not bread and wine, but *cuy* and *chicha,* or guinea pig and corn beer.

Corn was both bread and wine in the New World and particularly in Peru, for fermented corn did for the Inca what ash-processed corn did for the Hopi and lime-processed corn did for the Aztec. Not only did corn fermented from mash and malt make the drinkers of the brew happy in ways familiar to all drug-consuming cultures, but the enzymes of the ferment made the brew nutritious. In ancient Peru, the brewing of beer was held so sacred that it was entrusted to the hands of virgin priestesses, whose Christian equivalent would be the nuns of Mary. Even in modern Peru beer is a form of sacrament and no one drinks it before first pouring out a few drops on the ground to honor Mama Sara, the corn goddess, just as no one builds a house without putting a miniature bull and *chicha* jar on the roof, for luck and life.

My first taste of home-brewed *chicha de jora* sent me in search of a recipe for it. The earliest I found had been written by Girolamo Benzoni, in his *Historia del Mundo Nuevo* (1565), when he described how the Chosen Women of the Sun enhanced the potency of their brew by mixing the corn malt with saliva:

The women, taking a quantity of grain that seems to them sufficient . . . and having ground it, they put it into water in some large jars, and the women who are charged with this operation, taking a little of the grain, and having rendered it somewhat tender in a pot, hand it over to some other women, whose office it is to put it into their mouths and gradually chew it; then with an effort they almost cough it out upon a leaf or platter and throw it into the jar with the other mixture, for otherwise this wine would have no strength. It is then boiled for three or four hours, after which it is taken off the fire and left to cool, when it is poured through a cloth, and is esteemed good in proportion as it intoxicates.

Everywhere I went I came upon *chicha*. *Chicha* is the soda pop as well as the beer of Peru, and in one form or another everybody from nursing babes to toothless grannies drinks it. Children go for unfermented sweetened *chicha blanca,* which is made from white corn and sprinkled with cinnamon, or *chicha morada,* which is made from purple corn and looks and tastes like a strawberry milkshake. Adults move on to *chicha de jora,* made from sprouted and fermented corn, which produces a pale yellow-white brew with a two-inch head of foam and which tastes a bit like English barley water mixed with light pilsner, or like a shandygaff of ale mixed with cider or milk, once a country staple in both England and America. *Chicha picante* is the same brew zapped with lemon and the hot pepper sauce called *aji*. *Chicha frutillada* adds fresh fruit, such as strawberries, and *punchy* adds a shot of Pisco brandy to create a potent boilermaker.

In Peru today, women are still the brewers and every woman knows how to make home brew, whether for a *chicheria,* or beer joint, or just for her family and neighborhood friends. Long ago Peruvian women learned to share the work, and every rural village will sport above some doorway a red or white flag, nowadays usually plastic, which means "Here's where you get fresh *chicha* today." You may be sharing an earth-floored room with a few chickens and pigs, but like a pub the mood is convivial in proportion to the size of the glass consumed, and a quart-sized *caporal grande* costs but a dime.

My recipe search in Cuzco took me one day to a padlocked gate of sheet iron, beyond which was a dirt yard cluttered with antique ceramic *chicha* jars and scraggly plants native to pre-Inca Peru. The yard was enclosed by adobe walls covered with frescoes of the sun and moon and scenes of Inca life in

A nineteenth-century engraving by A. de Neuville of chicha drinkers in Cuzco, Peru.

the style of a Peruvian Grandma Moses. This was the studio-classroom of Professor Chavez Bellon, an elderly man in a baggy suit with a big smile and a lifelong enthusiasm for all things Incan. He swept me and a handful of students in his wake to his local, a *chicheria* called Rosas Pata, on Ciro Alegria. He led us through a small adobe house into a back room, so black with smoke from the brazier in the corner that I could barely make out the pair of women stooped

"[Chicha] *precipitates them into incest, sodomy and homicide, and there is rarely a drinking bout that is not mixed with heathen rites, the Devil often being visibly present, disguised in the person of an Indian.*"

—FATHER GARCIA MARCOS, quoted by Father Antonio de la Calancha in *Coronoica Moralizada del Orden de San Augustin en el Peru* (1638)

over the boiling black-iron pots. Near them, a batch of corn mash fermented in a straw basket, awaiting the addition of cold water from a long wooden trough. Next to the trough stood a bucket of foaming *chicha,* ready to pour into the glasses of the men in the adjoining room, where the air was dense with smoke and the benches with beer drinkers.

Professor Chavez did his best to explain the old and the new way of making *chicha.* Old-style *chicha* was made simply by letting ground corn and water slowly ferment, but the new way is to speed the process by adding yeast and sugar, plus a little trigo (a type of wheat). Since then, every Peruvian I've met in Cuzco and elsewhere has had his own contradictory way with *chicha,* some adding quinoa and barley, others the heavy dark-brown sugar called *chancaca,* others insisting on straw baskets for filtering and buried earthen jars for fermenting. The closest I came to a "definitive" *chicha* for the would-be home brewer was from Felipe Rojas-Lombardo, the late Peruvian-born chef of Manhattan's Ballroom restaurant, known for its fine tapas:

Take dry corn, then make it wet to sprout it. Keep it moist with burlap (or some other loose covering) until the corn grows two- to three-inch sprouts. Then spread honey on the *maíz de jora* and put it in the sun for a day. Forget how it looks, it's a mess. Just scrape it up, put it in a pot with water and add some dry soaked corn that is not sprouted, along with a piece of *chancaca* or more honey. Bring to the boil slowly and boil for five hours, adding water as it evaporates. (My mother always added cinnamon and clove.) Take it off the fire and when it is fully cool, strain it through cheesecloth [a grass-lined basket was traditional; any metal other than stainless steel will ruin the fermenting process]. Store the liquid in a ceramic pot or jar in a dark place for a week or two. In the Andes, they bury the pot in the ground, leaving just the long neck of the pot above the earth, covered with a cloth, because the earth maintains an even cool temperature. The longer it stays, the stronger it gets.

I tried many times but the mess stayed a mess—souring, rotting, molding, yes, but fermenting? No. My advice is to leave it to the *chicheria* women. If not everybody makes it, everybody drinks it, said the Cuzco guide who pointed out the *chicha* grooves cut in the stones of the fortress of Sacsahuaman, and who now sat me with me in Cuzco's best-known *chicheria,* La Cholla on Calle Pumacurco, where a baby dunked her head in her mother's *caporal grande* to the sound of her father's homemade-fiddle music. But for the chatter of Spanish and Quechuan voices, I might have been listening to a hootenany in Arkansas, and a few months later I was doing just that, picking up the beat of Paralee and her Swinging Strings with other folks who appreciated home brew.

It's a lot easier to find a *chicha* maker in Peru than an old-time moonshiner in Arkansas, but they share a brewer's knowledge of corn. If he is making good whiskey, an Arkansas moonshiner will begin with what he calls corn beer. In this country, whiskey originally was "pure corn," just like old-time *chicha*, without additional sugar or yeast. Mesoamerican Indians for centuries brewed beer from sprouted corn and cornstalks, as they distilled liquors from native plants and secretions like fermented honey to make a kind of mead, agave (or maguey) to make *pulque*, saguaro cactus to make a wine, peyote cactus to make a narcotic. Alcoholic beverages flourished wherever domesticated plants flourished, as dual signs of civilized life, but wheat-culture colonists brought their own ancient heritage of brewing techniques with them and had to learn to substitute corn malt for barley in the New World.

A colonial drinker taking his morning dram. North Wind Picture Archives

"Wee made of the same [mayze] in the countrey some mault, wherof was brued as good ale as was to be desired," Thomas Hariot wrote from Virginia in 1588. By 1620 Captain George Thorpe, who had set up a distillery at Berkeley Plantation on the James River, could write to a friend in London that he now made "so good a drink of Indian corn as I protest I have divers times refused to drink good strong English beer and chosen to drink that." Captain Thorpe, however, was unusual in his open-mindedness and was repaid for his generosity by being scalped two years later by Indians who had drunk too much of his corn.

In England, of course, the brewhouse was as important an adjunct to the farm as the dairy, and small beer was the drink of choice for every member of the household just as soft drinks are with us. On the farm, brewing was woman's work. When Richard Bradley, a professor of botany at Cambridge

University, undertook in 1736 to instruct *The Country Housewife and Lady's Director* in the Management of a House, and the Delights and Profits of a Farm, his first concern was "Instructions for managing the Brew House, and Malt-Liquors in the Cellar; the making of Wines of all sorts." The housewife's traditional brewing tasks provoked a Virginia colonist a century earlier to scold lazy American housewives for dereliction of beer duty. The title John Hammond gave his work in 1656 suggests that women were much on his mind: *Leah and Rachel, or, the Two Fruitful Sisters, Virginia and Maryland: Their Present Condition, Impartially Stated and Related.*

> Beare is indeed in some places constantly drunken, in other some nothing but Water or Milk, and Water or Beverige; and that is where the goodwives (if I may so call them) are negligent and idle; for it is not want of Corn to make Malt with, for the country affords enough, but because they are slothful and careless; and I hope this Item will shame them out of these humours; that they will be adjudged by their drinke, what kind of Housewives they are.

Spirits, or *aqua vitae,* were another matter. Distilling was man's work, and the early Scottish and Irish monastic tradition of distilling spirits from barley malt to make what the Celts called *usquebaugh,* or water of life, played an important role in the history of corn. It also, as I discovered with shock, signified in the history of my own American life. When I set out to find a moon-

A family in 1894 celebrates the Fourth of July with copious bottles of bourbon.
The Bettmann Archive

shiner who would give me a recipe To Make Corn Likker at Home, I had no notion that I would uncover the stills of my own teetotaling ancestors.

It wasn't easy to find Frank and Paralee Weddington in Butler Hollow near Beaver Town, total inhabitants fifty, in the wooded hills of northern Arkansas near Eureka Springs, but I got a little help from friends. The house we came to was a ramshackle weathered cabin, with rockers on the porch, barking dogs in the yard and a bluebottle tree out front. A bluebottle tree is one you make by putting empty blue glass bottles on the branches of a leafless tree to catch the sun and prettify the yard. Frank, bright-eyed and toothless, was tucked up in his overalls behind the big woodstove in the parlor. At eighty-five he doesn't hear or remember so good, but Paralee at a mere seventy-six, with short-cut hair and square-cut jaw, remembers for both of them. Since they've been married sixty years and have two daughters, six grandchildren and five great-grands to show for it, they have much to remember.

I asked Frank how he got started moonshining. "There wasn't work and I had to do something and I made a livin', " he said. "Back in the twenties, times was hard." Paralee took over: "Him and all his folk was always crazy about whiskey and I guess they didn't have no money to go buy it, so they went to makin' it. He growed up with boot jacks—a boot jack is a still," she explained. "We'd been married just nine months, Betty, the nineteenth of October and next July twenty-fourth he got caught and was in jail for eight months, so we spent our first anniversary with him in jail." Frank was caught just four days, I realized, before I was born.

It was a one-man operation, Frank told me. "I done everythin' meself." So when he gave me his whiskey recipe, I knew it'd been tested. Just as with *chicha,* however, there were an old and a new way of making corn whiskey. The old way was "pure corn" and slow fermentation. The new way was "sugar corn," with quantities of brown sugar substituted for grain because it was quicker and cheaper. For the purist, "sugar likker" was a corruption, but for the Prohibition moonshiner it was more like necessity. Frank's recipe was for "sugar corn":

You git your barrel, whatever you're goin' to put your mash in. If you're goin' to put up a whole lot, git you a sixty-gallon barrel, and put fifty pounds of chops [the chopped corn] in it and fifty pounds of sugar, and a package of yeast foam from the store. Stir that all up together and let it set three days till your still goes to pot and settles down. Put it on the far [fire] and go to burnin' it. Put somethin' under thar to catch your whiskey in. You start to boilin' your copper pot and the water come down to the boiler over into a barrel of cold water, so you got it coiling around and around and your whiskey comes out here. You got to watch it, when it gits down kinda weak, you're supposed to quit. Doublin' back, we call it, you catch a little and put it in your boiler for the next batch. Doublin' back, boy, it's pure dee alkeehol then.

A classical copper pot still of the kind used by distillers like George Washington at Mount Vernon, and by moonshiners everywhere, is now the property of the Bureau of Alcohol, Tobacco and Firearms, on permanent loan to the Oscar Getz Whiskey Museum in Bardstown, Kentucky. Courtesy Department of the Treasury, Bureau of Alcohol, Tobacco and Firearms

Most whiskey is made from a combination of mash (cornmeal of ground unsprouted kernels mixed with water and then fermented) and malt (cornmeal of sprouted kernels, dried and ground) from white flint, not yellow hybrid, corn. A breed like Holcomb Prolific was favored by the Georgia moonshiner quoted by *Foxfire,* who explained how Georgians sprouted corn: In winter they soaked it in a barrel of warm water for a day, then drained it and put it in a tub by the stove; each day for four or five days they covered the corn with warm water for fifteen minutes, then drained and turned it. Soon they'd have a good malt with shoots two inches long. In summer, they put corn in tow sacks in the sun, sprinkling the sacks with warm water once a day and flipping them. They had to watch it, however, for if the corn got too hot, it would go "slick."

They would take the sprouted corn to be ground at the mill or they'd use a sausage grinder at home. They'd need about 1½ bushels of corn sprouted for malt to put with 9½ bushels unsprouted for mash. They'd grind the mash fine, then boil it in water in batches and put it in the mash barrels. "It's like a woman making biscuits," said one Tennessee moonshiner. "If she don't know how to mix that dough in the bread bowl over thar, when she puts 'em in the pan, they ain't no count. You don't make likker in a outfit. You make it over thar in the mash barrels."

In each of his mash barrels, the Georgia moonshiner first thinned the mash by sticking a mash stick upright and adding water until the stick fell to the side. Next he added a gallon of malt to each barrel and a double handful of raw rye over the top. After five days the mixture would develop a thick foamy cap about two inches deep, a suds-and-blubber foam called a "blossom cap." Once the alcohol had eaten up the cap, this "distiller's beer" was ready to run. You had to catch it at just the right moment, he warned, or it would turn to vinegar. Both distiller and revenuer could tell by the "smack," the feel of the beer when you dipped your fingers in it, whether the liquid had the right stickiness or tackiness to begin distillation.

All a still needs is a firebox attached to a cooker that is attached to a condenser. The simplest kind was a "ground hog" or "hog still," built directly on the ground with a furnace of mud and rocks built around it so that the flames could wrap around the pot and exit through a backside flue. Vapors would collect in a barrel on top that was connected to a condenser, so that fermenting and distilling could be done in one operation and the still could be easily built and concealed in a creek bank or hillside. The most common still was a pot still, in which a copper pot shaped like a turnip with a tall neck could be made airtight with a lid and fired by a furnace below. Like fermenting, firing had to be watched to keep the temperature steady at 173 degrees Fahrenheit, the point at which alcohol vaporizes. Higher heat meant more water and impurities in the condensed liquor.

For a "singling" run, as it was called, you could expect to get fifty gallons of weak alcohol from eight bushels of corn. "You run them singlin's 'til as long as they got any strength in 'em, then you put your hands under the worm [the distilling coil], rub 'em and inhale," explained a distiller from Blairville, Georgia. "When they smell right sour, the alkihol's out." That's when the whiskey, as they say, "breaks at the worm." Moonshiners pride themselves on sensing the moment of break. "Lots of times I could tell when the bead broke because it changed that twist," said another Georgian. "I'd say, 'It's broke, boys,' and go over and test it and it'd be dead." To bring the liquor up to strength, you'd have to run the singlings through again for a doubling, what Frank called "doublin' back," and thus "pure dee alkeehol." From fifty gallons of singlings, you'd get maybe 16 to 20 gallons of "doublin' likker," or about 2½ gallons to a half bushel of cornmeal.

During Prohibition some hillfolk devised the thumper keg, which speeded up the doubling by distilling the vapors through a keg of beer inserted between the cooking pot and condenser. When the hot steam hit the beer, it began to bubble or thump. Beneath the condenser, the distiller put a funnel lined with a double layer of clean cloth and a double handful of clean hickory coals to act as a filter and remove the oil slick called "bardy grease." In the early days moonshiners were more likely to use a "bootleg bonnet," or felt hat, tacked across the top of the keg beneath the worm.

To test the strength of his doublin' likker, a moonshiner would proof it by shaking a sample in a glass vial and then looking at the bead. "If it's high

proof—say 115 to 120—a big bead will jump up there on top when you shake it," explained one man. "If the proof is lower, the bead goes away faster and is smaller." When a doubling comes through the worm, the first shots are as high as 150 or 160 proof, but it gets weaker as it continues until it gets below 90 proof, when it breaks at the worm, and from then on is called "the backin's," which can be mixed with singlings for the next run. The ideal 100-proof pure corn makes a bead about the size of a BB shot. That confusing word "proof" was a British import, and it meant the proportion of alcohol it took to make a small heap of gunpowder burn with a steady blue flame. Whiskey that was about half alcohol and half water "proved," by means of the gunpowder test, to be the best proportion for human palates and bloodstreams; the British settled on 57.1 percent to mean 100 percent fit for drinking, whereas Americans rounded off the figure to 50 percent. In the colonies, 100 proof meant, as it still means, exactly half alcohol.

Two variations on pure corn liquor involved souring and aging. To get a sour mash whiskey, a distiller took the "slops" left over in the cooker after a run and added it to a new batch of mash to repeat the fermenting process. "Sloppin' back" was like adding a sourdough starter to flour and water when making bread to give a little more character to the dough. Unaged whiskey was called "white lightning," for the liquid was as clear and colorless as vodka when it came fresh from the still. The Scotch whiskey makers who invaded this country in the eighteenth century were accustomed to aging whiskey in wooden barrels or casks, since the wood in symbiosis with the liquor helped to filter out impurities as the liquid evaporated and to ripen its flavor through the tannin and other extractives of the wood. The liquid also took on color and tasted as smooth and sweet as the Scotch whisky they brewed back home from barley malt.

Legend differs on which Scotsman in which county of Kentucky first aged his corn whiskey in a newly charred white oak cask to create the distinctive taste of American bourbon, but the chief contenders are both Baptists. According to Gerald Carson in *The Social History of Bourbon* (1963), the honors are usually given to the Reverend Elijah Craig, a capitalist-entrepreneur/preacher, who in 1789 included in his watery activities distilling, as well as baptizing, convenient to his gristmill, papermill and clothmill business at the Big Spring Branch of North Elkhorn Creek in Georgetown of Scott County. But two years earlier, in Bourbon County, originally part of Virginia rather than Kentucky, the Reverend James Garrard, who combined preaching with tavern-keeping, was charged with selling locally distilled whiskey without a license. In neither case are there any records of charred casks.

"Here's to Old Corn Likker,
Whitens the teeth,
Perfumes the breath,
And makes childbirth a pleasure."
—North Carolina folk saying

A. W. Thompson's drawing for Harper's Weekly, *December 7, 1867, captioned "Illicit distillation of liquors—Southern mode of making whisky," exemplifies Moonshine Romance.* Picture Collection, The Branch Libraries, The New York Public Library

In the next two decades the bluegrass counties of northern Kentucky, blessed with good limestone water, produced excellent whiskey at such a rate that Fayette County alone numbered 139 distilleries and the state 2,000. Before this time and until the Revolutionary War, rum was the distilled drink of choice of all the colonies, and New England was the pot still that condensed molasses and slaves into money and rum. New England ship owners who traded rum for slaves on the Guinea Coast, then slaves for molasses in the West Indies, finally turned molasses into rum. By 1750, the sixty-three rum distilleries in Massachusetts consumed 1,500 hogsheads of molasses a year. After the war, the distilling center moved from New England to the South as whiskey replaced rum and as bourbon, with its echoes of pro-French and anti-English sentiment, became the whiskey of choice.

The name "bourbon," however, didn't take hold until the mid-nineteenth century (1846 saw the first printed use), when home distilling began to move off the farm and into the factory. "Old Bourbon" became synonymous with good aged whiskey, a class drink. Old Crow, for example, was the name given by W. A. Gaines & Co. in 1856 to the bourbon they produced by the refined methods for souring mash developed some decades earlier by James C. Crow, a Scottish-born physician. When a Kentucky paper-maker named Ebenezer Hiram Stedman recalled an annual fishing week at Elkhorn in the 1830s that attracted the area's richest and finest, he remembered that they had "alwais The Best of old Bourbon" and that the bank president "alwais Kept his Black Bottle in the Spring and the mint grew Rank and Completely Hid the Bottle." Stedman, no bourbon snob, proclaimed the virtues of even the most ordinary whiskey:

> Every Boddy took it. It ondly Cost Twenty Five Cents pr. Gallon. Evry Boddy was not Drunkhards. . . . A Man might Get Drunk on this Whiskey Evry Day in the year for a Life time & never have the Delerium Tremers nor Sick Stomach or nerverous Head Achake. . . . One Small drink would Stimulate the whole Sistom. . . . It Brot out kind feelings of the Heart, Made men sociable, And in them days Evry Boddy invited Evry Boddy That Come to their house to partake of this hosesome Beverage.

After the Civil War, the increasing popularity of this hosesome Beverage turned whiskey-making into a major Southern industry. While men like Colonel Edmund Hayes Taylor, Jr., a nephew of General Zachary Taylor of the Mexican War, retained home quality in manufacturing his Old Taylor, Hermitage, Carlisle and Old Sinner brands in Columbia, Kentucky, others were less scrupulous. Grocers would bottle bulk whiskey from the spigot and with impunity slap on fraudulent labels like "Old Crow Hand Made Sour Mash Bourbon Whiskey." For a long time, the government's sole interest lay not in supervising labels that claimed aged bourbon where there was none, but in collecting taxes on the basis of alcoholic content. Not until 1896 did congressional hearings reveal that, of the 105 million gallons sold annually as Old Bourbon, only 2 million was genuine—the rest being "blended" with everything from ethyl alcohol to prune juice—leading to enactment the following year of the Bottled-in-Bond Act, which guaranteed federal government supervision of bourbon bottling at the source, demanding 100-proof liquor aged at least four years and distilled at the same facility. And not until 1964 did the government legally define bourbon as a whiskey containing at least 51 percent corn and aged in new charred oak barrels. By this time, Bourbon County itself produced no bourbon at all and was, in fact, teetotaling dry.

Kentucky bourbon was one thing, Tennessee whiskey another. The oldest registered distillery in the country is in the Cumberland Mountains southeast of Nashville, in Lynchburg, Tennessee, home of the Jack Daniel Distillery. It

"CORNED, p.p. Boosy, swipy, soaked, hog drunk, set up. (Very low and vulgar.) 'Hell hath no fury like a woman corned.' —Hector Stuart."
—AMBROSE BIERCE, *The Enlarged Devil's Dictionary* (1911/1960)

began on the east side of Mulberry Creek in a log cabin built by Davy Crockett in 1811, by the graveyard of the Bethel Baptist Church. On the north side of Mulberry Creek was a deep gorge of limestone cut by a stream. This runs from Cave Spring through Daniel's Hollow, and this is where Jack Newton Daniel set up his distillery around 1866 at the ripe age of eighteen. His nephew Lemuel Motlow joined him a few years later, and Motlow's descendants carry on the company and the legend today.

Although Kentucky bourbon and Tennessee whiskey share water from the same clear limestone springs for brewing and the same new-charred white oak barrels for aging, the difference, say Jack Daniel's producers, is in the filtering. In Tennessee the distilled liquor is filtered through charcoal made from local hard-sugar maple wood. Once called "Old Lincoln County Process," the leaching process begins in the rickyard, where the charcoal is made from maple sticks, stacked in ricks six feet high and burned to the ground, after which the charcoal is ground fine and packed twelve feet deep in vats in the mellowing house. You can watch the entire process if you take a tour of the distillery today, at the end of which you'll be handed a glass of lemonade for your trouble. Like Kentucky's Bourbon County, Lynchburg, Tennessee, is bone-dry.

By the time I found the Weddingtons in Carroll County, Arkansas, America had had four centuries in which to develop a complete lexicon of comic whiskey talk, from the beginning a dialect of subversion against the Establishment—religious, political, social. For the language of moonshine, there's no better compendium than Joseph Earl Dabney's *Mountain Spirits: A Chronicle of Corn Whiskey from King James' Ulster Plantation to America's Appalachians and the Moonshine Life* (1974). A journalist from South Carolina, Dabney knew how to find and talk to moonshiners like the Weddingtons all over the South, and while they are now a dying generation their language lives on.

Whiskey slang from the beginning was a language of comic burlesque, ridiculing those who made and enforced the rules. "Moonshine" is eighteenth-century English slang for white brandy smuggled at nighttime from France and Holland onto the coasts of Kent and Sussex to avoid the liquor tax. "Bootlegger" is nineteenth-century American slang for the smuggler who concealed flasks of spirits in his boottops in order to trade with the Indians after the colonies expressly forbade it. "Bootlegger" was given new meaning in 1871 with the first federal excise tax on whiskey, when bootleggers would conceal revenue stamps in their boots to stick on a bottle when challenged.

That challenge, dear to America's rebel heart, created a literary genre I call Moonshine Romance, which pits a legendary Outsider against the Feds or—even better—a pair of Outsiders against each other, Hunter and Hunted.

Whether fact or legend, moonshine tales are compelling in the way that man-against-beast tales are, as in Faulkner's *The Bear* or Hemingway's *The Old Man and the Sea,* because the antagonists confront the same primal wild and share the mutual respect of those crafty enough to survive it. For Prohibition moonshiners the only disgrace was getting caught. When I told Paralee that I'd seen an old still at the Heritage Center in Berryville, labeled "Last Moonshine Still Captured in this Area," she let out a hoot. "Why that was Frank's old still the sheriff tore apart," but not at the time Frank got caught and put in jail. "They didn't ketch ya without somebody'd snitched on ya," Paralee explained:

I guess the revenoo men had heard about Frank because they came looking for him and soft-soaped this real old man, telling him they wanted five gallon a whiskey. Frank didn't want to trust 'em. He's mousey—or whaddaya call it?—foxey. He's hard to slip up on and hard to fool. But Frank got 'em the whiskey and they paid him off and then two or three weeks later they came back when we was out at a beer joint over by White River bridge and these fellers pulled their coats back and said they was Federal men. That's when he stayed in jail. After that he really had to know a person afore he'd trust 'em. But they didn't git the still that time, they just got him for sellin'. They found the still several times after that and busted it up but didn't ever ketch him again.

While we were talking, the Weddingtons' daughters dropped by with their instruments, Helen with a guitar, Laverne a mandolin and June a bass. Paralee handles the fiddle, electric organ and harmonica, the last two at the same time. The walls were full of photos of Paralee and her Swinging Strings, along with prizes for fiddlin', singin' and jiggin'. It was part of her heritage, Paralee explained: "Fiddlin' I learned from my daddy. He just loved music, just like me. I don't know how my momma put up with him. But I learned to jig on my own 'cause I like the

Josh Billings, in Everybody's Friend *(1874), spoofs both Darwin and Whiskey at once.* AMS Press

DARWIN THEORY AND WHISKEE THEORY.

Man waz kreated a little lower than the angells—

—and haz bin gitting a little lower ever sinse. (11)

music. None a my ancestors ever had a squeakin' joint but I got my knees mashed up against the dashboard in a car accident, so I got arthritis bad and a cruel old Arthur he is. Frank, once in awhile, he'll git up and cut off a limb or two jiggin'." And sure enough, as Paralee and the girls lit into their fiddlin' and singin', Frank hitched up his overalls and started jiggin' by the far.

Since I was double Scotch-Irish like Paralee Kirk, I felt at home among these descendants of the typical eighteenth-century American frontiersman, whom Dabney called "a dogmatic Presbyterian, a hard drinker and a contentious cuss who carried his long Pennsylvania rifle with him at all times." But not until I learned about the great migration of Ulster Presbyterians first to Pennsylvania and then south through the Shenandoah Valley to the Appalachians and Blue Ridge Mountains did I discover my home was here I knew that a number of Harpers and Kennedys had come to America from County Tyrone in Northern Ireland, but I didn't know when or why until I hit the moonshine trail.

In 1608 when Ulster's two clan chieftains, the Earl of Tyrone and the Earl of Tyrconnel, joined their fellows in the "Flight of the Earls" to the Continent after the disastrous defeats at Kinsale, three million acres of land were left for the Crown's disposal. James I decided to plant Protestant Scotsmen there to tame Catholic Irishmen and to foster trade with England. But the Scots thrived so well in the woollen and whiskey trades, combining their native whiskey skills with those of Irish poteen makers, that England in 1640 imposed an "Act of Excyse" in the form of a punitive liquor tax. The Ulsters resisted and moonshining flourished, but as "rack-renting" Scottish landlords screwed up their rents, the Presbyters took off for America, where Pennsylvania offered both tolerance and land.

Between 1717 and 1776, some four hundred thousand Ulster Presbyterians worked their way south along the "western frontier" of Virginia, the Carolinas, Tennessee and Georgia. Fractious by temperament, they were as zealous fighting Indians as they'd been fighting British revenuers. Fired by their clansman Patrick Henry at the outbreak of the Revolution, they served General Washington at the rear while he commanded the van; their defeat of the Tory militia at the Battle of King's Mountain in South Carolina in 1780, when the Presbyters rallied to the Biblical cry of "The sword of the Lord and of Gideon," was a turning point in what George III called the "Presbyterian war." These were the men whom a minister of the Church of England traveling in South Carolina in 1766 called "a set of the most lowest vilest crew breathing—Scotch-Irish Presbyterians from the north of Ireland." And these were the men whom the Philadelphian Benjamin Rush compared to "the barbarous and indolent Indian"—a wild and disorderly people who grew nothing but corn.

"No nation is drunken where wine is cheap; and none sober, where the dearness of wine substitutes ardent spirits as the common beverage. It is, in truth, the only antidote to the bane of whisky."
—THOMAS JEFFERSON

These were my kind of people. A batch of Presbyterian ministers named Kennedy, the Reverends Gilbert, Robert, Thomas and John, all emigrated to America from Scotland or Ireland in the 1730s, some settling in Pennsylvania, some moving south to Virginia. My great-great-grandfather James Kennedy, born in Virginia in 1796, moved on to Kentucky and then Conneaut, Ohio. On the other side, a batch of Presbyterians named Harper—George, Andrew, William and James—all born in Ulster, emigrated in the 1780s to Pennsylvania, some moving into Virginia and some to Ohio. My great-great-grandfather James Harper settled at 20-Miles Stand, the first stagecoach station outside Cincinnati.

These were the settlers who as quick as they grew corn grew whiskey, as the best and cheapest way to transport their grain. Since they could distill eight pounds of corn into one gallon of whiskey, a mule could carry two eight-gallon kegs better than twenty-four bushels of corn. And besides, the price was right. During the Revolutionary War, good Monongahela whiskey sold for a dollar a gallon in Philadelphia and was a stabler currency than the coin of the realm. When Alexander Hamilton as Secretary of the Treasury decided to bail out the debts of the Revolutionary War by laying an excise tax on whiskey, he forgot that he was dealing with troops skilled in moonshining. Presbyterians were nothing if not Protestants and they protested vehemently the excise enacted in 1791 by the Congress of the new government they had fought for in order to end such taxes. It was West against East and Tom the Tinker's men against the Feds.

The Whiskey Rebellion came to a head in 1794 at Bower Hill near Pittsburgh, where rebel forces commanded by a former Revolutionary War officer, James McFarlane, stormed the mansion of General Neville, in charge of the revenue collectors. After McFarlane was killed while charging the hill, the rebels fired the mansion and, calling themselves "white Indians," marched on to Pittsburgh. They were joined by seventeen hundred insurgents while Washington hastily rounded up thirteen thousand army troops. But it was a wintry November and the whiskey army petered out before it reached the enemy. A handful of ragged prisoners were captured and driven on foot across the Alleghenies to the streets of Philadelphia to demonstrate the power of the new federal government. Jefferson repealed the unpopular tax eight years later, but the excise did much to spread the network and stiffen the resistance of illicit cottage whiskey farmers.

The whiskey interregnum lasted until 1862, when Congress needed to bail itself out from debts incurred in the Civil War. With the establishment of a Commissioner of Internal Revenue and a group of deputies to collect it, the

"A Recipe for Temperance Tipple:

Take one bushel cornmeal, 100 pounds of sugar, two boxes of lye, four plugs of tobacco, four pounds of poke root berries and two pounds of soda. Water to measure and distill."

—From the Asheville *Gazette News*, quoted by Joseph Earl Dabney, *Mountain Spirits* (1974)

*Temperance crusaders in 1879
clean out the leading saloon of
Fredericktown, Ohio.* Culver
Pictures, Inc.

excise tax rose in two years from twenty cents on a gallon of whiskey in 1863 to two dollars in 1865. Then there was the temperance movement, which made gains after the war with the founding of the Prohibition Party in 1869 and the Women's Christian Temperance Union in 1874. If taxes stimulated the sons of some illicit whiskey makers to new efforts, temperance turned the sons of others into staunch "tee (for emphasis) total" abstainers. The same language and culture that produced "teetotalers" also produced moonshiners and "pure dee alkeehol." There were purists on both sides of the barroom fence, and the quarrel between teetotalers and moonshiners was to some degree a family quarrel between Ulster folk who had kept to the old ways in the Appalachian hills and those who had moved on to the progressive frontiers of the prairies.

By the time Prohibition took off, after America's next big war—the World War now called First—my family was in thrall to a pair of household divinities, preacher Billy Sunday and axe-wielder Carry Nation. When Sister Carry swung her axe in the saloons of Medicine Lodge, Kansas, in 1899 she was pushing the heritage of her "white Indian" ancestors in a new direction. But there was no getting around it. Despite their Sunday preachments, my grandparents, praise the Lord, came from a long line of moonshiners. In the culture of corn, moonshiners and teetotalers were alike stubborn dissenters, brewed in the same mash, run through the same worm, but distilled into different bottles. Each had made his own accommodations to the ironies of heritage, and now it was my turn. After all, if an Inca painter in Cuzco three hundred years ago found it natural to compose a Last Supper of guinea pig and corn beer, surely I could come to grips with a United Presbyterian family in California who made a Last Supper of crackers and Welch's grape juice.

The Language of Commodities

SQUEEZING THE MOLECULE

INFUSED WITH THE SPIRIT of the brand-name age, my family shouted hallelujah in daily worship of the processed box, bottle and can. Presbyters who believed that wheat thins and grape juice could be transubstantiated into His Body and Blood could believe anything, anything but the equation of the "natural" with the "good." Fallen nature required redemption, and Christ was the soul's processor. We praised the manufacturers who, in imitation of Him, worked miracles of transformation. Instead of turning water into wine, they turned corn into starch, sugar and oil. Like the Indians, we too were the people of corn, but our corn was synthesized at the molecular level and extruded into the marketplace as the coin of the realm.

Today the corn synthesizers can transmute substances at will. "The primary message," the National Corn Growers Association declared in 1987, was that "anything made from a barrel of petrolcum can be made from a bushel of corn." These are corn farmers, mind you, representing eighteen thousand growers in forty-six states, headquartered in St. Louis, Missouri. Many come from preacher stock, and today they are preaching the message of ethanol and biodegradables to tribes who have run out of gas in a wasteland of boxes, bottles and cans. Corn is a cash crop, say the Corn Growers, to be pumped aboveground as crude oil is beneath. Joining the chorus are the nation's nine giant wet-millers, the kings of corn processing known as the Corn Refiners Association, the archdeacons of pumping and squeezing, who proclaim, "Corn refiners constantly search for new technologies and more uses which will squeeze even more value out of every bushel of American corn."

Today, the way to squeeze money out of corn is to squeeze the molecule and manipulate its structure in the tee (for total) commodification of corn, in which

"The most promising new market for corn starches is as a raw material for the production of many industrial chemicals which are today made from petroleum feedstocks. As petroleum supplies dwindle or become less reliable, the importance of having an abundant source of basic industrial chemicals takes on new proportions, and corn industry scientists are at work on new systems for producing industrial necessities from the versatile corn plant."
—Corn Refiners Association pamphlet (1987)

farmers are replaced by marketers, millers by refiners and machinists by biochemists. From the perspective of industrial farmers, corn is of value only as it can be transformed chemically into whatever commodity is most in demand. The methodology of nineteenth-century chemistry underlies the refining of corn as it does the refining of oil: analyze the system, fragment the parts, quantify the parts and synthesize at will. In such a system organic plants are but raw material for the processor, who fabricates products for which the manufacturer creates demand. Equally, consumers are raw material for processing and consumption by the manufacturer. The consumer becomes the consumed.

In this interchange, chemists rule. "Chemists of the Kernel," the CRA trade bulletin *Corn* hails those who control the chemical milling of corn, known as wet-milling because the process begins with wetting and squeezing the corn. Corn is steeped in a solution of water and sulphur dioxide in order to separate each kernel into its components—hull, germ and starch. Indian ash processing, as we've seen, helped to remove the hull by chemical action but kept the rest of the kernel intact. The function of modern industrial processing is to break up the interior matrix in order to separate germ from starch and starch from gluten, so that the kernel chemists can go to work. "In general, corn refiners manufacture *components* of consumer products," *Corn* says, "rather than the products themselves."

In the abracadabra of corn chemistry, starch is the magic component of consumer products because starch, in turn, is a raw material for processing. In 1987, out of 971 million bushels of processed corn, 128 million became industrial starch, 290 million became ethyl alcohol, and 303 million became a sweetener for beverages. All these are transformations of starch, and one of the ironies of industrial history is that cornstarch was originally a substitute for wheat.

Starch for all kinds of purposes had been leached from wheat and rice by the simplest water solution from the time of ancient Egypt and China. In the sixteenth century, American colonists imported wheat starch in some quantity to powder their wigs and starch their collars, until they developed wheat- and later potato-starch factories of their own. Not until the nineteenth century was there any major change in starch extraction, when in 1840 the Englishman Orlando Jones patented a method which used an alkaline as catalyst. Within four years, Colgate & Company had applied the patent to corn in

its wheat-starch factory in Jersey City. An employee, Thomas Kingsford, was so struck by the results that he set up a cornstarch factory of his own in Oswego, New York.

This extracted cornstarch was first sold culinarily as a flour, superior to finely ground wheat flour for the baking of cakes. The fact that starch did not have the same properties as flour presented problems for the manufacturer in promoting his product. A recipe pamphlet of 1877 explained to the housewife why some of the recipes called for a little wheat flour to be added to the cornstarch: "This is done because the Oswego Corn Starch is so rich in all its parts, that it will not hold together in cakes, biscuits, etc., without the aid of flour. Still, if you wish to make them entirely of Corn Starch, do so, but use a little less butter and sugar than is mentioned in these recipes."

Wright Duryea, who had worked as a millwright, opened his own starch factory in 1854, coining the word Maizena for his starch. By 1891 he had the largest starch factory in the country, grinding up seven thousand bushels of corn a day. A Duryea plant engineer of the time, Frederick Jeffries, has given us a good working-man's account, in *Grinding Corn as I Have Seen It* (1942), of how starch was made in these early plants, with their wooden tubs and starch tables and profligate waste:

There was not a motor or electric light in the place. Corn was put in wooden tanks, covered with warm water, and nature was allowed to do its worst. Considerable of the corn was shovelled, as the tanks were flat bottomed. It was then ground. Then came the sieving and washing on silk shakers. The resulting liquor went to wooden tubs, where it was treated with caustic soda and allowed to settle. The water went to the sewer, carrying, aside from the solubles, quantities of insoluble starch and gluten.

Now to the starch tables—which were twelve feet wide and gave little trouble. When settled, the water, together with the gluten remaining in the starch, was decanted to the sewer. The starch, with fresh water added, again was put in solution with revolving sweeps, and the operation repeated. This settling or "topping" as it was called, was done three times. . . . All of the steepwater went to the sewer. No germs were separated, so there was neither oil nor cake. The fiber or slop as it left the end of the shakers was combined with the run from the ends of the tables, or the gluten. No settling or pressing was done. The material "as is" was run into a number of large bins [where] the water leached through the burlap to the ground. In a week or so the "starch feed," as it was called, would have leached to a point where it was solid enough to shovel. Then it was sold to local farmers who came for it in wagons.

How much of the corn was lost no one knew. In the starch-washing they made sure to get rid of the gluten. As to how much starch also went to the sewer, no one knew. When the feed could not be sold, it went to the sewer. No doubt, at times, one-half of the corn was lost.

Starch tables of the 1930s or earlier, described by an engineer of the Duryea plant. Courtesy Corn Refiners Association, Inc.

As day follows night, merchandising followed manufacturing and brought riches to new starch entrepreneurs like Gene Staley. Staley was a farm boy who had done a turn with the Royal Baking Powder Company of Chicago before 1897, when he decided to repackage bulk starch, sold at two cents a pound, into one-pound packages he could sell for seven cents a pound. When miffed starch manufacturers cut off his supply, he purchased the Cream Starch trademark and set up business in Baltimore. His Corn Products Company (which in 1906 he renamed Corn Products Refining Company) was the father of today's leviathan Corn Products Company International. By 1922, *The Staley Journal* reported the success of a company that understood the world value of a trademark: "Since 1912 we have ground 35 million bushels of corn. If all that corn were to be loaded into freight cars the train would be 400 miles long. Our products are shipped to every part of the globe. On the streets of Cairo, it is not uncommon to see a fallaheen wearing a Staley starch bag for apparel. In Constantinople, many a rain barrel displays the Staley brand."

STARCH IS STILL EVERYWHERE, especially in every variety of manufactured product using sugar. Historically, the first attempts to turn corn in any quantity into sugar began when corn syrup became a substitute for molasses after the Molasses Act of 1733. Legend, however, prefers to credit Napoleon's sweet tooth, aching during the Continental System blockade of 1806, which prevented West Indian cane from reaching French shores. Motivated by Napoleon's offer of one hundred thousand francs to anyone who could create sugar from a native plant, a Russian chemist, K. S. Kirchhof, discovered that he could obtain a clear, viscous syrup by adding sulfuric acid to heated potato starch. Cornstarch would do the same.

Contemporary language explains that the acid, or enzymes, from malt or mold alter the molecular structure of the starch, just as the enzymes in saliva do when they convert starch into sugar so that the body can digest it. The result is glucose, or as we now call it, dextrose, meaning "right-handed sugar" (right being "the direction in which the molecules rotate a beam of polarized light"). Fructose, which is chemically identical with dextrose, is molecularly different and should be called "left-handed sugar." It should also be called super-refined sugar, since it is no more "natural" than ethyl alcohol and derives from the same chemical conversions.

In America the industrial conversion of cornstarch to sugar began with the Union Sugar Company in New York in 1865 and accelerated with the American Glucose Company in Buffalo a decade later. Chemistry was again the key.

In the language of corn refining, once the starch matrix has been separated from its protein gluten, the starch is converted by chemical action (an acid or enzymes, or both, are added to starch suspended in water) into "simple" sugar, called a "low-dextrose solution." Sweetness and texture (crystal or syrup) are controlled at every point to produce different products, depending upon how much starch is digested by the acid or enzyme. "We now know that starch consists of long chains of glucose molecules," Harold McGee has explained in *On Food and Cooking* (1984), "and that both acid and certain plant, animal, and microbial enzymes will break this chain down into smaller pieces and eventually into individual glucose molecules." By the same initial process through which the Hopi made "virgin hash," our modern corn refiners make glucose, maltose, dextrose and fructose.

The larger the number of these long glucose chains in the molecule, the more viscous the syrup, a quality important to the baking and candy industries because it prevents graininess and crystallization. Without corn syrup, no easy-to-make chocolate fudge. The more complete the digestion of starch, the sweeter the syrup, because the rate of glucose and maltose is higher. Maltose is a "double-unit" sugar produced, as in brewing, by enzyme-manipulated starch. By manipulating the glucose units with an enzyme derived from— unlikely as it sounds—*Streptomyce*s bacteria, the refiner can get a supersweet fructose called High Fructose Corn Syrup (HFCS). Today, this is where the king's share of cornstarch goes, because this syrup is the sweetener of choice (as long as it is cheaper than price-supported cane sugar) for the soft drink, ice cream and frozen dessert industries.

Although supersweet fructose tastes about twice as sweet as ordinary sugar, we do not as a result consume half as many soft drinks or ice cream cones. On the contrary, American sweetness consumption spirals ever upward, so that today, out of the 148 pounds of sweetness consumed per person per year ($\frac{1}{3}$ pound per day), 45 pounds come from corn syrup. Like new breeds of super-sweet corn, supersweet syrup intensifies desire and invisibly and silently manipulates the molecules of the eater.

If we take a single corn kernel of No. 2 Yellow Dent through the refining process start to finish, we can see what the mind of modern industrial man hath wrought in squeezing every drop of juice from nature's molecules and in devising uses for each drop squeezed. A kernel arrives at the plant in a load of 51 metric tons, where it passes through mechanical cleaners on its way to the steep tanks. Here the kernel soaks for 36 to 48 hours in 120-degree (Fahrenheit) water with sulfur dioxide, which toughens the germ and softens the protein in its starch matrix. The steepwater, which is highly nourishing, is then concen-

trated by evaporation and sold as a component in antibiotics (steepwater provided the mold for penicillin in World War II), vitamins, amino acids, fermentation chemicals and—above all—animal feeds.

The softened kernel now goes to the degerminating mills, which tear it
apart, loosening the germ and sloughing off the bran. This slurry of mixed
parts is then sluiced into flotation tanks, where a centrifugal hydrocyclone separates the lighter germ from the heavier parts, which can then be filtered,
ground and shaken. The germ is squeezed for oil (by expellers and solvent
extractors), filtered and refined into edible oil and coarser "soap stock." The
remainder, known as "corn oil cake," is ground into meal to be added, along
with the ground hull, to corn gluten feed and gluten meal.

After a final shake, the lighter gluten is separated from the heavier starch in
a high-speed centrifuge, and the gluten (70 percent protein) becomes the major
component of feedstuff for dairy and beef cattle, poultry, hogs and sheep. (In
poultry feed, the pigmentation of yellow corn, from a pro-vitamin called xan-
thophyll, is what turns chicken skin and egg yolks Perdue yellow.) The protein
zein is, in turn, separated from the gluten, and the zein is then used by the
pharmaceutical industry to make medicines in tablet form.

We are left with the industrial heart of the kernel—the starch. Some of it
goes to the dryers to be marketed for home cooking, for paper and textile mills,
metal casting and sand molds, laundry starches and—in the form of dextrins—

*A Siamese-twin train of corn
and Coke advertises the High
Fructose bond for the Corn
Products Refining Company.*
Courtesy Archer Daniels
Midland

for adhesives. Dextrin is simply roasted starch, and its properties were discovered, according to legend, when a fire broke out in a potato-starch factory in Dublin in 1821, at the very moment the locals were celebrating a royal progress of King George IV with quantities of Irish whiskey. In attempting to man the fire pump, six of the men fell into a tank of starch-water, hot from the fire, and emerged glued together. The superglue properties of heated starch were thus tested and proved. Even unroasted starch is so hydrophobic that it has become an essential dusting agent for every variety of manufactured goods from plastic cups to fur coats.

The larger part of the starch is converted to syrup by acid, enzymes, heat or a combination of the three. In the first stage of conversion, 15 to 25 percent is converted to dextrose after the purified starch slurry has been thinned by means of an alpha-amylase enzyme or acid. In the second stage, the starch converts to 97 or 98.5 percent dextrose in reaction to a glucoamylase enzyme, over a period of seventy-two hours at 140 degrees Fahrenheit. After it is evaporated, crystallized, dried and remelted, the starch molecule may then be "cleaved," "modified" or "cross-linked" to produce different forms of corn sugars and syrups. The degree of conversion is measured by its "D.E.," or dextrose equivalent. More than half the dextrose output goes to manufacturers of breads, other baked goods and breakfast cereals. Because dextrose caramelizes easily, it is used as a coloring agent and sweetener in baked goods and drinks like cola, root beer and whiskey, not to mention dry mixes for everything from iced tea to salad dressing.

Refiners, in their own inimitable language, list the seventeen basic properties of corn syrup valued by "food industry scientists":

bodying agent (to improve "mouth feel" of chewing gum), browning reaction (color to bakery products), cohesiveness (for frostings and icings), fermentability (brewing beer), flavor enhancement (jams and jellies), flavor transfer medium (dried fruit drink powders), foam stabilizer (ice cream), lowers freezing point (frozen or dried eggs), stabilizes moisture (frozen fish), moisture absorption (marshmallows), sweetness and nutrition (almost all food products), osmotic pressure (candy), sugar crystal prevention (pie fillings), ice crystal prevention (frozen fruit), sheen (canned fruit), viscosity (pancake and waffle syrup).

The family of corn syrups includes hydrol, or corn sugar molasses, a dark, viscous syrup useful in animal feed and in drugs; lactic acid, a colorless syrup useful as a preservative and flavorer for everything from pickles to mayonnaise; and sorbitol (dextrose plus hydrogen), an emulsifier that shows up in toothpaste and detergents as well as processed edibles. But the premium syrup is high-fructose corn syrup, first commercialized in 1967 by the Clinton Corn Processing Co. of Clinton, Iowa, which patented *Isomerose* (named for the enzyme xylose isomerase, which converts glucose to fructose). By 1972, the company had increased the sweetness from 14 to 42 percent fructose, to make it equivalent to ordinary sugar. As sugar prices rose, food and beverage industrialists began to replace more and more sucrose with "Isosweet." Within four years, production of the supersweet syrup jumped from two hundred thousand

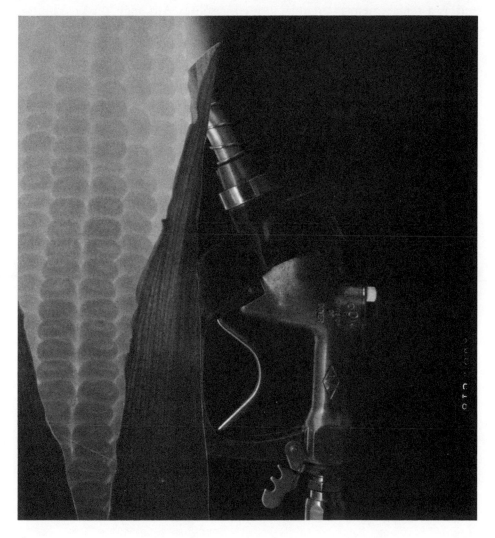

Corn fuels cars by way of ethanol. Archer Daniels Midland

to two and a half billion pounds a year, and within the decade it had become a major component of all major soft drinks. Today, HFCS can be made 25 percent sweeter than sugar (*Isomerose 600* contains 60 percent and *Isomerose 900* contains 90 percent fructose) and in crystalline form is an important rival to saccharin in the sugar-substitute industry.

This is the industrial alembic that makes corn and petroleum kin, for the same plants that produce high-fructose corn syrup also distill ethanol. In the 1970s, America's simultaneous oil crunch and pollutant anxiety revived the idea of fueling cars, as well as animals and people, with corn. Ethanol, or ethyl alcohol distilled from corn, began to be used both as a lead-free octane booster and as a replacement for regular leaded gasoline. Although the possibilities of fueling engines with ethyl alcohol had been contemplated from the beginning of car manufacturing, cheap oil made such experiments irrelevant until corn surpluses equaled oil shortages. Within six years, between 1978 and 1984, ethanol production jumped from 10 million to 430 million gallons, to make 4.3 billion gallons of the ethanol-blended gasoline called gasohol (10 percent ethanol to 90 percent gasoline). Those who laughed in the mid-1970s at the very word "gasohol" were sobered in the mid-1980s by the considerable tax benefits Congress granted in 1985 to gasohol producers.

Because it takes 56 bushels of corn to produce 2½ gallons of ethanol, corn growers could also boast that ethanol had raised the value of corn by three to seven cents a bushel. In 1984 the future of ethanol looked so bright that the General Accounting Office projected a production of one billion gallons of ethanol in 1990 to generate a net income for farmers of $3.59 billion. In 1990, however, the costs of energy consumption and environmental pollutants in the simple growing of corn clouded the picture, and enthusiasm shifted to nurturing the environment with biodegradable plastics.

For the past decade, starch makers have been experimenting with ways to make plastics photodegradable: that is, composed of chemicals sensitive to ultraviolet rays, which help to break up the tightly bound "polymers," or chains of hydrocarbon molecules, that characterize plastic. In the spring of 1989 the St. Lawrence Starch Company of Canada introduced Ecolyte plastic, in which the addition of cornstarch and a vegetable oil for oxidation would allow plastic trash bags, for instance, to disintegrate along with the trash. While the starch granules are eaten by bacteria, the oxidizer reacts with salts in the soil to break up the polymers into little bits of litter. Environmentalists skeptical of the hard sell of corn refiners point out that these remnant shards do not turn into soil, as advertisers suggest, but into permanent plastic dust.

In Decatur, Illinois, Archer Daniels Midland—"the world's largest commercial practitioner of biotechnology"—has been a major producer and promoter of cornstarch degradable plastics through its subsidiary A. E. Staley Manufacturing. The story of wet-milled cornstarch comes full circle in the "Castle in the Corn Fields," as the Staley plant is called, once the dominion of the farm boy turned starch salesman and now the mother lode of high-fructose corn syrup and corn plastics. Significantly, another major producer of degradable plastic bags is Mobil Corporation, father of Hefty bags, which neatly completes the refiners' equation of a barrel of petroleum with a bushel of corn.

In a curious linguistic conversion, the word "feedstock," which once referred to the substance of field corn consumed by hogs, has now become a metaphor for industrial corn consumed by chemistry. "Corn is a high-tech industrial feedstock which can switch gears to become a biodegradable plastic or an extremely hard, lightweight building material," says a research scientist at Purdue University. "Corn is the only biomass feedstock worth considering in the chemical industry," says the president of Bio En-Gene-Er, in Wilmington, Delaware. In a decade when corn is but a subcategory of bio en-gene-ering, the watchwords "Onward and Upward" of the Iowa Corn Promotion Board seem as quaintly innocent as a Presbyterian hymn.

WITH KARO, Kingsford's and Mazola, of the Corn Products Refining Company, a whole new cuisine was born, based on the promotion of processed corn products that were embraced with rapture by my parents' generation, true believers as they were in the onward and upward of process. As Kellogg extended his reach from Battle Creek, Michigan, to fill my cornflake bowl, so Edward Thomas Bedford, a founder of New York Glucose and first president of CPRC, infiltrated all our meals with his thickeners, sweeteners and emollients in the name of "purity and refinement." Aseptic purity is the appeal on the title page of a 1920s *Corn Products Cook Book:* "You are cordially invited to inspect our Refineries where Karo, Kingsford's and Mazola are manufactured

Brand names for "the three great products of corn" became household words in the early 1900s through ads and free recipe booklets published by the Corn Products Refining Company.

under the most hygienic and sanitary conditions. From the time the yellow kernels of Corn are unloaded from the cars at our Refineries until the Pure Food Products made from them reach the Consumer in the form of Karo, Kingsford's and Mazola, they are not touched by human hands." CPRC knew how to exploit the popular confusion of cleanliness with godliness in all parts of the American home, but particularly in the kitchen. In the era of domestic engineers, when kitchens aspired to the conditions of chemical labs, Juliet Corson admonished her students in her New York Cooking School, "Remember that the best cook always has the cleanest kitchen." Fifty years later, in 1934, the same message was headed "Points to be considered in marketing" in the manual of my seventh-grade home economics class: "Insist upon a clean grocery store and meat market; Insist upon clean, courteous clerks."

To those who'd worked the soil with their hands, hand-free products signified progress and ease. Ready-mixed baking powders and baking mixes were a boon, not a corruption. Because cornstarch was an essential preserving element in commercial baking powder, to keep the powder dry, the new world of Bisquick breads, Aunt Jemima pancakes and Pillsbury ready-mix cakes was built on invisible starch. Cornstarch, which fine palates today view as an abomination, we viewed as a refinement over vulgar flour when we came to thicken our sauces, puddings, cakes and pies. Cornstarch, in fact, got its current bad name from its ubiquitous use in the 1930s Depression as a quick, cheap thickener of Anglo-American pudding and Chinese-American sauce. Anglos had earlier turned French blancmange, thickened classically with pounded almonds, into a common pudding thickened with flour. Americans translated English blancmange into cornstarch pudding, preferably flavored with chocolate, and so it appeared in my home economics manual, with $\frac{1}{4}$ cup cornstarch thickening two cups milk. Americanized Chinese embraced cornstarch as a cheap substitute for water-chestnut powder or rice flour in sauces, reserving rice flour for puddings and cakes. A 1936 *Chinese Cook Book,* compiled by M. Sing Au of Philadelphia, gave three typical recipes for "Chinese gravy," each thickened by cornstarch.

Karo began as a cheap substitute for other syrups, but it soon created a dentist's fantasy of new candies and desserts. In our pantry there were always two bottles of Karo, one light and one dark. Crystal White Karo went into unthinkable tooth-dissolvers like Karo Pie: "Line pie plate with rich crust, and fill two-thirds full with Karo (Crystal White). Stir in lightly without touching the paste two teaspoons Kingsford's Cornstarch." While this *Corn Products* recipe even in the reading may set teeth aquiver, note that pecan pie, still beloved today, didn't become part of the American repertoire until Karo (Red Label, dark like molasses) came on the market.

The great advantage of Karo of both colors was that it didn't crystallize, and so formed a stable and simple sugar base for candies like fondants that were otherwise tricky in the extreme. Fudge making, which became a freshman rite in Eastern women's colleges in the 1890s, was a Karo offshoot. So were subcategories like my childhood favorite, peanut butter fudge (a recipe for it well-thumbed in my home-ec manual), and my grandmother's favorite, divinity fudge (sometimes called sea foam), made with eggwhites, nuts, dates and of course Crystal White Karo. Karo also substituted for molasses in chewy caramels and pulled taffies. A recipe for saltwater taffy in a *Products Cook Book* managed to incorporate Karo and Kingsford's for the taffy making and Mazola for the taffy pulling.

"The half billion bushels of corn utilized in corn sweetener production represents over 4.5 million acres of planted land, which is more than the number of acres planted to corn in the entire state of Ohio in 1985.

More than one million corn growers produce raw material for the U.S. sweetener market. The equivalent of twenty-five acres from every Illinois and Iowa corn grower's crop will end up in corn sweeteners in 1985."

—National Corn Growers Association promotion materials, 1985

In 1910, when the current vegetable oils were olive, cottonseed, poppy, coconut and palm, a chemist at CPRC found a way to refine corn oil for cooking. The first customers were a group of sardine packers in Maine, who substituted the cheaper corn oil for olive in their packs. When the trademark "Mazola" moved into Boston grocery stores the following year, customers resisted buying until company demonstrators went into the stores and deep-fried french fries and onion rings to prove the superiority of corn to bacon grease and fish oil. Later, corn oil had to compete with peanut, soy and sunflower oil, but corn helped form and maintain the standard for a pure, colorless and minimally flavored vegetable oil for cooking and salads.

Mazola was born the same year as Hellmann's mayonnaise, made by a New York deli man from Germany, Richard Hellmann. He bottled his wife's mayonnaise in glass jars and put a "Blue Ribbon" label on them, as Frederick Pabst had done with beer. Like other food entrepreneurs of his time, Hellmann was a good salesman, able to persuade housewives to buy ready-made dressing the way Heinz persuaded them to buy ready-made pickles. Although Hellmann's today is made with soy oil, corn oil was the original base for its emulsion of oil, vinegar and eggs. In our house, Hellmann's "real"—not fake and certainly not homemade—mayonnaise was the altarpiece of our dining table, removed only for ice-box protection between meals. With its proud blue-ribboned front, the

Richard Hellmann's original mayonnaise in 1912 wore a prominent blue ribbon to signify a winner. Courtesy CPC International Inc.

jar stood like a good angel to the right of my father's plate, since he could do without salt and he could do without sugar but he could never do without mayonnaise. At breakfast he spooned it onto his scrambled eggs; at lunch he slathered it top and bottom on the bread of his bologna sandwich. At dinner he scooped it onto his canned pineapple and Jell-O salad, onto his mashed potatoes and sometimes onto his Swiss steak.

He was, as I see it now, a mayo freak, gratefully processed by Hellmann salesmen like Paul Price, whose wife in 1937 made a chocolate mayonnaise cake, thickened with walnuts and dates, flavored with chocolate and made tender and moist by mayonnaise. For Hellmann's seventy-fifth birthday, a New York pastry chef updated the classic Hellmann version to make it suitable for microwaving. Behold—an American cuisine of molecular manipulation, start to finish. As a botanist of the old school and a cook of the old-fashioned range, my father knew little and cared less about molecules by the time he joined his ancestors. But I know how much he cared about mayonnaise, and I know he would have loved that cake.

FIVE

*The
Sacred
Round*

(overleaf) A boy in his festal costume of shredded cornhusks at the Atchison Corn Carnival of 1905 in Atchison, Kansas. From the Kansas Collection, University of Kansas Libraries
Girls in their festal costumes at a Corn Dance in Jemez Pueblo, New Mexico, in 1938. Photo by T. Harmon Parkhurst; Museum of New Mexico

The Language of Ceremony

DANCING UP THE CORN

CORN, BOTH NATURAL AND REDEEMED, invested with ceremony the tables of American settlers, but not their myths. These remained tied to the language of wheat, as formed by the English of the King James Bible. When my grandfather Doctor Charles Sumner Harper went west from Kansas, to leave farming for osteopathy, he landed in Greeley, Colorado, not far geographically from the mythical origins of the Tewa in the Lake of Emergence near Pagosa Springs, but light-years away from his own mythical origins in Adam's Eden. The geography of his tribe was entirely Old World, at the same time their migration across oceans, mountains and deserts rejected old worlds and old faiths for new. His journeying, like his language, was linear and progressive. Look onward and upward, never backward or downward. Upward was the direction of the pearly gates. Downward was the direction of the fallen earth, downward was the mouth of Hell.

My grandfather prayed in words, because dancing, in his language, was a sin. So was the body, so was all matter. Flesh and blood were of the earth, earthy, corruptible and corrupted, not God's but Devil's work, awaiting the lightning blasts of the Apocalypse and the trumpets of Armageddon. The split between body and soul was as complete as between man and God, Indian and white. In their westward migration, my tribal Presbyterians were aliens among the heathen and fundamentalists among the heretic. As self-willed exiles, they could not comprehend a people whose gods were rooted in this particular earth, both patch and globe, as strongly as stalks of corn. As self-appointed elect, they could not comprehend a people whose vision was egalitarian and inclusive, a vision which allowed Saints and Corn Mothers to live happily side by side.

My search for corn became a search to reconcile opposites that in my heritage were mutually exclusive. Even as my tribal ancestors mutated their "harvest homes" to cornhusking bees, their midsummer eves to sweet-corn feasts, their church steeples to corn palaces, still their division between corn savages and wheat saints seemed immutable. Even as I traveled from Nebraska to Cuzco, seeking connection, I was still my grandparents' child, preconditioned to square the circle of ceremony and myth by the Biblical language in which I was born. What good is an Indian peacepipe to a person taught not to smoke? Corn no more than tobacco figured in the ancient language of my heritage, but it was at the center of the land in which I lived. That challenge was one my ancestors had faced crossing the Atlantic. Now I would have to make my own crossings, searching in ritual and ceremony for the connections between opposites that elude reason and defy logic. I was a stranger in this land, no less than my ancestors, and my search for the hidden roots of corn was a search for a homeplace, a search ultimately for myself.

Watching the midsummer corn dance at one or another pueblo in New Mexico, I felt the shades of my ancestors rising in wrath. Not only was this a pagan fertility rite but the feast day of an abominated Catholic saint. The descendants

Hano Clowns—Koshare *of the Hopi, painted in watercolor by L. Honewytewa.* Museum of Northern Arizona

of the people of corn, however, had the logic of ceremony to connect opposites in a world altogether different, where time stands still and upward and downward are the same. In a desert as ancient as the sands of Samaria and Judah, this summer as every summer, the many tribes of the New Mexican Pueblos dance the rain down and dance the corn up. They dance while diesel trucks and cars speed past them on the superhighway between Albuquerque and Taos, while jets thunder overhead and space satellites circle far above, bouncing back signals to TV aerials that sprout like cornstalks on the roofs of their adobes.

At first, all I could take in at the pueblo of San Domingo, which holds the largest dance, were these weird conjunctions: the leafy shrine in the central plaza enclosing a life-sized image of Saint Dominic behind offerings of corn stew and Wonder Bread; the white leggings for winter dances crocheted by a devout Methodist lady in shrewd trade for turquoise and pots; the country-western blare from the carnival rides clashing with muffled drumbeats from the kiva; the gowned monk in a baseball cap laughing at the koshari clowns grabbing sno-cones and popcorn. And everywhere, as my grandfather had waited for the Second Coming, hundreds of spectators, natives and tourists, waiting hour after hour in folding chairs, under cowboy hats and sun umbrellas, for the coming of the dancers.

Restless and impatient for the dancing to begin, I remembered what Alfonso Ortiz had said about the Tewa traditions of his own pueblo of San Juan. "Westerners think of tradition as something static, frozen, opposed to progress," he told me. "For Indians tradition has always meant change, something living and organic—the Buffalo Dance now includes not only animals like buffalo and snakes but spacemen and rock stars." For the Tewa, who gather from around the country each summer to dance the sacred round of their ancestors, he said, the dance is a way of ordering their universe by a rhythmic beat, tuned to the energy of a universe that wires the galaxies of outer space to the germ within each single grain of corn.

When the Tewa dance, they pound the same "earth mother earth navel middle place" that their remote forefathers pounded in the courtyards of La Venta, Monte Alban and Copán. In the ancient rhythms of their dance, they invoke the presence not only of tribal ancestors but of Blue Corn Woman and White Corn Maiden, the summer and winter daughters of Mother Corn. They dance a universe of correspondences in a language so different from Latin and Greek that translation falters. Instead of the abstract signs of my root alphabet, the languages of the New World, though often carved, painted, sculpted and woven, were chiefly spoken, sung, chanted and danced, in the body language of ritual and ceremony.

It takes a poet to translate dance, a poet like D. H. Lawrence, who witnessed the corn dance at San Domingo in 1927. He described the koshari as "blackened ghosts of a dead corn-cob, tufted at the top," and the dancers of the sprouting corn as "some sort of wood tossing, a little forest of trees in motion, with gleaming black hair and gold-ruddy breasts . . . and the deep sound of men singing . . . like the deep soughing of the wind, in the depths of a wood." Others, like Captain John G. Bourke of the Third U.S. Cavalry in 1884, recorded the scene as amateur anthropologists. He noted the clowns painted black and white with bands of otter fur across their chests, cedar sprigs around

Young corn dancers at Cochiti Pueblo in 1935 are eloquent, even in a formalized camera pose, of the rhythmic language of corn. Photo by T. Harmon Parkhurst, courtesy Museum of New Mexico, Neg. No. 55189

their ankles and cornshucks woven into the whitewashed topknots of their hair. In the pine branch that each dancer waved, he found a symbol of green life, and in the gourd of dried corn kernels that each dancer shook a symbol of rattling rain.

A century later, I saw nothing but signs and symbols of corn. Painted cornstalks embraced the portal of the white-plastered church, invigorated the legs and thighs of the koshari, claimed kinship with the sun on "the cane." The cane was the sun's emblem carried by the leader of the dancers—a pole which bore on top a kilt, hung with eagle feathers and fox tail, surmounted by a gourd of seeds and a bright crest of parrot and hummingbird feathers. This was the ancient *huitziton,* the crest of the Aztec war god Huitzilopochtli, and the pole was the ancient serpent-staff of the Feathered Serpent.

Every motif had meaning in a language that voiced the unity of corn, man, sun and rain, but I couldn't decipher it without instruction. To submit to the boredom of eternal waiting in heat and dust while nothing happened, to the boredom of repeated shufflings and chants, I had to unshuck my ancestors. I had to be told that all dances, even winter dances, speak to rain because rain

Men and women, dancing together at San Ildefonso in the mid-thirties, choreograph the energies of earth, sun, corn, and rain. Courtesy Museum of New Mexico

mediates between sun and earth, between the father and mother of corn. I had to learn that as a summer dance, the Corn Dance is both a harvest celebration and a prayer for the new year, a feast of thanksgiving for the crop of ripe corn just reaped and a prayer for rain for next year's crop.

What exhausted me, Ortiz said, energized the dancers. Since time and space no longer count, the dancer is more refreshed at the end of the day than when he started, for he receives power from the energy of earth and sun, power that makes the rain come, power that is choreographed in circle and line. The circle is the kernel, earth navel, womb, globe. The line is rainfall, lightning, irrigation. To a stranger like myself, the rhythms of the dance changed unaccountably and continually, like desert clouds, like a secret language. I began to see how varied and subtle was this unknown tongue that had to be felt in muscle and bone before it could be seen and heard.

A koshari makes zigzag motions with his hands to imitate lightning; then with sweeping motions, palms down, he moves like sheets of rain. Others shake their gourds from sky to earth to send the rain rattling down. Male dancers bare to the waist wear white cotton kilts, embroidered with cloud and rain symbols, tied with the long tasseled rain sash. Hanging behind each dancer is a fox skin, tied to his right knee is a rattle of turtle shell and deer hooves, across his chest a bandoleer of seashells, on his head a cluster of parrot feathers to bring rain from the south, over his moccasins a skunk fur to ward off evil—all reminders of his brothers the animals, whose lives he shares. Female dancers wear black *mantas* bare on one shoulder, tied with a red and green sash. Their feet are bare, their heads covered with *tablitas,* thin boards cut in the geometry of mesas and clouds and painted with signs of zigzagged lightning, sun and stars. Everything is coded, including the colors: yellow for sun, green and blue for crops, black for thunderclouds, red for fire, white for purity.

The dancers dance in two groups, alternately, divided like the moieties of the pueblo, into Summer People and Winter People, Turquoise and Squash, the male bodies painted with blue-gray clay for Turquoise and with yellow for Squash. The koshari of the Turquoise, naked but for loincloths, are striped horizontally, skull to toe, in black and white; the Squash are painted vertically, one half the body white with black spots and the other half ochre. Jangling their belts of bone or metal bells, the koshari are licensed clowns like the spirits of All Hallow's Eve who mediate between living and dead, gods and men, kivas and moieties, fear and laughter. In Old World language, they are Masters of the Revels, healers and tricksters, who at one moment rescue a fallen toddler and at the next tumble a girl for a kiss.

"He partakes in the springing of the corn, in the rising and budding and earing of the corn. And when he eats his bread, at last, he recovers all he once sent forth, and partakes again of the energies he called to the corn, from out of the wide universe."
—D.H. LAWRENCE, "Dance of the Sprouting Corn," *Mornings in Mexico* (1927)

Men and women dance face to face in opposite lines, then join as couples, the man ahead, the woman behind. All day they dance in alternation, Turquoise and Squash, under the dipping banner of the Sun. All day the band of singers, a massed choir of fifty or seventy-five men, calls the rain from the four quarters of the earth to thunder here. Houses are open all day to anyone hungry for ham and hominy, slices of watermelon, adobe bread, fruit-filled pies, soda pop and Kool-Aid. Toward the end of the day the two groups join at last to dance as one, five hundred dancers together, old men, young girls, fat men, athletic boys, matrons with babies, wrinkled crones, white hair and black hair shaking together, bare feet and moccasins stamping in unison as thunderheads mount in the east. In midsummer the clouds mount every afternoon over the Sangre de Cristo mountains, potent with the fire that spoke to Moses in the burning bush, but that here, in deserts half a world away, speaks in forked lightning to fertilize the seed deep in the womb of Mother Corn.

GATHERING IN THE CORN

To THOSE OF US whose ancestors crossed the Atlantic with their sacred texts packed among the apple seeds and iron pots in their sea chests, the summer solstice is an odd time to celebrate the new year. My Christian calendar puts the birth of the celestial sun, Holy Son and new year at the winter solstice. It's true that the Christian calendar bears vestiges of pagan planting calendars in both midwinter revels and spring resurrections. God's son is related, after all, to the wheat-and-barley son of the Great Mothers Demeter and Ishtar, whose province was spring. But after the Great Fathers dethroned them and in due time amalgamated the calendars of Roman emperor and pope, the new year and its symbolic babe were born in the dead of winter. In the New World, where Mother Corn continued to reign, summer is the beginning of the new year symbolized by corn and celebrated in the Green Corn Busk.

"The only way the Peaux-Rouges helped the Pelerins was when they taught them to grow corn (mais). The reason they did this was that they liked corn with their Pelerins. . . . In 1623, after another harsh year, the Pelerins' crops were so good that they decided to have a celebration and give thanks because more mais was raised by the Pelerins than Pelerins were killed by Peaux-Rouges."

—ART BUCHWALD,
  explaining le Jour de Merci Donnant
  (Thanksgiving) to the French

Midsummer for my Grandfather Harper, when he was still raising sugar beets and corn and peaches in Edgerton, Kansas, was a season of hard labor that was not to be celebrated until the end of November, when the corn was in

the cribs. At that time, to be sure, the citizens of Edgerton sang hymns of thanksgiving in little white steepled churches and celebrated harvest abundance by eating fat turkeys. This ceremony, however, was an Old World "harvest home" they adapted to an alien corn. New World harvests were celebrated twice, first when green corn was gathered in midsummer and then when ripe corn was gathered in the fall. When Chief Massassoit and his men brought wild game and popcorn to the tables of the Pilgrims in Massachusetts, my ancestral fathers thanked God that the heathen were brought to His table for the salvation of their souls. That the Pilgrims themselves were guests, rather than hosts, at a seasonal corn feast as old and as sacred as Abraham and Isaac was literally unthinkable to those whose history and geography had been charted by Biblical maps.

Both my Grandfather and Grandmother Harper were born and raised in the fertile crescent of the Ohio and Mississippi rivers, which watered corn for the natives a couple of thousand years before they watered corn for the white man in parcels labeled Ohio, Illinois, Indiana, Iowa, Missouri. In Ohio, my grandmother was born not far from the world's largest serpent effigy mound, 5 feet high and 1,254 feet long, built by the Adenas in Adams County, Ohio, perhaps thirty centuries ago, at the time King Solomon built his temple in the kingdom of Israel. Ohio farmers tried to plow the mound flat, but the serpent with the egg in its mouth was obdurate. It was as native to Ohio as the serpent with an apple in its mouth to Eden.

Crossing the Mississippi River at St. Louis on their wedding trip from Ohio to Kansas, my grandparents could have seen the pyramidal earthworks called Monks Mound at Cahokia, covering sixteen square acres. But if they had, they would have seen a reminder of Moses' escape from the Pharaohs rather than vestiges of the high civilization of the Mississippians a millennium ago. And when they asked the Lord's blessing over the white starched cloth of their first Thanksgiving table, they would not have known that Woodland tribes from Florida to the Great Lakes had helped to shape that blessing of turkey and corn by the Green Corn Ceremony marking their new year.

Numbers of colonial travelers and settlers described that ceremony, each interpreting it by his own bent. Robert Beverley saw in the Creek ceremony in Virginia in 1705 a time of feasts, "War-Dances, and Heroick Songs." A later Creek chieftain, who learned to write English and adopted the unlikely pen name of Anthony Alexander M'Gillivray, concentrated on the fasting—which gave the ceremony the name "busk." While none were permitted to eat corn from April until July or August, "boskita" meant a three-day period of fasting accompanied by purging with the "black drink" of snakeroot, senneca or cassina, "which they use in such quantities as often to injure their health."

The explorer William Bartram was taken with the communality of the busk among the Creeks of Florida and Georgia in the late 1770s, and with their "proper and exemplary decorum."

> It commences in August, when their new crops of corn are arrived to perfect maturity: and every town celebrates the busk separately, when their own harvest is ready. If they have any religious rite or ceremony, this festival is its most solemn celebration.
>
> When a town celebrates the busk, having previously provided themselves with new clothes, new pots, pans, and other household utensils and furniture, they collect all their worn-out cloaths and other despicable things, sweep and cleanse their houses, squares, and the whole town, of their filth, which with all the remaining grain and other old provisions, they cast together into one common heap, and consume it with fire. After having taken medicine and fasted for three days, all the fire in the town is extinguished. During this fast they abstain from the gratification of every appetite and passion whatever. A general amnesty is proclaimed, all malefactors may return to their town, and they are absolved from their crimes, which are now forgotten, and they restored to favour.

On the fourth morning, the high priest, by rubbing wood together, produces new fire in the public square, from whence every habitation in the town is supplied with the new and pure flame.

Then the women go forth to the harvest field, and bring from thence new corn and fruits, which being prepared in the best manner, in various dishes, and drink withal, is brought with solemnity to the square, where the people are assembled, apparelled in their new cloaths and decorations. The men having regaled themselves, the remainder is carried off and distributed amongst the families of the town. The women and children solace themselves in their separate families, and in the evening repair to the public square, where they dance, sing and rejoice during the whole night, observing a proper and exemplary decorum: this continues three days, and the four following days they receive visits, and rejoice with their friends from neighbouring towns, who have purified and prepared themselves.

Where many white men found Christian echoes in this native ritual of purgation, purification, burial and resurrection, Thoreau found in Bartram's description a moral exemplum dear to his puritan heart. "Would it not be well if we were to celebrate such a 'busk,' or 'feast of first fruits,' as Bartram describes?" he asked. He wished to imitate not the feast but the fast, the stripping away of old clothes, old pots, old fires, old habits, old lives, a cleansing within and without to burn with a purer flame. He observed that "the Mexicans" practiced a similar purification every fifty-two years and concluded, "I have scarcely heard of a truer sacrament, that is, as the dictionary defines it, 'outward and visible sign of an inward and spiritual grace,' than this, and I have no doubt that they were originally inspired directly from Heaven to do thus, though they have no biblical record of the revelation."

No Biblical record certainly, but another record of revelation was at hand in the liturgical calendar the Aztec (Thoreau's "Mexicans") had inherited from preceding civilizations of Toltec and Maya, the shared calendar of the New World, which ordered ritual time according to the patterns of change they saw in the heavens and on earth. This was the great Calendar Round, based on fifty-two-year cycles, in which each new round was inaugurated by the ritual of fire-drilling. The same calendar timed the green-corn ceremonies in New England as in Tenochtitlán, reflecting how ancient and widespread were ceremonies of purgation, fire-drilling and gift-giving, how ancient and widespread the masking of a priest in the garments of a god.

Since the Woodlanders were hunters as well as planters, they needed shaman-priests to keep Sky-World and Earth-World in harmony. Their corn

"'We give thanks to our sustainers,' says the Senecan male leader during their Green Corn Thanksgiving. In their ceremonial march the female leader holds an armful of corn and a cake of corn bread and leads her band in a march around a kettle of corn soup."

—From JOHN PINKERTON'S *Collection of Voyages and Travels* (1812)

Iroquois masks made of corn-husks and worn by the Husk Face Society during midwinter festivals, when their dances were prayers for the rebirth of green corn in midsummer. Photo Ed Castle

ceremonies were different from those of the Pueblo planters: for the Pueblo peoples, corn was before time was; for the Woodland tribes, there was a time before corn. Hunter rituals are star treks, measuring the cycle of years, evoking the time when people fell to the earth like arrows from the sky. Planter rituals are earth-born and -bound, measuring the cycle of seasons, re-creating the emergence of people from the earth like seedlings.

Shamans were central to the green-corn dances of the Woodland Indians, which focused on fire rather than rain and connected earth fires to astral ones. The shaman's trance journey or vision quest lasted ritually eight days and nine nights, because that is the time it takes the planet Venus to make its west-to-east transit from morning to evening star. We can see from George Catlin's description in the 1830s of the green-corn dance of the Minataree, a small tribe on the Knife River in the upper Missouri, how the medicine men or priests orchestrated the event. Catlin called the dance "a ceremony of thanksgiving to the *Great Spirit,*" and the priests "doctors." First the doctors tested the corn's ripeness, then arranged for the corn to be boiled in a central kettle around which they danced with a larger circle of warriors. After the doctors sacrificed a few symbolic ears of corn on a pyre of sticks, they drilled new fire and incited the "unlimited licence" of surfeit and excess that characterize our own Thanksgiving feasts.

In this Woodland ritual, time and space are ordered in a linear narrative of four days, and meaning depends upon what happens in which order. The corn dance of the Pueblo peoples orders time differently, since everything happens within the round of a single day, from dawn to dusk, and in a single place. Its action is iconographic, like a Navaho sand painting, rather than like the pictographic narratives of Midewiwin scrolls or the recited narratives of Hiawatha.

Hiawatha is typical of the Woodland shaman-hero whose destiny unfolds in symbolic segments of time. For seven days he fasts to induce the vision quest; on four successive days he wrestles with Mondawmin until the god is overcome, dead and buried, and finally resurrected in the form of corn. The story tells of the sacrifice of an individual hero who concentrates in his own person the energy of the group and acts on their behalf. For the Pueblo tribes, on the other hand, the individual must submerge his unique identity and power with the inhuman energy of vegetative life. This is the force fused by the rhythms of the group, men and women, acting in concert—dancing rather than wrestling.

Among Woodland groups, the blood sacrifice common to earlier planting rituals continued to a surprisingly late date. George Will noted the ancient Pawnee midsummer tradition of sacrificing a human to the gods of the Sky-World: "At the summer solstice a human sacrifice was made to the Morning Star—a maiden captured from some hostile tribe usually being the victim." The Skidi Pawnee, he claimed, "kept up these human sacrifices until well on into the nineteenth century." Even

After the girl's death, her skin was flayed and worn by a dancing priest who impersonated the flayed god, Xipe Totec, a god like Xilonen of spring and regenerating seed. Here the Florentine Codex depicts a priest being vested by his acolytes in a flayed skin and feathered ornaments. Neg. No. 292758. Photo Llane L. Bierwers, courtesy Department of Library Services, American Museum of Natural History

where human sacrifices were not kept up, their meaning was part of the "sacrament" Thoreau attributed to divine revelation. Had he known that the Green Corn Busk was kin to the wholesale slaughter of the Mexica, he might have had second thoughts about the ceremony's exemplary decorum. Certainly the example of the shaman Quetzalcoatl was not the outward sign of an inward grace that my grandparents had in mind when they offered prayers of thanksgiving to the Lord God of Israel for turkey and corn.

TEARING OUT THE HEART

THE CREEK BUSKS that Thoreau extolled for enlightenment an Aztec priest would have deplored for ignorance and barbarism. To end the long fast with no more than a feast of corn was to miss the whole point. Where was the god in the boiling pot? The only proper end for a corn festival celebrating great generating nature was the killing and eating of the god, or goddess. At the midsummer festival celebrating the goddess Xilonen (*xilotl* meant "green corn"), Aztec priests selected a young girl pretty enough to wear the robes and crown of the goddess. For a month, women danced in her honor, shaking their hair loose over their breasts like corn silk, to encourage the corn to multiply

This horrific statue of Coatlicue, dug from the site of Tenochtitlán and now in the Museo Nacional de Antropologia in Mexico City, embodies the cannibal relation of life and death in the central skull at her belly, the serpent skirt, the necklace of human hearts and hands and, surmounting all, the twinned serpent heads that form her face. The serpent heads are the streams of blood that gushed from her neck when she was beheaded by her sons. Neg. No. 333855, courtesy Department of Library Services, American Museum of Natural History

and be fruitful. At the end of the month, Torquemada reported, "The girl was placed on the sacrificial stone, and with her death ended the celebration, and with it the day."

So much for decorum. It's as if we were to end our celebration of Miss America with her dismemberment on the boardwalks of Atlantic City. But slaughtering, like dancing and feasting, has its own rules of propriety which vary with time and place; and while today Americans sanction wartime sacrifice on a global scale, individual dispatchings distress us. That our Woodland tribes did not always or even usually end their ceremonies in human sacrifice says less about their moral nicety than their geographic and cultural distance from the centers of urban civilization in Mesoamerica. To the citizens of Tenochtitlán, the Creek and Iroquois were as Goths and Gauls to the Romans; and as Romans inherited the glory that was Greek, so the Aztec inherited the grandeur that was Toltec. Tenochtitlán was the heart of civilized life in a vast continent, and the pious Mexica symbolized that heart in a real and palpitating organ torn from living flesh.

The greatest sacrament of the year for the Aztec, as Easter for the Christian, was the harvest celebration of the ripe-corn goddess and Earth Mother, Coatlicue, or Chicome Coatl. This was sacred theater, dramatizing primitive narratives embeddedin the Green Corn Busk the way Christ's Passion dramatized earlier narratives of sacrifice told in Israel, Egypt and Babylon. When Father Sahagún described the ritual death of the maiden enacting the corn goddess at the September festival, Sahagún's imagination was informed by the ritual death of his own Lord. Sir James Frazer, translating Sahagún, spoke of the Aztec breaking their fast "as good Christians at Easter partake of meat and other carnal mercies after the long abstinence of Lent." Frazer's imagination was also informed by the fertility rituals celebrating one or another incarnation of the serpent goddesses of the Old World, and it is difficult not to read Coatlicue as a powerful manifestation of the Terrible Mother, in her skirt of serpents, necklace of skulls and shirt of flayed skin.

A moon goddess and mother of all the gods, Coatlicue had many guises: sometimes she appeared as the god of ripe corn, Cinteotl (*cintli* for "maize" and

and *teotl* for "god"); sometimes as her daughter Xilonen; sometimes as her son Xochipilli—"the Prince of Flowers," god of young love, spring and procreation, like Adonis or Osiris. Like other Great Mothers, Coatlicue had her son for lover, and spectators at the sacred ball game of the Aztec cried out to Xochipilli, "the great adulterer," when a player drove his ball successfully through the stationary stone ring at the side of the court. The mother's son who must be slain and reborn so that the green world may spring again to life is so familiar in Old World symbols and rites that it's easy to overlook the crucial feature in Mesoamerican rites—the visual shape of an ear of corn, at once phallus, face and knife.

Among Coatlicue's many sons, the Aztec chose for patron Huitzilopochtli, whom the Aztec associated with fire, sun and war. In his name the Aztec, with their genius for organization, institutionalized sacrifice on an epic scale. In his honor Moctezuma initiated the "flowery war," waged against six city-states to the east for the sole purpose of capturing suitable victims for sacrifice. Other peoples would not do because Huitzilopochtli could not abide the coarseness of their savage and barbarous flesh. "Their flesh is as yellowish, hard, tasteless tortillas in his mouth," an informant told Father Duran. Captives from the city-states, on the other hand, "come like warm tortillas, soft, tasty, straight from the griddle."

By the thousands, heads were chopped and hearts sundered on the round Sun Stone of Tenochtitlán, the very Calendar Stone that charted the course of the stars and the count of days, the flickering of fire, the breathing of winds, the flight of birds, the slithering of snakes, the undulation of waters and the ceaseless metamorphoses of matter and spirit. The rhythm of life engraved in the stone was also incarnate in the god whose mask the priest wore when he ripped from the victim's breast a heart pulsing to the same beat. At that moment the priest impersonated the greatest of the corn gods because he was the most mortal—the Feathered Serpent, Quetzalcoatl, twin to the god of war.

The Feathered Serpent was a descendant of the Maya god Kukulkan, legendary founder of the city of Chichen Itza, who sat at the center of the cross-shaped tree and embodied in his emblems of sprouting maize, fish, salamander and vulture the four elements of earth, water, fire and air. His day sign was Ik, the day of breath, and for the Maya he was

Carved probably in 1497, the great calendar stone of the Aztecs, 13 feet across, related human hearts directly to the sun at its center, "heaven's heart," on which the sacrificial victim was placed. Encircled by a pair of knife-tongued serpents, the stone dictated daily ritual in the present by the recorded history of the past. Neg. No. 318168, courtesy Department of Library Services, American Museum of Natural History

the god of resurrection, transmuted to the Creek and northern tribes as *the great master of breath,* the Great Spirit. The Toltec renamed him for the green-plumed quetzal bird of the rainforests of Guatemala and Chiapas and for the water serpent of the tropics. Sacred as jade, Quetzalcoatl became the priest-king who founded their city of Tula on the high plateaus, taught his people the arts, conceived their calendar and gave them maize. He was a mediator between gods and men, sky and earth, a mortal and immortal hero who sustained the sun with his fire-drill and the corn with his blood.

For more than a thousand years, from the rise of the empire of Teotihuacán in A.D. 250 to the fall of the Aztec empire in A.D. 1521, Quetzalcoatl ruled the cradle of civilization in the New World. He brought corn to man after he had transformed himself into a black ant to steal a grain from the red ants who lived in the heart of Food Mountain. To the later Aztec, his earlier reign in Tula was legendary and paradisal, a golden age of abundance in which pumpkins were so large "a man could hardly embrace one with his arms" and ears of corn so plentiful that "those that were not perfect were used to fuel the fires."

In the Codex Borbonicus, Quetzalcoatl, with a serpent in his hand, dances before his enemy Tezcatlipoca. Neg. No. 332117, photo Logan, courtesy Department of Library Services, American Museum of Natural History

In his time, it was said, every ear of corn was as strong and firm as a man.

Sahagún described his temple at Tenochtitlán as encrusted with precious metals and jewels: the room to the east was covered with gold, to the west with turquoise and emeralds, to the south with white seashells and to the north with silver. Another temple was lined entirely with four different colors of quetzal feathers, yellow, blue, white and red. The sacred jewels and colors reappear in the altars of the Hopi kivas, as Major John Wesley Powell noted in 1875: "In the niches was kept the collection of sacred jewels—little crystals of quartz, crystals of calcite, garnets, beautiful pieces of jasper, and other bright or fantastically shaped stones, which, it was claimed they had kept for many generations."

What set Quetzalcoatl apart from other creator sun-corn-rain gods in the New World was that he was also human; his flesh was mortal and he suffered as a man. To my ears his story was all too familiar. He prayed and fasted, did penance, was tempted and sinned. Thrice he was tempted and thrice fell. First vanity undid him. When his dread enemy Tezcatlipoca gave him a mirror, Quetzalcoatl was so appalled at his ugliness that he allowed Tezcatlipoca to dress him in a mask of turquoise and a mantle of feathers. Next gluttony undid him. He gorged on a meal of corn, beans, chili, tomatoes and wine mixed with honey. At first he refused the wine, but after tasting one drop he drank five gourds of it and called for his sister Quetzalpetlatl, who also drank. Then lust undid him, for they lay together in carnal sin.

When Quetzalcoatl woke to what must have been a stupendous hangover, he lay four days and nights in a stone casket, then threw himself into the flames of a funeral pyre and was consumed. His ashes rose as a flock of birds which bore his heart high into the heavens to become the morning and evening star, Venus. Now every night he journeys through the Underworld, repeating his first journey when he defeated the Dead Land Lord by piecing together the scattered bones of his father from which man was made. For the Aztec, man was made of bone ground into meal, stuck together with maize and moistened with penitential blood.

In the person of Quetzalcoatl, Aztec priests reenacted in bloody sacrifice the mystery of metamorphosis, "the fall" into matter and rebirth into spirit sung by the poets of many testaments in their psalms. The shape-changing of Quetzalcoatl sprang directly from the metaphoric relation of man to corn. The ritual act of tearing out the heart was figured in the husking of corn, which Erich Neumann has interpreted in Jungian terms: "The husking of the corn, the heart, is castration, mutilation, and sacrifice of the essential male part; but at the same time it is birth and a life-giving deed for the benefit of the world or mankind." The phallic shape of corn makes husking a logical, if startling, symbol of castration. But startling only to us, not to the Aztec, for whom the phrase "to bear a child" was interchangeable with three phrases of death and violence: "to die in childbed," "to take a prisoner," "to be sacrificed as a prisoner." The Aztec who glorified war and conquest did so in part to harvest captives as he harvested fields of corn, to sustain life at the source. The paradox of equating child-birth with prisoner-death, like the paradox of equating blood with corn, came easily to men whose world depended not only on the substance of corn but on its sym-

On a stepped pyramid altar, an Aztec priest holds the victim's husked heart aloft and offers it to his Royal Lord the sun, to sustain life for mankind at the source. From the Florentine Codex. Neg. No. 1731, courtesy Department of Library Services, American Museum of Natural History

bolic configurations, where rows of kernels appeared to be both protected and imprisoned by their husks, where husking appeared to be both castration and insemination, where corn-eating was both cannibalism and sacrament, a mystic communion with the sacrificed god.

Quetzalcoatl endured through centuries and civilizations because the metaphor worked as a figure of self-transformation: a carnal heart purified into the "precious eagle-cactus fruit" of the deified heart that blazes nightly in the transit of Venus. While Huitzilopochtli conquered the outer world of matter, Quetzalcoatl conquered the inner world of spirit, of penitence, of atonement for the guilt man was born with, or as my grandparents would have said, the guilt man was born for. Quetzalcoatl embodied what in other circumstances my grandparents would have called a change of heart.

DRINKING DOWN THE SUN

IF I FOUND CONNECTION in the rites of Quetzalcoatl, I lost it in Cuzco at the feast of Inti Raymi, celebrated at the summer solstice since the founding of the city and the Inca empire half a millennium ago. I found corn everywhere, but overwhelmingly in the form of drink. For a week, villagers come down from the mountains and up from the valleys to parade daily through the streets. For a week women in their Mad Hatter hats and Wizard of Oz skirts, behind tables improvised into bars with bottles of Pisco and rum, cry "Punchy, punchy," and "Chicha morada, chicha bianco, chicha picante, chicha chicha!" Cuzco's Plaza de Armas—enclosed by the spotlit fronts of the cathedral, the Church of La Compania and the Moorish balconies of the arcades—is a maelstrom of flutes, drums and harps, brass bands and conch shells, men in feathered capes and pointy caps, masked troops of children in top hats and wedding veils, youths in cloaks of Spanish moss waving yucca stalks, women in bowlers carrying plumed batons—everyone in costume, everyone dancing. To an American tourist like me, deafened by firecrackers and popped like a cork from the pushing, pressing, crushing, pickpocketing multitude, the festival is a combination Fourth of July, New Year's Eve and Mardi Gras, fused into one big drunken bash.

Inti Raymi so shocked the Spaniards that they forbade it, but to so little avail that after four centuries the Peruvian government officially restored it, in 1930, under the name "Indian Fiesta." In the Southern Hemisphere, the month of June ("Raymi") is the time of harvest, which belongs to the Sun ("Inti") and to corn. At the summer solstice, the reigning Lord of the Sun tallied the loads of grain, gold, feathers and coca leaves collected as tribute, arranged the marriages of young knights, distributed the year's chosen virgins, reviewed the year's oracles and punished the priests who had guessed wrong, numbered the different-colored flocks of llamas and ended the fast with a communion meal of *yahuar sancu,* little balls of raw corn mixed with the fat and blood of sacrificed llamas.

Sancu was a vestige of the cannibalism practiced in "ancient times," Garcilaso confessed, when tribes were so addicted to human flesh that they buried their dead in their stomachs: "As soon as the deceased had breathed his last, his relatives gathered round and ate him roasted or boiled, according to the amount of flesh he still had: if little, boiled, if much, roasted." Such practices, he explained, were more common to Indians of the jungle, where produce grew spontaneously, than to those of his native Cuzco, where men were required to plant maize and vegetables and so got themselves civilized. Where the civilizing power of the Inca did not reach, there were still barbaric tribes like the Anti, said to have come "from the Mexican area," who ate human flesh as a sacred thing—"without cooking it or roasting it thoroughly or even chewing it." Such tribes violated decorum. In his own enlightened times, Garcilaso continued, *sancu* was made only "by bleeding and not by killing the victims." First they half-baked the bread "in balls in dry pots, for they had no ovens," then added to the dough the blood of children between five and ten, "obtained from between the eyebrows, above the nostrils."

Only at the spring and fall harvest festivals, which resembled the fasting and feasting rites of the Aztec, did the Inca use corn for bread. Since they had other staples—quinoa, potato, cassava—they commonly ate corn in whole kernels rather than ground into meal. And because cornbread was sacred, "only pure young girls could grind the meal for it." These were the "wives of the Sun," who on the eve of both festivals worked all night grinding the corn flour to make bread in "little paste-balls the size of an apple." The main job of the pure young girls, however, was to brew *chicha* for massive consumption at the feast. When the Inca king broke his fast at dawn on Inti Raymi, he greeted the Sun, his father, with two golden vessels of the brew. Inviting the Sun to drink first, the king poured the sacred beer from the vessel in his right hand into a gold basin, from which it flowed through an underground channel into the fortress-temple of the Sun, so that "it disappeared as though the god-star had really drunk it." The Inca drank from the other vessel, then divided the rest among the gold goblets of his nobles, believing that the sanctified liquid "communicated its virtues to the prince and to all those of his blood."

"Each home kept a Corn Mother (sara-mama) of corncobs, wrapped in fine textiles, enclosed in a shrine. Since she represented the strength or weakness of the corn crop, if she was 'strong' during the year, she remained; if 'weak,' she was destroyed and replaced. After harvest, a new sara-mama *was made from the most fruitful of the corn plants. The ritual is observed to this day."*

—LYNN MEISCH, *A Traveler's Guide to El Dorado and the Inca Empire* (1977)

At the Sun temple, priests brought in lambs of the "Peruvian sheep" for sacrifice. The first sacrificed was always black, for this color was held most sacred because most pure and unmixed. (Even a white llama has a black snout.) After a priest slit the llama's belly to read its organs for auguries, large numbers of creatures were slaughtered and their flesh roasted on spits in the public squares for all to eat with the *sancu* bread: for "all Peru was one people during this feast." This custom, Garcilaso observed, led some Spanish commentators to assert that the Inca and their vassals took Holy Communion as Christians do. Garcilaso, however, was more cautious: "We have simply described what the Indians did and leave each reader to draw what parallel he wishes."

Christians who observed worshippers washed in the blood of the llama might well draw the parallel for themselves, particularly if they heard any hymns to the creator god Viracocha. One such hymn has come down to us through the knotted-rope language of the *quipu*, used not only to number flocks and crops, but to convey the formulaic phrases of Inca rituals:

> *peacefully, safely*
> *sun, shine on and illumine*
> *the Incas, the people, the servants*
> *whom you have shepherded*
> *guard them from sickness and suffering*
> *in peace, in safety.*

Pastoral metaphors of shepherding were possible to these highlanders because they had long ago domesticated llamas and found them proper for sacrifice, along with the usual pretty youths.

Blood sacrifice was as potent for Inca crops as for Aztec, but where the Aztec saw symbolic potential in "husking the corn," the Inca fixed on unhusked corn, young and green, with wrappers intact. Virgin purity was essential and, at earlier festival times, chosen youths of both sexes were kept in a pound, next to the llama pound, in the Field of Pure Gold before the Coricancha. While the llamas were slit open alive, the youths were first made drunk on *chicha* and then strangled before their throats were cut. Many pious parents, particularly in Cuzco, offered young daughters of their own free will, but more were purposefully "not very watchful with their daughters," Father Cobo wrote. "On the contrary, it is said that they were happy to see them seduced at a very early age."

Farmers used blood in practical as well as symbolic ways to fertilize their fields, just as they used guano. As late as the nineteenth century, a traveler in

Peru observed that on the feast day of San Antony, the natives of Acobamba, east of Lima, celebrated the day by staging a fierce fight in their plaza. The men divided themselves into two parties and battled until some fell wounded or dead. "Now the women rushed forth amongst the men, collecting the flowing blood and guarding it carefully," wrote the author of *Travels in Peru, 1838–42.* "The object of the barbarian fighting was to obtain human blood, which was afterwards interred in the fields with a view to securing an abundant crop."

The early Spanish Fathers were bothered less by the volume of bloodletting than by the volume of drinking. "Indians drank in the most incredible manner: indeed, drunkenness was certainly their commonest vice," Garcilaso commented. In his own day that vice had been mitigated by the shame Indians were made to feel from the good example set by the Spaniards. "If the same good example had been given them as regards all vices," Garcilaso the Inca added, "today all the Indians would be apostles and would be preaching the Gospel."

If the Aztec institutionalized wholesale sacrifice in his corn rites, the Inca institutionalized drunkenness. During Inti Raymi, feasting was followed by a drinking bout ritualized in a series of toasts. The invitation to drink was always extended with a pair of goblets so that host and recipient could drink equally: "The king has invited you and I have come in his name to drink with you." The bout lasted for nine days, the point being, as Father Cobo lamented, "to drink until they cannot stand up." To this end they preferred the strongest *chichas* and added other strong potions to "knock them out more rapidly."

If excess was the point, from what I saw at the festival of Inti Raymi in 1987, not much had changed. By the end of the week, back streets and hills were littered with bodies and here and there a bus that had toppled over the edge of a road. The body count was particularly heavy along the windy road leading to the fortress-temple of Sacsahuaman, which shares the view over Cuzco with a megalithic White Christ. Nowadays, the official climax of the week's festivities is a pageant performed inside the ruins of the Sun's House, built of cyclopean stones "so large that nobody who saw them would think they had been laid there by human hands."

The stones of Sacsahuaman become bleachers for spectators watching the procession of the Inca during the feast of Inti Raymi. Photo by Robert Frerck, Woodfin Camp & Associates

A native Cuzqueña celebrates Inti Raymi today as her ancestors did, by drinking chicha.
Photo by Mireille Vautier,
Woodfin Camp & Associates

The pageant had been laid by too many human hands, at least for the hundreds of foreign tourists who dozed on bleachers, while local performers enacting the Inca and his voluminous court proclaimed in Quechua, hour after hour, the glories of empire. Interest picked up when a real llama was lugged up the altar steps and the Inca lifted his knife, but the victim disappeared through a trapdoor before a drop of blood was shed. All about us, however, on the Field of Spears, where blood aplenty had been shed during the Great Rebellion of 1536, the hilltop seethed with life. The field was a giant earth oven, a *huatia*, with a hundred smoking chimneys, where hundreds of families camping here for the week baked in the earth their potatoes and oca roots and corn.

The real harvest festival was here, in Chuqui Pampa, not in our segregated bleachers, where scruffy bands of boys, scampering out of range of the guards, begged and fought over our tourist lunchboxes of Jell-O and hard-boiled eggs. The festival was in Chuqui Pampa and back at the Plaza de Armas. There the dancing and drinking had never stopped. There thousands still snaked past the rows of alpaca-sweater sellers, the display of the vampire bat and Brazilian tarantula, the small boys peeing at the curbs. There I sought refuge with a glass of European beer inside Chez Victor. I liked the taste of *chicha,* but the decorum of excess defeated me. At the restaurant I was divided only by a pane of glass from one *chicha*-bombed celebrant, who stood for an hour with his Inca face pressed against the window. Looking in as I looked out, he looked through me as if I were glass, as if centuries were gone in smoke, and he would stand there always, fixed and motionless as stone.

The Language of Carnivals
and Kings

HOOPESTON'S SWEET-CORN MAGIC

THE CORN RITES past and present of America's native civilizations kept me at a distance, but even those of the Midwest made me feel like a tourist. At 10:00 A.M. on Labor Day weekend, at the corner of Main and Sixth streets in Hoopeston, Illinois, I found men still unloading plastic folding chairs from the back of Ford pickup trucks for their womenfolk to sit on. In Hoopeston men wear their bib hats stiff and high; women wear their hair—colored blonde, white or blue—the same way. Men wear their jeans low and loose, cinched tightly below formidable bellies. Women wear their pastel polyester pants high, stretched tight across bellies worn proudly, even post-menopausally, as emblems of fertility. On Main Street, at the crossroads of what was once the north-south Chicago, Eastern & Illinois railroad line and the east-west Nickelplate line, Hoopeston's 7,092 inhabitants were gathering to celebrate their forty-third Annual National Sweetcorn Festival. Forty-three years is an eon out here, and the rites of this local festival are as decorously prescribed as those of the Pueblo, Creek, Aztec or Inca.

All over Illinois—not to mention Kansas, Nebraska, Ohio, Indiana, Missouri, Pennsylvania, Michigan—small towns, like an archipelago in a land-locked sea of corn, celebrate sweet-corn festivals. In Illinois I could have gone to Mendota for its thirty-ninth National Sweet Corn Festival, to Morris in Grundy County for its thirty-eighth, to Mount Vernon for its fourteenth Sweetcorn & Watermelon Festival, to Kewanee for its Annual Corn & Hog Days, to Bloomington, Urbana, Delavan, Warrenville, El Paso, Arcola. No town is too small to be without its Grand Parade, carnival rides and demolition derbies. I chose Hoopeston because it calls itself the Sweet Corn Capital of the World, not for corn in the field but corn in the can.

Hoopeston is built of cans. It was founded in 1871, in prairie between the Vermilion and Iroquois rivers, when a railroad was being laid along the north-south Hubbard Trail to Chicago. The Chicago, Danville & Vincennes line opened the following year, the same year as the founding of East Lynn next to Hoopeston and of the Sunbonnet Club of Young Ladies within Hoopeston. Shortly Hoopeston would have the first Illinois Canning Company, developed exclusively to can corn for the railroad to transport. Today Main Street divides the canneries of the north from those of the south, with names that have metamorphosed into Stokely-Van Camp, Green Giant and Pillsbury. To the north, the American Can Company supplies the cans and, to the south, the Food Machinery Corporation supplies the machinery for canning. In corn-pack season, when fifteen thousand acres of sweet corn in a thirty-mile radius around Hoopeston are ripe, Hoopeston cans around the clock seven days a week. As one festival booster, John McElhany, said, "It's a corn town."

John's dad, Clyde, is a dapper man of seventy-seven who's helped the Jaycees run the festival since 1938. I found Clyde joking with Pat Musk, a big woman with a Gertrude Stein haircut, who runs the National Sweetheart Pageant that began with a competition for Miss Sweetcorn. Now it's a "training pageant" for Miss America, said Pat, who is also town organist. Pat and Clyde go back a ways. "We used to smoke behind the barn together many years ago," Clyde said. "Yep, she played it on the organ out behind the barn." Pat heaved with laughter like a leaky bellows.

John was running the twenty-four-hour scavenger hunt this year—seven teams and 325 items—"some difficult, some embarrassing." He ran through the menu of events: the "I Like the Sound of America" pageant presented by the children's choir of the Church of the Nazarene, the Horseshoe Pitching Contest, the Horse and Pony Show, the "Festival of the Stars" Talent Show, Square Dancing with Merle Ponto and Mike Powell Callers, the Brownback Family Magic Act, and of course the parade. Baton twirling is big at the Hoopeston parade. The thin, the fat, the shapely, the squat, toddlers barely out of diapers—all strutted, swung, twiddled and dropped their batons in time to a thousand-and-one trombones. Local politicians like "Jerry Stout—Your Small Town Alternative" worked the crowd. The Shriners' Royal Order of Cooties invaded in motorized minicars like a plague of crickets. But the heart of the parade was cars, slick and penile, adorned with living dolls in organdy ruffles or glittering sequins, emerging like corn silks from the cob, waving smiles and bosoms for the title of National Sweetheart.

The entire festival celebrated engines and wheels: the Bigwheel/Tricycle Races, the Dual-Demolition Derby, the Sweetcorn Cruise, the Tractor Pull and the climactic King Krunch—a monster truck that stomped cars. Even the feast of "FREE HOT BUTTERED SWEET CORN" served to twenty-two thousand people a day, like a Midwestern potlatch, celebrated the machinery that can husk and steam some fifteen tons of corn for assembly lines of people, equipped with roasting pans, dish pans and plastic garbage bags to catch the Niagara fall of ears from the steamer. The Kids' Corn-Eating Contest was won by a freckled boy with no front teeth who turned his gums into a machine, "cleaning the cobs" round and round like a lawnmower. "Don't swallow," his brother yelled at him, "just chew." In the most casual talk cars figured: a man handed his busted shoe to the repair man with the words, "Blew out my tire."

The Kids' Corn-Eating Contest at Hoopeston's Annual Sweet-corn Festival. Photo by John McElhany

Machines are nature's way in Hoopeston; everyone works at one time or another for the canneries. "I used to work at Stokely cleaning smut," said the prim director of the Vermilion County Museum. "Awful stuff, you'd scrape it off and it'd get all over your glasses." "There are few hand jobs left now," said Bill Nichols at the present Stokely plant, and most of those are done by seasonal help, migrant Mexicans. But there is work running the machines that can Stokely's ten thousand acres of sweet corn, after they have been automatically husked and cut, cleaned for three hours, cooked for twelve minutes and cooled for five. Machines turn out 1.7 million cases of corn, one-third of it creamed.

Clyde Timmons, a well-kept man of sixty-six now retired, spent his life in the industry, as did his father before him. "I was pokin' cans at thirteen," he says, "for twenty-five cents an hour." He worked every "corn-pack" in high school and college until he came back from the army and went to work as a field man for Milford Canning, in charge of contracting and harvesting the sweet-corn crop. "Each company," he explained, "pays the farmer a contract price and furnishes the seed to control variety and timing, so that they can harvest everything during a four- to six-week period." When corn was all "hand snapped," they used to import Kentuckians and Missourians and mules to go with them to get the harvest in: "Each company had three hundred and fifty or so head of mules in their barns. At two-thirty every morning the workers would hitch a team of mules to a wagon that'd hold three ton a corn, they'd move out to the fields, jerk the corn to throw up into the wagon, then bring it back into the streets here with all the kids in town hollering, 'Git me a roastin' ear.' Each company had a muleskinner. He'd spend the whole year buying and selling the mules, too expensive to keep year-round, so they'd sell 'em after corn-pack and start again in the spring, buying 'em up for farming and jerking."

Mules were replaced by trucks in the late 1940s, hand snappers by mechanical harvesters in the mid-1950s. Hoopeston is the home of the first successful mechanical harvester, called the FMC Sergeant after the man who developed it in Iowa but didn't have "the finances" to continue. "We were among the first to put them in the field," Timmons said. In 1975 Alvin Slosser mounted a four-row harvester on a New Idea Uni-Harvester, which pulled a truck behind it, and that became the Byron Sweet Corn Harvester of today. When corn was shucked by hand, the shucker was given one brass coin per bucket, which he could exchange for money at the end of the day. But once William Sells developed a husker using iron rollers and then a feed machine called the "Peerless," the only major work left to automate was cutting kernels from the cob.

Originally whole ears of corn were canned, the first by Captain Isaac Winslow of Maine, who sold a dozen cans to S. S. Pierce of Boston in 1840. Three decades later, Barker's Semi-automatic Plunger Cutter paved the way for Welcome Sprague to create a cutter with rotating knives and an automatic silker. Sprague and Sells got together to form the company that became Food Machinery, with the aim of manufacturing all the machinery needed for canning corn. Soon a proper steaming kettle was invented by J. F. Rutter, who also devised a way to keep corn white in the can without bleach. In those days they boiled corn for three to four hours.

Today Hoopeston's canning companies may count on the fact that the taste for canned corn in the United States has not changed for the last twenty-five years: we still consume forty-two to forty-five million cases annually, of which Hoopeston produces eighty-one million cans. It is still a housewife's boon, said Timmons. "You just open it, heat it and dump it out." The voice of pragmatism in the rhythm of the machine and the ceremony of the can. I thought of the crowd's cheers when King Krunch stomped on cars in a monster sacrifice of metal. Where tin lizzies were enthroned with tin cans, King Krunch was Coatlicue. In the festival booklet labeled "Hoopeston's Sweet Corn Magic," an ad for one cannery boasted, "We built our plants right beside the cornfields in the heartland of America." Only to an outsider would that seem a contradiction.

COURTLAND'S CORNHUSKERS

THE LITURGIES OF INDUSTRIALISM boomed over the car radio on Sunday morning of that same weekend as I drove through minuscule Illinois towns, headed for Hog Days in Kewanee. A former Marine, now a born-again evangelist of the Church of God, pummeled me with questions: "Did you know that Jesus had short hair, was a taxpayer and dined with the wealthy as well as the poor?" I had been driving for miles through six-foot walls of corn, so mechanically uniform they looked like a Marine's dream of flat-topped Christian soldiers presenting arms to a short-haired Jesus. No wonder Khrushchev flipped when he saw the scale of these battalions, divisions, armies of corn, a rural proletariat regimented to military-industrial perfection. The paradox of the Midwest is that its farms and farmers are children of the industrial revolution, at once progressivist and conformist, like a capitalist Jesus—a paradox not lost on a Russian communist viewing for the first time America's machine-tooled factories of corn.

As an ex-Presbyterian, I saw the paradox of rural America celebrating Labor Day, a rite of the urban proletariat, with country corn festivals and churchgoing. For paradox, take Delavan, Illinois, where all but a handful of its two thousand inhabitants were attending the town's six churches before enjoying a communal barbecue in a cook-shed decorated with corn. First the eating, then the Frog Jumping Contest, Needle in the Straw, Tomahawk Throwing, Nail Driving, Corn Shelling, Lip Sync Contest and Cow Patty Throw—all played in the birthplace of factory corn. In Delavan in 1847, the corn that Robert Reid planted, and his son James crossbred, laid the foundations of America's corn industry—Reid Yellow Dent.

Kewanee, while far from urban, was more proletarian than Delavan or Hoopeston. At Kewanee the bars outnumber the churches, and beer is not sequestered in a tent. The bars were jumping along the Main Street midway and so was the World's Largest Pork Chop Barbecue, surrounded by mountains of deep-fried onion rings, foot-long corn dogs, lemon shake-ups for the temperate, deep-fried elephant's ears with maple glaze and funnel cakes with apples and candied cherries for the fatties. There's nothing genteel about Kewanee, Hog Capital of the World. The Mud Volleyball Tournament was as satisfying as a hog wallow and the geriatric square dancers as invigorating as a troop of dervishes. I missed the Hog Jog Stampede, the Hog Calling Contest and the Kiddie Tractor Pull, but I found Kewanee's secret treasure, the National Corn Huskers' Hall of Fame, and an ex-cornhusking champ, Bill Rose.

Bill, a tall, barrel-chested man of seventy-nine

Cornhusking tools from the trade catalog of Laymen & Carey Co., ca. 1890. From the Collections of the Henry Ford Museum and Greenfield Village, Neg. No. 103449

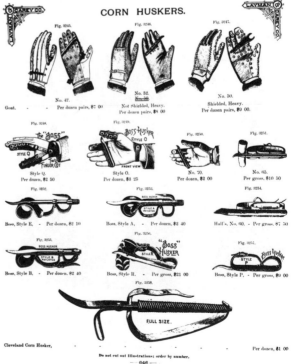

with hog-sized hands and thumbs like cigars, was selling raffle tickets for an afghan to benefit the Kewanee Historical Society, which devotes a corner of its building to the Hall of Fame. Bill pointed to a display of husking paraphernalia—the wrist hook, thumb hook, palm hook—and a wall of photos. "Here we're lined up waiting for the bomb to go off," he explained a *Life* photo of the 1935 national in Indiana. "Eighteen wagons, contestants from nine states, over one hundred thousand spectators mashed the corn down. There's Henry Wallace, he's the one started it in 'twenty-four in Des Moines, Ioway. I got fourth place that day in Indiana, got second in the state, won the county." Bill was off and running, recalling a world that ended as abruptly in 1941 as the pony express in 1861. For cornhusking, not only a necessity but a national sport in the 1930s, stopped when the war ended the contests and the combines ended husking by hand.

Years ago we planted with a wire with buttons, about three foot apart, so the planter would click and plant a kernel. Then we'd husk two rows at a time and the ears'd hang down. Now they plant the corn so thick we pick only one row at a time and you grab the ears different and got to hold onto 'em. They're bred for combines 'cause that's what's doin' the pickin'. Then a man'd do good to pick a hundred bushels a day, or about two acres. Now a combine picks eight hundred bushels an hour.

Cornhusking champions trained in the field, where they learned to break, strip and throw an ear against the "bangboard" of the wagon in a single motion.
Photo Grant Heilman, Agricultural Photography

In 1922 Henry Wallace challenged Midwestern farmers to improve the efficiency of their cornhusking (not just quantity but clean ears), Bill said, and offered a prize of fifty dollars for the best husking record for a day. The first contest took place in Des Moines and was won by Louis Curley, who picked 1,644 pounds. The following year Wallace doubled the prize and instituted rules: Wagons must be double-boxed, two boards high and twenty-six inches deep, with a forty-foot-square bangboard. Heats were to be eighty minutes, with a weight deduction for husks and a triple deduction for gleanings. County winners would go to the state contest, and state winners to the national. Farm magazines became sponsors, donating prize money and crowning husking queens. Churches got into the act, providing food and tents for husking banquets. Entertainment by bands and barbershop quartets, automobile and farm machinery exhibits, educational displays like Indian wickiups turned the contests into community fairs.

"In our opinion," Wallace said in 1923, after a horse named Zev had won the Kentucky Derby, "it should give the spectators as many thrills as the race between Zev and Papyrus or the Yale-Harvard football game." Here was a corn competition far more thrilling than the National Tall Corn Sweepstakes held annually at the Iowa State Fair, even though a world record was set in 1942 with a stalk of 26 feet, 10⅛ inches. Almost overnight champion corn-huskers became national sports heroes, sought by promoters to endorse everything from steak restaurants to insurance policies. About the time one husker was signed for a promised Hollywood movie about cornhusking, the farm papers required contestants to sign a pledge against paid promotions.

Wallace, himself no slouch at media promotion, used the pages of the *Farmer* to critique the husking techniques that were hotly debated by men and boys over suppers of creamed canned corn. Whetting their appetites for the match to come, Wallace compared the pinch-and-twist versus the free-swing methods of a pair of major contenders in the December 1923 issue of his *Farmer*:

> Both Rickelman and Paul use thumb hooks, one a Kees and the other a Clark. Their method of husking, however, is totally different. Rickelman uses almost invariably the pinch and twist husking method, grasping the ear at the butt with the left hand with the thumb up. The thumb hook on his right hand brushes the husks aside so that he can grasp the ear and give the twist which usually breaks the ear quite clean of husks. Occasionally, however, the Rickelman method results in a slip-shucked ear.... Paul uses the standard hook method, but he has a free and easy, rhythmical swing which makes his husking rather prettier to watch than the Rickelman husking.

By the 1930s the contests were covered by *Newsweek* and *Life,* by radio and newsreel, and President Franklin D. Roosevelt fired the opening shot from the White House. In 1940, the Nubbin Derby or Battle of the Bangboards, as NBC's *National Farm and Home Hour* called it, drew a record crowd of one hundred sixty thousand people, before the war ended contests already doomed by the advent of harvesting machines.

Machines may have supplanted the hands but not the hearts of veteran huskers. A few old-timers began to revive local contests in 1970, Bill told me, and revived the national in 1975 in Oakley, Kansas, purely for sport. Today

"At 12:45, when a five minute warning bomb exploded (upon signal from President Franklin D. Roosevelt in the White House) 160,000 people—more than have ever filled a football stadium—were throbbing with pre-kickoff excitement. The 18 contestants, each stationed in his own plot of land, waved aside photographers, radio announcers and reporters. Up floated an American flag, the starting bomb burst; and the 13th World Series of the Corn Belt started with a bang."
—From Newsweek, November 21, 1936

nine states—Kansas, Nebraska, Iowa, Indiana, Illinois, Ohio, South Dakota, Minnesota and Missouri—compete in the national, the host town and state varying from year to year. This year it was Oakley's turn again, Bill said, and I could watch the husking contenders warm up in the North Central Kansas Corn Husking Contest that takes place every September in Courtland, Kansas.

Courtland is just across the border from Hildreth, Nebraska, and is inhabited mostly by Johnsons and Thomsons, three generations of them, who run the show. Courtland is the kind of small town that wears its sporting heart on its shop windows: "Eat the Bluejays," says Gero's Cafe; "Bank the Panthers," says the Swedish-American Bank; "Flush the Bluejays, sink 'em," says Tebow Plumbing. I found the husking field on Highway 36, just three and a half miles east of Courtland. Horses and wagons were drawn up by privies labeled "HE" and "HER," with the footnote "Not Responsible for Accidents." A sign on a backboard said, "If you think nobody cares, just miss an interest payment on a couple of 8800 John Deere Combines." A sheet labeled "What We Named Our Horses" listed names like " 'Damn You Earl'—always called 'Damn You' by our children." When I pulled in, Esther Thomson was announcing the winners of the Patched Overalls and Jeans Contest—four divisions: largest, smallest, most unusual and most decorative.

Most of the folks were standing around waiting, waiting for the drivers to hitch up the wagons, waiting for the heats of each division to be announced, waiting for the starting gun to go off and then to go off again at the end of thirty minutes, waiting for the loads to be weighed and the results posted, waiting for the combine to finish off the picked rows, waiting in line to eat a porkburger and a lard-crust rhubarb pie and to drink a lot of lemonade to counter the hot dry heat. But no one's in a hurry in Courtland and waiting leaves plenty of time to talk. I talked to oldsters and youngsters and unhusked a whole new world of corn.

"This is my thirtieth contest," said Vernon Erickson, who is seventy-five and makes all the trophies for the contest by hand. His big competition is Gene Walker, a mere sixty-nine. "Gene won last year so Vernon's hot to win today," said Gene's wife. Gene said his best score was twenty-four pounds a minute, "but the corn is heavier this year and that slows you down." He showed me how a right-handed husker grabs the ear with his left hand, rips it open with the hook, shucks and tosses it in one motion with his right. It's the left hand that wears out quickest, and the men do exercises to strengthen it. As a boy he shucked from September to April, six days a week, with maybe two feet of snow on the cornfields. "You got ten cents a bushel and if you shucked a hundred bushels, ten bucks a day—ideal for a boy who wanted to get out and hustle."

As seniors, they don't compete with the age group designated Men's National, twenty-one to sixty-four. Of the seven divisions at each contest, this is the toughest, for the men have to pick for a full half-hour. Youths and seniors pick only for ten, women for twenty. "Ideal age is twenty to thirty but if you didn't grow up with it, it's kinda hard," said one husker, "gotta be able to do it blindfold." Waiting for all the heats of all divisions to end was like waiting for the Pueblo corn dances to begin. The contest drawled slow as speech through the hot afternoon, and I decided I could wait for the awards banquet that night to find out who'd won.

At seven o'clock sharp I joined the chowline with three hundred others in the high school gymnasium of a nearby hamlet, Scandia. Checked tablecloths stretched from one end of the basketball court to another, awaiting our paper plates of dry turkey, wet stuffing, mashed potatoes and corn. After the Doxology, the piano thumped out "Alexander's Ragtime Band." Everyone I met who was not a Johnson or Thomson was an Olson or Peterson. Across from me Orville Peterson, at eighty, had just competed for the fifty-eighth time. Next to him Roy Hubbard, at nine, had competed for his third and won first place in the sixteen-and-under division. Roy's father, Don, had won a prize for his horses—Most Popular Team—and Don began the evening's entertainment by reading Edgar Guest's "A Heap o' Livin'. " The poetry reading was followed by a barbershop quartet, a clog dance and a skit featuring Dumb Bunny, Agra Bear and Farmerette. Vernon's trophies were almost anticlimactic, but I found out that Bob Ferguson, a "super husker" from New Sharon, Ioway, and a three-time national winner, had won today.

Afterward, as I drove to a distant motel through a landscape totally black, totally flat, the horizon exploded. "We have a little bit of everything out here— floods, droughts, tornadoes," some Thomson had told me. "A little twister the other day hit Harding and leveled the town, you wouldn't believe the debris." I believed it now, watching pitchforks of lightning stab ricks of clouds, booming like Armageddon, obliterating on my radio *Big Joe's Polka Show* and *Your Radio Bible Class.*

I caught up with Bob Ferguson again at the Iowa state contest, held at the Living History Farms in Des Moines. I also caught up with Herb Plambeck, who's been broadcasting farm news on the radio for fifty years, with time out for reporting World War II and Vietnam, and for serving as assistant to former Agriculture Secretary Earl Butz. Herb, an intense, worrying man of seventy-nine, is the guiding spirit behind the husking revival and founder of the National Corn Huskers Association and its newsletter, *Shucks.* In 1984, Herb started the first National Corn Throwing Contest and devised the rules: two throws each, one underhand and an optional overhand. That same year saw the first Champion of Champions Contest, limited to former national champs and won by John Jackson, husking 509½ pounds gross in twenty minutes. These are the kinds of statistics Herb keeps in his head, together with memories of former heroes like Carl Seiler of Oneida, Illinois, who hung up his hook after setting a world record in 1932, in deep mud in an ice storm. Ferguson's competition today, Herb told me, was another national champ, Tony Polich of Johnston, Iowa, age seventy-three to Bob's sixty-two. "It'll be that close today, a whisker's gonna tell the story," one husker predicted, but Bob won handily and set a new world record of 867½ pounds in thirty minutes.

The theme song of all this cornhusking revival is, There's been a change. "In the old days a couple would pick together and put the baby in the back of the wagon," said Herb. "The whole family picked or the harvest wouldn't get done. Tried to get it done by Thanksgiving, get the house banked up to insulate against the cold, get the produce stored in the root cellar, get the livestock penned. Then it was three hundred and sixty-five days you had work to do. Now it's corn, soybeans and Florida."

There's been a change, said Joe Anholt, a former national champ from Fort Dodge: "We'd stay out of school six to eight weeks every fall to get the crop done. They don't allow that anymore." There's been a change, said Ernest Heidecker of Lakota: "Nobody's got cattle anymore so nobody's using silage. Most people store corn shelled, 'cause last year we shelled one hundred and five thousand bushels from six hundred acres and if you did that with ear corn we'd a had to have cribs from here to Kansas and back."

There's been a change, said Gary Kupferschmid, of Mediapolis, Iowa, who capitalized on change in 1981 by founding International Corn Hook Collectors. With more than a hundred members, they've expanded into all corn-related software and hardware, from corn sacks and shellers to Shawnee pottery, and now call themselves Corn Items Collectors. "About ten of us have got maybe three hundred to three hundred and fifty of them cornhooks, but I've probably got the biggest collection," Gary said, pointing to his display boards of antique pegs and

Poster for the Missouri State and National Championship meets at Marshall, Missouri, in October 1987.

hooks, with rare beauties like the "twin-spurred palm hook" or the "iron-mesh thumb stall."

But some things don't change, like the "two-buckle thumb hook" made since 1929 by Raidt Manufacturing of Shenandoah, Iowa, and used today by Tony Polich. Or like the husking mitts and gloves that Raidt sold for twenty years after the bottom dropped out of his business, in 1948, when they were selling forty thousand dozen pairs of gloves and a hundred thousand palm hooks a year.

Some things don't change, like the voices of American men talking corn-husking as if it were baseball or football or golf. "Good huskers are born, not made," said Ray Oroke of Oskaloosa. "It's rhythm and stamina," said another. "It's breathing and concentration," said a third. "You just work hard as you can," said Bob Ferguson. "Hard work, clean living and a fierce determination to win," said Bill Rose. Winning takes the gumption of Vernon Erickson, the trophy maker of Scandia, who in 1978 lost the middle finger of his left hand in a sawing accident before the state meet and defended his title with a taped stub. Winning takes the passion of Herb Plambeck, still broadcasting in the pages of *Shucks* the glory of champions who contend for honor on the fields of corn.

The World's Only Corn Palace

GLORY IS WHAT TOOK ME to South Dakota in search of Mitchell, home of the World's Only Corn Palace, built to the greater glory of corn before the sport of husking champions was born. In late October, I picked up I-90, which runs straight across the state from Sioux Falls on the east to Rapid City on the west, where the four stony heads of Mount Rushmore look down on Crazy Horse Monument, Calamity Park and Custer State Park. If those faces could look to the southwest, beyond Buffalo Gap National Grassland and Badlands National Park, they would see Wounded Knee. If they could scrunch toward the east, nothing on these limitless barren plains, burnished to a shine by iced winds straight from the Pole, would interrupt their vision for 250 miles until they saw, in disbelief, the Kubla Khan domes and minarets of the Corn Palace.

Mitchell's Corn Palace of 1904 carried on the tradition begun by Sioux City in 1887.

After hours of bleached corn stubble and withered sunflowers, lit now and then by the startling blue eye of a pond, I was glad to reach Mitchell. The plains howl with the ghosts of travelers stranded after dark, and I was cheered to see, in the utterly deserted crossroads of North Main Street, the little Christmas-tree lights that outlined the only remaining corn palace from a century ago, when such palaces signaled the triumph of King Corn over the last stand of Mother Corn. By that time, Mother Corn had already lost the prairies and was about to lose the plains.

It was hard to believe that the loss was so recent and so complete. The Indians of the United States had made their last stand in the rightly named Badlands but three generations ago. When South Dakota became a state in 1889, the Dakotas—last of the Louisiana Purchase lands to become a territory— were still half Indian. Just a year later came the massacre of the Sioux at Wounded Knee, the murder of Sitting Bull and the death of the Ghost Dance that promised the buffalo would come back and the invader depart forever. The year before, when the corn was in, my grandparents took a honeymoon trip upriver from their new home in Edgerton, Kansas, to Sioux City, Iowa, sixty miles south of Sioux Falls, to celebrate the Grand Harvest Jubilee Festival and take a gander at Sioux City's third Palace of Corn.

The new corn boom of the industrialites had already foretold the destiny of the continent and persuaded poet-prophets like Walt Whitman, traveling through prairies and plains a decade earlier, that one day they would feed the world. It was booster time, when new settlements vied to become towns, county seats and railroad centers, when booster talk turned hotels into People's Palaces and booster enterprise turned crops into Corn Palaces. It was the time when the nineteenth century changed gears, and Sioux City typified the speed of change. In less than a decade a farm town of seven thousand became a meat-packing metropolis of thirty thousand. The formula was corn plus railroads. What is striking in the sudden rise of these Midwestern cities is not the quick change from rural to urban but the fact that the urban preceded and shaped the rural before a field was planted or an ear of corn canned. In marveling at the way an entire continent packaged itself, Daniel Boorstin has written that the development of the American West is "one of the largest monuments to *a priorism* in all human history . . . a relic of the young nation's need to make a commodity of its land, and hastily to map and sell it, even before it was explored or surveyed." In the same booster spirit, the nation made a commodity of its crops; they were packaged and sold before planted. This despite the realities of a landscape biblically plagued by grasshoppers and locusts, droughts, tornadoes, prairie fires, white blizzards of snow and black blizzards of dust.

"We are strangers in the land where we were born."

—INSHTAMAGA
OF THE OMAHA

When the fathers of Sioux City got together in 1887 to give thanks for the rain that had spared them from the drought afflicting their neighbors, they didn't do a ceremonial dance as the Sioux would have done. These champions of liberty, who had fled Old World monarchies in the name of independence and democracy, built a palace, a palace that would sell their town as a center of commerce and culture inferior to none. "Palacing" their town was a way of packaging it. "St. Paul and Montreal can have their ice palaces, which melt at the first approach of spring," noted *The Sioux City Daily Journal* of August 21, 1887, "but Sioux City is going to build a palace of the product of the soil that is making it the great pork-packing center of the northwest."

The Sioux City Corn Palace of 1891, the fifth and last before Mitchell, South Dakota, took on the palace glory. Photo courtesy State Historical Society of Iowa—Special Collections

They would build a palace entirely of corn to celebrate a "Sioux City Thanksgiving and Harvest Festival and Corn Jubilee." The image of a corn palace inspired the citizens of Iowa when America was consciously searching for a symbol of national identity, and what better symbol for the union of science, commerce, agriculture and art than corn? Corn was no longer Indian wheat or Indian anything. Corn was 100 percent Made in the USA and therefore a prime symbol for a new nation, indivisible, that defined itself not by the generative life that bound its tribes but by the commodified life of its products. Since corn was the ground of the entire industrial empire that sprang from the prairies and plains, corn was appropriated symbolically to convey the white man's aspirations and achievements. Corn was the glue that bound one small community to another as tracks were laid across the plains.

These newest of New World settlers were too new to despise corn as inferior to wheat, for here the mere planting of corn was a symbol of white man's progress. The settlers were unaware that a thousand years before the white man set foot on the Plains, the Plains Indians were planters as well as hunters and that horses were not used in numbers until the middle of the eighteenth century. They knew nothing of the Woodland tribes, who had extended the Hopewell culture up the Missouri, of Sioux subcultures like the Mandan and Hidatsa who were tending their gardens of corn in North Dakota at the moment General Custer was hunting for Crazy Horse and gold. Did the white man conquer the Indian or did the Indian absorb the white man? Perhaps the battle of Wounded Knee did not so much mark the end of an empire as transform it into a new ceremonial mask in which Corn Mother became Corn King.

According to *The Sioux City Journal,* 1887 was the year Sioux City went "corn crazy." The architect W. E. Loft was commissioned to turn the northwest corner of Fifth and Jackson streets into "the Eighth Wonder of the World." He designed a hundred-foot cupola, thatched with green stalks, from which flying buttresses sprang to the four corner towers, representing the four-square states of Iowa, Dakota, Nebraska and Minnesota. The Sioux City and Pacific Railroad brought in 15,000 bushels of yellow corn, 5,000 bushels of variegated corn, 500 pounds of carpet tacks and 3,360 pounds of nails to cover the frame. Iowans were energized by the discovery of a new art material, available to all: "Everyone was experimenting with grain as a medium of artistic expression." Every man could be a Michelangelo in corn.

The corn palace as state booster, trumpeting Corn Belt science and art, was a mainstay at national expositions well into the 20th century. At San Francisco's Panama-Pacific Exposition of 1915, the North Dakota building enlightened the world with corn. Courtesy State Historical Society of North Dakota

The entire skin of the palace inside and out, every pinnacle, cupola and turret, was made of colored corn and other prairie grains, like sorghum and oats. The interior was a gallery of corn mosaics, executed by the Ladies' Decorative Association, creating allegorical scenes and panoramas not with gaud, tinsel or precious metals but with "an ear of corn, a handful of grasses, a bunch of weeds, a wisp of straw—the materials of nature's own painting." Rendered in corn, Hiawatha's Mondawmin joined hands with Demeter in a frieze around the dome. The Iowa State Seal was depicted in corn and cattails. Millet's *Angelus* and a map of the United States were alike figured in cereals. Even Ceres herself, the Great Mother of the ancient civilization of wheat, was robed in satiny husks on a stairway of yellow kernels and given a cornstalk scepter in homage to the King.

President and Mrs. Grover Cleveland, Cornelius Vanderbilt, Chauncey Depew and a party of "135 eastern capitalists from Boston and New York" led a hundred thousand visitors to celebrate the new empire. Through the corn-decorated arches of the streets marched a parade of industrial machines *and* a whooping procession of two hundred Omaha, Sioux and Winnebagoes in war paint, feathers and little else. The "fastidious are requested not to blush," warned the *Journal,* as the redmen performed their traditional corn dances in native undress. In the evening, fortified by "corn juice on tap even though Iowa is a prohibition state," the entire community dressed in corn costumes of husks, leaves and cobs to dance through city streets lit by seven thousand colored gas jets, past storefronts blazoned with harvest scenes, and into the armory for Iowa's first Corn Ball.

So successful was the first Jubilee Palace that Sioux City built four more in four years; the fifth, a cross between Moscow's St. Basil Cathedral and Washington's National Capitol, expired in a puff of glory, but floods and economic panic aborted a sixth. As an embodiment of progress, each successive palace had to top the last, with ever more voluptuous renderings of the royal treasury of corn: "Above the arch was a spacious balcony bounded at each end by stately turrets which were flanked by minarets overlaid with wild sage and white corn, giving the appearance of a chased silver column divided into diamond sections by bars of ivory." Visitors were tripled and quadrupled by publicity stunts like the Corn Palace Train, which toured the Eastern seaboard to receive the blessings of newly inaugurated President Benjamin Harrison and accolades from *The New York Times*—"Everything used in the decorations except the iron nails is the product of Iowa cornfields and the whole train is a marvel of beauty."

Corn palaces were the Midwest's answer to Eastern hauteur in the cultural line of literature, music and art. The Ladies of the Lilac History Club in Sioux City won first prize in the 1890 palace with a miniature corn library: "The walls of the library booth were adorned with [corn] pictures—a portrait of Dante, a winter scene, and a country maid with an apron of flowers. . . . Upon a table were quill pens of cane and oat straw, a corn lamp, a gourd inkwell, and several corn husk blotters." Nor were the dramatic arts neglected. The palace

The World's Only Corn Palace as it looks today, with its annual panels of corn and permanent domes of fiberglass.

of 1891 featured the balcony scene from *Romeo and Juliet* in white corn, the lovers in cornhusks and corn silk, shown at Romeo's moment of parting down a white corn ladder. In a medley of arts worthy of grand opera and lit by ten thousand of the city's first electric lights, King Corn was crowned in front of the palace, surrounded by Knights of Pythias mounted on steeds, while the Pullman Band of Chicago vied with the Ladies' Cornet Band of Clinton and a Mexican band played "Hail, Columbia." Proudly the city announced that the cost of decoration was $8,700 and of advertising $4,000. By happy coincidence the man crowned King Corn was James E. Booge, president of the Corn Palace Association.

In 1892 in South Dakota, Mitchell with upstart

The natural union of corn and railroads was celebrated by Atchison, Kansas, at their corn carnival of 1897 when they crowned corn king. Courtesy Kansas State Historical Society, Topeka

cockiness took up where Sioux City left off. Mitchell had begun as a railroad town, founded by Alexander Mitchell, president of the Chicago, Milwaukee and St. Paul line. But after a decade it had no more than a few dirt streets and wooden sidewalks in a land so hostile that the U.S. government provoked gamblers to settle it: "The government bets you 160 acres of land against $18.00 [or three cents an acre] that you will starve to death before you live on it five years." The government's wager seemed a sure thing after January 12, 1888, when a gale of forty miles an hour blew in a blizzard that reached 45 below zero and stayed there, leaving cattle frozen in the fields and snow banks sixteen feet high, which people froze their ice cream with on the following Fourth of July.

Mitchell decided to erect a Corn Palace in this unpromising landscape because it wanted to outdo its rival, Pierre, to become the state capital. "Sioux City has abandoned her Corn Palace," said L. O. Gale, town druggist and jeweler. "Why not build one here?" Fifty-nine days later, after every man, woman and child pitched in with labor and cash ($3,700 total), the Palace opened at Fourth and Main on September 28, 1892, at 4:30 P.M. with a May Pole Dance, as announced. "Sixteen of Mitchell's loveliest ladies attired in bewitching costumes will take part, and in their graceful evolutions will circle about and surround the living personification of Ceres, goddess of grain." The grain of fabled Greece and Rome had turned to corn.

True to form, the following year's palace was far grander, corn "nubbings" and husks now imitating stained-glass windows, Grecian scrolls, a New England kitchen, a bridal chamber and the Black Hills Crystal Cave. The Phinney (Iowa) State Band and the Santee Indian Band warred for listeners already distracted by a flower dance, a German parade, a reunion of Civil War veterans and a large Indian wedding. The *Mitchell Gazette* touted the benefits of the Palace as (1) aesthetic—a happy escape from work, (2) pragmatic and educational—new ideas for farmers and (3) promotional—effective advertising to show corn farmers from other states that South Dakota was a good place to grow corn. They were wrong about number three. After 1893, a severe drought canceled both palaces and crops for six years.

Undaunted, Mitchell organized a Corn Palace Commission in 1902 and has held a festival and exposition the last week of September every year since, even after they lost the contest for state capital to Pierre. What they won was a more unique distinction, which attracted celebrities as grand as John Philip Sousa in 1904, hired at the cost of $7,000 a day for a six-day engagement. When Sousa saw the mud streets of the town, he refused to get off the train unless he was paid—in cash, in sacks brought to his carriage. "Whatever you gentlemen lack in judgment," he is supposed to have said, "you certainly make up in nerve."

Mitchell nerve made for survival and Mitchell's palace survived where Sioux City's did not. In 1921 Mitchell made the building permanent and changed annually the theme of the exterior panels, which became a kind of corn mirror of the times. Egyptian motifs one year gave way to patriotic themes during the Great War, to scenes celebrating "Allied Victory" in World War II, to vignettes of "Relaxin' in South Dakota" in the 1950s and of "75 Years of Mitchell Progress" in the 1980s. For nearly a century, Mitchell's palace headliners mirrored the evolution of American entertainment. The minstrel shows and military bands of the first decade were replaced by revues and variety shows like Ernie Young's Golden Girls in the 1920s, by the big swing bands of Jimmy Dorsey and Paul Whiteman in the 1930s and by comedians like Red Skelton and Bob Hope in the 1970s.

From Jim Sellars, building manager, I learned that an arsonist had burned one of the palace's domes ten years ago, so its minarets are now fiberglass and its foundations brick and concrete. The outside panels, however, are renewed yearly to the tune of a thousand pounds of nails, a hundred thousand cobs of corn, two thousand bushels of sorghum, murdock, buffalo grass, broom grass, wild oats, milo, sudan grass, slough grass and "just plain weeds." Designs are projected onto tar paper, then nailed on wood panels numbered by color for the segments of corn. Mitchell farmers mix their palettes in the cornfield, breeding corn by color as the Indians did, to achieve pink, orange, calico, brown, green, smoky gray and black. Corn must be picked at precisely the right point of moisture and cobs must be cut to precisely the right thickness, so that the corn segments won't curl as they dry. "If they're cut right, the kernels won't blow out even in a high wind," Sellars explained, "and in Mitchell the wind blows quite hard." Outside, wind erosion is abetted by pigeons and squirrels; inside, erosion is abetted by kids who find ready ammunition in kernels during the heat of a basketball game.

Tossing kernels is also a tradition stemming from the days of corn carnivals at the turn of the century, as the empire of King Corn spread through Midwestern towns. Railroad towns that couldn't afford a palace created corn carnivals, such as the one Atchison, Kansas, staged in 1897 under the banner, "King Corn is supreme." Atchison's carnival was the brainchild of the editor of *The Atchison Globe,* and was heartily supported by the Burlington and later the Atchison, Topeka and Santa Fe railroad lines. "When one is separated by five hundred miles from a lake-shore, by as many from the mountains, and by a thousand miles from the ocean," wrote a *Topeka Journal* newsman, "it becomes a merit to conceive new forms of enjoyment dependent on none of these."

New forms were dependent, however, upon the wheels of spring-wagons,

The high point of the Atchison corn carnival of 1897 was the elephantine erection of the Burlington Route. Courtesy Kansas State Historical Society, Topeka

buggies, surreys and excursion trains. The corn carnival moved the old agricultural county fair into town. City merchants promoted the new street fairs and conjured the mixed carnival bag that provided city pleasures by means of country products. One of the chief pleasures was masquerading as corn people in suits, dresses and hats of shredded husks and tassels, a garb less surprising to Indians than to Easterners. "The Corn Milliner of Kansas," Mrs. H. J. Cusack, gained notoriety when she sent a dainty corn bonnet to the White House for President McKinley's wife. The carnival combined the mimes and mummeries of New Orleans's Mardi Gras with the genteel floats that would soon grace Pasadena's Rose Parade. A prairie schooner, covered with white poppies, disclosed a pair of corn kiddies; half-nude "Filipino savages" in cornhusk skirts were mimed by "the colored population"; fifty bright-eyed children sailed in a corn-covered ship; fifty more peeped from windows in a monster ear constructed from thirty-six bushels of corn. Not to mention marching bands, a giant cigar-store Indian of corn, an Old Glory of red, white and blue husks, minstrels dancing on street stages, boys holding red ears of corn like mistletoe above the heads of kissable girls and merrymakers buying bags of shelled corn to hurl like confetti until "the streets became veritable mills for the grinding of the corn." Welcoming all to the main carnival street was the Burlington Railroad's elephantine erection of an ear of corn four stories high, a fit symbol for the rising of King Corn in an age innocent of Freud.

King Corn had already informed the world of the grandeur of his territorial ambitions in 1893, at the World's Columbian Exposition in Chicago, America's first world fair. Here states competed side by side in erecting fantasies, deliriums, phantasmagories of corn. Photographs show corn draperies, columns, obelisks, pyramids, corbels, caryatids, Roman arches, Gothic arches, buttresses, arabesques. Every possible architectural motif that could be purloined from Victoria's Crystal Palace at the 1851 Great Exhibition in London was emulated by the new prairie metropolis that sought to conquer the world with corn. If the Crystal Palace was "a revelation of what could be done with steel and glass," America's state palaces were a revelation of what could be donewith corn.

A partial view of Missouri's corn towers, pyramids, curtains and cupolas at the Louisiana Purchase Exposition of 1904. Courtesy Missouri Historical Society

At the Fair, Iowa's palace was built "Pompeiian style," with a grapevine frieze of purple popcorn. The soil that produced such wonders was so sacred they exhibited it in long glass columns. Iowa's palace was rivaled only by Illinois's Corn Kitchen, ruled by the formidable Sarah T. Rorer of the Philadelphia Cooking School, there to tell the world of the superiority of corn over other grains as a cheap and nourishing staple and as an elegant dessert. When St. Louis staged its world fair in 1904 in the Louisiana Purchase Exposition, it was now Missouri that garnered kudos with its palace of corn. In addition to two corn towers, each thirty-eight feet high, flanking the Louisiana Purchase Monument and Emblem rendered in husks, the central Russo-Byzantine cupola stood sixty-five feet high and forty feet in diameter, giving rest to the weary in lounge chairs.

If the medium was the message, the message outlined was "The Agricultural Conquest of the Earth." Illinois, Iowa and Missouri were doing for corn what Pittsburgh was doing for steel, noted a magazine called *The World's Work*. The fair as a whole provided a history of corn in America, beginning with the single-rowed small ears grown "by blind choice" before Columbus came. "But the new corn, the ideal corn," the magazine said, was developed by "initiative and brains" and the kind of farmer-boy contests that created "a new kind of Olympic game!" From such exhibits the rest of the world would not only learn how to grow corn scientifically, but would also discover all the products that grow from corn. The familiar litany of hidden corn products was recited in 1904, two decades before Henry Wallace extended King Corn's empire around the world:

All the products of the corn plant are there—oils, paper, pith (that is used in battleships to stop shot-holes below the waterline), whisky. There are three kinds of sugar and two each of syrup and molasses. There are many food elements—different kinds of cellulose, vicose, proxylene, and anyloid. There are many products useful in the arts: celluloid, collodion, sizing, varnishes, films, filaments for incandescent lights, artificial silk, guncotton, smokeless powder, and fine charcoal. There are many varieties of starch and of glucose, several kinds of gum, grape-sugar, corn-rubber (used in buffers on railway cars), corn-oilcake and meal, malt, beer, wines, alcohol, and fusel-oil. One may see also shuck-mats and shuck-mattresses. How many products of corn there are nobody knows, for new products are evolved every year.

Corn's conquest of the world happened within my lifetime. An unexpected form of bio-botanical destiny linked the personal roots of my family tree to thehistory of my country and its place in the world. For me, the glory of Mitchell's Corn Palace was that it put together what had so long been kept apart, and I saw conjunctions in the most commonplace artifacts and events. In the auditorium, a triple-header girls' basketball tourney was framed by scenes of Indian life. In the lobby, a mounted buffalo head marked the main exit and an elk head guarded the popcorn machine. On the wall, a 1930s snapshot of Jean Darling, of Our Gang, showed her in Indian regalia, being initiated into a Sioux tribe. The chief designer and architect of the palace's exterior for twenty-five years was a Sioux from Crow Creek Indian Reservation, Oscar Howe, a Second World War veteran who became professor of fine arts at the University of South Dakota and "South Dakota's Artist Laureate." When I learned that "Mitchell of the Palace grand" stands on the site of an eleventh-century Sioux village, I realized that there might be a way to speak two tongues at once. There might be a way to connect in heart as well as mind the vision of a Chicago prairie poet, "The wind blows, the corn leans" with a proverb of the Sioux, "A people without history is like wind on the buffalo grass."

Iowa, at the State Fair in Des Moines in 1908, exhibits itself in unconscious parody as a Corn Belt Coatlicue, both the mother and maw of corn. Lake County Museum, Curt Teich Postcard Collection, Wauconda, Illinois

Closing
the
Circle

The Night of Shalako

THERE IS NO WIND and no grass where I stand now, alone in the cold on this darkest night of the year, at winter solstice, New Year's Eve for the Zuni and the night of Shalako. My boots make a sucking sound as I lift first one and then the other to keep from sinking deeper in the mud. My poncho stinks of wet wool while I stand and drip in the unrelenting rain. Other strangers have been waiting in the rain for a good eight hours outside one or another of the seven host houses on the Zuni mesa, but I am as much a stranger to them as to the people we stare at through large glass windows set in the house walls, shut out from the lit interior where men and women sit in chairs, laughing, smoking, dozing, greeting friends who come and go, catching up a loose child, waiting—like us—for the dancing to begin.

The dancing place is a long rectangle dug out of the earth floor, like the womb of the Underworld from which the Zuni emerged. The room is hung with fabrics, with dancers' white kilts embroidered in red and black, Spanish shawls dripping fringe, hand-loomed Navaho rugs and factory-made nylon rugs next to animal skins and deer heads. These are backdrops for the family jewels displayed like a trader's dream of Indian goods—huge silver belts looped over clotheslines, thick strands of coral and shell tossed casually over a shawl. Even the deer heads are looped with turquoise neckpieces, their antlers chained with silver. At the west end of the dancing place are the totems and signs of the wooden altar, painted white, red, blue, yellow, many-hued and black, which center the cardinal points, the up and down and the here and now of this place, this house. In front of the altar the prayer plumes and baskets of seed and corn have already been blessed by a sprinkling of sacred meal. And in the corner the giant mask of the god Shalako stands guard, stands empty, while his young impersonator, stripped to the waist, drinks coffee and smokes a cigarette before the ritual begins.

Once begun, the chanting, drumming and dancing will not stop until all that is has been *named*—all the rivers, mesas, rocks, skies and seas, all the animals, plants, peoples and seeds, all the stars, planets and constellations, every kind of bean, every kind of corn, every kind of god. The drumming will not stop until the chanters have sung and the dancers danced the entire story of how the Zuni were created and emerged, how they wandered in search of the Middle Place and how they finally found their home in the middle of the Middle Place, here on this mesa on the border of Arizona and the Navaho Reservation, south of Gallup and Four Corners, west of the Continental Divide and north of Bat Cave, where a young Harvard graduate student struck popcorn.

Once begun, the chanting and dancing will go on until dawn, but now it's two hours past midnight and still we wait, outside, inside. I have come by bus from Santa Fe, climbing though piñon and juniper forests and red rock canyons to a flat scrubland of sage and the four-winged saltbush, and now not even scrub—just a brown sea of mud from which a few low, flat, ugly houses emerge around the cardinal points of Western Auto, White's Laundry, Pat's Chili Parlor and Chu-Chu's Pizzeria. In the parking lot outside Thriftway, teenagers hang out in pickup trucks blaring the Kinks; inside the Zuni Tribal Building, tourists hang out over counters of silver, hoping to hammer down prices.

I came before sunset, to see through the drizzle the procession of gods and priests come down from Greasy Hill and cross the Zuni River, no more than a creek, by the footpath near White's Laundry. Tonight the gods are masked as Shalakos, the monster kachinas, led by one that is ten feet tall, twice the height of the dancer who walks inside him. The chief Shalako wears horns for ears, popped orbs for eyes in a turquoise face that explodes in feathers—a ruff of black crow feathers at the neck, an arc of eagle feathers on top and, behind, a sunburst of parrot feathers loosening a cascade of black hair that falls to the hem of his stiff white skirt. His bright blue beak with three white teeth goes snicker-snack—four times, like a vaudeville clapper—before the four shrill hoots of his cry send chills down the spine. As a stranger, I don't know whether to laugh or run.

Shalako is but one of the strange gods that have been summoned by the tribe. There is Longhorn, the Rain Priest of the kiva of the north, who appears in a black and white mask with eye-slits like a Sherman tank and a yard-long horn instead of an ear. There is Hututu, his deputy from the kiva of the south, who ululates the high-pitched sound for which he is named. There are the twins

"What is usually termed the 'Discovery of America' must be seen to entail the problem of who is entering whose history."
—GORDON BROTHERSTON, *Image of the New World* (1979)

The Shalakos in 1897 descended as they do today from Greasy Hill to cross the Zuni River at nightfall. Photo Ben Wittick, courtesy Museum of New Mexico, Neg. No. 16443

Yamuhakto of the east and west, who dangle feathered cottonwood sticks from their bright blue heads. And running in every direction are those "without place," the ten Mudheads, their mouths, eyes and ears like fat doughnuts in knobbed and lumpy adobe-colored heads, the progeny of incest. These are the clowns, like the *koshari* of the Corn Dances, who scare little boys and tweak dozing matrons awake. All are spirits of rain, summoned at this turn of the year, to renew the life of the crops and the life of the tribe.

Their chosen hosts have spent an entire year building new houses in which to receive them, and some of the rooms are only half-finished, but the dancing and eating rooms are done, for this is a feast. Strangers as well as visiting gods are welcomed at trestle tables of posole and cheese Danish and pots of hot coffee. The coffee tastes good after hours of wandering in the pitch black, looking for houses that are sometimes two or three miles apart. Skirting ditches but blinded by headlights along Highway 53, which runs straight through the village, I've fallen flat in the mud to emerge like a mud-volleyball player at Hog Days in Kewanee, or a Mudman in Zuniland. I've been lost many times this dark night because there are no maps for this territory and this is not my place.

"A curious thing about the Spirit of Place," D. H. Lawrence wrote, "is the fact that no place exerts its full influence upon a new-comer until the old inhabitant is dead or absorbed." On this night, this is a place where the old inhabitants are so long dead and so fully absorbed that it is a place chiefly of Spirit, not only of the masked gods, but of the animals sacred to each surrounding place—Mountain Lion in the Home of Barren Regions; Bear, old Clumsy Foot, in the Home of Waters; Badger, Black-Masked Face, in the Home of Beautiful Red Sunrise; Wolf, Hang Tail, in the Home of Day; Eagle in the Home on High; Mole in the Home of Low. Here there is a place for everything, as my Grandmother Harper would have said, and everything in the created world, if properly named, is in its place.

But in this place I am an intruder shut out by language. When the impersonators put out their cigarettes to put on their masks, to jangle the bells at their ankles, to clack their beaks to bird hoots and drumbeats, to begin the dance at last, I am outside, separated by a thick layer of glass. I am outside the blessing of cornmeal that the villagers have sprinkled on houses, walls, altars, hosts and dancing gods, and although I can follow the cornmeal path of the Shalakos to and from "the place whence they came" on Greasy Hill, I am but a spectator dripping mud.

Only once do I make connection, this in the darkness of the village itself, lit fitfully by the blue glare of television screens through open windows and doors. As I turn a corner by the little graveyard of the church, a window in front of me frames a face and a blanket-wrapped body in frozen profile. As I step close to make out what it is, the face turns slowly in my direction, a face so ancient I can see the skull beneath the skin, two holes for eyes, another one for mouth. My heart thumps and I turn and run. It is not the skull that unnerves me, it is the face. The face is my Grandmother Harper's the night she died.

THE BLESSINGWAY

"Yet one day the demons of America must be placated, the ghosts must be appeased, the Spirit of Place atoned for."
—D. H. LAWRENCE, "The Spirit of Place" (1923)

"I AM THE WAY, the Truth, and the Life." My Grandmother Harper pointed to each word when she first taught me to read from the little Bible cards she kept in her family Bible. The image on the card was of a pale bearded man in a white nightshirt knocking at a door, his head backlit like a picture of Lillian Gish. When I grew up I departed from the Way of my ancestors, blazing my own path through urban wildernesses as remote as possible from the rebel stock of which I was a rebel child. I was a traveler of other times and places and had circled most of the world before that first reunion of cousins in Lincoln, Nebraska, planted my feet for the first time on the prairie sod of my grandparents. Like other Americans dispersed to the four corners of the continent, I had trouble putting the coasts together with the prairies. It was easy to miss the center when there was so much ground to cover.

So many paths, so many dispersals, so many stranger tongues. Even in my own language, the King James Bible talk of my Grandmother Harper clashed with the *Origin of Species* talk of her son. It was hard to fit her Garden into his Galapagos; each place jostled for room on the family map, crowding the Brazilian jungles where Uncle Roy and Aunt Evelyn warbled "Bringing in the Sheaves." My parents were the last generation to inherit the American earth, at the turn of the century when America was still locked in land and clocked by the seasons. They were a generation glad to chuck annual blizzards in Kansas for an occasional earthquake in California, just as they were glad to chuck fresh corn for canned, horses for cars, trains for planes, full speed ahead.

From that first Culver in New England to the Harpers in Kansas and the Kennedys in Nebraska, they never looked back and they never looked down, down to the earth their ancestors had taken by God-given right. God's Will was theirs and their Way straight as Kansas corn rows and Union Pacific railroad tracks east to west. Their Way was lit by Old World myths which mutated into New World science, and the word of science was square. What wouldn't fit their straight and narrow was excised— the blood in the Garden, the transplanted mother who sickened and died in an orange grove.

But who had entered whose history? My people were deaf to ancient drumbeats and blind to the spirals, mazes and circles of people for whom the Word was round. Where my people shot into space, these people went underground, every year, year after year, for millennia. It was difficult to square space shuttles and earth navels, just as it was difficult to square the vision of those for whom only the future was real with the vision of those for whom the past was eternally present. This is the past Ivan Illich called "the lost time of the blue tortilla," made from the blue corn which shaped religious rites, hearthstones and lives long before Columbus or Cortez. The time of the blue tortilla my people had obliterated almost overnight with Reid Dent and the McCormick Reaper. The seeds of life preserved here for hundreds of generations my people had killed in the name of permanent shelf life. Different languages, different worlds. "Only by re-entering the

This drypainting, The Blessingway of the Black Cornfield, *was made by Maude Oakes, with singer Wilito Wilson, at Mariano Lake, New Mexico, in 1947. Pollen footprints lead up the cornstalk to Cornbeetle Girl and Pollen Boy, flanking a corn tassel beneath the double-arched rainbow. The painting is used "for anyone who has been harmed in a cornfield." Repainted by M. S. Hurford.* Courtesy Wheelwright Museum of the American Indian, PI21

present moment with knowledge of the lost time of the blue tortilla," Illich said, "will it be possible to establish a new way of seeing and a new set of terms."

Looking for just that, a new way of seeing, a new set of terms, a way to connect my people and this land, I stumbled onto the hidden corn road and the lost time of the blue tortilla. In a bowl of buttered popcorn, I found both Grandfather Harper and my son, microwaves and movie theaters connected to Peruvian corn poppers and Machu Picchu. Crunching into the sweet milk of fresh corn-on-the-cob, I found both Grandmother Kennedy and my daughter connected to the Green Corn Busks of the Moundbuilders in Ohio and Illinois. In a plate of mush I found Grandmother Harper connected to both Buffalo Bird Woman in her garden and Frank Cushing in his mesa. In a dried corncake I found the Empress of China and an African in Soweto. In Miss Sweet Corn in Hoopeston I found Xilonen of the Aztec, and in a bottle of Arkansas moonshine the *chicha*-drinking Inca. In the Corn Palace of South Dakota I found Palenque and Copán. In a box of Kellogg's corn flakes I found Grandma Helen Sekaquaptewa in Hopiland. Whether we knew it or not, America was corn land, and both native and immigrant Americans were corn people.

Wide Cornfield, *drawn by Maude Oakes, with singers Hosteen Yazzi and Tom Ration, at Smith Lake, New Mexico, in 1946/47, shows the pollen footsteps of Changing Woman and "the path of her mind" as she proceeds up the cornfield to stand between white male corn and yellow female corn under a rainbow arc. The ceremony is done in the cornfield to ensure good crops.* Courtesy Wheelwright Museum of the American Indian, P121

But what immigrant wheat people fractured, atomized and smashed, corn natives kept whole. For the Navaho that wholeness was inscribed in song and ritual as the Blessingway. The task of a Blessingway singer was to remember by heart each part of the ceremony that blesses the center of the hogan, the homeplace, the center of harmony to which we give the names holy and blessed. The Blessingway enacts in song and ceremony what Navaho sand paintings depict in images. Both are forms of speaking pictures which First Man gave to Changing Woman when he gave her the magic corn bundle containing four jewels of four colors—white shell, turquoise, abalone and jet—each carved into a perfect ear of corn, each wrapped in a translucent sheet of its own gem, each containing the power to create the inner forms of outward shapes, the forms of the natural world.

When Changing Woman buried the medicine bundle in the heart of the earth, she created Thought in the shape of Long Life Boy and Speech in the shape of Happiness Girl. Together they made

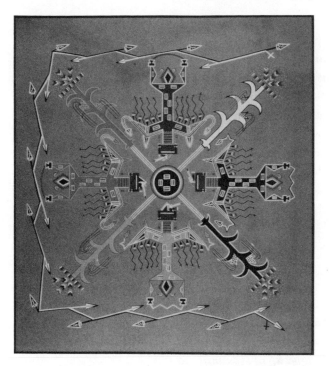

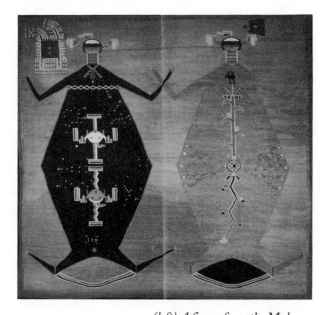

(left) A figure from the Male Shooting Chant depicts "The Home of the Thunder Gods," painted here by Hosteen Bezody. Because the number four to the Navaho represents order, wholeness and harmony, four thunder gods are paired with four corn stalks, radiating toward the four cardinal points. The encircling guardian line (here zigzag arrows of lightning) opens always to the east. Photo by Gene Balzer, courtesy Museum of Northern Arizona
(right) The paired figures are "Blue Mother Earth and Black Father Sky," painted on the fourth day of Male Shooting-way. Father Sky contains the sun, moon and Milky Way, Mother Earth the four sacred plants and a bird atop the corn-stalk. The guardian figures at their heads are "Corn Bugs." A sandpainting rug woven by Atlnabah. Courtesy Museum of Northern Arizona

That Which Continues, the progeny of White Corn Boy and Yellow Corn Girl, Pollen Boy and Cornbeetle Girl. Changing Woman created the Mating Songs of these first corn couples by painting their forms, running her hand over the corn ears of shell, turquoise, abalone and jet, drawing their root legs and tasseled faces. She then told the Corn People that through them the earth would be permanent, the sky, flowers, dew, pollen, young men, young women, death, birth and rain, and "by that we will go about in blessing." When she gave them speech, she gave them pollen words. "You will speak for us with pollen words. You will talk for us with pollen words." The word of Blessingway is pollen.

Pollen is the way, the truth and the light of the Navaho ceremony in which the singer draws two pictures in the cornfield and two in the hogan and links them by pollen trails. In these paintings, the path of life is a cornstalk, hung with twelve ears of corn as a ladder for footprints to climb to a cloud terrace where a bluebird sings. The person who seeks blessing places his feet in the pollen path to circle each painting clockwise, before he steps inside the circle and enters the painting, for the painting is "the place where the gods come and go." Here the One Sung Over is absorbed into the image and here the pollen placed in his mouth becomes the fine carved jewel in the mouth of the god, immutable as the inner forms of the holy. These are the images that, in the beginning in the worlds below this one, the gods painted on sheets of sky and gave to the Navaho to copy on the floors of their hogans. When the singing is done, the singer erases the painting, but the image stays, like the songs and stories in the memory of the singer. "It is like the plants, like corn and beans," says a Blessingway singer of this century. "When they mature you pick the seed and you plant it again."

In the New World, pollen words were sung by the warrior-hero who, planted as a stalk of corn in the fecund earth, was transformed into a poet. For the Toltec singer, it was the hunter Nacxitl who gave language and art to the snake-columned city of Tula before he climbed the sky to fall as quetzal plumes and clear water. This earlier skywalker, like Quetzalcoatl, was born again as the blossoming flower of the earth's flesh and as the emblem of perfection, an ear of corn:

> As white and yellow maize I am born,
> The many-coloured flower of living flesh rises up
> and opens its glistening seeds before the face of our mother . . .
> My song is heard and flourishes.
> My implanted word is sprouting,
> our flowers stand up in the rain.

"Corn is the Navaho staff of life, and pollen is its essence."
—DONALD SANDNER, *Navaho Symbols of Healing* (1979)

Star-trek returned to earth-surge bends the arrow and completes the circle. In that round, the oppositions between Sky Father and Earth Mother, between movement through time and growth within, between the way up and the way down, are equidistant from the center, fixed and immutable. "In the song, corn grows upward, rain comes downward," says the Blessingway singer. "If there's no down, there's no up."

The migration of my ancestors was across continents, up and away from the earth navel of fallen man. My own journey had been down, down into the muddy cornfield and below, into the darkness of seeds and roots to find my dead mother and her mothers, my father and his fathers, in the womb not of Eden but of Mother Earth, the living flesh of the land where I was born. Here corn was not silent or invisible, but sprouted in many-colored songs and images of my own language, if I would but open my ears to hear and my eyes to see. Singers of my own time and tradition had found pollen words, had sung of pollen paths, in their own searchings for connection. In the dreaming eyes of "A Girl in the Library," the poet Randall Jarrell saw "The Corn King beckoning to his Spring Queen." All this time the poets and myth makers of America were implanting words and images to make them blossom in new soil. In a mythical cornfield in Gatlin, Nebraska, the storyteller Stephen King planted seeds of bloody horror in the *Children of the Corn,* invoking primal gods who slaughtered the innocent on crosses made of corn. In a real cornfield in Iowa, W. P. Kinsella saw his novel *Shoeless Joe* transformed into a cinematic *Field of Dreams,* where the mythic spirit of the cornfield summoned lost baseball gods and fathers. "Is this heaven?" asked the father. "No—it's Iowa," said the son.

In the language of art was a new way of seeing, a new set of terms, though long drowned in our country by the language of science and industry, by the clamorous shouts for a future devoid of the past. While we plotted the cosmos and crunched it into numbers for our mental machines, while we lost touch with the earth, lost living connection to the fecundity of the land, still our singers could make us feel corn songs we'd never heard. Even if we'd never once stood in a cornfield, Jim Harrison in *Farmer* could give us a glimpse of the ancient sexiness of corn: "They walked a few rows into the tall corn with a slight breeze rasping the stalks and leaves together. They giggled and drank their beer and began kissing kneeling there. She raised her dress some, not wanting to get it dirty. He had his hands on her thighs. She took his thing out saying she had never touched one before. Even in the cornfield the music was loud and people were shouting with the light of the bonfire against the stalk tips."

Corn was the center that contained and ordered the oppositions of male and female, youth and age, sex and death, even in our own polyglot anarchy of races and kinds. The land bound us all together, the land to which we came as strangers and the earth from which we were increasingly estranged. Corn was the connection between the tyranny of slavers and the innocence of the enslaved, between the violence of rape and the tenderness of love. Just as the Blessingway singer had to hold the implanted word in his memory that the pollen path might be walked again and again, so Sethe, the runaway slave in Toni Morrison's *Beloved,* had to hold in her memory the silk and juice of new corn to feel again her husband's heart:

Looking at Paul D's back, she remembered that some of the corn stalks broke, folded down over Halle's back, and among the things her fingers clutched were husk and cornsilk hair.

How loose the silk. How jailed down the juice.

The jealous admiration of the watching men melted with the feast of new corn they allowed themselves that night. Plucked from the broken stalks that Mr. Garner could not doubt was the fault of the raccoon. Paul F wanted his roasted; Paul A wanted his boiled and now Paul D couldn't remember how finally they'd cooked those ears too young to eat. What he

"Always with one thought
We shall live.
This is all.
Thus with plain words
We have passed you on your roads.

This is our father's waters,
His seeds,
His riches,
His power,
His strong strong spirit,
All this good fortune whatsoever,
We shall give to you
To the end, my fathers
My children,
Verily, so long as we enjoy this light of day,
We shall greet one another as kindred.
Verily, we shall pray that our roads may be fulfilled.
To where your sun father's road comes out
May your roads reach.
May your roads be fulfilled."
　　　　　—Night Chant of Hekiapawa Shalako

did remember was parting the hair to get to the tip, the edge of his fingernail just under, so as not to graze a single kernel.

The pulling down of the tight sheath, the ripping sound always convinced her it hurt.

As soon as one strip of husk was down, the rest obeyed and the ear yielded up to him its shy rows, exposed at last. How loose the silk. How quick the jailed-up flavor ran free.

We too had our feasts of new corn, our rites of fertility shaped by husking the corn, loosening the silk, letting the juice run free. These were not just echoes of ceremonies indigenous to the first people of corn. We had formed rites in common, given them the accent of our multiple tongues, our Babel of voices. We made of the cornfields our own heaven and hell, transformed our own pollen words into immutable turquoise and jade, the inner forms "where the gods come and go." Corn was our mutual birthright, corn was our home. "Corn is the connection between my bottom and the chair," Wright Morris wrote of his own *Home Place* in Nebraska. "It's the cane seat Grandmother Osborn stretched between the long, long ago, and what she knew to be the never-never land. The figure in the carpet, if there is a carpet, is corn. Corn, I guess is the grass that grows wherever the land is—as Whitman put it—and sometimes it grows whether the water is there or not. No, it isn't the carpet. It's under the carpet. Corn is the floor."

What is the corn? The floor, earth, grass, leaves, the bluebird on top of the stalk, the evening and morning star, the man who tends it with his blood and the woman who grinds it with her sweat into meal, the lost time of the blue tortilla. "When the twelve Holy People came up to this world they made twelve paintings, each one his own, and they sang eleven songs, each one missing the hogan song except Changing Woman, who remembered it and sang it. While they sang during the night corn grew." So sang the singers of Blessingway, who remembered the pollen words. So sang the singer of Walden Pond, who believed in the forest, and in the meadow, and in the night in which the corn grows. So sang the singer of the Oglala Sioux, Black Elk, remembering his vision quest: "The life of man is a circle from childhood to childhood, and so it is in everything where power moves." Rain comes down, corn grows up, the way up is the way down, when the circle is complete. For a moment I completed my circle, where the way forward was the way back, where Coatlicue and the Couac monster were at my center as well as the Blessed Saints. "The old myths, the old gods, the old heroes have never died," said Stanley Kunitz, the singer of "Seedcorn and Windfall." "They are only sleeping at the bottom of our minds, waiting for our call." Waiting for the dancing to begin.

Photo by Gregory Thorp

SELECTED BIBLIOGRAPHY

In a library catalogue there is always too much and too little under the subject heading "Corn." In the New York Public Library alone there are more than a thousand entries, but 99 percent of them are technical works on agriculture, industry or economics. Corn as a generative force in works of mythology, anthropology, ethnology, geopolitics, poetry and fiction, folk ritual and art, food and drink is a hidden subject that must be hunted out. The works cited here are but a skeletal guide for the general reader who wants to explore some area of this vast territory without going corn mad. For a condensed map, take along Gordon Brotherston's *Image of the New World: The American Continent Portrayed in Native Texts* (London: Thames & Hudson, 1979). (Where relevant, I've cited a title in its original language with the probable date of composition or first publication, followed by its publication in English.)

GENERAL

Corn in the Development of the Civilization of the Americas. Eds. L. O. Bercaw *et al.* Washington, D.C.: Bureau of Agricultural Economics, 1940.

Corn of the Southwestern U.S. and Northwestern Mexico. Eds. G. Habhan *et al.* Tucson, Arizona: Native Seeds/SEARCH [n.d.].

Maíz: Bibliografía de las Publicaciónes Que Se Encuentran en la Biblioteca. Eds. A. Martinez and C. N. James. (Editorial material in Spanish and English.) 2 vols. and supplement. Turrialba, Costa Rica: Instituto Interamericano de Ciencias Agricolas, 1960–64.

Maize bibliography for the years 1917–1936; 1888–1916; 1937–1945. Ames, Iowa: Iowa State College, 1941, 1948, 1951.

Aliki. *Corn Is Maize: The Gift of the Indians*. New York: Harper & Row, 1976.

El maíz, fundamento de la cultura popular mexicana. Mexico City: Museo de culturas populares, 1982.

Giles, D. *Singing Valleys*. New York: Random House, 1940.

Hardeman, N. P. *Shucks, Shocks, and Hominy Blocks*. Baton Rouge and London: Louisiana State University Press, 1981.

Historical Atlas of the United States. Eds. W. E. Garrett *et al.* Washington, D.C.: National Geographic Society, 1988.

Longone, J. B. *Mother Maize and King Corn: The Persistence of Corn in the American Ethos.* Ann Arbor, Michigan: William L. Clements Library, 1986.

Nuestro Maíz. 2 vols. Mexico City: Museo national de culturas populares, 1982–83.

Visser, M. *Much Depends on Dinner.* New York: Grove Press, 1986.

MIDDLE AND SOUTH AMERICA

Acosta, J. de. (*Historia natural y moral de las Indias,* 1590.) *The Natural and Moral History of the Indies.* Trans. E. Grimston. New York: Burt Franklin [n.d.].

Bankes, G. *Peru Before Pizarro.* Oxford: Phaidon Press, 1977.

The Book of Counsel: The Popol Vuh of the Quiché Maya of Guatemala. Trans. M. Edmonson. New Orleans: Middle American Research Institute, Tulane University, Pub. 35, 1971.

Bray, W. *Everyday Life of the Aztecs.* London: Batsford, 1968.

Brundage, B. C. *Lords of Cuzco: A History and Description of the Inca People in Their Final Days.* Norman: University of Oklahoma Press, 1967.

Campbell, J. *Historical Atlas of World Mythology: Volume I: The Way of the Animal Powers.* London: Alfred van der Marck, 1983.

———. *Volume II: The Way of the Seeded Earth.*

Part 1: The Sacrifice. New York: Harper & Row, 1988.

Part 2: Mythologies of the Primitive Planters: The Northern Americas. New York: Harper & Row, 1989.

Part 3: The Middle and Southern Americas. New York: Harper & Row, 1989.

Cobo, B. (*Historia del nuevo mundo,* 1653.) *History of the Inca Empire.* Trans. R. Hamilton. Austin: University of Texas Press, 1979.

Coe, M. E. *Mexico.* London: Thames & Hudson, 1962.

———. *The Maya.* London: Thames & Hudson, 1966.

Davies, N. *The Aztecs.* London: Macmillan, 1973.

———. *The Toltecs.* Norman: University of Oklahoma Press, 1977.

Díaz del Castillo, B. (*Historia de la conquista de la Nueva España,* 1568.) *The Conquest of New Spain.* Trans. J. M. Cohen. Harmondsworth, England: Penguin, 1963.

Durán, D. (*Historia de las Indias de Nueva España e islas de la tierra firme,* 1574–81.) *The Aztecs: The History of the Indies of New Spain.* Trans. D. Heyden and F. Horcasitas. New York: Orion Press, 1964.

Frazer, Sir J. G. *The Golden Bough: A Study in Magic and Religion.* 3rd ed. London: Macmillan, 1966.

Galeano, E. *Memory of Fire: I. Genesis. II. Faces and Masks.* Trans. C. Belfrage. New York: Pantheon Books, 1985–87.

Garcilaso de la Vega. (*Los commentarios reales de los Incas,* 1609–17.) *Royal Commentaries of the Incas and General History of Peru.* Trans. H. V. Livermore. Austin: University of Texas Press, 1966.

Gauman Poma de Ayala, F. *Nueva corónica y buen gobierno* (1580–1620). Paris: Institut d'Ethnologie, 1936.

Handbook of South American Indians. Ed. J. H. Steward. 7 vols. Washington, D.C.: Government Printing Office, 1946–59.

Hemming, J. *The Conquest of the Incas.* New York: Harcourt Brace Jovanovich, 1970.

Joralemon, D. "A Study of Olmec Iconography." *Studies in Pre-Columbian Art and Archaeology No. 7.* Washington, D. C.: Dumbarton Oakes, 1971.

———— . "Ritual Blood-Sacrifice Among the Ancient Maya: Part I." *Primera Mesa Redonda de Palenque, Part II.* Ed. M. G. Robertson. Pebble Beach, California: Robert Louis Stevenson School, 1974.

Kubler, G. *The Art and Architecture of Ancient America: The Mexican, Maya and Andean Peoples.* 2nd ed. Harmondsworth, England: Penguin, 1975.

Landa, D. de. (*Relación de las cosas de Yucatán,* 1566.) *Yucatan Before and After the Conquest.* Trans. W. Gates. New York: Dover Publications, 1978.

Las Casas, B. de. (*Historia de las Indias,* 1552–61.) *Obras Escogidas de Fray Bartolomé de Las Casas* (1550). 5 vols. Madrid: Ediciones Atlas, 1957–58.

Laughlin, R. M. *The People of the Bat.* Washington, D.C.: Smithsonian Institution Press, 1988.

Lumbreras, L. G. *The Peoples and Cultures of Ancient Peru.* Trans. B. J. Meggers. Washington, D.C.: Smithsonian Institution Press, 1974.

MacNeish, R. S. "Ancient Mesoamerican Civilization." *Science* 143 (7 February 1964).

Maya Iconography. Eds. E. Benson and G. Griffin. Princeton, New Jersey: Princeton University Press, 1988.

Moctezuma, E. M. *The Great Temple of the Aztecs: Treasures of Tenochtitlán.* London: Thames & Hudson, 1988.

Neumann, E. *The Great Mother: An Analysis of the Archetype.* 2nd ed. Trans. R. Mannheim. Princeton, New Jersey: Princeton University Press, 1963.

Oviedo y Valdés, G. F. de. *Historia general y natural de las Indias* (1535–57). 4 vols. Madrid: Ediciónes Atlas, 1959.

Popol Vuh: The Definitive Edition of the Maya Book of the Dawn of Life and the Glories of God and Kings. Trans. D. Tedlock. New York: Simon & Schuster, 1985.

Robiscek, F., and D. Hales. *The Maya Book of the Dead: The Ceramic Codex.* Charlottesville: University of Virginia Museum, 1981.

Roys, R. L. *The ethno-botany of the Maya.* Middle American Research Series Publication No. 2, New Orleans: Tulane University, 1931.

————. *The book of Chalam Balam of Chumayel.* Carnegie Institution of Washington Publication 438, 1933.

Sahagún, B. de. (*Historia general de las cosas de Nueva España,* 1558–69.) *Florentine Codex: A General History of the Things of New Spain.* Trans. A. J. O. Anderson and C. E. Dibble. 12 vols. Santa Fe, N.M.: School of American Research and University of Utah, 1950–69.

Schele, L., and D. Freidel. *A Forest of Kings: The Untold Story of the Ancient Maya.* New York: William Morrow and Co., 1990.

Schele, L., and M. E. Miller. *The Blood of Kings: Dynasty and Ritual in Maya Art.* Fort Worth, Texas: Kimbell Art Museum, 1986.

Spinden, H. J. "A Study of Maya Art, Its Subject Matter and Historical Development." *Memoirs of the Peabody Museum of American Archaeology and Ethnology, Harvard University, VI.* Cambridge: Harvard University Press, 1913.

Stephens, J. L., and F. Catherwood. *Incidents of Travels in Central America, Chiapas, and Yucatan* (1841). Repr. 2 vols. New York: Dover Publications, 1969.

Taube, K. "The Classic Maya Maize God: A Reappraisal." *Fifth Palenque Round Table,*

1983, Vol. VII. Eds. M. G. Robertson and V. M. Fields. San Francisco: The Pre-Columbian Art Research Institute, 1985.

————. "The Maize Tamale in Classic Maya Diet, Epigraphy, and Art." *American Antiquity* 54 (1), 1989.

Thompson, J. E. S.. *Maya Hieroglyphic Writing.* Norman: University of Oklahoma Press, 1960.

————. *A Catalogue of Maya Hieroglyphics.* Norman: University of Oklahoma Press, 1971.

————. *A Commentary of the Dresden Codex.* Philadelphia: American Philosophical Society, 1972.

Torquemada, J. de. *Monarquía Indiana (Los veinte i un libros rituales i monarchía indiana,* 1613). Mexico City: Editorial Chavez Hayhoe, 1943–44.

NORTH AMERICA

Adair, J. *History of the American Indians* (1775). Ed. S. C. Williams. Johnson City, Tennessee: Watauga Press, 1930.

Bahti, T. *Southwestern Indian Ceremonials* (1968). Rev. ed. Las Vegas, Nevada: KC Publications, 1982.

Barlow, J. *The Hasty Pudding* (1793). Ed. D. J. Browne (*with A Memoir on Maize or Indian Corn*). New York: W. H. Graham, 1867.

Bartram W. *Travels of William Bartram* (1791). Ed. M. Van Doren. Reprint of 1928 edition. New York: Dover Publications, 1955.

Benedict, R. *Tales of the Cochiti Indians* (1931). Albuquerque: University of New Mexico Press, 1981.

Berkhofer, R. F., Jr. *The White Man's Indian: Images of the American Indian from Columbus to the Present.* New York: Alfred A. Knopf, 1978.

Beverley, R. *The history and present state of Virginia.* London: 1705.

Billington, R. A. *Land of Savagery, Land of Promise: The European Image of the American Frontier in the Nineteenth Century.* New York: W. W. Norton & Company, 1981.

Boorstin, D. J. *The Americans: The Colonial Experience.* New York: Random House, 1958.

————. *The National Experience.* New York: Random House, 1965.

Bradford, W. *Of Plimouth Plantation, from the Original Manuscript.* Boston: Wright and Potter, 1898.

Catlin, G. *Letters and Notes on the Manners, Customs, and Condition of the North American Indians.* 2 vols. 3rd ed. New York: Wiley and Putnam, 1844.

Champlain, S. de. (*Les voyages de la nouvelle France occidentale, dicte Canada,* 1632.) *Voyages.* Trans. C. P. Otis. 3 vols. Boston: Prince Society, 1878–82.

Cronon, W. *Changes in the Land: Indians, Colonists, and the Ecology of New England.* New York: Farrar, Straus & Giroux, 1983.

Crosby, A. W. *The Columbian Exchange: Biological and Cultural Consequences of 1492.* Westport, Connecticut: Greenwood Press, 1972.

Cushing, F. H. *Zuni: Selected Writings of Frank Hamilton Cushing.* Ed. J. Green. Lincoln and London: University of Nebraska Press, 1979.

Debo, A. *The Rise and Fall of the Choctaw Republic.* Norman and London: University of Oklahoma Press, 1934–61.

Driver, H. E. *Indians of North America.* Chicago: University of Chicago Press, 1961.

Dutton, B. P. *American Indians of the Southwest* (1975). Rev. ed. Abuquerque: University of New Mexico Press, 1983.

Earle, E., and E. A. Kennard. *Hopi Kachinas.* New York: Museum of the American Indian, Heye Foundation, 1971.

Fergusson, E. *Dancing Gods: Indian Ceremonials of New Mexico and Arizona.* Albuquerque: University of New Mexico Press, 1966.

Hariot, T. *A briefe and true report of the new found land of Virginia* (1588). Reprint of 1590 ed. New York: Dover Publications, 1972.

The Jesuit Relations and Allied Documents, Travels and Explorations of the Jesuit Missionaries in New France, 1610–1791. Ed. R. G. Thwaites. 73 vols. Cleveland, Ohio: Burrows Bros., 1896–1901.

Josephy, A. M., Jr. *The Indian Heritage of America.* New York: Alfred A. Knopf, 1968.

Kalm, P. *Peter Kalm's Travels in North America* (1753). Ed. A. B. Benson. Reprint of 1937 ed. New York: Dover Publications, 1987.

Kopper, P. *The Smithsonian Book of North American Indians: Before the Coming of the Europeans.* Washington, D.C.: Smithsonian Books, 1986.

Moulard, B. L. *Within the Underworld Sky: Mimbres Ceramic Art in Context.* Pasadena, California: Twelvetrees Press, 1981.

Mullett, G. M. *Spider Woman Stories: Legends of the Hopi Indians.* Tucson: University of Arizona Press, 1979.

Navajo Blessingway Singer: The Autobiography of Frank Mitchell 1881–1967. Eds. C. J. Frisbie and C. P. McAllester. Tucson: University of Arizona Press, 1978.

Neihardt, J. G. *Black Elk Speaks: Being the Life Story of a Holy Man of the Oglala Sioux.* Reprint of 1932 ed. Lincoln and London: University of Nebraska Press, 1979.

Newcomb, F. J., and G. A. Reichard. *Sandpaintings of the Navajo Shooting Chant.* Reprint of 1937 ed. New York: Dover Publications, 1975.

Ortiz, A. *The Tewa World: Space, Time, Being and Becoming in a Pueblo Society.* Chicago and London: University of Chicago Press, 1969.

Parker, A. C. *Iroquois Uses of Maize and Other Plants.* Albany: University of the State of New York, 1860.

Powell, J. W. *The Hopi Villages: The Ancient Province of Tusayan* (1875). Palmer Lake, Colorado: Filter Press, 1972.

Robbins, W. W., J. P. Harrington and B. Freire-Marreco. *Ethnobotany of the Tewa Indians.* Bureau of American Ethnology, Bulletin 55 (1916).

Rothenberg, J. *Shaking the Pumpkin.* Garden City, New York: Doubleday & Company, 1972.

Russell, H. S. *Indian New England Before the Mayflower.* Hanover, New Hampshire and London: University Press of New England, 1980.

Sander, D. *Navajo Symbols of Healing.* New York and London: Harcourt Brace Jovanovich, 1979.

Schoolcraft, H. R. *The Indian Tribes of the United States.* Ed. F. S. Drake. 2 vols. Philadelphia: J. B. Lippincott, 1884.

Sekaquaptewa, H. *Me and Mine: The Life Story of Helen Sekaquaptewa.* Tucson: University of Arizona Press, 1969.

Simpson, R. D. *The Hopi Indians.* Los Angeles: Southwest Museum, 1953.

Stratton, J. L. *Pioneer Women: Voices from the Kansas Frontier.* New York: Simon & Schuster, 1981.

Strickland, R. *The Indians in Oklahoma*. Norman: University of Oklahoma Press, 1980.

Swanton, J. R. *The Indians of the Southeastern United States*. Reprint of Bureau of American Ethnology, Bulletin 137 (1946).

Underhill, R. *Red Man's America*. Chicago: University of Chicago Press, 1953.

————. *Singing for Power*. Berkeley: University of California Press, 1938.

Viola, H. J. *After Columbus: The Smithsonian Chronicle of the North American Indians*. Washington, D.C.: Smithsonian Books, 1990.

Waters, F. *Masked Gods: Navaho and Pueblo Ceremonialism* (1950). Athens, Ohio: Swallow Press reprint, 1984.

————. *Book of the Hopi*. New York: Viking Press, 1963.

Will, G. F., and G. E. Hyde. *Corn Among the Indians of the Upper Missouri*. St. Louis: W. H. Miner, 1917.

Williams, R. "A Key into the Language of the Natives in That Part of America Called New England (1643)," *Complete Writings*. 7 vols. New York: Russell and Russell, 1963.

Wilson, G. L. *Buffalo Bird Woman's Garden: Agriculture of the Hidatsa Indians* (1917). St. Paul: Minnesota Historical Society Press, 1987.

Winthrop, J. *The History of New England from 1630 to 1649*. Ed. J. Savage. 2 vols. Boston: Phelps and Farnham, 1825.

Witthoft, J. *Green Corn Ceremonialism in the Eastern Woodlands*. Ann Arbor: University of Michigan Press, 1949.

The World of the American Indian (1974). Eds. J. B. Billard *et al.* Rev. ed. Washington, D.C.: National Geographic Society, 1989.

Wyman, L. C. *Blessingway*. Tucson: University of Arizona Press, 1970.

AGRICULTURE

Ainsworth, W. T., and R. M. Ainsworth. *Practical Corn Culture*.Mason City, Illinois: W. T. Ainsworth & Sons, 1914.

Alternative Agriculture. National Research Council Committee on the Role of Alternative Farming Methods in Modern Production Agriculture. Washington, D.C.: National Academy Press, 1989.

Anderson, E. *Corn Before Columbus*. Des Moines, Iowa: Pioneer Hi-Bred International, 1945.

————. *Plants, Man and Life*. Berkeley: University of California Press, 1967.

Beadle, G. W. "The Mystery of Maize." Field Museum of Natural History, Bulletin 42 (1972).

————. "Teosinte and the Origin of Maize," *Maize Breeding and Genetics*. Ed. D. B. Walden. New York: John Wiley & Sons, 1978.

Benz, B. F. "Racial Systematics and the Evolution of Mexican Maize," *Studies in the Neolithic and Urban Revolutions*. Ed. L. Manzanilla. BAR International Series 349 (1987).

Bird, R. M. "Systematics of *Zea* and the Selection of Experimental Material," *Maize for Biological Research*. Ed. W. F. Sheridan. Charlottesville, Virginia: Plant Molecular Biology Association, 1982.

Bonafous, M. *Histoire naturelle, agricole et économique du maïs*. Paris: 1836.

Bruce, R. V. *The Launching of Modern American Science 1846–1876*.Ithaca, N.Y.: Cornell University Press, 1987.

Candolle, A. de. *Origin of Cultivated Plants.* New York: D. Appleton and Company, 1887.

The Canned Food Reference Manual. Eds. R. W. Pilcher *et al.* New York: American Can Company, 1947.

Corn and Corn Improvement. Ed. G. F. Sprague. Madison, Wisconsin: American Society of Agronomy, 1977.

Crabb, A. R. *The Hybrid-Corn Makers.* New Brunswick, N.J.: Rutgers University Press, 1947.

Dick, E. *Conquering the Great American Desert: Nebraska.* Lincoln: Nebraska State Historical Society, 1975.

Emrich, D. *Folklore on the American Land.* Boston and Toronto: Little, Brown and Company, 1972.

Enfield, E. *Indian Corn: Its Value, Culture, and Uses.* New York: D. Appleton and Company, 1866.

Field, J. *The Corn Lady: The Story of a Country Teacher's Work.* Chicago: A. Flanagan Company, 1911.

Galinat, W. "The Origin of Sweet Corn," Massachusetts Agricultural Experiment Station, *Research Bulletin* 591 (1971).

———. "The Origin of Corn," *Corn and Corn Improvement.* Ed. G. F. Sprague. Madison, Wisc.: American Society of Agronomy, 1977.

———. "Domestication and Diffusion of Maize," *Prehistoric Food Production in North America.* Ed. R. Ford. Anthropological Paper 75. Ann Arbor: Museum of Anthropology, University of Michigan, 1985.

Gerarde, J. *The Herball, or Generall Historie of Plantes.* London: 1597. (2nd ed. 1633.)

Goodman, M. M. "The History and Evolution of Maize," *CRC Critical Reviews in Plant Sciences* 7, no. 3 (1988).

Grobman, A., W. Salhauna and R. Sevilla, with P. C. Mangelsdorf. *Races of Maize in Peru: Their Origins, Evolution, and Classification.* Washington, D.C.: National Research Council, 1961.

Hurt, R. D. *American Farm Tools: From Hand-Power to Steam-Power.* Manhattan, Kan.: Sunflower University Press for *Journal of the West,* 1982.

Iltis, H. H. "Maize Evolution and Agricultural Origins," *Grass Systematics and Evolution.* Eds. T. R. Soderstrom *et al.* Washington, D.C.: Smithsonian Institution Press, 1987.

———. "From Teosinte to Maize: The Catastrophic Sexual Transmutation," *Science* 222, no. 4626 (25 November 1983).

Jacobs, L. J. *Battle of the Bangboards.* Des Moines, Iowa: Wallace Homestead Co., 1975.

Jefferson, T. *Thomas Jefferson's Farm Book.* Ed. E. M. Betts. Princeton, N.J.: Princeton University Press, 1953.

The Journal of Gastronomy 5, no. 2. Ed. N. H. Jenkins. San Francisco: American Institute of Wine & Food, 1989.

Kahn, E. J., Jr. *The Staffs of Life.* Boston: Little, Brown and Company, 1985.

Maize. Ed. E. Hafliger. Basel, Switzerland: CIBA-GEIGY Ltd., 1979.

Mangelsdorf, P. C. *Corn: Its Origin, Evolution, and Improvement.* Cambridge, Mass.: Harvard University Press, 1974.

Mangelsdorf, P. C., and R. G. Reeves. *The Origin of Indian Corn and Its Relatives.* Texas Agricultural Experiment Station, *Bulletin* 574 (1939).

McClintock, B. "Significance of chromosome constitutions in tracing origin and migration of races of maize in the Americas," *Maize Breeding and Genetics.* Ed. D. B. Walden. New York: John Wiley & Sons, 1978.

Nabhan, G. P. *Enduring Seeds: Native American Agriculture and Wild Plant Conservation.* San Francisco: North Point Press, 1989.

Report of the Commissioner of Patents for the Year 1860. Washington, D.C.: Government Printing Office, 1861.

Roe, K. E. *Corncribs: History, Folklife, and Architecture.* Ames: Iowa State University Press, 1988.

Sargent, F. L. *Corn Plants: Their Uses and Ways of Life.* Boston: Houghton Mifflin, 1901.

Sauer, C. *Agricultural Origins and Dispersals.* New York: American Geographical Society, 1952.

Sturtevant, E. L. *Indian Corn.* Albany: Charles Van Benthuysen and Sons, 1880.

Usborne, J. *Corn on the Cob.* London: Rupert Hart-Davis, 1956.

Walden, H. T. *Native Inheritance.* New York and London: Harper & Row, 1966.

Wallace, H. A., and E. N. Bressman. *Corn and Corn Growing* (1923). Rev. 5th ed. New York: John Wiley & Sons, 1949.

Wallace, H. A., and W. L. Brown. *Corn and Its Early Fathers.* East Lansing: Michigan State University Press, 1956.

Weatherwax, P. *Indian Corn in Old America.* New York: Macmillan, 1954.

Wellhausen, E. J., L. M. Roberts and X. E. Hernandez, with P. C. Mangelsdorf. *Races of Maize in Mexico.* Cambridge, Massachusetts: Bussey Institute, Harvard University, 1952.

Whealy, K., and A. Adelmann. *Seed Savers Exchange: The First Ten Years.* Decorah, Iowa: Seed Saver Publications, 1986.

Wilkes, G. "Maize: domestication, racial evolution, and spread," *Foraging and Farming.* Eds. D. R. Harris and G. C. Hillman. London: Institute of Archaeology, University College, 1989.

Yearbook of the United States Department of Agriculture 1915. Washington, D.C.: Government Printing Office, 1916.

FOOD AND DRINK

Anderson, E. A. *The Food of China.* New Haven: Yale University Press, 1988.

Bayless, R. D., and D. G. Bayless. *Authentic Mexican: Regional Cooking from the Heart of Mexico.* New York: William Morrow and Company, 1987.

Benitez, A. M. de. *Cocina prehispánica.* Mexico City: Ediciónes Euroamericas, 1976.

Benjamin Franklin on the Art of Eating. Princeton, N.J.: Printed for the American Philosophical Society by Princeton University Press, 1958.

Carnacina. *La Polenta.* Milan: Fratelli Fabbri Editori, 1973.

Carson, G. *Cornflake Crusade: From the Pulpit to the Breakfast Table.* New York and Toronto: Rinehart & Co., 1957.

———. *The Social History of Bourbon.* New York: Dodd, Mead and Company, 1963.

Cobbett, W. *A Treatise on Indian Corn.* London: W. Cobbett, 1828.

Coe, S. "Aztec Cuisine," *Pétits Propos Culinaires* 19–21. London: Prospect Books, 1985.

Crellin, J. K. *Plain Southern Eating: From the Reminiscences of A. L. Tommie Bass, Herbalist.* Durham, N.C.: Duke University Press, 1988.

Cushing, C. H., and B. Gray. *The Kansas Home Cook-Book*. Reprint of 1886 ed. Ed. L. Szathmary. New York: Arno Press, 1973.

Cushing, F. H. *Zuni Breadstuff*. Reprint of 1920 ed. New York: Museum of the American Indian Heye Foundation, 1974.

Dabney, J. E. *Mountain Spirits: A Chronicle of Corn Whiskey from King James' Ulster Plantation to America's Appalachians and the Moonshine Life*. New York: Charles Scribner's Sons, 1974.

Eddy, F. W. *Metates and Manos: The Basic Corn Grinding Tools of the Southwest* (1964). Rev. ed. Santa Fe: Museum of New Mexico Press, 1979.

Egerton, J. *Southern Food*. New York: Alfred A. Knopf, 1987.

Eustis, C. *Cooking in Old Creole Days* (1904). Reprint ed. New York: Arno Press, 1973.
———. *Fifty valuable and delicious recipes made with corn meal*. Aiken, S.C.: 1917.

Furnas, C. C., and S. M. Furnas. *Man, Bread and Destiny*. Baltimore: Williams and Wilkins Company, 1937.

Getz, O. *Whiskey*. New York: David McKay Company, 1978.

Hazard, T. R. *The Jonny-Cake Papers of 'Shepherd Tom.'* Reprint of 1915 ed. New York: Johnson Reprint Corp., 1968.

Hesse, Z. G. *Southwestern Indian Recipe Book*. Palmer Lake, Col.: Filter Press, 1973.

Humphrey, R. V. *Corn: The American Grain*. Kingston, Massachusetts: Teaparty Books, 1985.

Jaramillo, C. M. *The Genuine New Mexico Tasty Recipes* (1939). Reprint ed. Santa Fe, N.M.: Seton Village Press, 1942.

Kamman, M. *Madeleine Kamman's Savoie*. New York: Atheneum, 1989.

Katz, S. H. "Food and Biocultural Evolution: A Model for the Investigation of Modern Nutritional Problems," *Nutritional Anthropology*. Ed. F. E. Johnston. New York: Alan R. Liss, 1987.

Katz, S. H., M. L. Hediger and L. A. Valleroy. "Traditional Maize Processing Techniques in the New World," *Science* 184 (17 May 1974).

Kavena, J. T. *Hopi Cookery*. Tucson: University of Arizona Press, 1987.

Keegan, M. *Southwest Indian Cookbook*. Weehawken, New Jersey: Clear Light Publications, 1987.

Kennedy, D. *The Art of Mexican Cooking*. New York: Bantam Books, 1989.

Kimball, Y., and J. Anderson. *The Art of American Indian Cooking*. Garden City, N.Y.: Doubleday & Company, 1965.

Lang, G. *The Cuisine of Hungary*. New York: Bonanza Books, 1971.

Leslie, E. *The Indian Meal Book*. Philadelphia: Carey and Hart, 1847.
———. *New Receipts for Cooking*. Philadelphia: T. B. Peterson and Brothers, 1852.

Maize on the Menu. Pretoria, South Africa: published by Muller and Retief for the Maize Board, 1971.

McGee, H. *On Food and Cooking*. New York: Charles Scribner's Sons, 1984.

Miller, J. *True Grits*. New York: Workman Press, 1990.

Murphy, C. J. *American Indian Corn*. New York and London: G. P. Putnam's Sons, 1917.

Myrick, H. *The Book of Corn*. New York: Orange Judd, 1904.

Navajo Curriculum Center Cookbook. Rough Rock, Arizona: Rough Rock Demonstration School, 1986.

Niethammer, C. *American Indian Food and Lore*. New York and London: Collier Macmillan Publishers, 1974.

Ortiz, E. L. *The Book of Latin American Cooking.* New York: Alfred A. Knopf, 1979.

Page, L. G., and E. Wigginton. *The Foxfire Book of Appalachian Cookery.* New York: E. P. Dutton, 1984.

Peruvian Dishes: Platos Peruanos. Lima: Brenuil, 1980.

The Picayune's Creole Cook Book. New Orleans: The Picayune, 1901.

The Pocumtuc Housewife. Deerfield, Mass.: Deerfield Parish Guild, 1805.

Powell, H. B. *The Original Has This Signature—W. K. Kellogg.* Englewood Cliffs, New Jersey: Prentice-Hall, 1956.

Quintana, P. *The Taste of Mexico.* New York: Stewart, Tabori and Chang, 1986.

Randolph, V. *The Virginia House-wife* (1824). Facsimile ed. Ed. Karen Hess. Columbia: University of South Carolina Press, 1984.

Rivieccio, M. Z. *Polenta, Piatto da Re.* Milan: Idealibri, 1986.

Rose, P. *The Sensible Cook: Dutch Foodways in the Old and the New World.* Syracuse, New York: Syracuse University Press, 1989.

Root, W. *The Food of Italy.* New York: Atheneum, 1971.

Rutledge, S. *The Carolina Housewife* (1847). Facsimile ed. Ed. A. W. Rutledge. Columbia: University of South Carolina Press, 1979.

Simmons, A. *American Cookery* (1796). Facsimile ed. Ed. M. T. Wilson. New York: Oxford University Press, 1958.

Southwestern Cookery: Indian and Spanish Influences. Facsimile ed. Ed. L. Szathmary. New York: Arno Press, 1973.

Spitler, S., and N. Hauser. *The Popcorn Lover's Book.* Chicago: Contemporary Books, 1983.

Super, J. C. *Food, Conquest, and Colonization in Sixteenth-Century Spanish America.* Albuquerque: University of New Mexico Press, 1988.

Traditional Navajo Foods and Cooking. Pine Hill, N.M.: Tsa'Aszi Graphics Center, 1983.

Wade, M. L. *The Book of Corn Cookery.* Glenwood, Ill.: Meyerbooks, 1919.

Wigginton, E. *Foxfire.* New York: Doubleday & Company, 1972.

Wilkinson, A. *Moonshine: A Life in Pursuit of White Liquor.* New York: Alfred A. Knopf, 1985.

Woodier, O. *Corn: Meals & More.* Pownal, Vt.: Storey Communications, 1987.

Index

Page numbers in italics refer to illustrations and their captions.

A NOTE ON THE TYPE

*This book was set in Granjon, a type named in compliment to Robert Granjon,
a type cutter and printer active in Antwerp, Lyons, Rome and Paris from 1523 to 1590.
Granjon, the boldest and most original designer of his time, was one of the first
to practice the trade of type founder apart from that of printer.
Granjon was designed in 1928 by George W. Jones, who based his drawings on a face
used by Claude Garamond (c. 1480–1561) in his beautiful French books.
Granjon more closely resembles Garamond's own type than does any
of the various modern faces that bear his name.*

Printed and bound by Halliday Lithographers, West Hanover, Massachusetts

Part title collages created by Arlene Lee

Designed by Mia Vander Els